72

7.50

FA·L

The
Cook's
Advisor

The Cook's Advisor

by Camille J. Stagg

The Stephen Greene Press
Brattleboro, Vermont
Lexington, Massachusetts

To my mother, Jeanette, who introduced me to the magic of her kitchen; in memory of my father, Stanley, who patiently supported my earliest childhood cooking experiments; to my brother, Steve, always a good sport and dependable taste-tester during all our growing years together; and to my special friend and colleague, writer-photographer Bob Bradford, whose immeasurable assistance and encouragement eased the editorial tasks and made this work possible.

Text copyright © 1982 by Camille J. Stagg
First Edition

Produced in the United States of America.
Designed by Irving Perkins Associates.
Published by The Stephen Greene Press, Fessenden Road, Brattleboro, Vermont 05301.

Library of Congress Cataloging in Publication Data

Stagg, Camille J., 1942-
  The cook's advisor.

  Bibliography: p.
  Includes index.
  1. Cookery.   I. Title.
TX651.S73   641.5   81-13285
ISBN 0-8289-0445-6   AACR2

Contents

Acknowledgments

Few authors have been fortunate enough to receive so much assistance and supportive interest from a host of professional colleagues and associates who offered their expertise to segments of this book. Particular appreciation to the following:

Reviewers: Chef Jean Banchet, Le Français Restaurant, Wheeling, Illinois, pâté en croûte, sauces; Robert A. Bemm, Creative Confections, Inc., Glenview, Illinois, candy/confectionery; Chef Carolyn Buster, The Cottage Restaurant, Calumet City, Illinois, ice cream, poultry, sauces; T. J. Goetting, Solait dairy food cooker, crème fraîche; Suzanne Checcha, former assistant food editor, *Cuisine*; Bob Finley, *Chicago Sun-Times* columnist, fish, seafood and shellfish; Roy Andries de Groot, nationally syndicated food writer and author; Arnold E. Landsman, wine; Phylis Magida, *Chicago Tribune* food writer and cookbook author, reviewed early segments; Peter Claudio Martini and John Kevin Robson, professors at Florida International University's School of Hospitality, baking, food spoilage/poisoning, pasta, pastries; William Rice, editor, *Food and Wine*, reviewed early segments when food editor of *The Washington Post*; Chef Jolene Worthington, baking, pastries, sauces, thickeners.

Researchers: Margaret Chaput, nutritionist; Joan Zak.

Recipe testers: home economists Jeannine Angio, JeanMarie Brownson, Paula M. Healy and Joyce O'Sullivan.

Editorial assistants: Cheryl Casey, Donna Kelleher, Charlotte London, Elsie Phalen, Margot Kopsidas Phillips, Paula Reger, and Karen Sanders. Special mentions go to Joan McLaughlin former assistant managing editor, *Cuisine*, and formerly of *Playboy* and *Oui*, for her editorial assistance, and to Joan Zak, formerly of *Cuisine* and *Playboy*, for a large amount of typing and for work on the index.

A special thanks to the following organizations: American Dairy Association; American Egg Board; Ball Corporation; International Institute of Foods and Family Living; National Live Stock and Meat Board; United Fresh Fruit and Vegetable Association; U.S. Department of Commerce; National Marine Fisheries Service.

Lastly, profound gratitude to my editor Bill Eastman of The Stephen Greene Press.

Introduction

Your dinner guests are due in half an hour. The table is set, and you're beginning the hollandaise, feeling well in command. You're pleased with the elegant simplicity of the menu: broiled herbed sea bass with lime, asparagus with hollandaise, leaf lettuce with peach vinaigrette, and meringue-topped strawberry tart. But suddenly, the once lofty soft meringue has shrunk to half its height and turned gummy—perhaps from the steam in the kitchen? You're addressing this problem when a phone call interrupts, and the temperamental hollandaise curdles. Another dilemma! What now? With only minutes left, your dinner party is headed for disaster!

Even the most advanced cooks and professionals encounter culinary emergencies—I admit to an occasional quandary myself! A fallen soufflé or a lumpy sauce have been known to provoke tears, panic—even violent behavior—in frustrated hosts and hostesses. How silly, you may think, until it's your turn as victim in the embattled kitchen arena, hopelessly remote from any professional expertise, left with only guesswork as your guide.

A primary reason for *The Cook's Advisor*. This exhaustively researched, intricately cross-referenced volume has the answers to multitudes of cooking predicaments. Also included are many common-sense solutions, as this is a comprehensive book. Now you can flip through alphabetically arranged entries to your particular foodstuff, pinpoint its problem, and find several suggestions and solutions as well as preventive measures for the future. Faced with the above mishaps, for instance, you would uncurdle and stabilize the hollandaise, then sprinkle the gummy meringue with a little sugar and slivered almonds before moving the tart to a cooler, drier place. (And when you're ready to slice it, get ice water for dipping the serrated knife.) With a minimum of fuss and delay, you've rescued your dinner, and even the most discriminating guests will not guess there were tense moments.

As a professional in food teaching and journalism for eighteen years—twelve spent as food editor of a major daily newspaper, nearly three as a key editor of a national food magazine—I was constantly aware of the critical need for a comprehensive cooking-problem-solving guide. My newspaper food department staff, like many others, became so inundated with reader calls that the phone service was discontinued. Letters still kept pouring in, but written replies were helpful only in preventing similar future perplexities. An entire library would be required to cover the range of questions a cook may face in a given week, and even if all those references were available, how impractical to drop the kitchen task at hand to do the research. Where was just one inclusive volume dealing with resolving and preventing cooking problems? There was nothing on the market.

So I conceived such a book. In gathering and synthesizing the material, I consulted with numerous top professionals in the field. Professors, executive chefs, pastry chefs, nutritionists, industry experts, and confectioners took a keen interest in the work and have reviewed specific sections germane to their expertise. I wanted to make certain the information was relevant, accurate, and current.

After years of research, consultation, writing, and testing, here at last is *The Cook's Advisor*, a hot line to food experts. Now the answers to common—and not so common—culinary questions and problems are at your fingertips.

The next time your gelatin fails to firm up, or you're wondering how to use some stale peanuts or too-rapidly ripening bananas, turn to the name of the particular food or general category (e.g., *Sauces*), then to the problem word—both alphabetized in chapter 1—and you'll quickly find the twofold answer: what to do *This time*, right now, and how to prevent a repeat occurrence *Next time.* Tips and references to recipes in chapter 2 offer concrete suggestions for how to use the food instead of wasting it. Explanations of why the problem happened are also included to satisfy curious minds.

For instance: a once high-and-mighty cake now looks like a deflated balloon. Look under *Cake, "Falls."* You'll get some recommended remedies that will enable you to transform the disaster into a delicious dessert, such as a pudding (recipe in chapter 2), and you'll find out what caused the collapse and how to prevent it the next time.

Getting acquainted with this book ensures reaping maximum value from it. Although designed mainly as a troubleshooting guide, it accomplishes much more. The information can preserve your time and energy, improve your kitchen skills, and save you money by preventing waste (as any good chef does). It also aids in conquering not-so-imminent problems. For instance, read the section on *Fires, burns* to know ahead of time how to prevent flare-ups and fires, and what to do in case of one. Likewise, *Food Spoilage, Poisoning* can clarify any uncertainties in this most serious area. *The Cook's Advisor* can make you more knowledgeable about food in general.

The second chapter, complete with index, contains recipes I have developed and perfected over the years to utilize cooking experiments that didn't quite make it, over-the-hill ingredients, and leftovers. Several recipes are from other good cooks, all adding up to a sample collection reflecting a healthful approach to cooking and intended to spark some creativity with resourcefulness. Keeping an open mind and an adventuresome spirit are key to transforming toss-outs into imaginative table fare.

Food authorities as well as both advanced and novice cooks tell me this is a most needed food volume. "Where is it?" cooking teachers were demanding months before its publication.

Keep this reliable guide at the ready in your kitchen. Use this book as a reference in conjunction with—not in lieu of—cookbooks. I'm confident you'll find it as trustworthy and useful as have the broad cross-section of manuscript reviewers. And take it to your armchair as well. Through personal experiences, anecdotes, and historical background, I enthusiastically share with you the joy that cooking and all things surrounding it can be . . . including the challenges. For without them, we wouldn't have much incentive to learn about this fascinating subject that provides one of life's greatest pleasures.

C.J.S.

Part I
An Alphabetical Guide to Common Foods and Cooking Problems: Solutions and Preventions

Alcoholic (too)—Dilute drinks with nonalcoholic ingredients (water, soda, etc.). Cooked dishes with alcohol can be simmered longer or ignited to burn off the alcohol; in both cases the flavor remains. For salvaging an alcoholic punch, see *Punch*.

Almonds—See *Nuts*.

Anchovy—The most common problem concerning anchovies is saltiness. See *Fish*.

Appetizer—See *Cheese; Fish; Sandwich* (for canapé questions) and other specific foods.

Apple—It got us thrown out of Eden. Its bounce off Newton's head inspired his law of gravity. Its daily consumption supposedly keeps the doctor away and the teacher happy. Occasionally, however, the apple poses problems.

DISCOLORED

This time: An apple discolors quickly when cut, but it's still perfectly edible. In fact, grated apple pulp, allowed to darken, can be used for treating an upset stomach. But if you're in top health, make applesauce instead, using cinnamon and other sweet spices. Then blend with another colorful fruit sauce, such as cranberry or rhubarb.

Next time: When serving cut apples in salads select varieties that do not brown: Golden Delicious or Cortland. Or as soon as apple is cut, rub cut surfaces with lemon juice. Pineapple and other acidic fruit juices work too, as does slightly salted water. But rinse after the salt treatment unless flavor is appropriate for intended use.

HARD

This time: When raw apples are too hard for eating, use for cooking instead. When the sautéed or broiled apple slices need softening,

3

cover to allow them to steam in their own juices. The texture of cooked apples is best when still firm, but when fruit is *really* hard, make applesauce.

Next time: Match the variety of apple to its intended use. A Greening, for example, is intended for cooking, although some tart-apple fanciers like myself love munching them raw, when sour and very crisp.

TOO JUICY

This time: This is hardly a problem except when baking apple dumplings, or something similar, when too much juice can make a dough soggy, or the cooked apple loses too much juice. Usually one does not know that the apples are too juicy until the dough is already soggy, and the juice leaks out and burns on the pan. Remove from the oven, spoon off excess juice, and brush bottom of dumplings with melted butter or margarine or a little jam. This will seal pastry and brown on further baking. You can always serve the dumplings topped with cream if they look less than perfect.

Next time: Where you need a baking apple without excess juice, select types like Rome Beauty, York Imperial, and Jonathan rather than the super-juicy ones like McIntosh, Winesap, Northern Spy, and Starr. When baking in pastry, make sure pastry is thick enough to hold juices, and the oven is hot enough to bake it crisp, usually 425 degrees.

MEALY

This time: Apples too mealy to be enjoyed raw may be cooked in a sweetened sauce, which helps them hold their shape, or made into applesauce, with enough water to prevent burning, then sweetened and sieved for a smooth sauce, if desired. Add spices to taste. Another use for mealy apples is in a stuffing.

Next time: Mealy apples are often old and overripe. Select firm, crisp-feeling apples without soft spots or a general soft touch. Store in a cool, airy, dry place for several weeks, or in the refrigerator for up to two weeks. Do not wash before storing.

SOFT, MUSHY (COOKED)

This time: Cooked apples that have lost their shape can always be turned into applesauce or incorporated in pudding, bread stuffing, or a casserole with sausage or ham.

Next time: Avoid cooking overripe apples, adding too much water, and overcooking. When cooking apples for a sweet dish, adding sugar at the beginning of cooking helps maintain shape and definition.

TOO SOUR (COOKED)

This time: The tart taste can be countered with sugar or another sweetener; adjust to taste.

Next time: Select apples known for their sugar content rather than their tartness. Yellow Transparent, Starr, and Greening tend to be tart.

TOUGH (COOKED)

This time: Purée in blender, perhaps with a little cream or milk and cinnamon, for a saucy pudding dessert, or for a sauce to be served over fruit gelatin or bread pudding. Or blend into yogurt for your own fruit-flavor version.

Next time: Select cooking apples for cooking. The sweeter eating types tend to toughen upon cooking.

Apricot—This velvety, golden stone fruit is a small cousin to the peach. The apricot is native to China where the trees were cultivated at least two thousand years ago, and traveled west to India, Armenia, and Persia. Spanish missionaries are thought to have introduced the first apricots to California, where the trees have thrived and still grow. However, the best I've ever tasted were served in Murcia, Spain. The season is all too short for these luscious little fruits—only June and July, sometimes August—and they are very perishable.

DISCOLORED

This time: Trim away darkened areas, then broil or bake halves with a little butter, brown sugar, and cinnamon. Add halves or slices to a spicy sauce for poultry, or mash or purée and cook with a little water, honey and red berries for use in puddings, sweet sauces, or yogurt. Or create a summery cold yogurt-fruit soup.

Next time: Select firm, plump, yellow to orange fruit with no soft or dark areas. Refrigerate in open or perforated plastic bag up to 4 or 5 days. Store cut fruit tightly covered in plastic wrap and rub cut surfaces with a little citrus juice to prevent discoloration.

GREEN

This time: Slightly green apricots should ripen in several days at room temperature (or faster in a ripening bowl); then refrigerate. If you're in a hurry, pickle or use with mango, raisins, etc., for chutney. Poach or stew in wine, fruit juice, or light syrup as meat accompaniment. Sweetened and spiced with cinnamon, nutmeg, ginger, and/or mace or other favorites, apricots take on flavor that allows them to stand alone as a dessert, perhaps with a dollop of whipped cream or ice cream. Or cook with other fruits in a compote. Halve or slice fruit and cook with meats or poultry in a sauce made of drippings and wine.

Next time: Select only fully ripe fruit, with a good golden color, that yields to slight pressure. Allow several days for hard fruit to ripen.

OVERRIPE

This time: When too soft to eat, purée, sweeten, and cook to a thick paste and use as pastry filling. Very soft fruit can also be mashed for sherbets and any variety of puddings. Apricot purée is a nourishing baby food, too.

Next time: To prevent fruit from getting too ripe too soon, see selection and storage tips above.

Artichoke (French or globe)—One restaurant in Rome serves the artichoke more than 100 different ways! The many unusual aspects and delicious subtlety of this vegetable were responsible for its rapid acceptance in France and England (where Henry VIII consumed large quantities for its supposed aphrodisiac effects). Most of our domestic supply comes from California, where the little town of Castroville calls itself the Artichoke Capital of the World. I sampled the artichoke there served 3 different ways: fried, in soup and— most unusual—in cake. Don't serve your finest wine with artichokes—for many people, the vegetable ruins the taste of wine.

DISCOLORED

This time: Raw artichokes darken quickly when cut. If the leaves or other parts have darkened considerably, you can scrape off the edible flesh, then mash and mix it with mayonnaise, sour cream, or yogurt for a dip or spread over artichoke bottoms or leaves. Or purée into a soup, blending with vegetable or chicken stock.

Next time: As soon as any cutting is done, place artichokes in acid water (about 2 to 3 tablespoons lemon juice or vinegar to a quart of water). Some people use only stainless steel knives since carbon blades—like iron and aluminum pots—darken artichokes.

OVERCOOKED

This time: If the leaves are falling off, remove them and serve separately—perhaps with sour cream flavored with lemon juice, parsley, and some chopped pimiento. Serve the hearts separately with a vinaigrette or combined with another vegetable, such as tiny onions or green peas. If extremely soft, scrape off flesh from leaves and purée for spread, dip, timbales (p. 333) or for cream of vegetable soup (p. 315).

Next time: Trim stem until almost flush with base; remove any tough, discolored leaves. Cut off a small portion of the top with a sharp knife. With kitchen shears, trim off the sharp tip of each leaf. Cook in water almost to cover, to which 2 tablespoons lemon juice, ½ teaspoon salt, and 1 tablespoon olive oil per quart have been added (for 2 to 4 artichokes). Stand upright snugly in tall saucepan, cover, and cook 20 to 40 minutes, depending on size. When base is just fork tender, remove from heat. Carefully lift out of pan and drain upside down. If they are to be stuffed, spread the leaves from the center, and, using a spoon, gently scrape out the choke.

OVERMATURE

This time: If artichokes are spreading, with hard-tipped leaf scales, and the center is purplish, they've been around a while, and will be tough or woody. Increase cooking time, and if they're still tough, scrape off flesh from leaves and mash or purée (see *Overcooked*).

Next time: Select heavy, plump heads with compact, tightly clinging, thick, green leaves. Size has almost nothing to do with quality. Large best for stuffing, small for stews and casseroles. Place in plastic bag or closed container and refrigerate until ready to use.

Asparagus—Known to both the Greeks and the Romans, this member of the lily family has been held in high esteem by epicures through the ages. Here in the U.S., the green thick stalks are favored and eaten with a fork. Europeans prefer the plump white stalks grown in earth mounds to prevent the greening effects of sunlight. The Chinese and Japanese like their spears sweetened. If you ever have the good fortune to taste wild asparagus, you may forever after be disappointed with the cultivated supermarket type. Like the date palm, asparagus has both female and male sexes—the lady plant identified by her seed pods and flowers. This romantic feature, plus the experience of anyone who has savored asparagus with the fingers, no doubt has given this delicate vegetable treat its long-standing sensual reputation.

DISCOLORED (OVERCOOKED)

This time: Mash or purée for sauce, vegetable timbale (p. 333), or cream of vegetable soup (p. 315).

Next time: Overcooking or an acid medium causes discoloration. Cook fresh asparagus upright in about ½ cup boiling water in asparagus steamer or bottom part of double boiler, covered, until stalk is just tender, about 10 minutes. One of the best ways to cook asparagus is in a glass dish in a microwave oven. A pinch (about 1/16 teaspoon) of baking soda per quart of water will help preserve the green color. If water is slightly alkaline, simmering uncovered in water to cover will preserve the color.

OVERCOOKED: See *Discolored.*

SHRIVELED, WILTED (RAW)

This time: Try cutting under water. If asparagus are too far gone, use them in a casserole, cover with a sauce, or purée for soup or timbales (p. 333).

Next time: Buy fresh spears, with firm heads made up of tiny close buds. To keep asparagus as fresh as possible for storage, trim or snap off tough ends (about ½ inch) under cold water and hold them there for a few moments to absorb some moisture. Wrap lower half of stalks in wet paper towel or place in jar partly filled with water and store in refrigerator. Try to use within 2 days.

Avocado—The avocado is the fruit of a tree originally found in Central America and Mexico. Three main varieties are grown here:

the California Fuerte—pear-shaped, generally medium in size, with pliable green skin and available mostly in winter; Hass—rounder summer variety with a pebbly skin that's green when mature but turns black when fully ripe, and the Florida Lula—at 14 to 24 ounces, the largest with smooth or corrugated green skin speckled with yellow. The California fruit is richer with a higher oil content.

DISCOLORED

This time: Once the fruit has been cut or peeled, the flesh darkens quickly and irreversibly. Color it a fresh green by puréeing with spinach and/or parsley leaves as a base for a dressing, soup, or sauce. Or add chunks to a Mexican-style beef casserole with tortillas and tomatoes. Darkened slices may be covered with cheese sauce. Or make avocado spread (p. 311).

Next time: Sprinkle lemon or lime juice on exposed flesh, after cutting, and keep pit stored in cut fruit. Stir a little lemon or lime juice in guacamole, and cover well with plastic wrap directly on mixture to store. When out of citrus juice, lightly smear cut surfaces with margarine before storing.

OVERRIPE

This time: When the fruit has gotten too soft for using as slices, mash with a fork and make a dip, such as guacamole or a spread (p. 311) or purée for drink, sauce, dressing, or soup. Also good for soufflé, mousse, and ice cream.

Next time: Select heavy, solid fruit of good color, without bruises or soft spots. When using immediately, choose fruit that yields to slight pressure. For later use, select firm avocados and store at room temperature for several days to a week. Then use or refrigerate up to another week; but do not chill very firm fruit.

VERY FIRM

This time: Store fruit at room temperature for several days until it gives a bit when gently squeezed, then place in brown paper bag to quicken ripening. If cut and found unripe, lightly spread margarine over cut surfaces, put back together with pit, and store in brown paper bag at room temperature to hasten ripening or dice and cook in a casserole or sauté with mushrooms for an omelet filling. Puréeing and cooking with chicken broth for a soup is yet another possibility. The sliced or diced fruit is especially compatible cooked with fish or chicken and citrus. Because of its velvety texture and bland flavor, it takes well to highly spiced foods, too. Cook lightly; the fruit can develop a bitterness from prolonged cooking.

Next time: See selection and storage tips above.

Bacon—*See Meat.*

Bacteria—*See Canning; Food Spoilage.*

Baking Powder—To test activity, mix 1 tsp. with 1/3 cup hot water; it should bubble vigorously if fresh. If inactive, it's useless.

Baking Soda—Must be used together with acid ingredients— usually sour milk or molasses—to have leavening power. Some recipes with little acidity back up the soda with some baking powder.

Bamboo Shoots

SOFTENED LEFTOVERS

This time: Place in cold water with some lemon juice or vinegar, cover, and refrigerate for several hours or overnight. If they are still not as crisp as you'd like, drain, then sauté them or fry in oil, then flavor with soy sauce, scallions, and garlic. Good with mushrooms, chicken, and meat.

Next time: Leftovers will keep for some time if covered with cold water in covered jar and refrigerated. Change water every two days or so, and avoid storing in the coldest part of the refrigerator.

OVERCOOKED

This time: Sauté or stir-fry quickly to help retain some outer crispness, or turn into casserole or soup where texture may not be as noticeable.

Next time: Add shoots at very *end* of cooking, allowing only about 3 minutes total time for canned. (Fresh may need to be parboiled first for 10 to 12 minutes.) Do not simmer or steam too long—texture and crispness will be lost.

Banana

DISCOLORED

This time: If thickly sliced, halve to make thinner slices and turn good-side up, brushing immediately with lemon juice. If you've got lots of thin, darkened slices, mash and use for milkshakes, chocolate-banana malt, or banana cake or bread.

Next time: Immediately after peeling, brush whole banana or pieces with lemon juice or other fruit juice or dip into acidulated water, or slice directly into gelatin, salad dressing or other food that will coat the banana pieces.

MUSHY, OVERRIPE

This time: Mash and blend with milk for shake or use in bread, muffins, cake, pudding, or for pie. If several bananas have over-ripened, slash peel on top side of each, add a bit of butter and cinnamon, then grill over coals or in broiler until exterior is blackened; spread peel apart from slash and eat with spoon. To slow maturation by a couple of days, ripe bananas may be refrigerated, contrary to common belief. If you have more soft bananas than you can use right now, mash with lemon juice (about 1 teaspoon per banana) or ascorbic acid, pack into freezer containers, leaving a little headspace, or in freezer wrap, and store in freezer for up to a year if desired. To prevent darkening, thaw before unwrapping or opening, then use for baking or shakes.

Next time: Decide on when and how you plan to use bananas. Then select accordingly the greener ones for several days hence; firm but yellow and fully ripe for same or next day—especially to use in salads—and softer, yellow with brown spots for mashing to use in baked products. Bananas last longer if bought by the bunch rather than singly. Avoid bruised fruit with cracked skins.

UNDERRIPE

This time: Serve sautéed, roasted, broiled, or baked instead of raw. Try soaking in butter or baking with fruit juice, honey, or jelly.

Next time: Buy yellow ripe fruit; avoid green unless you plan not to use them immediately. Ripening is hastened by leaving bananas at room temperature, unwrapped.

Barley—*See Cereal.*

Bass—*See Fish.*

Beans, Dried (legumes)

Basic directions:

1. Fast soaking method: bring washed and sorted beans and water (about 3 cups per cup beans) to a boil with a little butter in a large pot. Cover and cook 2 minutes; remove from heat and let stand about 1 to 2 hours, depending on size.

2. Overnight method: follow same directions as above, but allow to stand overnight.

Cook drained beans in plenty of water, covered, with a little onion, garlic, celery, ham trimmings, or ham bone for flavor. Latest research advises discarding soak water to enhance flavor and digestibility. The negligible nutrient loss in soak liquid would be lost in cooking anyway. Avoid salting or adding acidic ingredient, which tend to toughen beans. Salt after cooking; add tomatoes, wine, or lemon juice at end of cooking. Do not use a pressure cooker, as foaming may clog up air vent, creating a hazard. Cover pot, bring to boil, reduce heat and simmer from 45 minutes to 2 hours, depending on size. Beans are done when they are tender but still hold their shape.

BLAND

This time: A variety of seasonings always can be added. Ingredients compatible with beans are onions, garlic, herbs or spices, tomatoes, ham, celery, green pepper, and orange, to name but a few. Sauté onions, garlic, celery, or green pepper first before adding to cooked beans.

Next time: Add above vegetables or smoked pork hock or ham bone to cooking water for good flavor; beans absorb flavor during cooking. When using cooked beans in salad, add dressing to hot beans, which absorb the seasoning better. Or allow to marinate in flavorful mixture.

BROKEN SKINS

This time: Purée and use in soup or mash and use for bean dip (p. 313).

Next time: Avoid high heat and vigorous stirring.

FOAMY

This time: Skim off foam as it forms during cooking. Add dash of oil or butter.

Next time: Add a little butter to soaking water to prevent foam from developing.

HARD

This time: Cook longer, until tender (a microwave oven helps hurry the process; cook in plenty of liquid, uncovered. Let stand 5 minutes, covered, before serving).

Next time: Be sure to allow enough soaking and cooking time—more for the larger beans.

OVERCOOKED

This time: When the beans lose shape after cooking too long, mash or purée.

Next time: See proper cooking directions, above.

TOUGH

This time: Mash or purée.

Next time: See proper cooking directions, above. Avoid salt and acids, which tend to toughen.

Beans (fresh green and wax or yellow)

DISCOLORED

This time: Turn cooked beans into a casserole or soup, or cover with a rich cheese or mushroom sauce. Or purée pale beans with parsley and use in soup.

Next time: Steam or cook uncovered in boiling salted water only until tender—from 3 to about 20 minutes, depending on maturity and size. To be sure of a bright green in your beans (although there'll be some vitamin loss) add a small pinch (1/16 teaspoon) baking soda per 2 cups water to cover. Since storage time also discolors, keep fresh raw beans only a few days in refrigerator.

MATURE

This time: Tough or old beans need longer cooking, and richer sauces. Save the lightly seasoned butter for the young ones.

Next time: Select small, firm, bright green (or yellow) pods that snap easily. Seeds should be immature—rather small. Avoid large, dull-colored beans, unless they're a different variety that grows longer and thicker, like the pole. Wilted, shriveled, or scarred pods should be avoided. Store unwashed in plastic bags in refrigerator, up to 4 days.

OVERCOOKED

This time: Soft and mushy beans can be salvaged: purée and use for cream of vegetable soup (p. 315) or chop fine and use in casseroles, vegetable stews (a good blend with corn and carrots), or clear vegetable soups.

Next time: Follow proper cooking directions above.

SHRIVELED

This time: See proper cooking directions, above, then use in a dish where appearance is not too noticeable. Or purée and use as suggested, but avoiding clear soups (*see Overcooked*).

Next time: See proper selection and storage tips, above.

Beans (lima)—Baby limas (small and whitish) and Fordhook (large) are the limas mostly used for canning and freezing. Butter beans, a term used by Southerners, are not to be confused with the same reference New Englanders make to yellow wax beans.

DISCOLORED

This time: If raw beans are only slightly discolored, use immediately. When cooked, yellowing is due to alkaline cooking water, whereas browning can come from overcooking or from an iron utensil. Add about 2 teaspoons lemon juice or 1 teaspoon cream of tartar to enough water to cover discolored cooked beans, and simmer gently 1 to 2 minutes. Persistent discoloration can be camouflaged by a thick cheese or mushroom sauce, or by mashing beans and serving as a dip (see bean dip, p. 313) or puréeing for soup.

Next time: Shell raw beans just before cooking. Once shelled, they're very perishable, but in a pinch will keep about 3 days in covered container in refrigerator. Reheat cooked beans in small amount of salted water in noniron pot with a little lemon juice or cream of tartar; cover and simmer only until tender, 5 to 15 minutes, depending on age and size.

OVERMATURE

This time: Cook longer, with a dash of sugar in water, until tender. After cooking, draining, and buttering, stir in cream or half-and-half, season to taste, and heat thoroughly. Sprinkle with cheese, parsley, or paprika. Or mash for dip (p. 313) or purée and make into cream of vegetable soup (p. 315).

Next time: Buy bright, fresh, well-filled pods; shelled beans should be plump, green or whitish green. Tough skin and bulging large pods indicate overmaturity.

OVERCOOKED

This time: Mash for dip (p. 313) or purée and use for cream of vegetable soup (p. 315).

Next time: Follow proper cooking directions above.

SHRIVELED

This time: Shriveled raw beans indicate aging, and no doubt will be shriveled after cooking as well. Simmering in acidulated water helps, or cook in microwave, steamer, or pressure cooker. Mash or purée (see bean dip, p. 313, or cream of vegetable soup, p. 315).

Next time: See selection tips above.

Bean Sprouts—Chinese mung and soybeans can yield 10 to 12 times their volume when sprouted—quite an indoor harvest for so little effort! Mung sprouts are a great addition to salads and sandwiches; both kinds are good in cooked dishes. Because their protein-inhibiting enzyme is heat deactivated, soybean sprouts should not be eaten raw, only cooked. Nutritional value zooms when a bean sprouts; the starch converts to sugar, vitamin C is formed, and other nutrients multiply.

OVER THE HILL

This time: Sprouts tend to wilt and change color when stored too long. Avoid using tired mung sprouts in salads, but add them to soups and casseroles at the very end of cooking, just to heat through. Steam for several minutes or add to other vegetables or main dishes.

Next time: As soon as sprouts are ready for eating, rinse, place in jar with water to cover, close jar, and store in refrigerator for up to 4 or 5 days. Change water daily to keep sprouts fresh. For longer storage, blanch and refrigerate as above (but expect to lose some crunchiness and nutrients). Or parboil one minute, drain and freeze in plastic bag or tightly covered container for later cooking.

Beef—*See Meat.*

Beer—Freshly poured beer should have a nice head of foam. Flat beer can be used for cooking stews and various meat dishes, such as the famed carbonnade Flamande; it can be the liquid in a fritter batter, and it makes a flavorful marinade. There are beer soups, beer batters, and beer cakes—all good uses for stale beer.

Beet Greens—*See Greens.*

Beets—Believed to have originated in the Mediterranean, beets have been known to man since pre-Christian times. But in those days, the red roots were used as medical remedies and only the leaves were eaten. It wasn't until the start of the 19th century that beets were cultivated for eating both in Europe and here. Shortly thereafter the sugar beet was discovered as a source of commercial table sugar.

DISCOLORED

This time: When beets are no longer beet-red, add a little vinegar or lemon juice to the cooking water and watch the blue-purple disappear and the red reappear. If the beets turn bluish again from contact with an alkaline solution, the remedy can be repeated.

Next time: Add a bit of vinegar to the cooking water to ensure color holding. The color pigment is stable in heat and water soluble. Cook whole, unpeeled beets with some of the stem left on by steaming or half-covering with boiling water, covering the pot, and simmering until tender, about ½ hour for tender, little beets, or up to 2 hours for very mature, larger ones. Add more boiling water if needed.

OVERCOOKED

This time: When the beets are too soft to hold their shape as slices, chop and sauté with onions, then add a sweet-sour sauce (p. 329) which will help to give them some support. If they're so mushy they fall apart when chopped, make a blender borscht: to 2 or 3 cups beet mush, add a can of beef consommé, a minced garlic clove, and 1 cup of water (or ½ cup dry red wine and ½ cup water or ½ cup tomato juice and ½ cup water). Whir until well blended, reheat, adjust seasoning (salt, pepper, dash of vinegar, sugar, basil, etc.) and serve with dollop of sour cream in each bowl.

Next time: See Discolored.

OVERMATURE (TOUGH)

This time: Cook longer, and serve with a sweet-sour sauce (try adding chopped apple or orange juice and rind), which tends to mask the mature flavor and texture. Or make blender borscht (*see Overcooked*).

Next time: Select firm, unblemished beets with fresh greens. Avoid shriveled, withered roots and leaves. Smaller beets are usually more tender. Store, wrapped, in vegetable compartment of refrigerator for up to a month. If beets have tops, remove and use. (*See Greens.*)

Belgian Endive—This marvelous low-calorie vegetable is easily recognized by its elongated, compact cluster of white, crisp, 3- to 5-inch leaves with greenish tips.

WILTED

This time: Refresh slightly tired endive in an ice bath, drying and wrapping in towels and chilling about an hour. Badly wilted endive can be trimmed of outer shriveled leaves, then braised in butter with a small amount of seasoned chicken consommé, or cooked briefly, then covered with Roquefort cheese cream sauce and baked.

Next time: Select firm, tightly closed endives, creamy colored with light-green tips and no bruises or soft, loose leaves. Chill in plastic bag up to 4 or 5 days.

Berries—Wild berries generally taste better than cultivated. All berries are very perishable; store them covered in the refrigerator.

HARD, UNDERRIPE

This time: Allow to ripen at room temperature, or cook with sugar and water, and perhaps a compatible fruit juice, into a sauce, or into a spicy relish with other fruits. Firm, less ripe berries have more pectin and so are best for preserving. Really green fruit may never ripen properly, so it is best to cook it in a flavorful liquid.

Next time: Select plump, firm, clean berries with good color. Avoid green berries.

SOFT, OVERRIPE

This time: Whether soft from having been frozen or because they're overripe, use immediately. Their texture will be less noticeable when mixed with fresh firm berries. If very soft, stem and purée for milkshake, yogurt drink, soda; or mash and cook quickly in a light sugar syrup for a sauce to top ice cream or other desserts. Berry purée, thickened with yogurt or cream or combined with wine, makes a lovely cold summer soup. Winter cranberries cook up nicely with orange juice sparked with orange rind and sweetened; serve as relish to poultry. Sweetened a little more and spiced, the cranberry sauce makes a great pudding or ice-cream topper.

Next time: Choose firm, plump berries with no soft spots or mold. Avoid shriveled or leaky berries. Cover and refrigerate immediately. Do not wash or stem until just before serving. Use within a day or two.

Biscuits—*See Bread.*

Too Bitter—One of the four basic tastes—rather acrid. Harsh bitterness can be balanced by sweetness.

Blackberry—*See Berries.*

Blandness—While some foods are innately bland, others lack flavor that should be there. A squirt of lemon or lime juice will make the dullest melon come alive; honey, spices, herbs, and assorted condiments spruce up other dishes. Bouillon instead of water imparts additional flavor when cooking rice, chicken, meat, etc. See individual food headings for tips on counteracting blandness.

Temperature is a vital factor to the taste sensations. Be sure to taste foods at the temperature you intend to serve them, since cold inhibits aroma and flavor and warmth emphasizes them. Soup served cold requires additional seasonings. Fruits, cheeses, and wines, especially, give their fullest flavor at room temperature, or about 68 degrees. In fact, most foods taste their best between 68 and 105 degrees, although we often eat hot dishes at about 130 degrees.

Blintzes—*See Crepes.*

Blueberry—*See Berries.*

Bluefish—*See Fish.*

Bologna—*See Meat.*

Bombe—*See Ice Cream.*

Bones—*See Stock.*

Botulism—*See Canning; Food Spoilage.*

Bouillabaisse—*See Fish.*

Bouillon—*See Soup.*

Bouquet Garni—Fresh thyme and parsley sprigs, bay leaf, and fresh chervil, often tied together with celery and the white portions of a leek, add marvelous flavor to stocks and soups. Other fresh herbs may be substituted or added. When fresh are unavailable, dried herbs on stems or crumbled leaves may be tied in cheesecloth bags.

Boysenberry—*See Berries.*

Brains—*See Meat.*

Bran—*See Cereal.*

Braunschweiger—*See Meat.*

Bread—The staff of life since prehistoric man's first crude stone-baked version made of crushed seeds and water, bread is one of the most universal of all foods, although it varies greatly. The earliest breads were unleavened, and until the invention of the roller mill in the early 1800s, loaves were primarily whole grain and coarse tex-tured. White bread became beautiful because the pure milled flour lasted longer with the complete outer covering bran and germ removed. Also removed, however, were the nutrients, which are now replaced by fortification that customers pay for. So the return trend toward whole grains today makes good sense. While the broad category of bread includes unleavened types, the two general kinds covered here are yeast (yeast-leavened) and quick (baking powder or soda-leavened). This information should solve your bread problems any way you slice it.

Breads, Quick—Fruit and nut breads, muffins, biscuits, and other doughs leavened by baking soda or powder or eggs and steam. (For problems with dumplings, pancakes, popovers, and waffles see individual headings.)

DRY, CRUMBLY

This time: A dry sweet bread can be ripened like a fruitcake. Poke holes through bread with skewer, then saturate with a favorite liquor, flavored simple syrup, wine, or fruit juice, wrap in soaked cheesecloth and foil, and refrigerate several days. Several muffins may be wrapped together. Or split the loaf in layers and fill with jelly or jam, then wrap and chill before serving. A honey or molasses dip is a flavorful way of moistening dry breads, muffins, or biscuits. If not too crumbly, chunks of any of these baked items can be dunked into cheese or dessert fondues. Slices can be soaked in rum or sweet wine, topped with a custard or fruit sauce and fruit for a trifle-style dessert. Or make fruit roll pudding (p. 339).

Next time: Avoid overbaking or too hot an oven. Most 9-by-5-inch quick bread loaves are baked about 45 to 60 minutes in a 325-to-350-degree oven. Time and temperatures vary with the recipes, but any bread can be tested for doneness; a skewer inserted into center of bread should come out clean and crust should be golden-brown. Hint: fruit and nut breads slice better if wrapped in plastic wrap or foil and refrigerated overnight.

HEAVY

This time: Doughy, heavy-textured bread can be crumbled and used for numerous puddings (see fruit roll pudding, p. 339), and tortes. Soaked in rum or brandy, the crumbs can top fruit cobblers and chocolate or custard puddings. Even fruit or nut loaves can be crumbled and used in delicious fruited stuffings for poultry or pork roasts. Toast thin slices or sprinkle with sweet wine, spread with jam, and chill; just before serving top with whipped cream and slivered almonds.

Next time: Don't overmix, which condenses and toughens bread. Blend the dry ingredients well before mixing with the liquid. Do not beat unless recipe advises to do so. Make certain baking powder is active by mixing 1 tsp. with ⅓ cup hot water. Use it only if it bubbles enthusiastically. Greased sides of pans can prevent dough from rising.

PEAKED TOPS

This time: Level off top and frost with a confectioners icing or thick glaze. If the texture is undesirable near the top, cut the bread into chunks and dunk into dessert fondue or use in pudding.

Next time: Overmixing can cause peaking. Just combine the ingredients thoroughly.

STALE

This time: Crumbled stale bread is delicious soaked in liquor or wine, then topped with custard or fruit sauce or sprinkled over ice cream. Chunks can be turned into a bread pudding or stuffing. Or make fruit roll pudding (p. 339).

Next time: With the exception of the nut and fruit varieties, quick breads do not keep as well as yeast breads. Wrap and keep in cool, dry place up to two days. For longer storage, cover with moisture-vapor-proof wrap and freeze. Thaw in wrapping at room temperature. Reheat in 300-degree oven about 10 to 15 minutes. If wrapping is not heat-proof, unwrap, place in paper bag, and heat in 350-degree oven about 10 to 15 minutes for small items, about 20 minutes for loaves.

TUNNELS, AIR POCKETS

This time: Even the largest air pockets won't show when the tunneled item is crumbled and turned into a bread pudding, stuffing, or a pudding cake (pieces of cake or sweet bread covered with pudding and topped with fruit). Or soak crumbs in rum, top with preserves and chill. Before serving, top with whipped cream and nuts or make fruit roll pudding (p. 339).

Next time: Tunnels are an indication of overbeating. For most quick breads, slightly lumpy batter is okay. Mix dry ingredients before adding liquids, then blend batter with a rubber spatula. Do not beat.

Breads, Yeast

COLLAPSED

This time: Out-of-shape bread still tastes good. If the center is slightly doughy, toast it before eating, or remove, cook completely and use for crumbs. Misshapen bread can be used for stuffings, bread puddings (p. 339), or croutons.

Next time: Review this checklist of main reasons for collapse: overrising, inadequate flour strength, underkneading, jarring the risen bread, or uneven oven heat. Dough should not be allowed to rise more than double its original size (see *Overrisen Dough*, below). Use a good high-gluten bread flour—the free-form breads are even more dependent upon flour strength. Bread dough must be kneaded adequately to develop gluten; a well-kneaded dough should spring back as though it has life of its own when you press it lightly. Jarring the risen bread or very uneven heat in a faulty oven also may be responsible for your bread looking like a ski jump. Pamper risen bread like a baby.

DRY

This time: Make garlic or herb bread from your disappointing loaf and you'll be delighted with the transformation. Slice in thick wedges, brush with butter blended with garlic, onion, or herbs and grated Parmesan. Heat in moderate oven until toasted lightly; or bake bread cubes in clarified butter for croutons.

Next time: This texture problem can arise from several conditions, so review the reasons and take precautions. Too much yeast in the recipe dries out the bread. So does overrising (see *Overrisen Dough,* below). If the proofed dough has risen in too hot an area, the result will be the same; don't place in an oven set at low or on a burner. It is best to allow dough to rise, covered with greased plastic wrap, at room temperature (72 to 78 degrees F.), away from drafts. Too much flour causes dryness—add just enough to prevent dough from being sticky. Amount varies with humidity, so don't follow recipe exactly. Be sure eggs are medium or large, appropriate for most recipes. When using small eggs, increase number to make up difference (three small equal two large). Knead the dough more to work in the flour and develop gluten.

HEAVY

This time: Heavy bread thinly sliced often makes great toast when smeared with good jelly or jam. Thickly sliced, it can surprise you by being soufflélike after an egg–milk soaking for French toast. Other alternatives: cut into tiny cubes and toast for croutons; dry out for breadcrumbs; use in bread pudding. See also spinach quiche (p. 330), lentil-cheese meat loaf (p. 322), and fruit roll pudding (p. 339).

Next time: The delicious whole grains may be substituted for white flour, but they produce heavier loaves. To get lighter, higher loaves with the flavor of whole grains, mix with regular all-purpose wheat or high-gluten flour. Rye flour can be more of a problem, so be sure to include at least 50 percent high-gluten or 70 percent all-purpose wheat flour in your mixture. Rye flour has sufficient protein to develop gluten, but gummy substances in the flour prevent gluten from developing. Also, remember to add only enough flour to produce a workable dough. Compressed yeast produces a better volume and more open crumb structure than dry yeast (see *Dry*)

(TOO) LIGHT TEXTURED

This time: Warm bread right from the oven is tempting, but for nice slices, let it cool completely before taking a serrated knife to it. If the bread is very light and falls apart, try chilling first, then cut slices and toast. Or use for bread pudding or crumbs, or fruit roll pudding (p. 339).

Next time: Too light a texture is mainly the result of overrising. Let dough rise only as much as recipe suggests—usually until doubled in volume. (See *Overrisen Dough,* below).

MOLDY

This time: Discard very moldy bread; small moldy parts can be trimmed away. Use scraps of bread for stuffing or pudding (see bread pudding, p. 339).

Next time: Refrigerating bread retards mold but accelerates staling—fine if you want bread several days before using it stale. To keep bread both fresh and mold-free, freeze.

OVERRISEN DOUGH

This time: Remove putty dough from pan, place on floured board, and knead lightly. Reshape and put back in greased pan. Let rise only until almost doubled in volume—usually about 30 to 40 minutes for a regular loaf. Bake as usual, following recipe.

Next time: Retard rising by refrigerating dough covered in oiled plastic wrap. Later remove pan of dough from refrigerator, shape, let rise until doubled in size and bake. Dough also may be frozen.

STALE

This time: Make seasoned toast (see *Dry*), croutons, or crumbs. Stale bread is required for many recipes, such as French toast, stuffing, bread pudding (see fruit roll pudding, p. 339), crusts for individual quiches (see spinach quiches in breadcrumb crusts, p. 330), or meat loaf (see lentil-cheese meat loaf, p. 322).

Next time: Store bread in clean, well-ventilated, cool, dry place up to 2 or 3 days. Refrigeration accelerates staling, depending on bread. For longer storage, freeze.

UNEVEN SHAPE

This time: Sweeter yeast dough, such as coffee breads, can be trimmed and frosted to camouflage their shapes. If badly mis-shapen, use in puddings or stuffings.

Next time: Use proper-sized pans for recipe. Too much or too little dough in a pan affects the bread shape. Allow enough space for expansion on or in pans. Shaping should be done evenly to form proper-size product. Check oven temperature. If the bread looked well balanced when going in but came out lopsided, it's likely the oven heats unevenly. Leave space between pans on oven racks so air can circulate freely.

DOUGH WON'T RISE

This time: Dissolve 1 package active dry yeast and 1 teaspoon sugar in ½ cup warm water (110 degrees). Mix in ½ cup flour. Let stand in warm place for 10 minutes or until spongy. Beat this mixture into unrisen dough, then knead in enough additional flour for correct consistency. Proceed as usual by placing dough in warm place to double in size. The first rising is the slowest.

Next time: Check date on yeast package. If unsure of freshness, proof yeast by dissolving a little of the cake with sugar and a little of the dry in warm water (105 to 115 degrees); in a short time both should bubble and rise slightly. If no action, yeast is dead. If unable to use before expiration date, store in freezer. Yeast can be killed with too-hot water. Dissolve active dry yeast in water 105 to 115 degrees (or up to 130 degrees when dry yeast is added to dry ingredients) and compressed yeast in 85 to 95 degree liquid.

Freezing Dough: Wrap shaped dough in pan in moisture-vapor-proof wrap, seal and freeze. Or freeze in pan without wrapping just until hard, then remove from pan, wrap, and return to freezer immediately. Store up to 2 weeks. Replace dough in pan before thawing. Thaw in wrapping in refrigerator overnight. Brush tops with oil, let rise in moist, warm place until doubled, and bake as usual.

Freezing Bread: Cool bread after baking; wrap in moisture-vapor-proof material, seal, and freeze up to 6 months. Thaw in wrap at room temperature or remove wrapping and place in 300 degree oven 20 to 30 minutes.

Breading—See *Deep-fried foods.*

Broccoli—Very closely related to cauliflower, this vegetable is a latecomer in this country. Although grown by Thomas Jefferson in Monticello in the early 1800s, and known to be eaten for about two thousand years in Europe, broccoli wasn't commercially produced here until the 1920s, when Italian immigrants and California vegetable growers furthered its cause.

DISCOLORED

This time: Mash or purée for vegetable timbale (p. 333), or cream of vegetable soup (p. 315).

Next time: Overcooking or an acid medium causes discoloration. When broccoli is very young, cover and steam it like asparagus:

upright with stems in about ½ cup boiling water until just tender, about 10 to 12 minutes. Or remove tough parts of stalk and large, tough leaves (save for steamed greens or soup), slash large stalks to facilitate more even cooking. Soak in cold water a few minutes, drain; then cook in small amount of salted water or stock, uncovered first minute or two, then covered until tender. The vapor acids that first come off the vegetable tend to discolor it, so let them escape the first few minutes. If quite mature, cook like cabbage and other sulphur-containing vegetables—covered with water in an open utensil until tender, about 15 minutes. Save any cooking liquid for sauces or soups, since the vitamin C from the vegetable is water soluble. To ensure a bright green color, add a pinch of baking soda per quart cooking water. Add lemon juice, tomato sauce, or other acids at very end of cooking to prevent yellowing.

OVERCOOKED: See *Discolored.*

SHRIVELED, WILTED (RAW)

This time: Once very wilted, it's difficult for broccoli to recover. Try trimming the very ends of stalks under cold water, holding them under a short time; stalks may absorb some moisture and freshen a bit. A second remedy is to cut into small pieces and use in a casserole or sauced dish. Or mash or purée for vegetable timbale (p. 333), or cream of vegetable soup (p. 315).

Next time: Select heads with green, tight bud clusters and fresh green leaves; yellow, open bud clusters and woody stems indicate age. For optimum freshness, store properly; trim any tough ends of stalks under water, wrap unwashed vegetable in plastic wrap or bag, and keep in vegetable bin of refrigerator. Try to use within 2 to 3 days.

SMELLY

This time: Try the old wives' trick of dropping a piece of rye bread into the pot. If the smell has already made itself at home, simmer cloves in a little vinegar.

Next time: The odor is caused by overcooking—cook young broccoli until just tender.

Broth—See *Soup.*

Brown Betty—See *Apple; Pudding.*

Brownies—See *Cookie.*

Brown Sugar—See *Sugar.*

Brussels Sprouts—Named after the city where they supposedly were first grown many centuries ago, these plum-size descendants of the wild cabbage did not become a crop of substance in this country until the early 1900s. They gained wide popularity as a frozen vegetable after World War II. Sprouts grow in rows on one large cabbage head. A good winter vegetable, they are best when small.

DISCOLORED

This time: Chop and incorporate into soufflés or omelets, purée for vegetable timbale (p. 333), cream of vegetable soup (p. 315), or turn into a casserole or saucy dish. Add a little soy sauce or sugar to help counter any heavy sulphur taste from overcooking. An orange sauce made with grated rind is particularly good with sprouts. Another appealing treatment is grated nutmeg with butter and bread crumbs, or grated Parmesan and garlic butter. To best camouflage their appearance, use a heavy cheese, mustard, or mushroom sauce.

Next time: Acid or overcooking will cause discoloration. Cut off stems; gash ends. Soak in cold salted water a few minutes before rinsing, draining, and steaming, or cooking in rapidly boiling water to cover. Reduce heat and simmer, uncovered, just until tender, about 10 minutes. Or drop into small amount salted boiling water, cook uncovered 3 minutes; cover and continue cooking 2 to 7 minutes. To ensure a bright green, add a small pinch of baking soda per quart of cooking water. Add lemon juice, vinegar, tomato sauce, or other acid at very end of cooking.

OVERCOOKED: See *Discolored.*

WILTED (RAW)

This time: Once wilted, it's difficult to bring Brussels sprouts back to a pleasing appearance. Trim off any yellowed outer leaves. If sprouts still aren't palatable, treat as discolored/overcooked, above.

Next time: Choose green, firm, compact sprouts with no yellow spots or wilted leaves. Smaller are more desirable. Store in plastic bag or wrap in refrigerator. Use within about 4 days, if possible.

Buckwheat Groats—*See Cereal.*

Bugs—No reflection on your housekeeping. The saw-toothed grain beetle and his cousins thrive in flour, biscuit mix, cornmeal, and other cereals (except whole-grain which they can't penetrate), crackers, raisins, sugar, spices. Fresh packages from the store are often infested with one of the life stages of a bug. Suddenly your shelves are alive and crawling. Don't worry—the bugs carry no diseases and are harmless. But how do you clear them out of the kitchen?

This common pantry pest is quite prolific. One female can lay 45 to 285 very hearty eggs in a single cluster. They hatch in 3 to 5 days at approximately 80 degrees; give them 17 days in cooler weather. "All you need is one female and one male and you're in business," says entomologist Eric Smith of the Chicago Field Museum of Natural History. "The lower the moisture content, the more they thrive. For instance, old dried raisins will have more attraction for them than fresh fruit. The eggs are very impervious to liquids, so even mild insecticides won't work." He offers some of the nonchemical tips below for ridding your pantry of these pests. For those really plagued by insects he recommends *Urban Entomology,* by Walter Ebling. Smith says that no matter what type foodstuff these pests may infest (dried meats or vegetable products) they all have similar biologies. The grain beetle is the most common. The basic advice that follows can be applied to all these crawling critters.

This time: Discard badly infested items—those with only one creature might be salvaged. Smith advises transferring items to tightly sealed glass jars or heavy plastic containers (the bugs can chew through plastic wrap). Clear shelves and vacuum, using a brush to get into crevices, and wash with soapy water. As a precautionary measure, some swear by bay leaves scattered on shelves. The bugs are repelled by the bay leaves, but the question still remains, "Where do they go?" Others recommend placing a stick of spearmint chewing gum into the flour canister. (Just remember to remove it when measuring flour for bread.) To be really sure, place new products into a zero-degree freezer for 24 hours. The deep freeze kills eggs, larvae, and adult bugs; (and my crackers didn't get soggy when I tried it). Other experts recommend heat treatment, but placing flour in the oven dries it and would affect the outcome of recipes. Crackers could be heated successfully, however. And of course cooking a cereal would take care of any hidden life.

Next time: Shop at a store with fewer infested products and follow any or all suggested methods above.

Bulghur—*See Cereal.*

Burn—*See Fires, Burns.*

Butter—By law, butter must contain a minimum of 80 percent milkfat—about ten quarts of milk are needed to make one pound. Butter probably was discovered when milk carried by nomads churned itself during their travels. And man has found numerous uses for the animal fat ever since, from cooking to medicinal and beauty-aid purposes. Even brides were sometimes bartered with butter. Until an Iowa creamery launched the U.S. butter industry in 1871, churning was a home chore. For years now the yellow spread has been lathered on bread, creamed in doughs, melted over waffles, piled onto baked potatoes and brushed over broiled fish.

To clarify: Melt over low heat in heavy saucepan. Milk solids sink while the fat rises. Skim off white froth on top, then pour off clear butter, leaving sediment behind. Keep clarified butter in covered container up to several weeks in refrigerator, or longer in freezer. Clarified butter will withstand higher temperatures without browning—very good for quick sautéing, for example.

ACID TASTE

This time: U.S. Grade B butter may have a slight acid taste. If you don't like it plain as a spread, use for cooked piquant dishes— herbed lemony vegetable mixture, sautéed, is one idea. Or use in recipes requiring the heavier taste of browned butter. This sour butter is also compatible with mustard, horseradish, cracked peppercorns, garlic, and a host of other flavorings that can be mixed into it.

Next time: Buy U.S. Grade AA or A butter if the taste of tangy

Grade B is not to your liking. Also avoid processed butter, usually sold in bulk, which is butter rechurned with milk to overcome undesirable odors and flavors. Store butter tightly wrapped in cold part of refrigerator; loosely covered butter can absorb odors and flavors of other foods.

BROWNED (BY MISTAKE)

This time: Browned butter is called for in many recipes where a more robust flavor is wanted. It's especially good on fish, meat, and some vegetables, so even if you hadn't intended the browning, try it. If the butter was browned preparing a baked product, though, melt a fresh batch and save the browned for a cooked dish.

Next time: Melt butter very slowly over low heat, in top of double boiler or according to manufacturer's directions in a microwave oven. Or add a little salad oil; the blend doesn't burn as readily as butter alone.

FROZEN (OR TOO HARD)

This time: Butter can present a slight problem when it's stone cold and hard and you need it now. The best way to thaw it is slowly, in the refrigerator. But to quick-thaw, invert a bowl that has been rinsed in boiling water over the butter. Microwave-oven owners can use the slow-thaw cycle. When you want to mix or whip the butter, as in a dough, cut into small pieces and it warms up faster.

Next time: As soon as the refrigerator butter dish is empty, replace from the freezer. Butter freezes well in its original container up to 1 month. For longer storage, overwrap in moisture-vapor-proof paper.

(TOO) HARD: See *Frozen.*

(TOO) SOFT

This time: The logical solution is to get the butter cold again. Depending on your time, you may put it in the refrigerator or freezer or (wrapped in a plastic bag) in a bowl of ice. For some recipes that require cold butter, such as puff pastry, you may even knead the butter in ice water, working with your hands until it is pliable.

Next time: Keep butter stored in cold part of refrigerator; one stick kept in the butter keeper of refrigerator gives you some at spreadable consistency. When warming butter up to room temperature, leave on counter about 1 hour beforehand, away from heat of range or oven. Less time is needed during hot weather. In very hot kitchens and for more control over softening, rinse bowl with boiling water and invert over butter on dish or bowl.

STALE

This time: Old butter can develop a stale flavor. Avoid serving it plain as a spread. Instead, use for cooking and add seasoning to camouflage taste. A dash of butter flavoring might help, or brown to intensify flavor and serve over vegetables, fish, or meat.

Next time: Select a top grade butter, U.S. Grade AA or A. Store in its original package in coldest part of refrigerator at 40 degrees or lower. Try to use within several weeks. For longer storage, freeze after overwrapping in moisture-vapor-proof paper. Butter should be kept in a covered dish or compartment and used within several days. Salted butter lasts longer than sweet.

Buttermilk—*See Milk.*

Butternut—*See Nuts.*

Cabbage (red)

DISCOLORED

This time: So your red cabbage is no longer red? Don't worry. Blue or purple cabbage can return to its original color. Add a little vinegar or lemon juice to the cooking water, then stir, covering all parts of the blue cabbage, and watch it turn red.

Next time: The color pigments called anthocyanins give the red, blue, or purple color to plants. They are readily water soluble but stable to heat. From the above experiment, you know the color is intensified with acid and altered to a blue-purple in alkali; the change is reversible. To ensure color retention when cooking red cabbage, cook in a little water in a glass or unchipped enamel pot, cover after a few minutes, and cook only until tender, about 10 minutes for large wedges, longer for a whole head. Add a little acid to hard water. Avoid using aluminum or iron utensils.

OVERCOOKED: *See Cabbage (white).*

Next time: Follow cooking directions above for red cabbage (see *Discolored*).

OVERMATURE

This time: Steam or boil longer than usual. Cover very mature cooked cabbage with a sauce to camouflage and complement its age: a sweet-sour sauce or an Oriental soy mixture is especially apropos.
Next time: See Cabbage (white).

SMELLY: *See Cabbage (white).*

WILTED: *See Cabbage (white).*

Cabbage (white)

DISCOLORED

This time: If the discoloration occurred during cooking, add 1 to 2 teaspoons vinegar or lemon juice per quart of water. If color doesn't reverse itself enough, remove cabbage from water and toss with sprinkling of vinegar or lemon juice. If necessary, camouflage color by sautéing, incorporating in a brown-stock soup, or tomato sauce, or by baking with a sweet-sour sauce, etc.
Next time: The color pigment flavone is water soluble and turns gray-brown if overcooked; alkali brings out a yellow hue; acid makes it almost colorless. So avoid baking soda, very hard alkaline water, and overcooking. To insure retention of white color, add a bit of acid to water. When intending to eat cabbage raw, select a compact, fresh white head. Trim off any discolored leaves. Store no more than a week wrapped in plastic in covered container in refrigerator. Avoid cutting until ready to use. When making coleslaw, immediately place shredded cabbage in vinegar or lemon juice.

OVERCOOKED

This time: Drain, pat dry, shred, and sauté in oil or bacon fat until browned and slightly crisp. Season with caraway or fennel seeds, other herbs of choice, and sautéed onion. Or prepare a cabbage soup. Try giving the soup an Oriental twist by adding soy sauce, bean sprouts, and sliced scallions. There's always hope!

Next time: Drop cabbage in rapidly boiling water, reduce to simmer, and cook uncovered until just tender: about 10 minutes for large wedges, longer for whole head. Some of the vitamin C will be lost in the water and will evaporate without a cover, but this method produces a more palatable product. Eat raw for maximum vitamins.

OVERMATURE

This time: Cut out center and drop sliced or shredded cabbage into boiling milk for a couple of minutes. Drain and combine with a white sauce made from the milk, cheese sauce, or another sauce derived from the white. You can use the cooked milk for a cream of cabbage soup. Another use for old heads is to boil them.

Next time: Select firm heads heavy for their size with crisp outer leaves of fresh green color. Avoid heads that are very white or puffy, or those with leaf bases separated from the stem, indicating overmaturity and coarse texture. Store unwashed in plastic bag up to a week for firm heads, only a few days for softer ones.

SMELLY

This time: Add a piece of rye bread to the pot. If the smell has already permeated the air, simmer cloves in a little vinegar, or try any other method of perfuming the air: pomander, potpourri, airfreshener. If you prefer another food odor, crush garlic and sauté. But be prepared to leave the kitchen.

Next time: Soak cabbage in ice water a short time before cooking to help eliminate the odor. Cook just until tender, uncovered (see *Overcooked*).

WILTED

This time: Soak in ice water, with a bit of acid if water is alkaline. Drain, shake dry. (If cooked and wilted, see recommendations for *Overcooked.*) If wilted beyond repair, the only remedies are recipes that disguise the texture: sauces, soups, etc.

Next time: See selection and storage tips, *Discolored.*

Cake—The earliest cakes were crude honey concoctions that ancient Egyptians and Greeks offered to their gods. The two main types of cake can be classified by the method of mixing the batters: creaming (those made with fat) and foaming (no or low fat). Weather also affects cake; see *Weather.*

Creaming Method: Exemplified by pound and layer cakes, where shortening or butter and sugar are creamed together, giving leavening power in addition to the usual addition of baking powder or soda.

BREAKS, CRUMBLES

This time: Chunks of crumbly cake can be turned into delicious desserts by sprinkling with liqueur and topping with a custard or fruit sauce or dipping into a chocolate fondue. Small squares or rounds can also be frosted as individual cakes.

Next time: Be sure batter is mixed well enough by hand or use a faster mixer speed. Sugar is a tenderizer and aerating agent, and too much in a recipe, just like too much baking powder (which is bitter), can cause a crumbly texture. Or perhaps the recipe needs more eggs; use medium or large eggs, unless otherwise specified in the directions. If the cake stuck to the pan, grease and flour pan or line bottom with greaseproof paper. Best to use seasoned cake pans that are never washed, only wiped with paper toweling. To season cake pans, grease well with a high-smoking-point shortening; bake in 350-degree oven 3 to 5 minutes. Cool; regrease and sprinkle inside with cake flour. Cakes are very delicate when just out of the oven. So unless specified in recipe, allow to cool in pan on wire rack 10 to 20 minutes before removing from pan.

CRUSTY, SUGARY CRUST

This time: Cover with a tart fruit or liqueur glaze rather than a sweet, sugary frosting. A very heavy crust can be trimmed by the careful working of a serrated knife before glazing or frosting.

Next time: Excess sugar produces a dark, caramelized crust; when sugar crystals are too large in batter, cake will have brown spots. Use a finer granulated sugar, and perhaps less. Examine the recipe and compare with a reliable source. Be sure the butter and sugar are sufficiently creamed and the eggs are beaten properly. Overbaking causes a thick crust.

DRY, HEAVY

This time: Although a dry, heavy-crumbed cake can be disappointing to serve as intended, it absorbs moisture from custard or fruit pudding and becomes a delicious base for a sweet treat. Thin slices can be soaked in rum or sweet wine, spread with jelly or jam, bathed in custard sauce, and chilled trifle fashion. Just before serving, top with whipped cream and slivered almonds. Or poke holes throughout and pour over a sugar-water-liqueur syrup; let stand before serving. A quick way to solve the dry-cake problem is to sprinkle with liqueur, then top with ice cream and more liqueur.

Next time: Unless otherwise specified in recipe, use cake flour. Add more baking powder if all-purpose flour was used. When recipe calls for sifted flour, be sure to sift before measuring. Sift after measuring when amount of flour is followed by "sifted." Recipe may need more fat. Underbeating ingredients also can cause a heavy cake, but, reduce beating time on a warm day. Avoid overgreasing and overfilling the pans. Check oven temperature for accuracy; overbaking will dry out the cake. Bake cake just until cake tester inserted in center comes out clean. Cool about 10 minutes in pan before turning out and cooling on wire racks.

FALLS

This time: Slice into thin layers, trim edges, spread with ice cream (or other favorite filling), and roll up. Wrap well in foil and freeze, then slice ice-cream roll to serve. Or cut cake into chunks and use in cake pudding with a favorite sauce. (See fruit roll pudding, p. 339.)

Next time: Possibly too much baking powder (cake will taste bitter) or sugar was used; use reliable recipe and level measurements. Avoid opening oven during baking while cake is rising, since a draft or jarring could cause cake to fall. Do not remove cake from oven until completely baked. (Cake is baked fully when it begins to pull away from sides of pan and no imprint is left when top is lightly touched with finger.)

LOPSIDED

This time: A slightly lopsided cake can be leveled with the aid of a knife and frosting. Another choice is to cut into pieces and use in pudding cake or slice and make trifle (see *Dry*).

Next time: Uneven heat or incomplete mixing of ingredients can cause cake to be lopsided. Mix baking powder with flour thoroughly before sifting. Check oven thermostat; avoid opening door during baking.

OVERBAKED: See *Dry*.

PEAK OR HILL IN CENTER OF CAKE

This time: A serrated knife and steady hand will do wonders to remove the peak; frosting does the rest.

Next time: Overbeating, too much flour, or insufficient fat in recipe can cause the problem. The mixture toughens through over-mixing after flour has been added. Examine pans to make sure they're not warped. Check oven temperature, and do not cover bottom of oven with foil—this causes uneven heat reflection and improper air circulation, which can result in an unevenly baked cake. Do not overfill pans. Always spread batter to sides of pan, leaving a slight depression in center, unless otherwise specified. Do not place pan too near top of oven.

RUNS OVER PAN

This time: Put a baking pan on the rack beneath the overflowing cake pan to catch dripping batter. Do not place cake pan directly on baking pan; moving it may cause cake to fall and the larger pan directly under it can prevent proper heat circulation. When cake cools, trim away excess; frost as desired. Use leftover trimmings for pudding cake or make crumbs, soak in liqueur, and sprinkle over ice cream.

Next time: Be sure to use pan size recommended for recipe. Never fill pans more than ½ or ⅔ full. Bake any remaining batter in cupcake pans. If correct pan size was used, select a slightly higher oven temperature next time and bake the cake on lowest rack position.

SOGGY

This time: A soggy texture won't matter when you soak the cake in rum or other favorite liquor. Cut into squares or crumble, soak in your favorite spirit: top squares with fruit, whipped cream, ice cream, or custard sauce; sprinkle liquor-soaked crumbs over ice cream, pudding, cream pies, and anything else that will benefit from their rich flavor. When there's time, allow the supermoist cake to dry out, preferably in a very low oven; then soak. Texture will have more substance.

Next time: Double check proportion of ingredients in recipes; too much sugar, liquid, or leavening—especially eggs—can result in soggy cake. Eggs moisten and aerate their own weight in flour. Be sure to mix ingredients well.

STALE

This time: Slice thin and make trifle (see *Dry*) or use for fruit roll pudding (p. 339). Stale cake actually holds up better than fresh when combined with a custard or fruit sauce.

Next time: Very moist or perishable cakes (with whipped cream or custard) must be stored in the refrigerator; but most others keep well in a cake saver or other covered container in a cool, dry place for several days. Freeze for longer storage.

Foaming Method: No- or low-fat cakes in which leavening is achieved by beating air into eggs; e.g., angel food, sponge, chiffon.

FALLS WHILE BAKING

This time: A fallen cake may be more compact in certain areas, but the texture will not show when cut up and used for fondue or pudding. Another choice is to make crumbs, which can be frozen for future use. Soak in liquor and use as topping.

Next time: Add a little more flour. Be sure oven temperature is accurate. Avoid opening oven door during baking, especially at the beginning. Bake cake until it tests done with cake tester and springs back when lightly pressed with finger.

FALLS OUT OF PAN DURING COOLING

This time: Immediately place cake on wire rack, still inverted, to cool thoroughly. If the cake broke when it fell, serve slices or hunks with fruit sauce or custard sauce, fruit, and perhaps whipped cream.

Next time: Do not grease the pan. Sometimes a new, very smooth pan is the cause. Place new tinware angel-food-cake pans in a 350-degree oven for several hours. Also, lightly rub bottom and sides with steel wool. This treatment is not required for aluminum pans. Be sure to bake cake long enough.

HEAVY

This time: A thin layer of a heavy foam-type cake forms a nice base for a baked Alaska or any number of fillings and toppings. Try sprinkling with sweet wine, covering with whipped cream cheese, and spooning a fruit sauce over. Or cut into chunks, then arrange in

Bundt pan with fresh fruit and pour pudding around; chill for a delightful fruit-pudding-cake dessert.

Next time: Too much flour or all-purpose instead of cake flour can cause a coarse, tough, heavy texture. Perhaps the recipe requires more eggs; egg whites should be beaten until stiff for best volume. Overfolding, overbaking, and too high a temperature can also cause the problem. Remove the cake from the pan only after it has cooled, never when still warm. Follow directions for inverting cake when cooling. Cake shrinks back if allowed to cool right side up. The exception is certain types of sponge cake, which must be removed after 5 minutes.

SOGGY BOTTOM

This time: It's easy to peel or trim off a soggy outer layer with a knife. The surgery won't show if this part becomes the bottom of the cake. When a substantial amount of the bottom section is very moist, you might slice it off as a layer, dry in a low oven, then soak with liquor and top with sauce and fruit or ice cream. Or crumble and use in pudding. Remainder of cake can be left intact, frosted or sauced according to plans. For example, a cut-down sponge cake could still be used for strawberry shortcake.

Next time: Check recipe for excess liquid or possibly fat. Be sure egg whites are sufficiently beaten. Foam cakes should be removed from pans within 1 hour if cake is very close to the table when inverted; this causes condensation of steam and a soggy bottom.

STICKY TOP

This time: A heavy glaze with pieces of fruit will cover the top. To make it easier to spread, you might find it better to scrape or trim off the stickiest top part.

Next time: Use less sugar, bake cake several minutes longer, or raise oven temperature during last several minutes of baking.

TOUGH

This time: Slice very thin, cut out shapes with cookie cutters, and frost. Great idea for a children's party, and the kids will love helping to decorate the little cakes. Or use these cut-outs as decorations on a larger cake or other desserts. If cutting up isn't your style, then use a thin cake layer as a base for various toppings (see *Heavy*). Or turn cubes into puddings or soaked crumbs into toppings.

Next time: The recipe may need more sugar, which is a tenderizer. Avoid overbeating egg whites until very dry; beat only until stiff, straight peaks form. Overmixing or using all-purpose instead of cake flour also toughens as does overbaking. Foam-type cakes are done when cracks in top feel dry and no imprint remains when top is lightly touched.

TUNNELS

This time: There's hope for the cake that resembles Swiss cheese. Slice it thin or cut up and serve smothered with a custard or fruit sauce, whipped cream, and fruit. Crumbled into bite-size pieces, it makes a delicious sweet treat when chilled in a pan with pudding and fruit. Then there is always the crumb alternative; freeze crumbs in container if desired, then soak in liquor and use as dessert topping.

Next time: Insufficient blending of sugar and flour with egg whites can cause large holes; blend well with rubber spatula or wire whisk. Cut through batter several times before placing cake in oven. Another insurance against air pockets is to lightly tap pan on table before baking.

Cake Icing—*See Icings, Glazes.*

Canadian Bacon—*See Meat.*

Canapés—Bite-size open-face sandwiches with a bread or pastry base and a spread or filling; served hot or cold as appetizers.

Candy, Confectionery—Confections—sugar itself, in fact— were once enjoyed only by the wealthy and titled. Traces of early sweets made of honey and seeds have been discovered in the ancient tombs of several Egyptian monarchs. Sugar made its debut in the New World thanks to Christopher Columbus, whose mother-in-law owned a sugar plantation. He brought sugar cane cuttings on his second voyage. Cane crops quickly flourished in the Caribbean region, then in various countries of Central and South America. By the 19th century, modern sugar-refining techniques had removed the sweetener from the ranks of exclusive luxuries. Sugar cookery is fascinating because it changes character as the temperature is increased. Cook the same sugar-water mixture to five different stages and you get five different products!

General tips: Unlike many foods, once candy is a failure, it is difficult and sometimes impossible to correct; so follow these tips to prevent problems.

1. Sugar (syrup) temperature is critical to successful candy making, so use a good reliable candy thermometer. Read thermometer at eye level—looking down on it can make a difference of up to 3 degrees. Some advise keeping the thermometer in a container of hot water when not testing sugar, but other confectioners merely leave it on the counter.

2. Avoid overflowing by choosing an extra large pan for cooking candy mixtures. Most candy mixtures, especially caramels, produce voluminous bubbles.

3. Use a clean, heavy-bottomed saucepan that conducts heat well to avoid scorching. Professionals use unlined copper, but aluminum or stainless with aluminum clad is fine for fudges, caramels, etc.

4. Stir candy mixture with a wooden spoon in figure 8 pattern to avoid scorching. Wooden stirring utensils are best and do not scratch.

5. Avoid candy making on humid days, since candy absorbs moisture from the air. Caramels, nut brittles, toffees, and nougats are most susceptible to humidity. Pros adjust for humidity by cooking candy mixtures 1 or 2 degrees F. higher.

Problems of basic sugar cooking in candy making

CRYSTALS FORMED

This time: Dip a pastry or vegetable brush into cold water, shake off excess drops, and use to "wash down" side of pan—a kind of crystal magnet. (One pro confectioner I know uses a toilet brush!) Some candy makers prefer covering the saucepan for at least 2 to 3 minutes when mixture comes to a boil; the steam dissolves any crystals. Watch carefully so syrup doesn't boil over. When saucepan is uncovered, place thermometer into candy. If crystal formation on the thermometer makes it difficult to read, remove and wipe off crystals with damp cloth or brush.

Next time: Be sure all sugar is dissolved before mixture comes to a boil. Stir mixture carefully, only enough to dissolve sugar and to prevent sticking to pan and scorching. Cook candy (except caramels) at steady boil without stirring; best to prevent heat from fluctuating. Remove any sugar crystals that form on side of pan when mixture is coming to a boil. Remove thermometer as soon as candy is cooked, since large crystals tend to form around it (especially if returned to pot after having been set on counter). These can make the candy grainy. Do *not* scrape the pan, particularly with caramels. Scraping and agitation will create large crystals. Egg whites, used in some candies, retard crystallization.

CURDLED (CARAMELS)

This time: Cool candy before beating and you'll probably see it become smooth. Stirring or beating warm candy quickly forms crystals. If not creamy enough, return to pan; add a little water or milk and boil it again; then follow directions. When you have exhausted patience, crush or chop grainy candy and use as topping for ice cream, frozen yogurt, iced cakes, or parfaits.

Next time: Follow recipe directions precisely for mixing ingredients steadily (e.g. folding, stirring, beating, etc.). Remove thermometer as soon as candy is cooked to prevent large crystals from forming and causing a curdled or grainy texture. If directions advise cooling to warm (about 100 to 110 degrees F.), test bottom of pan with backs of fingers (more sensitive than tips); it should feel just barely warm. Be sure to allow candy to cool properly before beating. Find recipes that call for corn syrup (usually used in ratio of about 2 tablespoons per cup sugar), which is credited by pros for the creaminess of fudge and penuche. Corn syrup, known as a "doctor" in the trade, regulates crystallization of the sugar. Milk and cream can curdle, so gradually add room-temperature milk, never quite "killing the boil."

Divinity

TOO STIFF TO SHAPE

This time: If too stiff to drop from a spoon, fold in a few drops of hot water.

Next time: Avoid overbeating egg whites to dry stage before adding cooked syrup; whites should be stiff but still glossy. Use medium eggs; if there is too much egg white in proportion to sugar, product will be dry and too stiff.

TOO THIN, DOES NOT SET UP

This time: Fold in one teaspoon sifted confectioners sugar; if still not stiff enough to use as candy, use as icing on cake. Or add lots of chopped nuts, spoon and pat into lightly oiled parchment-lined square dish. Let stand at room temperature until top has a firm crust; invert if desired; cut into squares. Or roll soft divinity into small balls and dip into finely chopped nuts for a crunchy special confection. Or continue to beat in mixer until cold. Beat in enough whipped sweet butter to make a stiff buttercream icing (may be stored in closed jar in refrigerator at least a week, or frozen). Or make mock marshmallow fluff (good ice-cream topping) by beating until cold in mixer, about 8 to 10 minutes, depending on quantity and consistency of mixture. Also, can thicken by adding melted tepid bittersweet chocolate to color, then beat until cold; add chocolate slowly while beating. Can store mock marshmallow fluff in airtight container in refrigerator about 2 days.

Next time: Be sure to beat egg whites to proper glossy but stiff-peak consistency before adding cooked syrup very slowly in thin, steady stream; beat vigorously until very stiff. Make certain bowl is grease-free. Or perhaps syrup wasn't cooked to a high-enough temperature. Check accuracy of thermometer and be sure to cook syrup to about 260 degrees F. on a dry day, to about 265 degrees F. when humid. Cool a few minutes before adding to egg whites.

Fondant

A creamy smooth confection made from sugar, water and some substance such as corn syrup (or milk and butter for rich candy centers). Fondant has more uses than any other cooked sugar mixture, from shiny frostings on wedding cakes and bonbons to rich candy centers, the most common type being coating fondant (or so-called water fondant). Fondant stores well for months in a cool, dry place when tightly covered. See also *Icings, Glazes, Cooked*.

CRYSTALS FORMED: *See problems of basic sugar cooking.*

LOSES SHEEN

This time: Beat in 1 tablespoon egg white to every cup of heated fondant.

Next time: Do not heat fondant over about 110 degrees F. or glossy appearance will be lost. Heat fondant in double boiler, adding stock syrup or water to thin.

Fudge
GRAINY
This time: See *Crystals Formed,* above.

Next time: Do not scrape bottom of fudge pot while pouring cooked fudge in pan. Don't stir fudge while cooling to 110 degrees. Add vanilla when cooled and ready to be beaten.

TOO STIFF TO SPREAD
This time: Add a few drops of hot cream to bring fudge back to spreading consistency.

Next time: Adjust recipe by cooking a couple of degrees lower.

Peanut Brittle
Peanut brittle is crisp and "brittle" because carbon dioxide from the baking soda is incorporated into the sugar mixture and from pulling the brittle into thin sheets.

TOO THICK AND TOUGH
This time: Chop fine or crush; use as topping for ice cream, cakes, and puddings. Break into very small pieces; dip edges in chocolate.

Next time: As soon as you can after spreading the brittle, when it lifts off the greased marble slab, loosen with spatula and begin stretching, wearing cotton gloves. Holding at opposite ends, pull, rotating to stretch brittle as evenly and as thinly as possible.

TOO STICKY
This time: Dry in moderate oven a few minutes.

Next time: Make peanut brittle on dry, fair day. Do not place in boxes until completely cooled.

To freeze candies:
Best on a dry day. Layer between wax paper in tightly covered container; store in freezer for several months. Thaw in refrigerator, then bring to room temperature before opening.

To store candies:

For several weeks store chocolates in boxes, and others in closed containers in cool place away from odors.

Canning—Putting up food, to use an old-fashioned term, is an exacting procedure. Both ingredients and equipment must be in perfect condition and directions must be followed explicitly. It is best to get a reliable up-to-date canning guide. Some good ones are available from the government and canning jar companies. The term *canning* here encompasses all foods so preserved, with a breakdown of general problems followed by those particularly relevant to fruits, jelly, etc. When any food has mold growth, is sour, becomes smelly, or in any way seems unsavory, discard.

General problems

BOTULISM THREAT (DUE TO INADEQUATE PROCESSING OF LOW-ACID FOODS)

This time: If any doubt, throw out! This most dreaded of food poisonings is caused by a deadly toxin that is produced in a sealed jar of low-acid food. Spores of the bacterium, clostridium botulinum, commonly found in soil and raw plant foods, thrive in tightly sealed jars of any underprocessed low-acid food and produce the toxin. This bacterium cannot grow in air or an acid medium. The spores are not killed by boiling. Therefore all meat, fish, poultry and low-acid vegetables must be adequately processed in a steam-pressure canner. Usually there are no obvious changes in food infected with the toxin. So a safety precaution, whenever doubtful, throw food out. *Do not taste!*

Next time: Follow up-to-date canning cookbook for explicit directions for canning the particular low-acid food.

CLOUDY LIQUID

This time: The unclear liquid may denote spoilage. To be safe, *do not use.* Use only when you're positive the murkiness was caused by minerals in the water, starch in a vegetable, or ground spices.

Next time: Follow precise canning procedure and length of time. Use soft water. The minerals in water or the starch in a vegetable could be a cause. Sometimes fillers in table salt could trigger clouding. Use a pure refined salt.

DARK SPOTS ON INNER SIDE OF METAL LID: SAFE UNLESS JAR UNSEALED

Spoilage is evident when a sealed jar unseals itself. *Do not use.* Otherwise, this is a harmless deposit from natural compounds. These brown or black deposits occur normally with some foods and cannot be prevented.

DISCOLORING AT TOP OF JAR

This time: As long as the seal is intact, the food is safe to consume. Scrape off darkened portions and use the rest.

Next time: Make certain food is completely covered with liquid before sealing jar. Leave correct amount of head space and remove air pockets by running a rubber scraper around inside of jar. Follow directions for processing method and length of time.

GRAYING OR BROWNING (SEAL INTACT)

This time: Discard. Not very common. Usually due to reaction with a metal, which may cause illness.

Next time: Use only soft water. Chipped enamelware, worn tinplate, or copper and iron utensils can be the cause. Minerals in either the water or cookware may react with acids and other natural food substances to produce discoloration.

JAR DOESN'T SEAL

This time: Use food immediately or store in refrigerator and treat like any opened canned food; use within several days. Or reread processing directions to analyze the cause, and reprocess.

Next time: Inspect jar and cap carefully and be sure to follow directions for specific type used. Check to see if any bits of food have moved up between jar and lid during processing, thus preventing a complete seal.

JAR UNSEALS

This time: Contents of jar that had appeared to seal and then came open *should not be used.* The condition is from food spoilage caused from a fine crack in the jar, underprocessing, or food fragments left on the jar's rim.

Next time: Use only jars and lids in good condition; examine carefully. Diligently follow canning directions for particular food in an up-to-date guide. Using a very clean, damp cloth, wipe threads and sealing surface of jar before adding lid.

Fruits

DARKEN UPON REMOVAL FROM JAR

This time: Discard. Probably due to underprocessing, so not safe to eat.

Next time: Process longer to destroy enzyme in fruit. Discoloration occurs when enzyme remains active. Begin counting processing time when full boil is reached in canner.

DISCOLORED

Sometimes a chemical change during cooking causes apples, peaches, pears, and sometimes quinces to turn pinkish or blue-purple when canned. Cannot be prevented, but eating quality is unaffected. Use in baking, sauces, or fillings if you prefer to camouflage.

Jelly

BLAND

This time: A mild-flavored jelly can be added to others with strong fruit taste; the blend is fine for use on toast and pancakes or in dessert fillings. Just before serving, perk up jelly by adding bits of fresh fruit. Melt for glaze (spike with mustard for ham, spices for poultry, or liqueur for cake). Jelly also can be cooked with wine, liqueur, or fruit juice for a dessert sauce.

Next time: Select full-flavored, tree-ripened fruit for best jelly. Flavor can be lost if storage conditions are not right or jelly is very old. Keep in cool, dark, dry place; use within 1 year.

BUBBLES

This time: When jelly resembles champagne complete with bubbly motion, don't use it. You're witnessing spoilage in action. The airtight seal probably was broken. Still bubbles, though, indicate nothing more than air that was suspended within the hot jelly during pouring. Jelly in this case is fine to use.

Next time: Use vacuum seals and test seals before storing to prevent risk of spoilage. To avoid suspended air bubbles, hold utensil near jar top and pour jelly quickly.

CLOUDY

This time: Only appearance is affected; the jelly tastes just as good. To camouflage, it may be blended with cream cheese for a sweet spread—great on muffins and toast. Or use as filling for jelly roll or cake. Melt for sauce or glaze.

Next time: Use firm, ripe fruit; if too green, jelly transparency will be lost. Overcooking before straining can be another cause; cook fruit until just tender. The juice must be allowed to drip through jelly bag at its own pace; do not press. However, the jelly maker must work quickly when pouring. To ensure clarity, jelly should be poured into jars and sealed as soon as jelling point is reached.

CRYSTAL FRAGMENTS IN JELLY

This time: Heat and use for baking, sauces, or glazes. The particles will dissolve when jelly is heated.

Next time: Use less sugar. The crystallization might have been caused by too much sugar, or incomplete dissolving of sugar due to undercooking. Extended cooking can cause excessive evaporation, resulting in the same condition. When undissolved sugar adhering to pan is visible, ladle juice into jars carefully to avoid getting these crystals in jelly.

FERMENTED

This time: Sour fermented odor and broken paraffin indicate spoilage. *Do not use*. As jelly spoils it usually breaks through paraffin and weeps.

Next time: Use vacuum seal and test seal before storing. When seal is not airtight, yeasts enter and grow.

MOLDY

This time: Best to discard—but a little mold at the surface can be spooned off and the jelly used.

Next time: Mold indicates incomplete seal. If using jelly glasses, melt paraffin and seal top of jelly properly. When using jars and vacuum lids, wipe jar top after filling; add hot lid with sealing compound down; screw band on tightly. Invert jar a few seconds and stand upright to cool. Test for good seal before storing.

SOFT

This time: A runny jelly makes a delicious dessert sauce when blended with wine, fruit juice, or other liquids. Combine with Worcestershire sauce, mustard, horseradish, or numerous other condiments for a piquant meat glaze. Or mix with frosting or cream cheese for a rich cake filling.

Next time: Recipe probably needs more sugar, which aids the jelling. Never double or in any way increase a reliable recipe. A regular batch uses about 1 to 1½ quarts juice. Increasing the amount prepared at one time produces a soft jelly.

STIFF

This time: Incorporate air by beating lightly and perhaps blending into cream cheese for a spread. Or melt and use for cake or jelly-roll filling, sauce or glaze.

Next time: Not enough sugar, too much pectin, or overcooking might have been the cause. Use riper fruit. Add less pectin if used. Cook for shorter period. Use a proportion of about 1½ cups sugar to 2 cups juice for most fruits when not adding pectin.

WEEPING

This time: If not fermented, use as planned. The weeping (syneresis) is more common in jellies that set quickly and does not affect quality.

Next time: The amount of acid, pectin quality, and environment all affect this condition. The last one can be controlled. Store jelly in dark, dry, cool place to prevent weeping.

Pickles

DISCOLORED

This time: Discard. May cause digestion upset if due to spoilage.

Next time: Ground spices, or whole spices packed in the jars, can cause darkening. Use only whole spices to flavor pickling liquid, and remove before packing. Since minerals can cause discoloration, use soft water and avoid iron, copper, brass, and zinc utensils. Check reliable guide for proper processing.

HOLLOW

This time: Fill with a favorite cheese (blue or cheddar are good choices) or chicken spread, then slice and serve as individual appetizers or as canapé garnishes, depending on size. Or chop and use in relish, spread, or salad.

Next time: The cuke grew that way. But you can separate the hollows from the solids by soaking. The hollow ones tend to float and can be separated from those intended for pickles. The hollowed specimens can be chopped for relishes. Use fresh cucumbers for pickling. Age sometimes dries out centers.

SHRIVELED

This time: Although safe to sample, product probably will be very tough, vinegary, and unpalatable.

Next time: The beginning solution of brine, vinegar, or sugar should be weak. Work up gradually to full amount in recipe.

SOFT

This time: A spongy texture is evidence of spoilage, so *do not use.*

Next time: Use heavier brine with pure, refined salt and more potent (4 to 6 percent) vinegar. Make certain pickles are totally immersed in liquid at all times. Remove scum during brining process and fill each jar while boiling, capping one at a time before filling next. Boiling temperature should be maintained throughout process, about 10 minutes.

Vegetables

BROWNING OF GREEN VEGETABLES

This time: Discard. Spoilage due to underprocessing is a possibility.

Next time: Prolonged cooking before canning or overmature produce can cause this problem. Select the freshest possible vegetables and time all cooking and processing carefully. Make certain liquid completely covers vegetables.

PALING OF GREEN VEGETABLES

Instead of showcasing them as a separate dish, combine with other ingredients and a sauce, such as in a casserole, to hide appearance. Chlorophyll decomposes with heat; the canning process has this effect on green things.

WHITE SEDIMENT (IN BOTTOM OF VEGETABLES)

This time: An overall murkiness usually indicates spoilage. If food feels soft and squishy, *do not use*. A little sediment at the bottom, however, is probably from minerals in the water or starch in the vegetables. Use food as intended.

Next time: Process vegetable according to specific directions, calculating exact time. Use soft water.

Cans—They're thought to give an eternal life to the foods packed within, and properly stored canned goods do last a long time. But like organic matter, they must have just the right environment to survive. Take two cans off the same factory line, ship one in a temperature-controlled truck to an air-conditioned store and then keep it in a cool, dry kitchen, and it will last for years. Transport the other can through intense heat, then store it in a place with radical temperature changes, and it may not last a month. Because no shopper can be sure how the product was handled before purchase, it's a good idea to rotate canned goods on the home shelf. Try to use within a year. The major concerns with cans are those with bulges, dents, or leaks.

BULGING

This time: Do not open or taste. This is one time you don't want to salvage the food. But don't throw it out. Call your local Food and Drug Administration office or the board of health to report it. By tracing the can serial number, an entire lot can be recalled. *Do not* open the can. If you already have, *do not* taste and do not feed it to the dog. The popped-out can appearance indicates gases produced by spoilage inside. However, one cannot assume that because a can doesn't bulge that it's free of botulism. Botulin toxins are the most potent known poisons. A tiny fraction of an ounce can be lethal for thousands of people. Low-acid foods, especially home canned, are susceptible (see *Canning*). When in doubt *discard*. Boiling does *not* destroy clostridium botulinum bacterium spores.

Next time: Never buy bulging cans, and report any you find. When canning low-acid foods, carefully follow reliable directions.

DENTED

This time: Slight dents can be the result of rough handling. Use contents as planned if, after opening, the product looks, smells, and tastes as usual. If appearance is not right, *do not taste.* Dispose of contents of badly twisted cans down the drain, where neither children nor dogs can retrieve them.

Next time: Examine cans carefully, avoiding any badly dented ones—especially those so badly crushed the seams are leaking. Properly handle and store cans. Don't let the kids play catch with the canned tomatoes.

LEAKY

A leak indicates air has seeped in and there is spoilage. *Do not use.*

Cantaloupe—*See Melons.*

Capers—Buds of the caper bush preserved in vinegared brine. Their concentrated piquant taste and striking gray-black color make them favorite additions to seafood and meat dishes or accompanying sauces or salads. To reduce saltiness somewhat, rinse capers in cool water.

Capon—*See Poultry.*

Caramel—*See Candy, Confectionery.*

Carrots—A joy for the cook; it's one of the least problematic of the vegetables—it stores well, holds its color in cooking, can be eaten raw or cooked numerous ways, has a refreshing, popular sweet flavor, and is very rich in vitamin A.

OVERMATURE

This time: Soak raw carrots in ice water with a little vinegar added for a few hours before using. Scrape carrots to retain nutrients; do not peel unless withered and darkened. Cooking helps to hide the age, especially if a little sugar is added to cooking water. If you think carrots still show their age, serve them with a dill white sauce, tarragon cheese sauce, or glaze. The latter is easily done by dipping cooked carrots in honey and gently heating, or by heating drained cooked carrots in equal parts butter and sugar until glazed and hot. Or grate and use in carrot pudding or cake.

Next time: Find firm, nicely shaped bright-orange carrots, free from cracks. Tiny baby carrots are the most tender and sweetest. Most carrots are sold topless in plastic bags. If possible, buy with tops still on, provided greens are fresh and not wilted. To store, remove tops, wrap in plastic wrap, and place in covered container, or leave packaged carrots in their bag and refrigerate up to a month.

OVERCOOKED

This time: Chop fine and use in soup, or mash as you would potatoes, with a little cream and/or butter, season with ginger, or nutmeg, and serve—pretty when presented in alternating mounds with mashed potatoes or turnips. The mashed carrots also can be placed in a heatproof dish, sprinkled with grated cheese, and broiled until golden.

Next time: Scrub and scrape (young carrots need no scraping), steam, about 25 minutes if young, up to 1 hour if old. Or cook in a little water, covered, until just tender: about 20 to 25 minutes for whole medium; 10 to 15 minutes for sliced; 5 to 10 minutes for diced or shredded.

Casseroles—Derogatory remarks about casseroles—such as "tonight's casserole reveals last night's supper" —are unfair! Many casseroles, like French cassoulet and Greek moussaka, are comprised of original ingredients cooked to order. Your own personal culinary blend can be exciting and just as delicious as a classic.

BLAND

This time: Even when the dish is finished baking you can still season the top with appropriate herbs and spices, squeeze over some lemon juice or grated cheese. Another idea is to serve with an accompanying sauce—chutney for a lamb or curry-flavored dish; a curry mayonnaise for a chicken-fruit-rice mixture; a rémoulade for a seafood casserole; a mustard-yogurt topping for a beef and mushroom bake.

Next time: Taste as you prepare the dish, keeping in mind that ground spices cook out quickly. Use fresh seasonings and crush whole spices or herbs for more intense flavor. Or more ground spices may be added. Season the binding sauce according to taste with hot pepper sauce or spicy sauce blend, distributing well throughout. Overcooking can destroy flavor, so watch timing.

DRY

This time: Add consommé, stock, tomato juice, wine, sauce, or fruit or vegetable juice, stirring gently. To avoid disrupting layers, drizzle the liquid over and cover for remainder of cooking (reducing oven temperature to prevent overcooking if necessary) to create steam. When the sauce has almost bubbled away in a casserole but the rest of the dish is not yet cooked, you have several choices: cover the dish, add more sauce, or stick a straw or long piece of hollow macaroni in the center. The first method preserves moisture by creating steam within the casserole, but the steaming effect will soften any crisp coating. The second choice is fine if you have extra sauce. Adding a little water may help, but it dilutes the flavors. The last method helps the intense heat within the food to escape, preventing further drying.

Next time: Try to balance liquid with dry ingredients. Casserole mixture should be moist and saucy. Cook just until done; avoid too hot an oven. Check periodically during baking. If casserole appears to be drying out quickly, add more liquid and cover to finish cooking.

TOO LIQUID

This time: Vegetables and fish, especially, tend to release moisture. Spoon off excess juices and save for soup, stew, or stock. Or thicken (see *Thickeners*) and blend back into casserole and cook until cooked through.

Next time: When using high-water vegetables, such as zucchini, use fewer liquid ingredients or more thickener. Cook longer, without overcooking. If casserole was covered, too much steam developed and caused the runny consistency. Remove lid toward end of baking.

To freeze:

Most casseroles freeze well. Avoid those with hard-cooked egg slices since egg gets tough in the freezer. When preparing for the freezer, line dish with heavy-weight foil, leaving ends extending over sides.

Fill and cook casserole. Cool to room temperature, then freeze. After it's frozen, remove foil and food from dish, overwrap, label, and freeze. Thaw casserole in refrigerator or microwave oven before replacing in casserole and reheating in low oven.

To prebake:

Most casseroles take well to this treatment: bake ahead of time, removing dish 20 minutes before completed. Refrigerate. Thirty to 40 minutes before serving, bake in low oven, then increase temperature to cooking temperature in recipe and heat through.

Cauliflower—Like artichokes and broccoli, cauliflower is the flower portion of the plant. Also like broccoli, it belongs to the cabbage family and can be smelly if not properly cooked.

DISCOLORED

This time: Add a little milk or lemon juice or vinegar to the cooking water to cover and cook a little longer, uncovered. Color change is reversible, especially if brownish or grayish from overcooking, or yellowish from alkaline water. Iron turns cauliflower and other white vegetables green. If your cauliflower refuses to whiten to its original pure state, serve it with a cheese, hollandaise or creole sauce. These provide a color contrast to make the cauliflower appear whiter.

Next time: Add a little lemon juice or vinegar to alkaline cooking water, or simmer in about an inch of milk. Avoid iron utensils and cook only until tender; subjecting the vegetable to heat for a long time will darken it, and iron causes greening.

OVERCOOKED

This time: Overcooked may also mean discolored (see *Discolored*). To treat the most prevalent overcooked symptom, soft and mushy texture, incorporate in casserole, purée, or mash. Cauliflowerets that still hold their original form can be turned into a casserole, perhaps mixed with broccoli or another compatible vegetable. If the vegetable has lost all characteristic shape, however, purée and use for timbales (p. 333), or cream of vegetable soup (p. 315); or mash like potatoes, top with cheese, and bake. Another good idea is to blend mushy cauliflower until smooth, then add butter or margarine, skim milk, and seasonings until a saucy consistency develops. A great low-calorie substitute for white sauce.

Next time: Prepare a medium-size head by trimming off tough end and leaves and soaking, head down, in cold salted water for several minutes. If leaving whole, cut gashes in stalks, steam or cook in small amount of boiling milk, or use salted water to which about 1 tablespoon of lemon juice has been added. Cover and cook a few minutes, then partially uncover and continue cooking until just tender, 15 to 20 minutes total. Flowerets take only 5 to 8 minutes, and chopped about 3 minutes.

SMELLY

This time: Change the water, add a slice of bread, or start cloves simmering in vinegar.

Next time: Cook partially covered; do not overcook. (See *Overcooked.*)

OVERMATURE

This time: Add pinch each of sugar and salt to cooking water to help retain flavor and color.

Next time: Select bright, firm head with tight buds and no brown spots. Avoid shriveled, dried cauliflower with signs of decay.

Caviar—Sieved fish roe which is lightly pressed and salted. The eggs are taken from several fish, the most prized of which is the beluga. The highest quality is packed in tins and must be kept in the coldest part of the refrigerator. Use as soon as possible; it's highly perishable.

Celery

OVERCOOKED

This time: Because of its high water content, celery needs little cooking, and if overdone, will be soft and mushy. If you were planning to serve it braised or as a crisp addition to a cooked dish, forget it. If you have more raw celery, use it to substitute for the mushy celery, which can be scooped out of the dish. The overcooked batch can be added to canned celery soup or puréed into a wonderful cream of celery soup (see cream of vegetable soup, p. 315). Or make into a celery sauce by starting with a simple roux— cooking equal parts butter and flour (about 2 tablespoons each per cup of sauce), then stirring in 1 cup chicken stock, or a combination of stock and white wine or milk, plus about ½ cup soft cooked celery. Season to taste, cook until thickened. Serve over fish or chicken and rice.

Next time: Cook gently and time carefully to avoid overcooking. Celery hearts can be boiled or braised to tenderness in 8 to 10 minutes; slices or strips will be tender-crisp after 2 or 3 minutes of frying, and tender if cooked in boiling liquid after 3 or 4 minutes.

OVERMATURE

This time: Old celery usually is also tough. After scrubbing well, peel off tough outer strings and edges. Outer ribs are toughest, so use those for cooked dishes, and the inner, more tender ones for raw salads and appetizers.

Next time: If intending to use raw, select celery hearts, or stalks that are firm and crisp with no pithy, spongy, or brownish parts. Leaves should be fresh, not wilted. Seed stems are a sign of maturity; they appear as a roundish stem replacing the heart formation.

WILTED

This time: Like asparagus and broccoli, tired celery stalks are often revived by a soaking in ice water. After washing celery, stand upright in pitcher filled with ice water and a tablespoon of lemon juice or vinegar (cider and tarragon, especially). Store in the refrigerator a couple of hours, and you'll then see perked-up celery. If it's still not crisp enough to use fresh on a relish tray, cook it.

Next time: Select fresh celery (see *Overmature*). Rinse under cold tap water, shake off excess water, pat dry with paper toweling, and store in plastic bag in refrigerator vegetable crisper. Use within 1½ to 2 weeks.

STRINGY

This time: If raw, peel with paring knife; if already cooked, try to remove strings, or purée mixture and sieve.

Next time: When using outer stalks, first peel with paring knife, pulling off strings. For relish trays or salads, select celery hearts or inner stalks.

Cereal—This major food group is composed of edible grass seeds. The common ones are wheat, rice, corn, barley, oats, and rye. The cultivation of grains considerably altered the history of mankind. In the pre-grain era, primitives relied on hunting for their main food. The farming of cereal crops liberated them from the enslaving survival syndrome, enabling them to depend on a storable food supply and freeing their time for developing arts and crafts. In time, man learned to crush grain with stone implements—the push mill and mortar and pestle. Eventually the grain was ground to meal and used for breads, flours, pastas, and breakfast foods—also given the name "cereals." Unfortunately, today's refined milling removes most of the vitamins and minerals for the sake of extended storage time. Cereal enrichment programs are now returning the lost nutritive values to these foods. As farmland shrinks per capita in the face of the multiplying population, grains are gaining importance as a food supply. For more details on corn and rice, turn to those headings. This information applies to cereals as we find them: cooked, ready-to-eat and quick-cooking.

BLAND

This time: Fresh, dried, or canned fruits enliven any cereal bowl. Spice up the combination with cinnamon, nutmeg, allspice, ginger, or coriander. A sprinkling of toasted almonds or pecans gives welcome crunch to a soft cooked cereal. Nuts mixed with seeds, fruits, and dry cereals contribute to granola mixtures. Some people like cereal salted, but most like it sweet. Molasses, maple syrup, brown sugar, and honey offer more flavor than granulated sugar. To get assorted cereal flavors with every spoonful, try mixing several. I've often blended wheat germ with a crisp flake and raw oatmeal for an interesting texture contrast. Another way to add flavor dimension is with a flavored milk: chocolate, malted, or eggnog stirred over or into cereal might get the kids to eat breakfast more often.

Next time: Experiment with various cereals until you find several with good flavor you prefer. Generally, the whole-grains have more taste and texture than the refined. The blandest are farina, cream of rice, and cream of wheat.

LUMPY (COOKED)

This time: When your cream of wheat isn't creamy, it can be returned to smoothness by passing through a sieve. A faster remedy is to whir it in the blender. Lumpy cooked cereal is edible as long as the clumps are cooked through.

Next time: Sprinkle cereal very gradually into boiling water to avoid the problem. Stir well during thickening, then reduce heat and cook according to package directions.

MUSHY

This time: Add more of the same cereal and cook longer. Or cook more cereal, adding much less liquid to get a thick mixture, then blend into the mushy, soft cereal and reheat slowly. Mushy barley, farina, oatmeal, and many others can stretch and thicken soups and other liquidy mixtures. Some are good when they gain texture from frying and browning. For example, fried corn meal mush usually is made from slicing the set mixture, but even mushy mush can be dropped in globs and fried.

Next time: Measure both cereal and water carefully. The rule of thumb for granular cereal is ½ cup to 2½ or 3 cups water; only 2 cups water are required for cooking the same amount of whole-grain cereal.

SOGGY (READY-TO-EAT)

This time: Spread over shallow pan and heat for several minutes in 375 degree oven.

Next time: Store cereal tightly covered in cool, dry place.

Chard—*See Greens.*

Cheese—Although it is established that cheese was made by the Sumerians, Egyptians, and Chaldeans, frequently mentioned in the Old Testament and used abundantly by the ancient Greeks and Romans, its origin is not certain. Many countries claim its discovery, and harken back to the legendary traveler who carried milk in a saddlebag made from an animal's stomach. Later that day he found whey and curds—the first cheese. Rennet (from the enzyme rennin found in the stomach lining) converts milk into the two components, and is almost always used in cheese making today. For all its great beginnings, cheese fell into surprising disfavor during the Renaissance and Elizabethan periods. Physicians warned against cheese consumption and Shakespeare referred to it disparagingly. But man's longtime passion for this versatile wine of foods overcame superstitions, and cheese was soon reinstated. Because of its great storage life, cheese has been the mainstay of many world travelers.

Dutch cheeses were packed in the *Mayflower* on the Pilgrims' journey to the New World. Cheese is big business—one-fifth of our domestic milk supply goes into its manufacture. Cheeses can be classified as soft, semisoft, hard and very hard, with the soft being the most perishable. Hard cheeses have long life. When your cheese presents a problem, don't throw it out. Keep on reading.

DRIED OUT, HARD

This time: Grate or shred dried-out cheese and keep in covered container in the refrigerator. Flavor may have diminished somewhat, but it will be fine for cheese sauce, soup, soufflé, or cheese-filled crepes. One splendid use for bits and pieces of leftover cheeses is the brandied cheese crock (p. 314).

Next time: Both soft and hard varieties will remain freshest if stored tightly wrapped in refrigerator. Drying ("oils-off" process) is quickened by exposure to heat and air, so cut only the portion needed and return remainder to refrigerator. Soft varieties should be used within 2 weeks; hard last several months, depending on type and freshness.

FROZEN

This time: Except for Roquefort, Neufchatel, and a few others, most natural cheeses freeze well for up to 2 months if tightly wrapped in moisture-vapor-proof paper. Allow 1 pound of frozen cheese to thaw 1 day in the refrigerator. Use soon after thawing. If texture has been altered (because of long storage, improper wrapping, or type of cheese) save for cooking.

Next time: Avoid freezing Roquefort and Neufchatel. Preferable to store cheeses unopened up to 2 months for most, about 4 months for pasteurized process. Rewrap opened packages in moisture-vapor-proof paper and store. It is best to freeze pieces 1 pound or less, not over 1 inch thick, tightly wrapped to prevent moisture loss.

Substitutes: Any similar cheese can be used in place of another—Herkimer for Cheddar, or Romano for Parmesan.

MOLDY

This time: A small amount of mold on cheese may be harmless but not very palatable, so scrape deeply; rewrap remainder tightly in plastic wrap. If flavor is slightly altered (do not use if moldy-tasting) use in a spicy cooked dish or make the brandied cheese crock (p. 314). When a piece of cheese is permeated with mold, discard. The National Dairy Council states that the practice of trimming mold is controversial, and advises against using moldy cheese unless cut is made deeply. And it warns that potentially harmful mold may not be totally destroyed in cooking.

Next time: Select fresh-looking cheese free of mold. Store cheeses in original wrappers in refrigerator, preferably in cheese keeper. Once opened, wrap tightly. Avoid leaving out of refrigerator for extended periods, since exposure to heat and air causes drying; the cheese "oils off," thus furthering possibility of mold growth on the moist, oily surface. Moist conditions will hasten mold on natural cheese. Store soft, unripened cheese (e.g., cottage) tightly covered in coldest part of refrigerator; use within days of date on carton. Hard natural cheeses can be refrigerated for several weeks. Long storage of cured cheese will result in additional sharpness of flavor. Process cheese and cheese spread can be kept on the shelf if unopened, but refrigerate and wrap tightly once opened.

OILY

This time: Cheese tends to "oil off" when exposed to air and warmth, such as when uncovered on a cheese board for some time. Dab with paper towel to absorb oil, then wrap tightly in plastic wrap and chill. Use soon. Once moisture has been lost, the longevity is shortened. If quite dry, see *Dried Out.*

Next time: Keep cheese tightly wrapped and refrigerated. Cut just the amount of cheese needed, and return rest to refrigerator.

TOO SOFT

This time: Lower temperature hardens cheese. But when time is short and the cheese has softened too much (such as on a hot summer day) dip cheese knife in hot water and slice. Or add softened butter, seasonings, and some wine (fortified wines like sherries and port are good choices) and you have a wonderful spread for crackers. Add cream or more wine until you have the consistency of a sandwich spread. Or use for a cheese sauce over vegetables or perhaps a cheese soup, topped with croutons.

Next time: Cheese comes to full flavor at room temperature, so allow 30 to 60 minutes from the refrigerator before serving, less in hot weather. Avoid placing cheese board or platter near oven or other heating unit.

STRINGY, RUBBERY

This time: Best remedy for a stringy, rubbery mass of heated cheese is to break it down in a blender at low setting, then return to the pan or top of double boiler and heat slowly over boiling water. Now, if on the thin side, thicken by adding more small pieces of cheese to the pot or by adding browned flour (bake on cookie sheet in 250-to-350-degree oven, stirring occasionally, until browned); continue cooking and stirring for 2 to 3 minutes.

Next time: Cut cheese in small pieces to ensure even blending in less time. Melt over low heat in the top of a double boiler, making certain top part doesn't touch boiling water below. Heat just until cheese is melted and blended. High heat and long cooking cause stringiness and toughness. Add to other ingredients at the last moment. Pasteurized process cheese melts more readily.

TOO STRONG FLAVORED

This time: Whether Limberger, an ammoniated soft-ripened cheese, or just one that smells like dirty socks, the flavor (and odor) will be diluted by mixing small amounts with a very bland cheese. Blend with a cream cheese to make a spread or dip; or grate, chop or crumble for casseroles or baked goods.

Next time: Taste before buying from a cheese shop; check dates on packages; store individually wrapped in the refrigerator and use within a reasonable period.

UNDERRIPE (SOFT-RIPENED CHEESE, SUCH AS BRIE OR CAMEMBERT)

This time: When the center is chalky and hard while the cheese above and below bulges out, Brie or Camembert will never ripen properly. Once cut from the round, it cannot continue ripening normally. So use the hard heart for sauce or soufflé, or for a marvelous filled omelet.

Next time: When purchasing a cut Brie, examine through

cellophane wrap to make sure there's no hard chalky core. When it's bulging, it's ripe and ready for consumption. The white crust of Brie becomes red-brown when very ripe, then deteriorates and becomes ammoniated. Open Camembert to make sure it's springy and plump to the touch. Look for "optimum ripeness" or "pull" dates on some cheeses, and buy from a reliable dealer.

Equivalents: When recipes call for 1 cup shredded, crumbled, or grated cheese, use 4 ounces. For equivalent nutritive value, substitute 1½ ounces Cheddar for 1 cup whole milk, skim milk, or buttermilk.

Cheesecake—The recipes vary from light and fluffy whipped cream or gelatin fillings to rich blends made with sour cream with fruit toppings. All should be refrigerated. If hard to slice, wet the knife first. See *Pie* for crust questions; or individual ingredients.

Cherry—Early settlers brought the fruit to this land; the cherry tree was a common sight in a colonial backyard. We all know George Washington's family didn't have one after he chopped it down. Unintentionally, our country's father immortalized the little red fruit.

BLAND

This time: Cherries sometimes look great but taste blah. Soak them in cherry liqueur such as kirschwasser or cherry kijafa, or another complementary flavor, such as orange, and serve over ice cream, pudding, or cake. Or marinate in lime juice and turn into a cherry-flavored gelatin mold. Neutral-tasting fruit will absorb the flavors of other ingredients, so consider pairing them with poultry or pork and herbs or spices. Might add to rum pot (p. 337).

Next time: It's hard to tell a bland fruit by looking; snitch a taste at the market. Produce clerks shouldn't mind if a customer samples a little before buying. They get annoyed when there's a lot of tasting and no buying.

OVERRIPE

This time: When soft and losing texture, cook instead of using raw (see *Bland*). Or cook for cherry soup, sauce (for ham or poultry), chutney or a glaze for cheesecake; or combine raw with pears or peaches for pie.

Next time: Select firm, clean fruit with bright color. Avoid fruit with soft or brown spots.

TOO SOUR

This time: Sweeten to taste when cooking, canning, or freezing. Can be combined with sweet cherries or another sweet fruit for pudding, pie, sauce, or dumplings.

Next time: Buy sweet cherries for eating, and the darker sour for cooking.

Chestnut—Whether roasted in your fireplace or by a street vendor, the rich smoky-sweet taste of chestnuts is unsurpassed on a chilly day. When not roasted, this flavorful nut is usually boiled, and it mixes well with game, fowl, vegetables and desserts. Chestnuts were known by the ancient Greeks and Romans, and the huge trees flourished in America before most were wiped out by a fungus early in this century. Today, the trees in eastern America are disease-resistant hybrids crossed with Japanese and Chinese species. On the Pacific coast grow the European and Spanish chestnuts, which are mostly eaten boiled, roasted or even raw.

DRY, OLD

This time: Simmer peeled nuts in stock, broth, water, or wine (or a blend) about one hour, or until tender, or steam. Chop and add to stuffings, rice pilaf, Brussels sprouts, or other vegetables; purée and blend in butter and seasonings; or purée and sweeten, and fold in whipped cream for a rich dessert.

Next time: Gather plump, firm nuts with glossy, unshriveled smooth shells without cracks. Store in covered container in dry, cool place. Try to use within a week.

MUSHY, OVERCOOKED

This time: Purée overcooked mixture in blender or food processor. By adding consommé or stock, seasonings, and cream, you'll have a great soup. When your preference is a dessert, sweeten the purée, stir in vanilla, melted chocolate, brandy or rum, and whipped cream.

Next time: Simmer whole peeled nuts 45 to 60 minutes, depending on size and age; cook purée from 1 lb. nuts in 1½ to 3 cups liquid (stock, wine, or simmering milk) about ½ hour, just until tender.

Chicken—See *Poultry.*

Chicory—See *Endive.*

Chilies (hot peppers)—Probably the only vegetable that requires cautious handling, because their volatile oils can scald skin and eyes, long before its slow burn on your tongue and throat.

BURNS

This time: For skin, wash area thoroughly with soapy water and rinse well. For eye burns, flush well with clear tepid water. If burning doesn't subside, call a doctor. For burning sensation in mouth, eating a piece of bread or other flour-baked item helps. So does lemon juice or pulp; beer, and tomato. This is one fire that only rages hotter with water.

Next time: When working with fresh, hot chilies, wear rubber gloves. Do not touch your face, eyes, or skin. Wash gloves well with soapy water when finished; scrub cutting surface and knife before using them for other preparations. Rinse under cold running water. Fresh chilies may be soaked in salted cold water for 1½ hours to lessen potency.

OLD

This time: Trim off any browned or decayed spots, rinse under cold water, stem, and seed. If texture is soft from age, cook.

Next time: Select firm, fresh peppers with no mold or decay spots. Avoid soft, broken-skinned chilies. Store unwashed in refrigerator crisper drawer, and try to use within a week. If any of the chilies grow mold, remove and sort peppers to prevent mold from spreading.

Chocolate—Made from a blend of roasted cacao beans, cacao butter, and sugar. The first Europeans to learn of this New World item were Cortez and his followers when they invaded Mexico, where spiced, unsweetened chocolate was a common drink. The Spaniards brought it back across the Atlantic and within half a century it was becoming popular throughout Europe. It's no surprise that the early American colonists knew and loved it enough to start a chocolate factory in Dorchester, Massachusetts.

CRUMBLES (WHEN SHAVING OR MAKING CURLS)

This time: Bring chocolate to room temperature for making curls or shavings. Use a vegetable parer or sharp knife, making longer strokes for longer curls. Store in refrigerator to help keep shape. When you're facing a substantial amount of crumbled chocolate, use in some baked product where its shape doesn't matter. Or melt and use in recipe calling for melted chocolate.

Next time: Allow enough time for chocolate to come to room temperature. It is best to store chocolate between 60 and 75 degrees F. in a dry place. Stored properly, fresh wrapped chocolate has about a 1-year shelf life. Age may cause crumbling, so buy from a reliable source and keep inventory on home supplies.

MELTED (ACCIDENTALLY)

This time: If the wrapper has an oily appearance, the chocolate's life expectancy is probably shorter. Taste to make sure its flavor hasn't been lost. Very soft chocolate that has melted in the wrapper is best used immediately in a recipe calling for melted chocolate. Or it can be transferred to a container with a rubber scraper and chilled slightly until solid enough to work with. When chocolate is melting onto hands while grating or shaving, chill chocolate and grater; hold chocolate with waxed paper or dip hands in ice water, then dry before handling. Work as quickly as possible.

Next time: Store chocolate in cool, dry place, between 60 and 75 degrees F. Chill before working with it. Have grater cold and dry, and have waxed paper and/or a bowl of ice water handy to chill hands. Some prefer using light plastic gloves that may be chilled first.

SCORCHES, STICKS TO PAN

This time: A rubber scraper is handy for separating the melted chocolate from the scorched part. Scorched chocolate has a bitter flavor, which can be turned into an asset if not badly burned; add butter to the pot and heat slowly while stirring. Flavor with an appropriate liqueur (mint, coffee, or orange), strain, and use as bittersweet topping over ice cream.

Next time: Melt chocolate slowly in top of double boiler about 10 minutes. The low setting of a microwave oven is ideal for chocolate melting. To save pot washing, float chocolate in a foil "canoe" over hot water until melted. Scrape melted chocolate off and discard foil after use. Cool chocolate to about 80 degrees F. before adding to cake batter, cookie dough, or pudding. Even without scorching, chocolate tends to cling to the pan; butter utensil lightly before melting chocolate to enable contents to slip out easily without sticking. One of the best convenience foods is premelted (or liquid) chocolate in individual packets.

STIFFENS WHEN MELTED

This time: Add small amounts of butter, stirring until smooth and of right consistency.

Next time: Use melted chocolate immediately upon bringing down to about 80 degrees F. Melt over hot water in top of double boiler, remove top part, then cover while cooling slightly.

WHITE SPOTS, GRAYISH BLOOM

This time: Use where appearance isn't important. Neither flavor nor quality is affected, although chocolate loses attractiveness.

Next time: This is a common problem during warm weather, when the higher temperatures cause the cacao butter to come to the surface and form a bloom. Store chocolate in tightly covered container in cool, dry part of kitchen, between 60 and 75 degrees F., for optimum appearance.

Equivalent: 1 (1-ounce) square chocolate yields 4 tablespoons grated.

Substitutions

1 oz. unsweetened chocolate can be substituted in baking and cooking with 3 tbsp. cocoa plus 1 tbsp. shortening. 1 envelope premelted unsweetened chocolate can be substituted by 1 oz. square melted unsweetened chocolate or ¼ cup cocoa plus 1 tbsp. melted shortening. 1⅔ oz. semisweet chocolate can be substituted by 1 oz. chocolate plus 4 tsp. sugar.

Chocolate Milk—*See Chocolate, Hot Chocolate, Milk.*

Chocolate Sauce—*See Sauces.*

Chowder—*See Soup.*

Clams—See *Shellfish*.

Clostridium Botulinum—See *Food Spoilage, Poisoning.*

Cocoa/Cacao (Bean)—The word (usually spelled cacao when referring to the bean) applies to both the powdered product and the hot drink made with it. The powder is made from cacao beans grown on tropical trees whose botanical name translates to "food of the gods." Today, large crops are produced mainly in Brazil, Ecuador, and the Dominican Republic, and parts of Africa. Cacao beans were used as money in early Mexico. They are also the source of chocolate, made from grinding roasted dried beans and adding cacao butter. The remainder is put through a second grinding to make cocoa powder. See also *Hot Chocolate*.

LUMPY

This time: Cocoa powder that has become lumpy can be sieved or placed in a blender before using. A lumpy cocoa drink (whether never fully dispersed or settled out) can be whipped vigorously with a whisk or blended. Another corrective measure is to sieve the drink, then mash the cocoa bits with a little sugar and small amount of liquid; heat to dissolve, then gradually stir in remaining drink.

Next time: Store cocoa powder tightly covered in a cool, dry place. High temperatures and moisture cause lumpiness. To ensure a smooth drink, combine cocoa with the sugar or mix in blender with a small amount of the liquid before heating. Gradually add the liquid while stirring. Instant cocoa dissolves readily and Dutch process stays dissolved, avoiding the settling-out problem.

SKIN FORMATION

This time: A wire whisk or rotary beater eliminates the skin and fluffs the drink. Or skim and strain.

Next time: The steam formed by covering the pot while mixture heats prevents skin formation. Heat gently, preferably in top of double boiler.

Coconut—That dried stuff on birthday cakes is nothing like the sweet, succulent flavor of what is inside the hairy shell.

DRIED (GRATED OR PIECES)

This time: Heat in steamer or sieve over hot water or soak in milk. For use as toasted coconut: spread on shallow pan and bake 15 minutes in 350-degree oven.

Next time: Store in tightly covered nonporous container or wrap tightly in plastic wrap to prevent pieces from drying out. Store in refrigerator up to a week, or freeze up to 8 or 9 months.

OVERRIPE, DISCOLORED

This time: When cut coconut flesh has been stored too long, it begins to brown. At the early stages, trim off discolored spots and grate remainder for use in cooking. One idea is to make coconut milk, required for curry sauce: simmer equal parts grated coconut with cow's milk, stirring until foamy, about 2 minutes. Strain. Then toast leftover grated coconut following directions above under *Dried.*

Next time: Select coconuts that sound liquid when shaken and that are heavy for their size. Avoid those with wet or moldy eyes. Whole coconuts will store nicely at room temperature up to 4 to 6 months, depending on age and environmental conditions. Once opened, the fresh milk and meat (milk in plastic containers, meat in plastic wrap) can be refrigerated up to a week.

UNDERRIPE

This time: Underripe meat is gelatinous, but still can be used cooked.

Next time: I never considered this a problem until I was selecting one from a coconut grove in the Yucatan. Natives advised choosing one that sounded full of liquid. The nuts without milk sloshing around indicates dryness or underripeness; the latter means the liquid is incorporated in the underdeveloped gelatinous meat, which often is spooned as a dessert. Since both can make very good eating, it's worth taking chances.

To crack: Actually not that tough a nut to crack when you know these tricks. If not removed, the outer husk must be hacked off. Drain the milk from one of the "eyes" (three dark spots on one end of shell) by punching one of the indentations with ice pick or other sharp tool. Then place either in a 350-degree oven for about 12 to

15 minutes or into a freezer for about an hour. Remove, cover with towel, and hit sharply with a cleaver or hammer. The shell should fall apart, the meat separating from it easily. Peel off dark skin before using.

Cod—See Fish.

Coffee—Believed to have originated in Ethiopia, this sociable brew has long been America's traditional eye-opener and round-the-clock hot pick-me-up. Americans consume more coffee than the residents of any other country. Even the skyrocketing coffee bean costs of 1976–77 scarcely altered their addiction to the brew. According to some Arab sources, coffee was not introduced to Aden until the mid-1400s. From there it spread to Mecca and Medina, where the first public coffee houses opened in 1470. The coffee house was a gentlemen's domain and the coffee habit soon became the mark of a worldly man. Mid-16th-century Constantinople had numerous coffee houses where guests were honored with a cup of hot "coffa." The retreats became popular in Europe and later in colonial America. This information is designed to rescue your coffee-gone-wrong.

Tips

For best brew, coffee maker must be scrupulously cleaned with 1 or 2 tsp. baking soda, dissolved in water and scalded, before reuse. Coffee maker should be at least ⅔ full to produce good coffee. Water between 200 and 205 degrees F. is ideal for extracting coffee flavor without the acids. Grind only enough coffee to be used; open one can at a time. Use fresh coffee, fresh, cold water and the drip method for best quality. Never reheat coffee (unless in microwave oven). To cut down on caffeine, seek out decaffeinated beans or bean varieties, such as the Puerto Rican, that have substantially less caffeine than Brazilian coffee.

BITTER

This time: Dilute bitter coffee with water, then freeze in cubes for iced coffee or punch; the cubes prevent dilution. Bitter coffee lends robust taste to dark rye or pumpernickel breads, strengthens both color and flavor of gravies, and can be used in mocha frosting or sauce recipes calling for strong coffee. Or try the famous French morning drink, café au lait—half hot coffee and half hot milk.

Next time: Be sure the coffeepot is very clean; use soft (not softened or hard) water and freshly ground coffee. Never boil or reheat the brew; boiling brings out the bean's tannic acid, giving a bitter and cloudy product. Never reuse coffee grounds. Time coffee brewing accurately. If an average size coffee maker takes more than 8 minutes for the brewing process, it probably produces a bitter product. Use drip method if possible. When using percolator, do not let perked coffee stand with the coffee grounds; remove grounds as soon as coffee is perked. Shop around for a suitable coffee blend; some inferior beans or heavily roasted ones tend to be bitter.

CLOUDY

This time: When there's no time to make more and the brew is very cloudy, serve with milk or cream or blend with cocoa (cocoa mixed with milk); rum, brandy, or a liqueur can be added to make a more festive cup. Cloudy coffee still makes a nice enrichment for gravies and dessert sauces. It can also add flavor and color to breads, cakes, and puddings.

Next time: Boiling coffee produces both a bitterness and a cloudy appearance. To ensure a clear, bright brew, my grandmother always added a few eggshells to the coffee while it was heating. The same grounds-settling trick is used by professional woodsmen, whose clear morning potions can sharpen the edge of an axe. Be careful, however, to strain out any shell fragments before serving.

STRONG

This time: Dilute with boiling water or add cream or milk or even cocoa for a mocha drink. To err on the strong side is better than on the weak side.

Next time: Measure accurately, using a standard coffee measure (2 level tbsp.) of grounds to ¾ cup or 6 oz. water. Brewing time is essential to good coffee flavor. Any coffee maker that requires more than 8 minutes to brew tends to produce a strong, bitter product. The drip process is the best coffee-brewing method. It maintains the least contact between boiling water and coffee, keeping caffeine to a minimum. Some brands are heavily roasted to produce a strong, robust taste that may not be yours.

WEAK

This time: Coffee strengthens as it keeps warm. When using a percolator, let perk a little longer. But rather than risk overbrewing and a bitter taste, it's safer to brew some fresh, very strong coffee, measuring a heaping measure to ¾ cup water; then blend the strong with the weak. A quick remedy is to fortify the weak brew with a little instant. Mild coffee can be used in baking or dessert sauces.

Next time: Be sure coffee is fresh. Buy according to amount used. Accurately measure coffee and water, using no less than 1 level coffee measure to ¾ cup water. Check coffee maker; if water doesn't get hot enough or brewing time isn't long enough, the result will be a weak brew. Also match the grind to the brewing method and time. A coarse, regular grind can produce a weak coffee by the drip method.

Coffeecake—*See Bread.*

Coleslaw—*See Cabbage, Salads.*

Collards—*See Greens.*

Confections—*See Candy, Confectionery.*

Conserves—*See Canning.*

Consommé—*See Soup.*

Cookie—Derived from the Dutch word *koekie,* meaning "small cake." The English have biscuits, which tend to be less sweet and of more similar form than the American cookies.

Cookie-baking tips
Softened butter or margarine creams the best.
Shiny, level cookie sheets help ensure even browning.
Bake a few trial cookies so adjustments can be made before proceeding with entire batch.
Be sure baking sheet is cool before adding more cookies.
Bake cookies of similar pattern and size on same cookie sheet; they will finish baking simultaneously.
For best results cool cookies on wire racks before storing; cookies cooled on solid surface can become soggy.

Avoid storing crisp and soft cookies together. Store crisp cookies in crock with loose cover in cool, dry place; recrisp softened cookies on baking sheet about 5 minutes in low oven. Store soft cookies in tightly covered tin in cool place. Dried cookies can regain moisture by storing a piece of apple or bread in the container, or by adding a dampened paper towel loosely wrapped in foil to the tin. Soft bar cookies may be stored tightly covered right in their baking pan in a cool place.

Drop: Of soft-dough consistency to fall from a spoon; produces thick, round, crispy, soft-centered types such as chocolate chip, oatmeal, and peanut butter.

DOUGHY

This time: Liquid or flour may need adjusting in dough. A doughy texture usually can be improved by further baking. Or run cookies under broiler about 6 inches from heat until desired color and texture are achieved. Cookies too doughy to be eaten as cookies can be dried in a low oven, then crushed or ground in food processor and used in crumb pie crusts or puddings.

Next time: Always bake samples first, then adjust liquid or flour in dough, or adjust oven temperature. Place cookies in preheated oven and bake long enough at proper temperature. Watch baking time carefully.

DRY, HARD

This time: Add 1 or 2 tbsp. milk, cream, or fruit juice, depending on recipe, to soften dough. Dry, hard cookies can be finely ground in food processor and enough melted butter added to hold mixture together; press in pie plate to make crumb crust. Peanut-butter-cookie crumbs make a great apple-crisp topping. Crumbs can also be saturated in liquor and used to top puddings, pies, and ice cream.

Next time: Use less—or softer—flour. The same cookie recipe may require less flour on a dry winter day than in humid summer weather. Overmixing can cause hard cookies. Check oven temperature. Overbaking or too low a temperature can dry and harden cookies. The baking sheets should be positioned on racks at least 2 inches from oven walls.

SPREADING OUT OF DOUGH

This time: When the first few cookies spread out too much they can be used as crumbs; add a little more flour to remaining soft dough; chill before baking. Wrap and place in freezer for quick-chill. Be sure to allow baking sheet to cool before reusing and make certain oven is preheated to correct temperature. A too-low temperature can cause dough to spread instead of quickly baking it.

Next time: After working with drop cookies awhile it will be easier to recognize proper dough consistency. Be sure to cream butter and sugar sufficiently. Hold back on liquid or add flour to adjust. Make a few test cookies first to see if they properly increase in size.

Bar: Examples are brownies, lemon squares, and toffee bars.

CRUMBLY

This time: Dip the knife in water before each cut; use a sharper or serrated blade. Serve crumbly bars in dessert dishes with ice cream, yogurt, or whipped cream.

Next time: Warm cookies tend to crumble; cool completely before cutting. Overmixing toughens dough, resulting in a hard, crusty top, which doesn't cut well.

DOUGHY

This time: Slightly doughy texture can be remedied by further baking or a higher temperature. Very pasty but completely baked dough can be molded into small balls, rolled in confectioners sugar or nuts, and served as a confection. They make attractive garnishes for desserts such as puddings and cakes.

Next time: Check ingredients in recipe; perhaps more egg or leavening is needed. Use medium or large eggs, not small. Place dough in correct size pan. Smaller or deeper size will require longer baking time.

DRY

This time: Dry bar cookies make a delicious crumbled base for pudding; or they can soak up liquor and form a delicious layer in a trifle or top ice cream, sherbet, or cream pie.

Next time: Add an extra egg if a more moist, cakier bar is desired. Use proper size pan; dough is thinner in a larger one, so baking time would have to be reduced. Avoid overbaking. Oven temperature may have to be increased. Remove from oven as soon as cake tester inserted in center comes out clean.

Refrigerator: A very short dough that must be chilled and ripened before rolling, slicing, or shaping; examples are crisp-tender sugar cookies and vanilla refrigerator cookies.

CRUMBLY

This time: Flatten with spatula dipped in ice water to help hold dough together. Slice with sharp knife, reshaping dough by hand if necessary. Very crumbly dough can be reworked with egg white or more liquid or pressed into bottom of a pan and topped with a filling.

Next time: Cutting amount of shortening and/or baking powder or soda may help. Wrap rolled dough very well in wax paper, plastic wrap, or light-weight foil, twisting ends. Do not store dough in refrigerator more than a week; freeze for long storage. When adding nuts to dough, chop fine; coarsely chopped nuts cause dough to crumble.

DOUGH HARD TO SLICE

This time: Chill rolled dough or to hasten the process, place in freezer. Or drop in mounds on cookie sheet.

Next time: Allow 12 to 24 hours for thorough chilling of rolled dough. Cut cold dough with a thin, sharp knife.

Molded: Usually a short dough often chilled for easier handling; examples are thumbprint cookies, ambrosia balls, and gingersnaps.

BROWNING UNEVEN, POOR TEXTURE

This time: Uneven browning during baking won't show if the cookie is covered with ice cream, pudding, or some favorite sauce, or crumbled for dessert topping. For rest of batch, check oven temperature and heat flow; use level pans. Be sure dough is smooth. Roll dough to desired thickness between palms of hands.

Next time: Mix ingredients until a smooth-textured dough is achieved. Do not use warped pans.

DOUGHY

This time: Reshape remaining dough into flatter, smaller cookies. Doughy baked ones can be returned to the oven for further cooking. Crumble problem specimens, soak in liquor, and sprinkle over pudding, custard pie, or cheesecake.

Next time: Use less dough for individual cookies, making them flatter so they'll bake more thoroughly.

Rolled: Made of stiff dough, usually chilled, and rolled with rolling pin and cut out.

TOO CRISP

This time: Place in blender and make crumbs. The crisp texture adds crunch to apple brown betty, ice cream, and pudding desserts; makes a nice textured crumb crust for pies. Cookies will soften if stored in an airtight container; add a slice of apple or piece of bread for thick, crisp cookies. Or crumble and stir into a pudding.

Next time: Roll out dough thicker than before, lightly and evenly. The thinner the dough, the crisper the cookie. Overbaking also causes overcrisping.

DRY, HARD, TOUGH

This time: Hard cookies will soften if stored in an airtight tin with an apple wedge or a slice of bread. Or use large crumbles in puddings, finer ones as topping. Try sugar cookie crumbs over chocolate ice cream and ginger cookie crumbs over baked apples or applesauce.

Next time: The main cause for a compact rolled cookie is excessive rolling and too much flour on the board. Remove from the refrigerator only the part of dough that will be rolled at one time; keep the rest cold. Incorporate scraps from previous batch into present one; never save all scraps for one batch or it will be tough. Always bake a few samples first, then adjust dough if necessary by adding a little more liquid to soften. Avoid using a high-gluten flour and baking too long or at too low a temperature. Long refrigerator storage (especially of poorly wrapped dough) also causes the problem. Freeze dough if it cannot be used within a week.

STICKY DOUGH

This time: Warm dough tends to stick, so refrigerate or quick-chill in the freezer. If the cold dough is very soft, work in a little more flour. Dip cookie cutter in flour, shaking off excess before cutting. Rub flour onto rolling pin.

Next time: When dough feels too soft and sticky after thorough chilling, work in slightly more flour; too much will toughen dough. Remove only the portion you will work with at a time, leaving remaining dough to chill until needed. Avoid working near the oven or another heat source. Have extra flour nearby when rolling, so cutter and rolling pin can be floured. Roll a sticky dough slightly thicker on floured pastry cloth. Chill rolling pin to prevent dough from sticking to it.

STUCK TO BAKING SHEET

This time: The phone rang and the cookies have cooled and stuck to the baking sheet! Return to the oven to warm, wrap with a towel, and let stand a few minutes to loosen.

Next time: Grease pan when recipe advises; remove cookies while still warm to wire racks.

Pressed: Stiff dough pushed through a cookie press to form shapes dependent on the tips used; spritz are the classic example. When dough is of right consistency, it's not necessary to exert force on handle of press.

TOO SOFT DOUGH

This time: Quick-chill dough in freezer, or, add slightly more flour for thicker consistency. Can be baked as drop cookies.

Next time: Avoid overcreaming shortening-sugar mixture. Add enough flour to get workable consistency. To prevent the addition of too much flour and getting a tough cookie, chill dough slightly before placing in press. Work in cooler area of kitchen away from hot oven.

TOO STIFF DOUGH

This time: Gradually mix in a little egg yolk or white or a whole egg, depending on recipe.

Next time: When creaming the shortening-sugar mixture, be sure

butter or margarine is at room temperature and that mixture becomes light and fluffy. Avoid adding extra flour, which could result
in a stiff dough. When time permits, try chilling a soft dough first to
see if it firms up.

Corn—Historically the cornerstone food of emerging civilizations in
the Western Hemisphere; the true American cereal. A gift from the
Indians, it is still a very popular vegetable, although not quite the
mainstay in our diet that it was for the early colonists. Surprising to
some, popcorn was served at the first Thanksgiving. Cornmeal was
used for breads and puddings and to thicken numerous dishes,
many of which are still served regularly in the South and the East.
The problems here deal with fresh corn.

OVERMATURE

This time: Kernels of older corn are large and tough. Instead of
serving on the cob or plain, make a chowder, casserole, or
cornbread with whole kernels. Add sugar (about 1 teaspoon per
quart) to cooking water. Never add salt to boiling water, but 1 to 3
teaspoons sugar help preserve sweetness. Drop ears into boiling
water, then return to boil. Cook 3 to 5 minutes and remove immediately when done to prevent overcooking. A great treatment for
aging corn is to grate 4 ears corn, season with salt, pepper, and
coriander (curry spices, nutmeg, etc.), add 1 tablespoon maple
syrup (or molasses) and about ½ cup milk. Makes about 2 cups.
Place in buttered or oiled casserole and bake in 350-degree oven
30 to 40 minutes. Serves 4.

Next time: Select ears with tight green husks and brown silk.
Kernels should be plump and firm and fill the rows. Avoid spots and
signs of worms. Use as quickly as possible; much flavor is lost the
first day after picking and the sugar turns into starch when cooked.
Wrap unhusked corn in plastic bag with a damp paper towel and
refrigerate until ready to use.

TOUGH: See *Overmature.*

Corned Beef—See *Meat.*

Cornish Hens—See *Poultry, Game Birds.*

Cornmeal—See *Cereal.*

Cornstarch—See *Thickeners*.

Cottage Cheese—See *Cheese*.

Crab—See *Shellfish*.

Crabapple—This wild little apple is bitter when raw; cultivated for tartness in cooking and for decoration.

BITTER

Because of this natural characteristic, the fruit is suitable mainly for jellies or pickling. Wash; core and quarter if desired. Cook in water, sugar, and spices (cinnamon stick, cloves, cardamom seeds) about 30 to 50 minutes until tender and well flavored.

Crackers—Stale or slightly soggy crackers can be refreshened by baking several minutes in a 350-degree oven. Store crisp crackers in tightly closed container in a cool, dry place.

Cranberry—See *Berries*.

Crayfish—See *Shellfish*.

Cream—Several different types of cream exist. The U.S. Food and Drug Administration's standards of identity are employed if cream is shipped in interstate commerce. The different creams are listed here with their standard minimum milkfat (also called butterfat) requirements and respective information. Most regions carry several, but few have all types.

Light Cream: Coffee or table cream—at least 18 percent milkfat.

FROZEN
This time: When cream accidentally freezes, thaw in refrigerator; stir to blend any separated fat. The product is safe, although it may have lost some palatability. Use within a couple of days, preferably in baking or cooking (see cream of vegetable soup, p. 315).

Next time: Store at 40 degrees in refrigerator. For long-storage cream, buy ultra-heat-treated or ultra-pasteurized half-and-half, which lasts 60 to 90 days refrigerated in its unopened carton. Once opened, store as usual.

SKIN FORMATION: See *Milk*.

SOURING: See *Milk*.

SOURING: See *Milk*.

Substitute (for cooking only): About ⅞ cup milk plus 3 table-spoons butter equals 1 cup light.

Half-and-Half: A homogenized mixture of milk and light cream, with a minimum of 10.5 percent milkfat content.

FROZEN: See *Light Cream*.

SOURING: See *Milk*.

Substitute: About ⅞ cup milk plus 1½ tablespoons butter (melted, if appropriate) equals 1 cup.

Light Whipping Cream: At least 30 percent milkfat.

FROZEN: See *Light Cream*.

Light whipping cream may not whip after freezing, so plan to use in liquid state. For long-storage cream, buy ultra-pasteurized whipping cream (see *Heavy Whipping Cream*).

WON'T WHIP

Doesn't whip as readily as heavy whipping cream. Have cream, bowl, and beaters well chilled. Use straight-sided deep bowl and whip quickly. Or add 1 unbeaten egg white or ¼ teaspoon gelatin and whip some more. Sometimes several drops of lemon juice help. Don't try to whip thawed cream. Also, see *Weather*.

Substitutes (for liquid use in cooking and baking): Approximately ⅞ cup heavy whipping cream and 2 tablespoons half-and-half replaces one cup. Or ¾ cup milk plus ¼ cup butter. For whipped, substitute heavy whipping cream.

When cutting fat from the diet, substitute whipped evaporated milk or whipped instant nonfat dry milk, following these directions:

Whipped evaporated milk: Place in freezer until partially frozen. In cold bowl with cold beaters, whip rapidly until stiff enough to hold peaks. After whipping, stabilize with 1 tablespoon lemon juice for each cup measured before whipping. Evaporated milk triples when whipped.

Whipped instant nonfat dry milk: Mix with equal parts water or fruit juice at room temperature for optimum stability and volume.

Add about 2 tablespoons lemon juice for each ½ cup dry milk after soft peaks have formed to help stabilize the whip and accent taste. Add flavorings and sugar after stiff peaks form.

Heavy Whipping Cream: Minimum 36 percent milkfat. Heavy cream usually doubles, sometimes triples in volume, depending on beaters and other factors.

FROZEN

This time: Thaw whipping cream slowly in the refrigerator. Before using, stir well to blend. Plan to use in the liquid state, since it doesn't whip well after freezing; texture becomes heavy and grainy.

Next time: Whip first, then freeze. A convenient method is to freeze dollops of whipped cream on a foil-lined cookie sheet until firm, then store in closed plastic bag in freezer. For long storage purposes, shop for the ultra-heat-treated or ultra-pasteurized whipping cream. This product lasts 60 to 90 days refrigerated in its unopened carton—a real convenience. It freezes well, too. Once opened, however, the ultra-treated cream has the same life span as the regular. To prevent cream from freezing accidentally, store on refrigerator shelf at 40 degrees. When intentionally freezing, leave in its carton—unopened, if possible. Once opened, close tightly before freezing.

OVERWHIPPED

This time: The overwhipped quality will not be as noticeable when chopped or sliced fruits and a touch of liqueur are added. Serve layered with ice cream in parfait glasses, or blend part of overwhipped cream into softened ice cream, then freeze. When serving roast beef, tongue, or corned beef, add horseradish to overwhipped cream. When cream is only slightly overwhipped or on the verge, add 1 or 2 tablespoons half-and-half or evaporated milk to thin it, whip briefly to blend. Another alternative is to whip further until you have homemade butter. Beat until solid, drain off liquid, chill until hard. Knead cold butter to press out liquid. This sweet butter is delicious alone or blended with mustard, minced parsley, anchovy paste, or crumbled blue cheese for sandwich spreads.

Next time: Cream needs your full attention when whipping. Easier to control with wire whisk. When using electric beaters use medium speed until it starts to thicken, then low. Stop as soon as soft peaks form that still have gloss. This is a delicate state, so prepare just before serving when you want it this soft. For stiffer cream (such as for cake decoration) beat a little longer, watching carefully for just the right split second. Whipped cream can be stored about 1½ hours in refrigerator.

WON'T WHIP: See *Light Whipping Cream.*

Substitutes: None has the same good quality of honest whipping cream. In baking or cooking, ¾ cup milk and ⅓ cup butter can be used in recipes calling for 1 cup heavy whipping (not whipped) cream.

Whipped evaporated milk or whipped instant nonfat dry milk (see *Light Whipping Cream*) can be used as toppings flavored with vanilla, a little sugar, liqueur, instant coffee, toasted coconut, or nuts to improve texture and taste. So can whipped light cream with gelatin: dissolve 1½ teaspoons gelatin in 3 tablespoons cold water. Add ⅓ cup scalded half-and-half or light cream and sweeten with 2 teaspoons fine or confectioners sugar. Add a little vanilla or other flavorings. Chill about 5 hours, stirring occasionally. Beat in chilled bowl with chilled beaters at least 5 minutes. Yields about 2 cups.

Commercial whipped toppings (some nondairy) also may serve as toppings. I personally would rather do without.

Crème Fraîche: See below.

Sour Cream: See p. 271.

Cream Cheese—*See Cheese.*

Cream Puff—*See Pâte à choux.*

Cream Soup—*See Soup.*

Crème Fraîche (cultured 30 to 36 percent whipping cream)—A tangy-sweet, thick cultured cream commonly used in French kitchens and growing in popularity in the United States. This rich staple of *la nouvelle cuisine* has appeared commercially in some supermarket dairy cases while food experts have been teaching home cooks how to simulate it by culturing whipping cream with a starter of either buttermilk, thick yogurt or commercial crème fraîche. A relatively new nonelectric dairy (cultured) food "cooker," called Solait, simplifies and controls the process of homemade crème fraîche, yogurt, and other cultured foods so the results are uniform; it comes complete with dairy thermometer and dry starter cultures.

Crème fraîche has a longer refrigerator shelf life than ordinary cream. Its velvety texture and thick consistency add smooth body to sauces; and it doesn't curdle as plain cream does when heated. Its nutlike tartness gives new flavor dimension to anything from soups and main dishes to desserts. Crème fraîche whips beautifully and won't separate as readily as whipped cream, thus producing more stable soufflés, mousses, and pastries. Served with fresh fruits soaked in liqueur, it transforms simple ingredients into an elegant finale. Although it's easier to work with than plain cream, it does have its trying moments.

STRONG-FLAVORED

This time: Blend with robust blue-veined cheese and herbs for a spread or add to a full-bodied sauce for meat or game. If small amount of mold develops on top, scrape off; use the remaining crème fraîche unless mold has permeated it. Avoid using the strong-flavored item for delicate pastries or fruits.

Next time: Store in refrigerator up to 3 weeks. Longer storage or higher temperature will produce quicker aging and stronger flavor.

TOO THICK

This time: Whisk it a little—it should break down slightly. If using it fresh, bring to room temperature. Or heat if using for cooking—it will thin. Add whey or other liquid to thin when using for a sauce.

Next time: If 36 percent butterfat whipping cream was used, try 30 percent for a less rich product. Cut culturing time slightly.

TOO THIN

This time: If crème fraîche hasn't been refrigerated yet and you don't need it for 10 hours, pour into a large coffee drip filter and let hang for 4 hours; about 1 cup of whey will drip out, increasing butterfat by 10 percent. Chill at least 6 hours before using. If you need it almost immediately (it will be sweeter, less tangy), place in pan over medium heat; bring to boil, whisking frequently. Whisk while cooking over medium-low heat; bubbles should break at surface. Allow about 20 minutes to reduce 1 cup by 50 percent (without continuous whisking, some risk of separation with 30 percent cream). Reduction is sufficient if crème fraîche thickly coats back of spoon. Cool or chill to thicken further. (Quick-chill in ice-water bath.) If mixture never cultured, may be reused; but first heat to 180 degrees F., then cool to 100 degrees F. before introducing new starter.

Next time: Allow sufficient time for culturing and chilling. If cream still hasn't thickened, may be reused (see *This time*). Be sure starter is active; freeze-dried tends to be more dependable. When using buttermilk or crème fraîche starters, make certain products are fresh; or try a different brand.

To freeze: Whip to stiff peaks, drop in dollops, then freeze until firm; store in freezer bags.

Crepes—The elegant appearance of delicate crepes belies their preparation—contrary to popular opinion, crepes are not difficult to make.

HARD, OVERCOOKED

This time: Soaking hard and dry crepes in a thin sauce, crepes-suzette style, moistens them and restores their palatability. Once they're soft again, fold in quarters and serve with the sauce. When you're faced with at least 6 crepes in this condition, layer with a favorite filling, wrap the entire stack, and chill overnight. Dessert crepes can then be sliced and served cold with whipped cream or sweet sauce. Reheat seafood, poultry or vegetable crepes wrapped in foil in a moderate oven. To serve the torte, cut into wedges. Allow 2 to 3 crepes per serving. Don't attempt stacking with crepes smaller than 6 inches in diameter.

Next time: Correct heat or adjust time after first two test crepes. Pour batter into hot bubbly butter in the crepe pan, tilting quickly to coat bottom evenly. When heat is sufficient, crepe should set almost immediately, and may be ready to turn within 30 seconds. The second side requires even less cooking—about 15 seconds. Crepe batter with sugar browns more readily than plain, so watch carefully.

SOGGY

This time: Turn up heat and lightly brown both sides. Filled crepes that have become soggy can be browned carefully in a skillet or under the broiler. Dessert crepes sprinkled with sugar and glazed under the broiler take on a delicious crusty texture. If the soggy filled crepes can be handled, dip in an egg-milk mixture, then in bread crumbs, and sauté for a crisp coating.

Next time: Increase heat if first crepe is soggy. If next few still suffer the problem, correct batter by gradually stirring in a little flour. Serve crepes as soon as they're filled to prevent moisture from penetrating. When cooking, do not turn crepe until browned on the bottom.

STICKING, TEARING

This time: Correct batter if not all cooked; adjust heat, see *Next time* (below). Broken crepes can be trimmed evenly, rolled around filling, fastened with picks, and served as appetizers. Or serve pieces in dessert dishes soaked in sauce and topped with ice cream. Scraps can be turned into a bread or cake pudding, or crumbled and soaked in liquor for a dessert topping.

Next time: Allow batter to rest at least 1 to 2 hours at room temperature or several hours in the refrigerator. This ripening makes handling easier. The batter consistency when ready to cook should be similar to whipping cream. If too thin, the batter may stick. Although it's easier to thin a batter it may be thickened by gradually stirring in a little flour. If a dessert crepe, cut amount of sugar. Make sure crepe pan has enough butter to coat bottom to prevent sticking. Too high heat can also cause the problem.

BATTER THICK

This time: When the batter is thicker than whipping cream, thin by gradually adding a little water or main liquid used. A too-thick, cakey finished product (closer to the characteristics of a pancake) can be cut into strips, browned in butter and topped with a delicious saucy seafood or chicken filling. Sprinkle with buttered crumbs or grated cheese and bake until crispy. Dessert crepes treated in similar fashion might be combined with a fruit sauce and flambéed.

Next time: Be aware of batter consistency before resting period. It should be slightly thinner than the consistency of whipping cream. It thickens upon ripening. Use only about 2 tbsp. batter for a 6-inch crepe pan.

To store: One of the conveniences of crepes is that they can be made ahead and either refrigerated or frozen. Stack in piles of 6 with wax paper in between, overwrap the pile, and refrigerate up to 2 days, or overwrap in foil and freeze.

Croquembouche—*See Pâte À Choux.*

Croquette—*See Deep-fried Foods.*

Croutons—*See Bread.*

Crumbs—*See Bread.*

Crustaceans—*See Shellfish.*

Crystallization—*See Candy, Confectionery; Canning.*

Cucumber

BITTER

This time: Salt the slices allowing the bitter juices to draw out on paper toweling. If still too bitter for your taste, dress in a sweet-sour vinegar-dill dressing, or cook in water with some lemon juice and sugar, drain, press dry, and use in cooked dish or for a hot cucumber soup.

Next time: Select cucumbers fresh and firm and well shaped with bright green color. Some varieties are whitish around the tips. Very hard, compact little cucumbers tend to be the most bitter. Shriveled cukes also tend to be tough and bitter.

OLD

This time: Soak whole cukes in cold water in refrigerator 1 to 2 hours before serving; peel, slice, salt on paper toweling, refrigerate, then drain. The procedure crisps them. Or cut off the peel (a vegetable peeler doesn't work well on a soft cuke), then slice thick or chop coarse and taste. If still firm enough to be eaten raw, prepare in sweet-sour vinegar or sour-cream–dill dressing, or mix chopped cucumber into yogurt that has been blended with a crushed garlic clove, pepper, lemon juice, and dill—for jajick. If too soft for relish or salad, cook in boiling salted water with a bit of vinegar or lemon juice, just until heated through. Drain well, add sour cream or butter and parsley, or add to a vegetable-tomato stew. Or purée and use for cream of vegetable soup (p. 315).

Next time: Choose green, firm, but not too hard cukes that show no signs of shriveling or soft spots. Most commercially sold cukes are waxed, to retard spoiling. Wrap in plastic and refrigerate; use within a week.

Cupcake—*See Cake.*

Curdling—*See Egg; Sauces; Yogurt.*

Custard—*See Pudding.*

Dandelion Greens—*See Greens.*

Date—Dates are among the most ancient of cultivated fruits, from earliest Egyptian tomb evidence. The date palm is also a symbol of majestic beauty, often growing to 100 feet and with a longevity of two centuries. Historically, the trees have always thrived in Middle Eastern subtropical climates where human civilizations first began. Fifty years ago, the date industry was introduced to California desert land, where the bountiful crop today is exported to many other countries.

CRYSTALLIZED SURFACE, OLD, DRIED-OUT, STUCK TOGETHER, HARD

This time: Cover with boiling water; drain off after ½ hour, chop or grind, and use for breads or pastries. When there's more time, marinate dried dates in dry or semidry sherry or white wine or tart fruit juice overnight in refrigerator, so dates can absorb the liquid. Store leftovers in refrigerator for weeks, and serve with whipped cream and nuts, or combine with fresh fruits such as orange or tangerine segments or apple or pineapple chunks.

Next time: Select plump, soft dates with smooth, shiny brown skin. Store in tightly covered container in dry, cool place; once package is opened, cover, refrigerate, and use within a couple of months.

SINKING IN BATTERS

Toss date pieces lightly in flour to help suspend them. Or save about a fourth of the dates to sprinkle on top of batter in the pan. They'll distribute themselves during baking.

STICKY WHEN CUTTING

Dip shears into flour or cold water periodically when snipping.

STUCK TOGETHER (NOT DRY)

Rinse in warm water.

Deep-fried Foods—When perfectly cooked, deep-fried items are brown and crisp on the surface and moist on the inside. As the food is immersed in the hot fat the exterior should brown quickly, sealing in the juices and preventing the fat from entering the food.

GREASY

This time: Remove cooked food with wire drainer or basket. Drain thoroughly on paper toweling, gently press out excess fat.

Next time: To insure fast cooking, food for frying should be pre-cooked or cut in small pieces (about 2 inches in diameter) and at room temperature. Make sure temperature of fat is as hot as recipe recommends; use a thermometer to be accurate. Add a few pieces of food at a time to prevent lowering temperature of fat.

Deer—*See Game.*

Dessert—*See* specific types.

Dips—*See Cheese; Sour Cream;* or other main ingredients in dip.

Discoloration—*See* specific fruits and vegetables.

Doughnuts—*See Bread, Deep-fried Foods.*

Dressing—*See Salad, Salad Dressing; Sauces; Stuffing.*

Drinks—*See Alcoholic; Milk; Punch;* or specific items.

Duck—*See Poultry, Game Birds.*

Dumpling—Steamed or boiled globs of dough made from flour, crumbs, potatoes or some grain. The liquid added to the starch is most often water, broth or milk. The dumpling is sometimes fattened with shortening and leavened by egg, yeast or baking powder. Some versions incorporate liver or cheese. The German spaetzle, Italian gnocchi, and Jewish matzo balls (knaidlach) are all in the dumpling family. Central European countries specialize in making delicious variations of these little puffy dough balls. Some are cooked alone in boiling water; others simmer on top of a stew or in soup. Occasionally they cause cooks distress by bursting or becoming "sinkers." Read on to end all dumpling mishaps.

BLAND

This time: Few table offerings fall flatter than a tasteless hunk of boiled dough. Sprinkle with favorite herbs and spices, and if available, add a gravy or sauce. A topping of seasoned buttered breadcrumbs will also add both texture and taste.

Next time: Dumplings simmered in a flavorful soup or stew or filled with a spicy mixture need less seasoning than plain. Season an austere dough with thyme, dill, sage, oregano, parsley, or other favorite herbs. Minced onion or grated Parmesan can also be added directly to the dough. For apple- or plum-filled dumplings, some appropriate spices are nutmeg, coriander, and cinnamon.

BURST

This time: Filled dumplings can be a real problem when they explode in the pot. They can be chopped and incorporated into soup or stew. Serve the fruit-filled dumplings in a dish topped with sour cream or another sauce.

Next time: Mold enough dough around the filling to completely enclose it, sealing well. Cook in simmering water. Do not overcook or leave in rapidly boiling water. If dough tends to disintegrate, it may need more egg.

DOUGHY, GUMMY

This time: A sticky dough will drop more easily from a moistened spoon. When the finished product is doughy and gummy, cut into smaller pieces and simmer longer.

Next time: Add more flour or less liquid to the dough. Cook in ample liquid in a wide-topped pot. Never crowd the pan; each dumpling needs room for expansion. Cramped quarters can cause the doughy texture.

HEAVY, TOUGH

This time: Even the heaviest rocks will taste lighter when chopped and added to soup or broth. Or grind and mix with sautéed vegetables for a meat stuffing.

Next time: Less flour or more liquid or leavening (yeast, egg, or baking powder) produces a lighter texture. Keep dumplings steaming on top of simmering liquid; never boil. Boiling or long cooking without a cover can cause the toughness.

THICK

This time: When those little dough puffs have ballooned to enormous proportions, slice and serve like boiled potatoes with gravy or a sauce. A seasoned topping of buttered crumbs adds a touch of crunch.

Next time: Use smaller spoonfuls. Be prepared for much expansion when recipes use more than ¾ tsp. baking powder per cup flour.

THIN

This time: Thicken a thin batter by adding more flour, breadcrumbs, or whatever starch is used in the recipe. Depending on recipe, dough should have enough substance to hold shape when dropped from a spoon, molded or rolled. Once cooked, the thin, floppy result can be served in bowls topped with creamed chicken or stew. Or cut into smaller pieces, roll in melted butter, then in crumbs, and brown in a skillet.

Next time: Overbeating might cause the problem. Use larger portions of batter or thicker layers of dough. Make sure liquid is kept simmering throughout cooking. It's best to cover the pan with a tight-fitting glass lid and watch the batter increase in size. Do not lift lid until dumplings look fluffy. Test for doneness as you would a cake by inserting a wooden pick or cake tester through center. When the tester comes out clean, they're ready.

Eclair—*See Cream; Pâté à choux; Pudding.*

Eggs

General Tips

To center yolks (for hard-cooked): Turn eggs constantly when beginning the cooking in cold water. When water reaches simmering, cover and proceed with directions, allowing about 15 minutes for hard-cooked eggs.

To clean up egg when dropped: Pour salt over and let stand about 15 to 20 minutes. It should then be easier to scrape off.

To clean eggy utensils: Use cold water for soaking, which loosens the coagulated protein. Silver polish or salt helps remove sulphur stains from silver pieces.

To distinguish between raw and cooked: Play spin-the-eggs. The spinners are cooked; the wobblies are raw.

To preserve shape when poaching: Add several drops of vinegar or lemon juice to the cooking water.

Stuck to carton: Dip carton into water; the egg should come free without cracking apart.

To peel easily: Rinse in cold water immediately after cooking and chill to make peeling easier.

To remove eggshell pieces: When small parts of the shell fall into the raw egg, scoop out with an eggshell half.

To remove bits of yolk from white: Scoop out with eggshell half. When there are many little particles of yolk, moisten a clean cloth with water and let the two make contact. Yolks like to cling to wet cloths.

To separate easily: Yolks and whites part company more readily when fresh and cold. Cover and allow to come to room temperature after separating.

To slice easily: Chill egg first. For uniform slices, use an egg slicer. A very warm knife, cheese slicer, or carefully maneuvered thread also does the trick, but more tediously.

To test for freshness: Place in bowl of cold water. The sinkers are fine for use. Floaters should be discarded.

COAGULATED TOO QUICKLY

This time: So the egg coagulated before it could thicken a hot mixture! Try passing the lumpy blend through a sieve. If you get a pretty clear liquid with the clumped egg remaining behind, then add more egg to the liquid; but this time add a little hot mixture to the beaten egg or yolk first, then gradually stir into remaining hot mixture, stirring constantly. That procedure will not work too well with a thick sauce. Turn mixture into a casserole instead, adding wedges of hard-cooked eggs and topping with cheese or seasoned breadcrumbs, and bake.

Next time: Always add a little hot mixture to the beaten egg first, then gradually stir into remaining hot mixture, stirring constantly.

TOO COLD (AS FOR BAKING)

This time: Soak in lukewarm water a few minutes to bring to room temperature.

Next time: Remove from refrigerator ½ hour before use.

CRACKED

This time: Dirty cracked eggs can be contaminated, so it's safest not to use them. If only slightly cracked it can still be hard-cooked by wrapping very tightly in foil, then cooking as usual. When timer rings, transfer to bowl of cold water immediately to stop cooking. When eggs crack during cooking, add about 1 teaspoon salt or a dash of vinegar or lemon juice to the cooking water; the remedies prevent the egg from seeping out.

Next time: Examine eggs carefully before purchasing, and handle carefully to avoid cracking. When you notice a cracked one, use it soon to prevent drying out. Use one of the long-cooking methods to kill any bacteria. Add 1 teaspoon salt or dash of vinegar or lemon juice to cooking water in case an egg cracks while cooking. Good precautionary measures to follow are to gently pierce each egg at one end, bring eggs to room temperature, and to cover with cool water before cooking (see *Discolored, Next time*).

DISCOLORED

This time: It's easy to remove the green ring from hard-cooked egg yolks; halve eggs, gently remove yolk from each, and rub lightly with finger. Sometimes it helps to dip finger and yolk into cool water first. When dealing with several green-ringed egg yolks, however, it's more efficient to camouflage somehow. Make deviled eggs with a fresh green-herb filling. When the entire egg has discolored from cooking in an aluminum pan with a metal spoon, cover with tomato sauce and lots of chopped green pepper and onion.

Next time: The correct term is *hard-cooked,* not *boiled*—when eggs boil, the yolks develop green rings. To properly hard-cook eggs, place in saucepan one layer deep, cover with cool tap water. Bring to quick boil, cover pan, remove from heat. Let stand about 15 minutes. Cool in cold water and chill. Avoid cooking eggs in aluminum utensils, since there's a chance of discoloration.

FROZEN

This time: Thaw in refrigerator; use soon afterward.

Next time: Place whole eggs or yolks in quantities you will use in freezer containers, add a little salt or sugar, mix, and seal before freezing. Omit salt or sugar for whites alone.

NOT VERY FRESH

This time: Eggs that have been around for a while may be perfectly good for baking and cooking purposes. Avoid using them for soufflés, angel food cakes, and creations that need the strength of fresh egg whites. And to keep them from showing their age too much, don't serve as table eggs.

Next time: Try to select fresh eggs from a reliable source, store them broad side up in the refrigerator egg keeper or in their carton, and try to use within 10 days for optimum quality. Eggs are usable for a month or more, but they thin out.

OVERCOOKED

This time: Coarsely chop overcooked eggs and place in buttered casserole. Top with a white or cheese sauce sparked with wine (dry sherry is appropriate), herbs, spices, and perhaps a dash of hot pepper, and bake a few minutes in a low oven until heated. A microwave oven is perfect for this reheating. Or cool, chop, and use in sandwich filling or over salads.

Next time: The lower the heat the better for eggs. They must be carefully watched and the temperature regulated. Remove from heat just before they are done, for they will continue cooking in a hot pan. Transfer to plates immediately when right consistency has been reached.

THIN

This time: Avoid frying, poaching, or using in soufflés. Okay to scramble or use in cooked dishes, or for baking.

Next time: Select Grade AA for poaching or frying, and Grade A for most table use, baking, and cooking. Store broad side up and use within 10 days.

WHITES WON'T WHIP

This time: A speck of fat will prevent whites from beating up, so remove any visible yolk. Use clean beaters and bowl with rounded bottom. If whites are cold, allow to warm to room temperature. If they still don't beat up, there must be fat mixed in or they are very watery, so use in baking or cooking and start with fresh egg whites.

Next time: Select fresh, top-grade eggs. Separate whites carefully from yolks, place in clean round-bottomed bowl, cover, and bring to room temperature. Using clean beaters, beat well. Volume can increase and stabilize with the addition of a small amount of salt or acid. Beat to foamy stage before adding about ⅛ teaspoon cream of tartar or ½ teaspoon vinegar or lemon juice for every 3 egg whites.

Substitutes: When you're 1 egg short for a baked or cooked dish, use about 1 tablespoon cornstarch instead, which has the approximate thickening power. Commercial egg substitutes can also be used to replace whole eggs, but not in recipes where whites must be separated from yolks.

Equivalents: 1 small egg = generous 2 tablespoons; 1 large egg = generous 3 tablespoons.

Eggnog—*See Alcoholic; Cream; Egg; Milk.*

Eggplant—Can be a bit intimidating. Its juices are sometimes bitter, it holds a lot of moisture (undesirable in some preparations, such as frying), it readily absorbs oil and discolors after cutting. Following are the remedies.

BITTER

This time: Add a little sugar or, if the dish can accommodate it, tomato sauce or chopped tomatoes. Any sweetness will counter the bitterness.

Next time: Before cooking, place slices on absorbent paper, salt well, and weigh down with plate about ½ hour to drain off excess water, which is bitter. Peel a mature eggplant, since skin can be bitter.

DISCOLORED

This time: Sprinkle with lemon juice to prevent any further darkening and camouflage with a sauce, such as tomato or cheese. Most preparations for this vegetable require combining it with other ingredients, frying, or cooking with a sauce, so discoloration is not that noticeable.

Next time: Immediately rub cut surfaces with lemon juice; or cover with salty ice water, drain, then gently press dry on paper toweling. This last method works best for fried eggplant, or where it should maintain a firm texture. Cook in glass, enamel, or stainless steel.

OILY

This time: The eggplant was fried or sautéed in oil and absorbed too much? The only alternative is to press out the oil, using paper toweling. This is guaranteed to destroy the shape and texture, so change your preparation plans and place mashed eggplant in dish or purée, top with grated cheese, and broil.

Next time: Soak slices in salty ice water, drain, and dry before frying, which causes much spattering, but prevents oil absorption (and thus excess calories). Use a little oil; make sure it's hot. For deep frying, oil should be about 3 inches deep and at least 375 degrees.

OLD

This time: Trim away any brown spots, peel if skin is withered, salt slices (see *Bitter*), and cook in a tomato-basil sauce, or another sauce that will support its texture and cover its aging flavor (see gingered sweet-sour sauce, p. 329). Sweet Spanish onion is another compatible ingredient that lends sugar.

Next time: Select smaller firm, smooth fruit with a uniform glossy color. Avoid any with spongy spots. Store in refrigerator 3 to 4 days. Use soon—it's perishable.

OVERCOOKED

This time: Overcooked means soft and mushy, and about the only use for shapeless eggplant is in some saucy dish where its contour will not be noticeable. Purée it with fresh mint sauce, and you have a complement for lamb, or blend purées of eggplant and cauliflower with horseradish for roast beef. Try either sauce over a vegetable medley such as onion slices, green pepper strips, and carrot or zucchini rounds.

Next time: For preparations that look best when the eggplant keeps its shape, soak in salty ice water, drain, then gently press with paper toweling. Or salt slices, weight and allow moisture to drain off. For stewed or simmered dishes, sauté pieces quickly before cooking in liquid to help retain shape. Simmer pieces until tender, usually about ½ hour. Baked slices, ½-inch thick, take about 15 minutes, turning once, in 375-degree oven. A medium-size whole eggplant bakes in about 45 minutes at 350 degrees. Stuffed halves, with precooked filling, heat to serving in about 15 minutes in 350 degree oven.

WATERY: See Oily and Overcooked.

Elk—*See Game.*

Endive (Escarole, chicory)—The curly-leaf type is generally labeled endive or chicory, and the straight-leaf type is marketed as escarole. Two more varieties of chicory are grown: one for its roots, which are dried and turned into a coffee supplement and another elongated tight-leaved cluster, the elegant Belgian endive. Endive is almost always used raw for salads in this country, but its refreshing bitter, nutlike taste lends itself well to cooked dishes too.

OVERCOOKED

This time: Use in soup or purée and make cream of endive soup (*see cream of vegetable soup,* p. 315).

Next time: Shredded escarole takes only 3 to 5 minutes to braise or stir-fry.

WILTED, FLABBY

This time: Dip in hot water, then ice water with a little vinegar or lemon juice; chill 1 to 2 hours. Or chop and add to most vegetable or meat soups; purée and make cream of vegetable soup (p. 315). Or try this recipe for 1 head wilted greens, torn in bite-size pieces: 2 slices crumbled fried bacon, 3 to 4 tablespoons slightly sweetened oil-vinegar dressing and chives; boil, pour over greens, steam 5 minutes. Toss and serve. Slightly wilted leaves sometimes can be crisped by washing in cold water, wrapping in paper toweling, and storing in refrigerator several hours. If needed immediately, coat leaves with tiny bit of oil before adding dressing.

Next time: Select firm, crisp heads with fresh leaves. Although the center forms a yellowish heart, avoid yellowing outer leaves or wilted ones with brown spots. Wash in several rinses of cold water, drain, dry, and wrap in paper toweling or kitchen towels; store in plastic bags in refrigerator up to several days.

Escarole—*See Endive.*

Espresso—*See Coffee.*

Farina—*See Cereal.*

Fat—Fat is essential nutritionally. It stores fat-soluble vitamins A, D, and E in our bodies and is both an important energy source and a carrier of essential fatty acids. The standard American diet tends to be too high in solid animal fat. Although the cholesterol subject is controversial, nutritionists and heart experts generally advise altering the average diet to decrease saturated fat and to increase polyunsaturated fats. In cooking, the term *fat* includes oils, but there is a technical difference between the two: At ordinary room temperatures fats are solid and oils are liquid. Fats and oils differ in three other basic ways as well.

1. Melting point: Oils or fats with higher amounts of saturated fatty acids have higher melting points than those with a lower percentage of fatty acids.

2. Smoking point: The temperatures at which fats begin smoking and decomposing vary greatly. Generally, oils and hydrogenated shortenings are recommended for deep-frying because they can be heated to a higher temperature without smoking than butter, margarine, and lard.

3. Shortening effectiveness: Judged by flakiness of baked products. A flaky pastry is called "short"; one that is tough and hard is not. The low saturated fats tend to have more shortening power. Shortening effectiveness is increased if the fat is incorporated in large pieces so it forms a layer between two layers of the pastry mixture as it is rolled. Temperatures also affect this quality.

SMOKING

This time: If the fat is just beginning to smoke, remove from heat immediately and cool down by adding a cold food (raw potato, onion, etc.) to the pot. Fat may be used at a lower temperature if it hasn't smoked very much.

Next time: Use a deep-fry thermometer or thermostat-controlled electric pan. Follow recipe directions for type of oil and temperature to avoid overheating. Fats may be reused for frying, but repeated use lowers smoking temperature.

SPATTERING

This time: A dash of salt tends to quiet spattering fat during frying. Dry any remaining foods well before adding to fat.

Next time: Because of their density certain foods, such as kidney and liver, pop and spatter during frying. Pierce them in several places before cooking to prevent this, and dry any foods thoroughly before adding to hot fat. When adding liquid to fat, stir in gradually to prevent excessive spattering action and smoke.

STRONG-FLAVORED

This time: When a sample of fried food tastes of a previous fried food, change to a fresh oil. Or cool and strain fat through filter paper and clarify by slowing frying sliced raw potato, which absorbs some of the decomposition products. When oil has a more robust flavor than desired (in salad dressing made with olive oil, for instance) dilute with more of the dressing made with a milder oil.

Next time: Maintain the correct temperature during frying to prevent excessive flavor absorption, using a thermometer or an electric thermostatic-control skillet. Never re-use oil unless strained and clarified. Store fat used for frying fish separately. When a milder-flavored oil is desired, use corn or cottonseed instead of the more distinctive peanut or olive.

Fig—Frequent in biblical reference, peace symbol to the ancient Hebrews, and object of worship for the Romans, this oblong little fruit has made a distinct mark on history. Fossils found in Italy and France record wild figs millions of years ago. The unique method in which figs are pollinated is undoubtedly the reason for the fruit's symbolism of fertility. Some figs must be cross-pollinated, as with the ancient method used for the famous Smyrna fig, the best dried variety. Cross-pollination is done by the tiny fig wasps that breed inside the inedible Capri fig. Other types are self-pollinating, yielding fruit especially suited for table use.

Fresh summer figs are truly an experience. Served with thinly sliced prosciutto, they are a favorite Italian appetizer. One of my fondest memories is of eating succulent fresh figs and feta cheese on a beach near Athens. In the semiarid climates where the tree thrives, the fresh fruit may begin the day served with bread and cheese, and end it as a dessert bathed in cream.

BLAND (MOSTLY APPLIES TO FRESH)

This time: Occasionally the flavor of what appears to be a fully ripe fig is disappointingly neutral. Amazing what a little water spiced with cinnamon and cardamom, or port or other sweet wine, can do. When properly plumped with the wine, serve in dessert dishes with a touch of whipped cream or whipped cream cheese. Try a squeeze of lemon or lime juice over fresh, cut figs. Or turn another figleaf and allow the fruit to soak up a bit of vinaigrette, then listen for the compliments when you serve it in a salad—stunning with Greek olives, feta, and cucumber chunks.

Next time: Condition of fruit can't guarantee flavor, but reduce the risk of bland figs by selecting tree-ripened fruit that is soft to touch. They are extremely perishable; store in refrigerator and use within 2 days.

OVERRIPE, SOFT

This time: Fresh figs are delightful when soft enough to eat out of the skin with a spoon, but when very soft, peel, then purée pulp and turn into puddings or sauce (for fruit gelatin or applesauce cake), or blend with sweetened whipped cream for a rich dessert. Cooked down and sweetened, figs also make a delicious filling for tortes and pastries.

Next time: Avoid very soft, mushy fruit; should be free of brown spots. Choose soft figs, then refrigerate and use very soon.

SOUR ODOR

This time: Very overripe fruit, especially that stored in a warm place, may give off a sour odor from the juice fermenting inside. Make wine if there's enough. Uncontrolled fermentation may be harmful; it's not advisable to eat spoiled fruit.

Next time: Avoid very soft, mushy fruit, especially with any brown spots. Refrigerate as soon as fruit is ripe.

DRIED, STUCK TOGETHER, STICKY WHEN CHOPPING

Heating the glued mass of figs in a low oven should loosen the grip. You may want to poach them in syrup with lime juice. They double in bulk when cooked. Keeping flour nearby when chopping will help control your temper. Periodically dip scissors or knife into flour or even water. When sticky business persists, dip figs in flour too.

UNDERRIPE

This time: Generally, overripeness is the problem. But if you come across hard, underripe figs, you can store them at room temperature for a day or two to soften. Firm figs can be stewed in spiced fruit juice or syrup, perhaps with a touch of sweet wine. Especially compatible with rhubarb. Or purée and cook into a filling for pastry. Pulp may be chopped and steamed or simmered and used in puddings and compotes. Try blending it with raw banana and pineapple.

Next time: See Bland.

Filbert—*See Nuts.*

Filet Mignon—*See Meat.*

Fillets—*See Fish.*

Filling—*See Icings, Glazes; Sandwich;* or specific ingredient.

Fires, Burns—Almost every cook can tell of a fire experience—in the broiler, in the toaster, or on the burner. I've had several at various times, and the best advice I can give is to move quickly but stay calm so you remember what to do when seconds count. Read through this information carefully, then take the precautionary measures to increase your chances of safe cooking.

BURNS

This time: Hold ice cube or clean cloth wrapped around ice cube to burned area; fingers or hand can be dipped in ice water. Protect burned skin from air. Cover with thick, dry dressing, such as baking soda. Or apply the sticky substance from a snapped-off shoot of an aloe plant, if you have one. *Seek further medical aid for bad burns*—this is not a first-aid book. Unplug small appliance or turn off burner or broiler to stop further fire, smoke, steam, or spattering. If leaving area to get first aid, be sure everything is under control and there's no chance a fire could break out.

Next time: These safety measures will protect against burns.

1. Place a metal spoon or fork into glass to absorb some of the heat when pouring in hot liquids, to prevent the glass from cracking.

2. Do not carry full pots of boiling water from stove to sink. Ladle out water into another container to make the pot lighter.

3. The range should be level to prevent pots from sliding and tipping. Select well-designed flat-bottomed pans to prevent tipping.

4. Keep hot pads and long-handled utensils handy near range and grill.

5. Carefully lift cover of pot with boiling liquid so steam escapes away from you.

6. When pan-frying, keep pot cover or colander nearby to partially cover pan in case of spattering.

7. Wear long asbestos mitts when stirring a viscous, sputtering mixture like jelly.

8. Position pots of boiling water on back burners, out of reach of children.

9. Turn pot handles toward back of range so they don't overhang edge, where they can easily be bumped.

10. Slide pan out on oven rack or remove pan from oven. Do not try to reach into a hot oven.

11. Keep an aloe plant growing nearby and/or plenty of baking soda.

FIRES

This time: First turn off broiler or burner or unplug appliance involved without risk of being burned. Quickly cover grease fire with large pot lid to smother flames. Close broiler door for fire in that unit. If you have a fire extinguisher, use it. If not, throw baking soda or salt on a grease fire. *Never throw water on burning grease.*

Next time: Help prevent cooking fires with the following tips.

1. Keep a small fire extinguisher spray can handy in the kitchen or near outdoor grill.

2. Have a good supply of baking soda and salt nearby.

3. Trim off excess fat from meats to avoid flare-ups in broiler or grill. Avoid placing rack holding broiler pan of meat right next to heat source.

4. When grilling, follow directions carefully if using a fire starter. Keep grill far enough away from house or garage so that if wind changes, sparks cannot start a fire. Arrange charcoal so fire is not directly under food—especially long-cooking meats or poultry with lots of drippings.

5. Use only electrical equipment in good shape.

Fish—This section refers to finfish from both fresh and salt water. For specific information on mollusks and crustaceans, see *Shellfish*; for information on miscellaneous seafood, see *Seafood.* Considering the world is almost 75 percent water, it's surprising that fish isn't a stronger part of the American diet. Our fish consumption is tiny compared with the Chinese, Japanese, Scandinavians, French, Russians, and most other people around the globe. Ancient Egyptians venerated fish. In Chinese culture, it is a symbol of good fortune on the table.

Because of its delicacy (to say nothing of its low fat and calorie content), fish generally has long been my own menu preference, so I've sampled it in many places. The most memorable were rather simply prepared: a grilled sea bass brushed with lemon-butter in southern Spain; a poached salmon with caper mayonnaise in Eastern Canada; broiled bluefish in Boston, and sea trout Provençal at the French Port Restaurant in Chicago. The owner, Matt, once worked on a commercial fishing boat in his home Mediterranean waters. Now his fishing expeditions are early-morning rounds in Chicago markets. I asked him how he stores the fish until serving. He advises squeezing lemon over, then covering with lots of ice and refrigerating. When it's necessary to freeze fish, he recommends rinsing or quickly soaking it in cold water, then wrapping in a plastic bag and freezing. The water forms a thin ice glaze around the fish, preventing loss of juices. He suggests thawing in the refrigerator before cooking. Properly done, freezing need not detract from original fresh fish palatability. One of my favorites is frozen baby halibut. Broiled with a dusting of herbs and butter, it emerges slightly crusty on top and succulent throughout. Served with fresh lemon squeezed over, it has become a quick, never-fail delicacy.

Although some aversion to fish stems from improper freezing, most prejudice comes from improper cooking. The most common mistake with this delicate flesh is overcooking, which results in either too dry or mushy texture. The old "cook until it flakes easily" guideline is actually too much cooking by today's nouvelle cuisine standards.

BLAND

This time: Rub broiled or baked fish with a cut clove of garlic and add herbs (dill is great with salmon, thyme with halibut and many others, tarragon with mackerel). Ground spices (especially coriander, curry, and ginger) can be sprinkled over fillets and steaks. Squeeze lemon juice inside a whole baked fish and serve almost any fish with lemon wedges. Orange and lime are milder additions. Or put the flavor into fish through a delectable sauce or butter; an herb butter is especially appropriate for broiled fish, while a caper mayonnaise or rémoulade embellishes a poached fish. Tartar is the usual accompaniment for fried.

Next time: Add whole spices to cooking liquid; use wine and stock instead of water. Remember that long simmering cooks out ground spices; make sure herbs and spices used are fresh. Rub inside and skin of whole fish, especially the gill areas, with onion, lemon, and seasonings, before baking. Brush fillets and steaks well with seasoned butter before broiling. Add seasoning to coatings for fried fish; and when pan-frying, add garlic and onion to fat in pan.

DRY

This time: Simmer gently in broth, wine, or sauce. Serve with lots of lemon squeezed over.

Next time: Do not salt before broiling or grilling—salt draws out natural juices. Avoid very high heat. Add fat or liquid to lean fish.

FISHY FLAVOR, ODOR (assuming the fish is fresh; old or bad fish is a condition that cannot be corrected)

This time: The odor of boiling fish can become strong—usually from the boiling fish fat. A few celery leaves added to the pot help. The flavor will dissipate slightly if fish is left to stand in liquid after cooking. Skim off fat; discard. When the subject is fried fish, do not reuse smelly cooking fat. Ginger and sherry help mask the fishy flavor; sprinkle one or both into the sauce or mix with melted butter and lemon. An acrid citrus fruit is another ingredient that cuts strong fish flavor. Lemon, vinegar, or salt rubbed on hands before washing them helps remove odor. Wash pots in baking-soda water.

Next time: Avoid steaming or poaching fatty fish, since their natural oils become smelly and contribute the flavor known as "fishy." Celery leaves added to a pot of simmering fish help destroy strong odor. Fish that is a day or two old can be greatly improved by marinating in a piquant acid medium (wine, lemon juice, or vinegar-based mixture with garlic, green onions, ginger, and other contents of the spice rack). A spectacular illustration of the boiling technique can be experienced at the celebrated "fish boils" native to Wisconsin's charming Door County peninsula, sometimes called "the Cape Cod of the Midwest." These outdoor group-feeding affairs are indeed similar to seacoast clambakes. Presided over by a "boil master," the seemingly casual procedure is an arcane art of touch and instinct. First, potatoes and onions are dumped into a giant cauldron of boiling salted water over roaring logs. Then, at a precise moment, the master adds large pieces of lake trout or whitefish. Later, he tosses inflammable liquid on the fire. Flames leap skyward, making the pot boil over and carrying away all traces of coagulated oily fish protein.

OVERCOOKED, FALLING APART

This time: Whether too dry from overcooking by dry heat or mushy from long simmering, pick up the pieces (or crumble) and add sauce, then serve over rice or pile into pastry shells. Little chunks of poached fish are perfect for chowders, creamed dishes, and many casseroles and salads. (See *vegetable timbale*, p. 333.)

Next time: Fish is edible when internal temperature reaches 140 degrees. Ten degrees higher breaks down the tissues, permitting flavor and juices to escape. Fish continues cooking on a hot platter, so it's best to remove from heat as soon as done. The fork test helps determine readiness when fish begins to flake. Overcooking and excessive heat produce a dry product with less flavor and fewer vitamins. To prevent delicate fish from falling apart, handle as little as possible. Serve in ovenproof dishes instead of transferring.

SALTY

This time: A 5- to 10-minute bath in fresh cold water helps remove salt from raw fish. Then rub with lemon before cooking. Overly salty fish broth (such as for poached) can be slightly desalinized by adding a raw cut-up potato, which absorbs salt like a sponge. Discard the potato or add to pot when boiling more potatoes. Vinegar added to the salty cooking liquid also improves it. An acidic (lemony or vinegary) or sweetened sauce (sweet-sour is perfect) counter saltiness of cooked fish.

Next time: Season toward end of cooking or after. If raw fish is known to be salty, soak briefly in water or milk before cooking to avoid delay. Prepare a tangy citrus or sweet-sour sauce in advance. It can always be used, even with bland fish.

SCALY

Although dressed fish and fillets with skin supposedly are scaled, the star dinner attraction often needs some last-minute detail. The fastest, easiest method of loosening those well-fastened scales (which indicates freshness) is to plunge the fish into boiling water, then quickly into a cold bath. Use a small serrated knife to scrape the scales off.

STICKING TO PAN

This time: This problem applies to broiling and pan-frying, so pieces may be browned and dry. Add moisture by saucing, or add to a moist casserole. Even browned pieces make a nice chowder or soup, and can be marinated in salad dressing and tossed with other vegetables for a main-dish salad.

Next time: Always oil broiler pan. Do not turn fish during broiling. Make certain skillet is well oiled and very hot before frying fish and turn to brown both sides.

Servings: Estimate the following raw weights per serving: 1 lb. whole small fish; ¾ lb. dressed; ½ lb. steaks; ⅓ lb. fillets.

To refreshen: A common problem in hot weather. Wash not-too-fresh fish in vinegar-water and dry on paper toweling. Fry in very hot fat. The high temperature kills any bacteria that could multiply at lower heat. Serve immediately with lemon. Do not try to salvage spoiled fish; when odor is bad, return it to market if it was just purchased.

To select: When choosing fish with head on, eyes should bulge, gills should be reddish and scales on a fresh fish adhere firmly to the side. Flesh on all fresh fish should be firm to touch, scales should have a high sheen and there should be no offensive odor, especially around belly or gills.

To store:

1. *In freezer:* When working with whole fish, clean and remove gills, leaving heads on. Wash well (do not dry so a glaze forms) and place in open plastic bags in freezer until hard. Rinse in cold water again and return to freezer. When glazed, close bags tightly and store up to 2 or 3 months for best quality.
2. *In refrigerator:* Sprinkle with salt and lemon juice and pack with ice. Keep in coldest part of refrigerator (below 40 degrees, preferably closer to 32 degrees) and use within 2 days.

To thaw: Frozen fish should be left in its wrapper and thawed slowly in the refrigerator (about 6 hours per pound) before cooking.

Flambé—Any complementary high-proof liquor may be used; brandy and rum are popular choices. Usually warmed liquor poured over hot food is ignited. Desserts are often set ablaze by soaking sugar cubes in liquor, then flaming them when they are placed over the food. When a hot dish doesn't flambé readily, heat both food and liquor well before trying again. Make certain the alcohol is not aired out and has a high proof.

Flan—See *Pudding.*

Flapjacks—See *Pancakes.*

Flounder—See *Fish.*

Flour—See *Bugs; Thickeners;* and related problems.

Flour, Browned—Spread flour over baking sheet; bake in slow or moderate oven, shaking pan occasionally until flour is lightly colored. Use it to enrich flavor and color of sauces and gravies. Since its thickening power is halved by the browning, about twice the amount of all-purpose flour must be used.

Fondue—Fondue is communal table-top cooking, and all its variations fall into 2 basic groups: those in which foods are coated in sauce (such as the classic Swiss cheese fondue or dessert chocolate), and others (such as boeuf bourguignonne), which include actual cooking of foods in hot oil or liquid. The Swiss are credited with inventing the original cheese-wine fondue, but there are several versions of its beginnings. One tells of a lonely Alpine shepherd varying his usual cheese-bread-wine meal by melting the cheese in the wine and dunking the bread. Another, more elaborate story explains how, long ago, the Swiss made cheese and bread in the summer to last through the cold winter. Both foods hardened so much that the bread had to be chopped with an axe and the cheese melted to be eaten. One day, perhaps, someone spilled his wine into the cheese and discovered the true fondue. The wine softens and flavors the cheese; regulated heat keeps it at just the right velvety consistency for coating the bread. Today's fondue fans are more concerned about texture and flavor than the hungry Swiss peasants of yesteryear.

FLARE-UP

This time: Quickly place a pot cover over the burning area or toss baking soda at the base of the flames. A fire extinguisher also does the job well. Turn off or cover heat source if possible.

Next time: Use good quality equipment in top condition. Set on a level table and out of reach of children. Turn handles away from table edge to avoid bumping. Have safety equipment nearby. Keep hot pads, mitts, and long-handled tongs handy. Treat minor burns by wrapping an ice cube in a clean towel around the area or holding under cold water for 10 to 15 minutes. Then prevent air contact by applying a dry dressing such as baking soda. Major burns need medical attention. (See *Fires, Burns.*)

HEAT HARD TO CONTROL

The chances of an accident or food burning increase when the heating element cannot be regulated properly. A ceramic open pot, recommended for Swiss fondue, is not suitable for the beef version; it might crack from the heat of boiling oil. Use a metal pot for fondue bourguignonne. One good all-purpose 1- to 1½-quart metal pot can be used for all recipes. Butane-gas heaters regulated by a lever or dial give the most efficient control and highest heat. The popular canned fuel and alcohol burners offer a medium heat range. Canned heat generally will adjust heat with a swinging lid cover. Other burners have either a lid or a series of adjustable air holes.

Beef (fondue bourguignonne); vegetable: The first is a misnomer—it uses neither burgundy wine nor is part of the provincial repertoire. But the name is understandable considering the famous French vineyards of that region are near the Swiss border. Prepared by dipping tender beef chunks in boiling oil, then dipping the cooked meat into various sauces, this specialty has become a great après-ski meal. Made on short notice, it also frees busy innkeepers by having guests do their own cooking. The information below also applies to vegetable fondues. Peanut oil or a good quality corn oil are recommended.

OIL COOLS

This time: The oil may have to be transferred to another container and reheated on the range, if the pot is not electric. Drain and gently press in paper toweling any foods that soaked up warm oil, then cook in hot oil.

Next time: Before starting, preheat oil to about 375 degrees. A good temperature test is when a 1½-inch bread cube browns in ½ minute. Fill fondue pot about half (about 3 cups oil in average pot). Avoid dipping too many forks into the pot simultaneously. Have meat and vegetables at cool room temperature, but not cold. Regulate heat throughout cooking.

SPATTERING

This time: Add 1 teaspoon salt to the oil to reduce spattering. Dry foods well before dipping.

Next time: Allow enough time for meat and any vegetables to reach cool room temperature before frying. Blot off excess moisture on all foods, but especially frozen meat.

To re-use cooking oil (see Fat, Strong-Flavored): Cool and strain through cheesecloth, filter paper, paper towels or a fine sieve. Clarify it by slowly browning several slices of raw potato in the hot oil. Remove potato, cool oil, store in covered jar in refrigerator. Oil must be filtered after each use. But when a change in flavor or texture is detected, throw the old oil away.

Cheese fondue: The Zurich style, considered basic, begins by rubbing the pot with garlic, then adding dry white wine and a little lemon juice. Shredded or minced aged Emmenthaler (Swiss cheese) coated with flour is gradually stirred in until melted before flavoring with kirsch, nutmeg, and pepper. This regional version includes twirling the bread in kirsch before dunking. When a Swiss lady loses her bread in the dunking process, she kisses the man next to her. The man who lets *his* bread get away must buy the next bottle of wine. More wine causes additional bread to be dropped, so fondue parties often go on and on with heart-warming consequences. A cheese mixture that has been heating for some time develops a browned crust. I for one believe this to be the best part.

LUMPY

This time: Store the mixture in the refrigerator, then cut up and use for cheese omelet or taco filling. Another remedy salvages the fondue: thin it with more wine, whir until smooth in blender, then return to pot and thicken by slowly stirring in more floured shredded cheese.

Next time: Shred, grate, or chop natural aged cheese. Dip in flour and add gradually while stirring over low heat. Follow fondue pot directions. Domestic Swiss cheeses sometimes cause a grainy, lumpy texture. Shred Gruyère and melt in double boiler, *slowly.*

SEPARATING

This time: Place pot on range-top burner and whip briskly with wire whisk. To bring the mixture completely back together and keep it there, add about ½ teaspoon cornstarch diluted in small amount of water and wine. Cook briefly.

Next time: Separation should not occur if shredded cheese is added gradually and stirred vigorously to blend with the wine over low heat.

STRINGY

This time: Spaghetti-strand cheese may be too stretched out for fondue but still fine for baked products and other dishes. Cool and store wrapped in refrigerator. Chop and incorporate into bread doughs, omelets, casseroles—almost any cooked dish that can take a cheesy texture. Sprinkle over ovenproof bowls of onion soup (or another hearty potage), then bake in hot oven until cheese bubbles and browns slightly. Or add to pizza.

Next time: High heat or not enough stirring can cause the texture problem. Regulate heat and keep low while stirring mixture. Use a chafing dish to ensure a low holding temperature.

THICK

This time: Add just enough wine to maintain a creamy consistency. It might be easier to remove pot to range-top burner to do this.

Next time: Turn off heater if fondue will have to keep for some time; transfer to a double boiler or chafing dish for long holding.

THIN

This time: Simply adding more shredded cheese dipped in flour (in the same manner) thickens the mixture. When the Emmenthaler or Gruyère has run out, another similar natural cheese can be used. Otherwise, serve thin fondue as a cheese sauce over cooked vegetables, chicken, fish, or eggs. Or place the crusty bread chunks from the fondue into a buttered baking dish and top with the cheese mixture, then bake until bubbly.

Next time: Check proportions in recipe: 2 cups of wine take about 1 pound cheese and 3 tablespoons flour. Use more cheese and flour if the mixture was too thin.

TOUGH

This time: The addition of a little wine and gentle reheating can thin a tough cheese blend so it's no longer chewy. When wine has run out, cool cheese, cut into pieces, and use in bread doughs or omelets. A very compact mixture can be shaped into ½-inch balls, dipped in beaten egg and fine dry breadcrumbs, then deep-fried until golden. The centers should ooze out when the crunchy shell is bitten. These appetizers are so wonderful you'll want to make them again—but instead of getting a cheese fondue to toughen, next time cut natural cheese into ½-inch cubes.

Next time: Keep cheese mixture at a uniformly hot temperature so it slowly bubbles. This helps it maintain the desirable molten consistency.

Dessert (chocolate, fruit, or jelly sauce): Chocolate fondue was invented by the Switzerland Association in New York to promote Tobler's chocolate bars. So most of the recipes involve melting the bars down with cream and flavoring with either kirsch or brandy. Whether made with milk chocolate or bittersweet, the rich blend is a luscious coating for fresh fruits dipped in the pot.

DARKENED FRUITS

This time: Fruit for fondue usually is cut thick, so trimming off the discolored surface won't be noticeable. Dip trimmed slices briefly in lemon juice or another citrus juice to preserve fresh color. Very browned fruit slices can be used for pie fillings, puddings, sauces, cakes, or any number of dishes where their appearance won't matter.

Next time: Brush fruit with citrus juice immediately after cutting. Do not slice much in advance of serving.

SCORCHED

This time: Even if the bottom has scorched, the rest of the fondue is fine to use as long as there's no burned taste. Do not scrape bottom. Lightly scorched chocolate can be loosened gently by heating with a little brandy and/or cream. The combination may be added to strong coffee for a robust cup of mocha or thickened and used as a dessert sauce. Try bitter chocolate (with or without the coffee) over ice cream with toasted slivered almonds.

Next time: Dessert fondues scorch easily because of their sugar content. They only need warming, not cooking. Use the bottom setting on an electric fondue pot; control the heat on others to very low. Prepare in double boiler on top burner, then bring it hot to the table. Use a chafing dish to keep the mixture warm for extended periods. Stir periodically.

THICK

This time: Fondue expert John Davis of Geja's Wine and Cheese Café in Chicago suggests thinning a chocolate fondue with a little coffee (also a great use for the leftover stale brew). He also says an excellent consistency can be obtained from blending fudge sundae sauce with sweet chocolate. A little extra brandy, cream, or whatever liquid is used in the recipe should be stirred in to thin down the mixture.

Next time: Don't keep the fondue warm for long periods over direct heat. Simmering will thicken it.

THIN

This time: Gradually blend in more crumbled or grated chocolate, stirring until correct consistency is reached.

Next time: Thinning can result from dipping moist fruits. Drain juicy fruit pieces well before using. When adding brandy and other liquids, add gradually while stirring and watching consistency. You may not need all the liquid called for in recipe.

Food Spoilage, Poisoning—It's one thing to resurrect over-cooked broccoli or a curdled hollandaise—quite another to attempt to avoid waste by eating chicken salad that's been in a warm picnic basket for hours. No matter how expensive the food or how hungry you are, whenever doubtful, throw out! As my college microbiology professor once said, "If you don't die from the food poisoning, then you'll wish you could. It can be so miserable, you fear you'll live through it."

Sanitation and Food Safety Tips:

1. Keep cold foods cold (below 40 degrees F.) and hot foods hot (above 140 degrees F. when holding). This 100-degree range is easy to remember. Test temperatures occasionally to make certain equipment is functioning properly. A good refrigerator should maintain a temperature below 40 degrees, and a heated serving unit should keep foods above 140 degrees. Never let food remain at room temperature longer than necessary during preparation (within 2 hours maximum). To bring the temperature quickly down on a large amount of hot food about to be chilled, transfer to smaller containers and quick-chill in a sink of cold water, then refrigerate. Avoid placing steaming hot foods in the refrigerator or freezer, since that will bring the total unit temperature up. Alternate rechilling and reheating is also to be avoided, since temperature fluctuation stimulates bacterial growth.

2. Cover foods well; when exposed they're more vulnerable to contamination. Place leftovers in sealed containers.

3. Use perishable leftovers (custards, cream fillings, etc.) within 1 or 2 days; the less perishable foods (cooked meats, vegetables) within several days.

4. When cooking foods, heat to a high enough temperature (usually boiling temperature, 212 degrees F.) to destroy most harmful bacteria.

5. Avoid refreezing thawed raw foods—especially large, dense items. It's safer to cook thawed foods, then refreeze.

6. Discard any questionable foods.

Food Spoilage Agents

1. MOLDS

Present in air in spore form; thrive in warm, damp, dark places. Aerobic (need oxygen to grow). Fuzzy in appearance; often gray-black, blue-green, or orange-red. Do not require as much moisture as bacteria or yeast. Have a tolerance for acid; can cause other forms of spoilage in low-acid foods. Killed by boiling temperature. Many mold byproducts in foods are toxic. Some molds are desirable, such as those used to cure certain cheeses (blue-veined).

This time: Safest to discard food (although many of us use discretion and cut off light mold and area of food around it). Always discard heavily molded items.

Next time: Keep foods generally in cool, light, dry places. Although the inside of a refrigerator is dark, its cold is an even more important storage condition. Some molds grow in the refrigerator, but usually in an old, opened food: yogurt, jelly, tomato paste, and cheese are several common victims. To prevent mold growth in canned foods, process low acid foods under pressure and acidic foods in a water bath. Make certain seals are tight.

2. YEASTS

Microscopic plants in the air that require moisture to grow. Some strains are used to leaven breads. The leavening process is caused by the production of carbon dioxide gas, a fermentation, which also causes spoilage of some foods—mostly those containing sugar. This fermentation usually occurs in the presence of oxygen, but sometimes without it. This kind of spoilage is most likely to occur in canned fruits and fruit juices in which air remained during canning.

This time: Boil slightly fermented fruit for 10 to 20 minutes to destroy yeast. A lower temperature (about the 180 degrees F. required for pasteurization) will do the job if maintained about 20 to 60 minutes, depending on texture of food and size.

Next time: When canning fruits and fruit juices, be sure to select appropriate processing method and time.

3. ENZYMES

Elements present in foods that cause ripening; when not checked, the ongoing process causes spoilage. These catalysts are necessary and desirable to mature produce or meat for optimum palatability. But then the food must be served, cooked, or stored to prolong its life.

This time: As soon as a food reaches maturation, the enzyme activity must be curtailed to preserve the food. Cook the food to destroy the enzyme, then consume. Or refrigerate to retard enzyme growth, or freeze to arrest further ripening until thawing.

Next time: Watch fresh foods carefully to catch them at their peak of flavor and texture.

4. BACTERIA

Microorganisms present in air, in soil, and on plants. Some are necessary for nitrogen fixation and fermentation; others cause food spoilage and diseases. Some food spoilage is obvious from the condition of the food: slimy, sour, or putrid characteristics. The more insidious spoilage is not so obvious, but precautions can prevent them. Here's a run-down of the more common types of bacterial spoilage. The first four relate to canning.

a. *Flat-sour:* Determined by acid formation without gas; mostly caused by heat-resistant bacteria. Low-acid vegetables are vulnerable. Food is not poisonous, but considered inedible. Preventative measures are good sanitation, adequate processing, rapid cooling, and maintaining a cool storage temperature.

b. *Swelling in cans:* Gas and acid have formed, causing cans to bulge; in jars, look for a frothiness and a broken seal. Examine canned foods about a month after canning; the condition usually develops within this time. Do not use food; it's inedible. Follow same preventative measures above (see *Flat-sour*).

c. *Putrefactive anaerobic spoilage of low-acid foods:* Caused by soil organisms that grow without oxygen at room temperature. Evidence may be a slimy texture together with gas formation. Sometimes the brine may be cloudy and have an off odor. Do not use food.

d. *Clostridium botulinum:* A potentially fatal putrefactive anaerobe, found in soil and plant foods and most likely to cause problems in low-acid canned foods at room temperature. Spores of this bacterium thrive in well-sealed jars in a low-acid medium, creating the deadly toxin botulism. The toxin is not killed at the boiling temperature. All low-acid foods (meat, fish, poultry, most vegetables) must be adequately steam-pressure-processed to be safe. *Do not taste any suspect food. Throw out!* This poisoning affects the nervous system. If some of the contaminated food has been eaten, see a doctor immediately. Antitoxin is available.

e. *Staphylococcus Aureus:* "Staph" produces a poison that grows rapidly at warm room temperature. This bacteria has ruined many a picnic, when the potato salad quickly became poisonous on a warm summer day. The spoilage tends to occur in moist, low-acid foods: custards, cream fillings, light, creamy salad dressing, (e.g., egg, macaroni or potato salad), poultry, ham and tongue. Prepare these foods just before packing or serving and keep very cold (below 40 degrees F.) or hot (above 140 degrees F.). Avoid advance preparation—even refrigerated—more than one day. Add more acidic ingredients if possible. *Do not sample suspect food. Discard!* Symptoms of poisoning are gastrointestinal problems, sometimes accompanied with fever and chills. A Chicago internist advises trying to analyze which food caused the problem so a doctor can properly diagnose. Then see a doctor or, in severe cases, go to a hospital.

f. *Salmonella:* Grow best in nonacid foods, especially meat, poultry, and cream fillings. (See precautions for *Staphylococcus,* above.) Marinate cooked foods (potatoes, meat, etc.) in tart dressing and chill until ready to prepare salad. Increased acidity reduces chance of this spoilage. Keep prepared food very cold until serving. *Do not sample suspect food. Discard.* Symptoms of this poisoning are gastrointestinal, sometimes accompanied by fever and chills. See a doctor.

g. *Miscellaneous:* There are many food-borne diseases, such as dysentery, trichinosis, typhoid, and diphtheria. Except for trichinosis, no longer common in pork, the others can be prevented by good sanitation and use of approved and inspected products. *See Meat, Pork.*

Fowl—See *Poultry, Game Birds.*

Frankfurter—See *Meat.*

French Fries—See *Deep-fried Foods.*

French Toast—See *Deep-fried Foods; Pancakes.*

Fritters—See *Deep-fried Foods.*

Frog Legs—See *Seafood.*

Frosting—*See Icings, Glazes.*

Fruits—*See* individual names; *Canning.*

Fruitcake—*See Cake.*

Fudge—*See Candy, Confectionery.*

Game—Whether the game is bagged or bought, the material here deals only with what perplexes the cook. Hunters need a detailed book with directions for preparing the catch—drawing, cleaning, cooling, hanging, etc. Fat should be removed from game before freezing or cooking, since it tends to get rancid quickly and often is strong flavored. Some fat may be left on freshly killed young animals since it is not as "gamy" as that of older animals. Because fat is trimmed and most wild animals use their muscles a great deal, the meat can be tough. It often requires marinating and cooking with moisture, or larding. For most problems a cook encounters with large game see *Meat.* For questions related to game birds, *see Poultry, Game Birds.*

GAMY, STRONG-FLAVORED

This time: When you suspect the meat will be gamy from improper handling or because the animal is old, marinate before cooking. Moderately strong-flavored meat will be delicious after a soaking in a salted wine-vinegar marinade. Strong-flavored flesh is more palatable after an overnight bath in equal parts vinegar and beer with salt added. Then drain and cook in salt water 15 to 20 minutes; drain and stew. Waterfowl is often best after a milk bath. When the gaming item is cooked, serve with a spicy or sweet sauce that complements its robustness.

Next time: Often the cook is faced with game of questionable age and handling. Then it's best to marinate. But when the cook has some influence about how the animal is treated after the kill, here are some tips. Trim off all fat before freezing or cooking. Never cook meat in the animal's own fat, unless properly rendered from a young animal. Animal should be hung at refrigerator temperature according to recommended procedure in a game book. Generally small game birds and animals require 2 days, large young animals, 1 week, and large old animals, 2 weeks. Allow enough time for marinating mature animals or those not prepared properly.

Game Birds—*See Poultry, Game Birds.*

Garlic—No flowery fragrance from this member of the lily family! A little of this odoriferous bulb's distinctive flavor can penetrate meats, vegetables, salad dressings. (A dab of its potent oil has long been a favorite additive to mobster bullets!) Long essential to Mediterranean cuisines such as Provençal, garlic was not widely used in the United States until after World War II, when returning GIs introduced its European popularity. As a war baby myself, I happily was not acquainted with pregarlic American cooking. I love a touch of garlic and use it frequently to enhance many things from a Middle Eastern jajick (cucumber-yogurt relish) to ratatouille.

BITTER

This time: Browned garlic tends to be bitter. Lessen the taste by wrapping in small amount of cheesecloth and simmering in a little boiling water with lemon juice, then draining.

Next time: Use low heat; stir and watch garlic during sautéing to avoid browning.

OLD, SPROUTING, OR SHRIVELED

This time: If sprouting, there's still some merit in using. But if terribly shriveled and dry, boiling whole may help it give off some flavor, but not much. Can be crushed or minced and used in a cooked dish, after sautéing first in a little oil.

Next time: Select firm bulbs, heavy for their size, with clean, unbroken skins. Watch out for soft bulbs, or those which are sprouting or shriveled or have decay spots. Store in a cool, dry, well-ventilated place up to 1 month. If possible, use this storage tip from my mother: garlic cloves stay fresh longer if refrigerated in a tightly capped jar (although they tend to soften after several weeks).

TOO STRONG

This time: One alternative is to add more of the other ingredients—perhaps to double the recipe except for the garlic. Another is to add more lemon juice, sugar, or tomato sauce (if it's a tomato mixture) or to cook a bit longer. Freezing also lessens strength, so if you can save it for another time, give it the deep freeze.

Next time: Use raw garlic with discretion. Mashing it exudes more of the volatile oils than chopping or slicing. The mildest way of using it is cooking unpeeled cloves, which yield a sweeter taste that is actually rather subtle and leaves little or no breath odor.

To peel easily: Hold cloves under hot water, or drop in boiling water for ½ minute or so, then dip into cold water and the peel should come off easily.

Gazpacho—*See Soup.*

Gelatin—This granular protein substance softens and swells in cool liquid, dissolves in hot liquid, and firms up upon chilling. When dissolved, it is as clear as the liquid it binds, turning it into a sparkling showcase for suspended fruits, nuts, vegetables, and other added ingredients. Exacting cooks insist upon the European-style leaf gelatin, available at specialty cooking shops and supply houses. Lovely as they can be, gelatins can react to temperature, handling, and ingredients. More than once I've watched a hostess turn out a lovely layered mold only to find it suddenly running over the platter and onto the floor.

FLOATING OR SUNKEN FRUIT

This time: Sometimes a mold with all the fruit at the top or bottom is attractive and guests will think it was designed that way. But if the fruit settled unevenly, there's no need to serve on a platter. Serve in individual dessert dishes topped with whipped cream, sour cream or yogurt instead, or layered in parfait glasses.

Next time: Chill gelatin mixture to consistency of unbeaten egg whites (between 20 and 45 minutes) before adding fruit. Canned fruits and fresh orange slices and grapes sink; sliced bananas, apples, pears, grapefruit sections, and chopped nuts float. Assorted fruits can artistically arrange themselves top and bottom for a lovely mold.

GRANULAR

This time: Granular texture indicates gelatin is not fully dissolved, so continue heating and stirring. If liquid has already cooled or been poured into a mold, reheat to dissolve.

Next time: After regular gelatin is softened in cold liquid, be sure it is thoroughly stirred and dissolved in hot. Mixture should lose all graininess before the addition of other ingredients. To dissolve leaf gelatin, place sheets in cold water to cover about 10 minutes, until very limp; gently squeeze out water and melt in top of double boiler over hot water.

LAYERS DON'T ADHERE

This time: You slice through a two-layered creation and the lemon veers to the right while the lime takes a left. Whipped cream cheese can make a delicious mortar to hold the two in place. Separating the top from bottom without breaking them up is easier if the mold is sliced first. Another solution is to cut slices into cubes and serve in dishes with a sauce or topping.

Next time: The first layer is ready for the second when it is just firming up to consistency slightly thicker than unbeaten egg whites, about 1 hour depending on amount. Once completely jelled, it will not attach to the second layer. Timing and frequent checking are essential. An already jelled mixture can be softened quickly by placing mold in pan of warm water.

RUBBERY

This time: Melt down the rubbery mass and dilute it with appropriate liquid in the recipe (ice cubes can replace the cold liquid). Then quick-chill by placing in bowl of ice water. When thickened, place in freezer for a few minutes, then finish chilling in refrigerator.

Next time: Too much gelatin results in a product as rubbery as an inner tube. The finished gelatin should be quivery, not rigid, when moved. The rule-of-thumb proportion for clear gelatin is 1 tablespoon gelatin to 2 cups liquid for a consistency firm enough to unmold after 2 hours of chilling. Gelatin with fruits, vegetables, nuts, etc. added requires 4 hours of chilling. For a heavily fruited mold, add slightly more gelatin. When doubling a recipe that calls for 2 cups liquid, use only 3¾ cups. Pastry chef and cooking teacher Jolene Worthington offers this rule of thumb for correct amount of leaf gelatin: use 1 leaf to stabilize whipping cream for a 10-inch torte; use 2 leaves for a 10-serving standard Charlotte Russe.

STICKING TO MOLD

This time: Dip mold in hot water. Another aid to easy removal is to loosen edges all around with a pointed knife. Invert a moistened plate over the mold, invert the mold quickly, and shake gently once or twice in an up-down motion until the mold drops down. Lift mold off slowly and position gelatin on plate. Repeat procedure if unsuccessful in first try.

Next time: Before filling mold, rinse inside with hot water or oil lightly.

TOO THICK (FOR ADDING FRUIT, ETC.)

This time: Warm the gelatin mold by placing in pan of hot water or by heating in pan. When it reaches the consistency of unbeaten egg whites, add the ingredients and rechill until firm.

Next time: Begin checking after 20 minutes of chilling, or control chilling by stirring over ice water.

TOO THIN

This time: Quick-chill in a bowl of ice water or place in freezer briefly. Do not freeze or gelatin will get rubbery. Soft gelatin can be served in dishes with a sauce and fruits, or blended with yogurt and cottage cheese.

Next time: Check consistency before unmolding. Next time you make the recipe, add more gelatin for the proportion of liquid, or cut down on liquid. Allow sufficient chilling time. (See *Rubbery, Next time,* above.) Be careful not to boil gelatin or it will lose about half its jelling power.

WILL NOT JELL

This time: Add more dissolved gelatin to mixture; chill sufficiently. Remove any fresh or frozen pineapple since it has an enzyme that prevents gelatin from solidifying. Allow enough time for setting. For meat aspics, trim meat of visible fat because gelatin resists setting up in high-fat mixtures. Add more dissolved gelatin, and allow ample chilling time.

Next time: Use canned or cooked pineapple, but never fresh or frozen. Check proportions, be sure gelatin has fully dissolved, and plan sufficient jelling time. Trim fat from meats intended for aspics.

Gingerbread—*See Cake.*

Glaze—Hot poultry and meat dishes are frequently glazed with concentrated stock and sometimes with fruit syrups, whereas desserts usually derive their smooth, mirrorlike finish from sugar, syrup or various jams. Cooking to the correct temperature is important in obtaining the perfect consistency. See *Icings, Glazes.*

Gnocchi—*See Dumpling.*

Goose—*See Poultry, Game Birds.*

Gouda—*See Cheese.*

Grain—*See Cereal.*

Granola—*See Cereal; Nuts; recipe, p. 342.*

Grapefruit—Some claim it's truly American and that we introduced it in European citrus-growing areas; others say it has descended from the shaddock of India. Whether a hybrid or not, grapefruit was so named because it grows like grapes, in clusters. The tree came to Florida from the West Indies in the 16th century, but it wasn't until the early 1900s that the fruit caught on. Now available year round, grapefruit is most plentiful in winter and spring, with supplies from California, Texas, Arizona, and Florida.

BITTER

This time: Add honey, sugar, or sugar substitute or soak segments in sweet fruit juice, liqueur, or sweet wine. Broil halves topped with brown sugar or honey. Grapefruit is compatible with numerous ingredients, so try marinating it in an herb oil-and-vinegar dressing for an avocado-greens salad, or use juice and segments in poultry and meat dishes, which can be enhanced by the bitter taste. Salting slightly supposedly brings out its sweetness.

Next time: Select Duncan or Burgundy varieties, which tend to be sweeter and of excellent flavor. The seedless Marsh and Thompson pinks tend to be tart. Green-tinged fruit does not indicate underripeness—it's an occasional chlorophyll-regreening phenomenon to already ripened fruit. Avoid fruit with pointed ends or puffed appearance.

DRY

This time: Pithy, dry fruit can pick up flavor and replump if marinated in a favorite liqueur, liquor, wine, or sweet fruit juice so flavored. Or cook in sweetened juice or water that has been spiced, then chill and serve as compote. The grapefruit flavor is especially enhanced by the richness of prunes and figs. When still uncut, rolling around on flat, hard surface helps to make the juices flow.

Next time: Choose fruit that is firm, heavy for its size (to indicate juiciness), and springy to the touch. Stay away from puffy, very coarse-skinned fruit, which tends to be drier.

GREEN

Same chlorophyll-regreening phenomenon (see *Bitter*). Also true with oranges. Doesn't affect flavor.

HARD-TO-PEEL

This time: If already cut, dip grapefruit in hot water for a minute; white membrane should then require little coaxing.

Next time: Drop whole grapefruit in boiling water; remove from heat and let stand in water several minutes. The peel will slip right off.

SQUIRTY

This time: To avoid the classic cartoon setup of a grapefruit half squirting you or your neighbor in the eye, use a grapefruit knife to loosen pulp from membranes holding it. It also helps to use a serrated-edge grapefruit spoon. Turn your face away and hope for the best.

Next time: Try eating the grapefruit another way, by cutting it into "smiles," sections still on the rind—or peel and cut into segments or pieces. Enjoy with the eyes open.

OVERRIPE

This time: The juice from a slightly overripe grapefruit is still good. If you want to use the flesh, marinate segments or pieces in liqueur, liquor, or wine, or spiked fruit juice. By cooking slightly with some liquid (stock, bouillon, juice, wine, seasoned water) and thickening, the texture of the soft segments may be preserved and used for a poultry or meat dish. A sweetened version can be used over puddings, gelatins, and cheesecake.

Next time: Choose firm, well-shaped fruit that springs to the touch, free of soft spots or decayed areas. Avoid wilted, shriveled fruit. Fresh grapefruit can be kept at room temperature a few days. For longer storage, refrigerate in plastic bags in fruit bin up to a couple of months.

Grape Leaves—A prized essential to Middle Eastern cooking where tender, young leaves are wrapped around spicy fillings of meat and rice. How sad to think of all the vine leaves in this country that go to waste. Jars of grape leaves preserved in brine can be found in Greek shops, but there's nothing like young, fresh leaves.

TOUGH

This time: Add a bit of lemon juice to the water, then cook about 15 minutes, or until fork pierces easily. If still chewy, remove tougher stem part.

Next time: Pick only young, tender leaves. Simmer slowly in boiling water about 8 to 10 minutes, until tender. Note: for dried and brine-preserved, rinse thoroughly in colander with cold water, then drain before using.

Grapes—Grapes and grapevines are mentioned in both the Old and New Testaments, recorded by ancient Egyptians thousands of years ago, and painted by artists throughout the ages. One of the most decorative fruits, both in the vineyard and on the table. The following information should help remove any sour grapes from your cooking.

OVERRIPE

This time: When grapes get soft and almost mushy, press them for juice or add them to saucy dishes such as chicken in grape sauce or fruit compote. Add seeded, halved grapes to stuffing for fowl. Cooked, sieved pulp can be used for pie fillings and puddings.

Next time: Gently shake a bunch of grapes to make sure they're well fixed to the stem, indicating freshness. Fruit should be plump and have good color. Look for white or green varieties turning to amber for optimum flavor; dark-colored types should be without green areas. A few under- or overripe grapes do not spoil the bunch, but avoid bunches with many shriveled, sticky grapes or brittle stems. Store unwashed in loosely covered container or open plastic bag in refrigerator up to 3 days.

SOUR

This time: If time allows, ripen at room temperature several days. If not, pierce with cake tester or halve and seed before marinating in liqueur or other sweet sauce; fruit juice with a touch of brandy or another liquor does wonders. Or use grapes for a cooked dish with many spices, herbs, and preferably some sweet ingredients such as tomato paste, fruit juice, liqueur, or honey.

Next time: Taste before buying. Avoid underripe grapes, which may not be fully developed in flavor.

TOUGH-SKINNED

This time: If the pulp is delicious, I believe it's worth the trouble of chewy skins that may have to be spit out. But when you don't want to bother, cook the grapes to boiling, then rub through a sieve or food mill to remove skins and any seeds. Add cornstarch, honey, and perhaps grated lemon or orange rind and seasonings for pie or tart filling. Thickened grape sauce is a nice topping for some cakes. Reduced to a glaze, before adding cornstarch, it can crown a cheesecake.

Next time: Select thin-skinned varieties, such as Emperor, Olivette Blanche, Thompson seedless, or Eastern Delaware. Avoid Almeria, Cardinal, Red Malaga, Ribier, Tokay, and the Eastern slip-skins: Catawba, Concord, and Niagara.

UNDERRIPE

This time: Very hard grapes may ripen to fuller flavor if left at room temperature for a few days. When you can't wait, use for compotes, puddings, pies, or sole véronique. Another idea is to pierce each grape with a cake tester, poach lightly, then use in a hot chicken salad with mayonnaise and toasted almonds. The cold counterpart with fully ripe grapes is also wonderful.

Next time: See *Overripe.*

Gravy—*See Sauces.*

Grease—*See Fat; Fires, Burns.*

Green Beans—*See Beans.*

Green Onions—*See Onion.*

Green Pepper—*See Pepper.*

Greens—These are the greens usually served cooked as a vegetable, and a popular part of soul food—beet tops, collards, dandelion greens, kale, mustard greens, Swiss chard, and turnip tops. (Salad greens are listed under *Lettuce* or their respective names.) These flavorful dark green leaves can be boiled and enhanced by lemon juice, salt, and pepper, or cooked in bacon or ham fat and served with onions. They're extremely nourishing—high in vitamin A, a good source of other vitamins and minerals, and low in calories.

BITTER

This time: Sweeten slightly with a sweet-sour dressing, or camouflage with a ham and onion mixture. The bitterness often develops during cooking.

Next time: Serve young kale raw in salads if you don't like the bitter taste that develops in cooking. It's delicious to some. Most of the leaves of older greens can be cooked, the young ones often eaten fresh. Lighter-colored, cultivated dandelion greens are less bitter.

OVERCOOKED

This time: Purée and cream mushy greens as a vegetable accompaniment. Or add more liquid while puréeing to make a cream of greens soup. (See cream of vegetable soup, p. 315.)

Next time: Greens cook in the water that clings to them (with perhaps a little water or butter added), in 4 to 5 minutes, depending on tenderness.

WILTED

This time: Refreshen by giving an ice-water bath, then dry and store in toweling in refrigerator about 1 hour. If too wilted to serve raw, or if no time to refreshen, steam or braise and the shriveled leaves won't matter. Cooked greens can be added to soups, stews, and casseroles for added good flavor. Creamed greens is a nice side dish.

Next time: Look for fresh, green leaves that seem tender and clean, free of decay or shriveled areas. Usually leaves are juicier if roots are still attached (on dandelions and turnips, for instance). Remove roots if attached, discard damaged leaves; wash, dry, store in plastic bag in refrigerator up to 4 or 5 days.

Grill Fires—*See Fires, Burns.*

Grits—*See Cereal.*

Groats (buckwheat)—*See Cereal.*

Grouse—*See Poultry, Game Birds.*

Guacamole—*See Avocado.*

Guava—In Hawaii and South America it's available in many forms: fresh, canned, juice, jelly, paste. Here, one finds it mostly canned or preserved (for a treat, try the paste spread on toast), although it may be available fresh at some markets.

BLAND

This time: Fresh guava can be enhanced with a squeeze of lemon or lime juice, and when you want a sweetening boost, remember honey. As an alternative, cook for fruit compote or for a spicy dessert sauce or bake with sweet potatoes, seasoned with spices, orange juice, butter, and pecans.

Next time: Settle for nothing but the very ripest fruit, soft but spotless. If very firm, allow to ripen at room temperature.

OVERRIPE

This time: When mushy in texture, guavas are still good cooked into a sweetened dessert sauce (great over cheesecake or puddings), or cook down further into a very thick paste, delicious with cream cheese.

Next time: Avoid mushy fruit with spots. Store in refrigerator only 2 or 3 days after ripened.

UNDERRIPE

This time: Underripe fruit makes the best jelly and jam. Firm fruit can also be cooked with currants, mangoes, and spices for a chutney. Allow fruit to ripen at room temperature if planning to eat it raw.

Next time: Select soft fruit for eating raw, firmer specimens for jelly making.

Guinea Fowl—*See Poultry, Game Birds.*

Haddock—*See Fish.*

Ham—*See Meat.*

Hamburger—Go to Greece, Spain, the Caribbean, or Japan and everyone knows the American hamburger. Unfortunately many people, even our own citizens, are familiar only with the fast-food-operation version. There are so many bad burgers around that it takes quite a search to find a respectable one. But when a deliciously seasoned, browned, crusty exterior gives way to a pink, juicy center, one wonders why so many tolerate the ground-out masses of tasteless flattened rounds of dry meat in soggy buns. Hamburger also refers to ground meat, which I prefer to call just that (for more information, see *Meat*). Here the remedies apply to the All-American patty.

CRUMBLY, STUCK TO PAN

This time: Toss with sautéed raisins and almonds and cooked rice, then season with curry spices and rose water for a great pilaf. Crumbled hamburger can be incorporated into a casserole or served over noodles topped with sauce.

Next time: Form patties firmly but gently with as little handling as possible. Select a meat with more fat content, such as 75 percent lean ground beef or ground chuck. Egg can be added to the mixture to bind it. Avoid flipping burger many times during cooking. Sprinkling pan lightly with salt helps prevent sticking. When using lean meat, lightly grease pan.

DRY, OVERCOOKED, TOUGH

This time: Slightly dry burgers are made palatable served with a sauce (try barbecue, cheese, or mushroom). Steam in a little water first, then add sauce. Very tough specimens should be crumbled and incorporated into a casserole or added to sauce and spooned over rice or noodles.

Next time: Hamburgers should be handled as little as possible. Much working and shaping makes them less juicy and tender. Broil 1-inch-thick burgers 3 to 4 inches from heat about 4 to 5 minutes first side, 3 to 4 minutes flip side for medium rare. Pan-fry the same thickness about 5 to 6 minutes per side for medium rare. Select a ground beef with about 75 percent lean. Lean meat creates a dry end result.

WON'T BROWN

This time: Smear lightly with browning sauce or sweet sauce and zap with high heat.

Next time: Make certain patties are dry. Thawed burgers, especially, may have much moisture. Flour lightly before cooking to help browning.

Hare—*See Game.*

Hazelnuts—*See Nuts.*

Heart—*See Meat.*

Herbs—Sprinkled on graves by ancient Egyptians, and experimented with by medieval physicians who were keeping current in their profession, herbs have long inspired mysticism and curiosity. Throughout the ages, herbs have been used for medicinal and cosmetic purposes as well as for flavoring foods. Columbus was only one of numerous explorers given the mission to seek out additional sources, since supplies were scarce and expensive in areas where they did not proliferate. Indonesia, the Caribbean islands, and India were veritable spice and herb farms, and the cuisines of these places still reflect the seasonings grown there. Today gardeners grow a variety of herbs indoors and outdoors. Dill and chives are as common to the average American cook as the beef and potatoes they put them on.

SLIMY

This time: If the texture comes from freezing, use in cooked dishes. When the sliminess comes from fresh herbs gone bad, however, there's no salvation. If only a few leaves have turned, they may be discarded and the rest frozen or dried for future use.

Next time: Some herbs, such as chives, become slimy after freezing. Do not thaw; use frozen in about the same amount as fresh. Use only for cooked dishes, since texture will not be up to standard for fresh salads, etc.

TOO STRONG

This time: No problem unless you've already added too much. In that case, scoop out whatever you can, and add more of the other ingredients or a little lemon juice, tomato product (sauce, juice), or starch (rice, potato, or breadcrumbs), depending on the dish. Without overcooking, simmer or bake a bit longer to allow flavor to evaporate.

Next time: The sniff test will reveal herb potency. Judiciously add a little of an herb, then taste before adding more.

TASTELESS, IMPOTENT

This time: Herbs that have lost their potency may regain some of it by soaking a few minutes in hot water, then in cold. When the recipe is appropriate, steep in wine, broth, milk, or a little butter. Pulverize dried herbs first. This soaking revitalizes dried herbs. Use more of the herb when it has lost potency.

Next time: Use the freshest, best-quality herbs possible. Store them properly and add them at the right time in cooking. Seeds and large leaves (bay) should be added at the beginning of cooking, whereas crushed or ground leaves are best added toward end of cooking. For uncooked foods (marinades, dressings) add herbs with other ingredients and allow flavors to blend at least an hour or two. Taste foods at the temperature you intend to serve them; cold dishes require more seasoning.

Dried: Keep in tightly covered ceramic or dark glass containers in cool place. Or when in clear glass, store in a closed cabinet. Do not store near heat, no matter how handy it is to have herbs near the range. Purchase herbs from a store with big turnover and proper handling, so you can be sure of a fresh supply. Pulverize just before use for maximum flavor retention. Dried leaves last longer than ground herbs. Add toward end of cooking for optimum aroma and flavor. The larger herbs, like bay leaves, can be added at the beginning of long-cooking dishes.

Fresh: I once went marketing with Jovan Trboyevic, a French restaurant owner, who explained, "If you can't smell the parsley from an arm's length, it's not fresh." Although this rule may not apply to all herbs, since they vary in strength, it is true that fresh herbs should be aromatic. Select fresh-looking leaves, avoiding those with decay spots or that appear wilted. Store those still on stems in a jar of water, like flowers; cover with plastic wrap and refrigerate. Or wash, dry in toweling and place in plastic bag in refrigerator. Mince and crush, and add toward end of cooking for best flavor.

Frozen: Use frozen in sauces, dressings, stuffings and cooked dishes. Avoid using for garnish or in raw salads, since texture will not be as good. To quick-freeze, dip herbs on the stem in cold water, bring to boil, blanch for about 10 seconds; then plunge into ice water for about 45 seconds and dry with paper toweling; finally, place in freezer containers or wrap tightly with freezer paper.

Substitute: The recipe calls for dried thyme and you have only fresh, or vice versa. Generally, a rounded ¼ teaspoon ground or ½ to 1 teaspoon crushed dried herb is about the equivalent of 1 tablespoon chopped fresh. The variables are age and potency, so taste is always the final test.

Herring—See *Fish.*

Hickory Nuts—See *Nuts.*

Hollandaise—See *Sauces.*

Hominy—See *Cereal.*

Honey—The only principal sweetener until the 18th century. Most of the honey used in this country is "extracted" (clear liquid separated from the comb), and is without floral designation on the label because it is a blend of different types. More than half the U.S. honey comes from bees having worked clover and alfalfa.

CRYSTALLIZED

This time: Place the jar in a pan of very warm (not boiling) water until crystals melt away, or place in 150 to 200 degree oven for same effect. Crystalline honey can be used as a spread or whipped to a fluffy consistency. Try blending it with soft butter for a delightful honey butter that's irresistible on biscuits and pancakes.

Next time: Store in tightly covered container at room temperature in a dry place. Kept this way, it should remain pourable for several months. Crystallization occurs when honey is kept a long time and is hastened by refrigeration. But the product is still good.

STRONG-FLAVORED

This time: Aging honey often grows darker, thicker, and stronger in flavor. To lighten the taste, mix with lighter honey or make a delicious spread by blending with butter and a little orange juice and rind. Or dilute with cider or fruit juice to make a syrup or a glaze for ham or poultry. Use judiciously in baking. Strong-flavored honey will best complement dried fruits and nuts in spicy breads or cakes.

Next time: Select lighter-colored honey, which tends to be milder than dark. (See storage tips above, *Crystallized.*)

STUCK TO UTENSILS

This time: Narrow and wide rubber scrapers are an essential kitchen tool—especially at times like this when the stubborn honey clings to the jar corners or refuses to remove itself from the measuring cup. Warming the utensil in a pan of warm water will help loosen the sweetener's grip.

Next time: Before measuring honey, lightly oil the spoon or cup. Gently warm honey, place container in pan of warm water, and watch the thick mass become less viscous and easier to pour.

To substitute: Honey has greater sweetening potency and moisture retention than sugar, so alter recipes as follows: substitute 1 cup honey for 1¼ cups sugar and reduce liquid in recipe by ¼ cup. Honey's absorption qualities (so desirable in moist breads and cakes) can cause problems in some crisp cookies or confections. In these items, it may be necessary to experiment with the amount of flour.

Hors D'Oeuvre—See specific ingredients.

Horseradish—Its pungency can knock you dead or at least clear the sinuses. So be forewarned before grating the fresh root or sniffing a new jar. Some Polish old-timers clamp a wet towel around the nose and mouth while grating. Native to southeast Europe, the hot herb has been used since pre-Christian times. One of five bitter herbs used in the Seder service of Jewish Passover, the roots are sold fresh, preserved with vinegar and/or beet juice (for the red type), or dried, in order of decreasing pungency.

BITTER

This time: When volatile acids leave (as in old horseradish), bitterness is sometimes the resulting taste. Still lends a nice touch added to cream or mayonnaise, enhanced with a touch of honey or corn syrup and perhaps lemon juice. Also good in tomato sauce.

Next time: Use soon after purchase; store in refrigerator (except dried).

TOO MILD, AIRED OUT

This time: Combine old, mild-flavored horseradish with some fresh hot, or use straight on roast or corned beef, perhaps mixed with a bit of lemon juice and mayonnaise.

Next time: Use freshly grated when you want the most overpowering flavor. All types of horseradish except dried should be tightly covered, refrigerated, and used fairly soon to prevent loss of volatile oils and a resulting bitter taste.

TOO STRONG

This time: If your mouth simply can't handle the blast, blend the hot grated root with whipped cream (great for roast beef or boiled tongue), mayonnaise (nice on corned beef sandwiches), white sauce, sour cream, or yogurt. A touch adds just the right zing to a rather neutral seafood cocktail sauce.

Next time: Buy creamed horseradish instead of grated. Milk products act as a buffer to neutralize the pungency.

To reconstitute dried: Add ¼ cup water to 2 tablespoons dried about 20 minutes before using to allow full flavor to develop. Use soon thereafter, however, to prevent flavor loss. Refrigerate leftovers tightly covered.

Hot Chocolate—Unsweetened but spiced, it was the Aztecs' royal drink. Montezuma drank his from a golden cup, and to this day Mexicans love their chocolate. But now they tend to sweeten and flavor it with cinnamon or orange rind. Brazilians mix in another of their main crops, coffee. The French blend milk or cream into the chocolate pot and the Viennese top cupfuls with copious puffs of whipped cream. Americans drop a marshmallow or two into a steaming cup of chocolate, then drink the liquid through the melted sweet topping. Cinnamon or peppermint-stick candy stirrers contribute a spicy flavor as they melt. Here are several tips, whatever your chocolate preference.

BURNED ON BOTTOM OF POT

This time: Carefully scoop out liquid without scraping bottom; the burned chocolate has a bitter flavor. If bottom is only lightly scorched, you might try adding a little butter, heating, and sweetening with a syrup or liqueur for an ice-cream topping.

Next time: The safest way to heat hot chocolate is in the top part of a double boiler over hot water. When using pan over burner, use a low heat and stir frequently.

LUMPY

This time: Using a wire whisk, whip vigorously until smooth, or whip in blender. Stubborn lumps can be removed by passing the mixture through a fine sieve; then mash the chocolate bits with a little hot water and cook to blend before stirring in the warm milk. The chocolate fragments also can be used in baking.

Next time: Begin by cooking chocolate with a little water first before stirring in the milk.

SKIN FORMATION

This time: The skin can be eliminated and the drink fluffed with the work of a whisk.

Next time: Cover the pot while heating mixture to prevent skin from forming. Gentle heating in top of double boiler is another preventive.

Hot Cross Buns—*See Bread.*

Hot Dog—*See Meat.*

Hydrogenated Fat—*See Fat.*

Ice Cream—George Washington was an ice-cream fanatic. Mrs. Alexander Hamilton is credited with having first hooked him on ice cream at a dinner party in 1789. And our third president, the gourmet Thomas Jefferson, had a file of favored ice-cream recipes, many of them acquired in France. He especially savored the icy dessert served in warm pastry and treated guests at state dinners to such delicacies as baked Alaska. Dolly Madison impressed dinner guests with a high mound of pink ice cream on a silver platter. She also served strawberry ice cream in 1812 at the Inaugural Ball.

Despite all this political favor, not until 1851 did the first manufacture of wholesale ice cream begin, in Pennsylvania, and the business was an instant success. The ice-cream soda was born in Philadelphia in 1874 and, thanks to a strange blue law forbidding soda to be sold on Sundays, the sundae developed between 1896 and 1900. The soda fountain emerged in 1903, and the next year the cone was introduced at the St. Louis World's Fair—quite by accident, when an ice-cream vendor ran out of dishes and a waffle vendor came to the rescue by rolling his thin Syrian product into cone-shaped containers. There was no stopping this ice age explosion. Eskimo pies and dry ice dispensers made the sweet treat more available to impulse buyers. Ice cream hit the road even more after the Good Humor bar was developed in 1922. Another surge occurred in 1930 with the development of home refrigeration and homemade ice-cream recipes. But the commercial product still wins out in consumption.

Today federal and state regulations define ice cream and frozen desserts. The minimum milkfat is 10 percent, but some manufacturers add more for a richer product. America's most popular dessert comes in more flavors than any other food—over 400! Vanilla is the nation's favorite; chocolate is second, with strawberry and nut varieties close runners-up.

CRYSTALLIZED, DRIED, GUMMY

This time: The surface is usually the most affected. Long storage and heavy crystallization causes excessive drying and unpalatability, so discard any portion so ruined. The remainder may show signs of texture and flavor loss; doctor it up by blending in fruits, nuts, and other flavorings and topping with liqueur or some favorite sauce.

Next time: Purchase only what can be used within 2 months stored at zero degrees, or within a few days in the frozen-food compartment of the refrigerator. For more than a few days' storage, overwrap carton with aluminum foil or freezer wrap. Once opened, cover surface of ice cream with plastic wrap or other protective covering, then reclose carton tightly.

GRANULAR (ESPECIALLY HOMEMADE)

This time: When the ice cream lacks smoothness, soften it slightly. Add whipped cream if desired and appropriate ingredients that overpower any graininess—toasted chopped nuts, chocolate chips, raisins and crushed macaroons soaked in rum, toasted coconut, or crumbled candies such as peanut brittle or peppermint stick. Refreeze and serve as soon as possible for best quality.

Next time: A grainy product comes from packing the mixture with too much salt, cranking too quickly, or adding too much cream mixture to the container. Follow a dependable recipe and manufacturer's directions for your ice-cream freezer, but generally use 4 parts cracked ice to 1 part coarse ice-cream salt. To allow for expansion of the ice cream, fill the container only about ⅔ full. Begin by turning slowly (a turn every 1½ seconds) until a resistance is felt, then turn quickly for about 5 minutes.

MELTED

This time: Melted ice cream makes a wonderful sauce over a warm pudding or cobbler. When more ice cream melts than you can use, there are several alternatives. If it's vanilla (or a compatible flavor), make Jeanette's mandarin-ice-cream mold (p. 340). Following the recipe as a guide, substitute other flavored gelatins, fruits, and ice creams. When your dinner party ice cream melts, stir it into hot coffee, add a favorite liqueur, and give it an impressive name. Who'll ever know? Another suggestion, if time permits, is to partially refreeze the melted ice cream, then add chopped dried fruits, nuts, or other flavorings and refreeze. Texture may be a little more coarse because of refreezing, but the ice cream is safe as long as kept clean and cool. Refrozen ice cream also may be saved for malteds and shakes.

Next time: Buy ice cream last when shopping, make sure it's wrapped in an insulated bag, and put it away first when unpacking groceries at home. Keep in coldest part of freezer. Remove only what you need and return rest to freezer immediately.

RUNNY, TOO SOFT (HOMEMADE)

This time: Assuming manufacturer's directions are correct and have been followed, an excess of either sugar or alcohol could be the problem. In the case of sugar, Carolyn Buster, chef–owner of The Cottage Restaurant, in Calumet City, Ill:, adds a bit of lemon juice or dehydrated lemonade crystals to the ice cream and rechurns it. If there's an excess of alcohol, she serves runny ice cream as a sauce.

Next time: Before beginning, check manufacturer's directions for ice-cream maker; double check amounts of alcohol and sugar in recipe to ensure proper consistency.

STICKING TO DIPPER

To prevent ice cream from sticking, immerse dipper or spoon in cold water—just like a soda fountain jerk. Shake off excess water; otherwise you'll be adding crystals to the ice cream.

To unmold: Unlike gelatins, bombes should not be immersed in warm or hot water. Dip mold briefly into cool water; loosen edges with a spatula; invert onto cold platter and freeze to harden. Another method is to loosen mold around edges, and invert onto a platter. Cover mold with wet hot cloths until mold can be loosened. Return to freezer to firm up before serving.

Icings, Glazes (fruit and chocolate)—Icings and their general problem areas are here divided into two main categories; cooked and uncooked. No attempt is made to categorize further, since an entire book can be devoted to the various types. These finishing touches, like candies and confections, are all considered sugar cookery. For more information as it applies to some cooked icings see *Candy, Confectionery.*

Yields for all icings: Allow 1½ to 2½ cups for 2 (9-inch) layers, top and sides. Allow 1 to 1½ cups to frost a 9 × 5 × 3-inch loaf, and 3 cups to cover a 10-inch tube cake.

Cooked: Boiled white icing, seven-minute frosting, fondant icing, and fudge and caramel frostings.

CRYSTALS FORMED: See *Candy, Confectionery.*

FONDANT LOSES SHEEN: See *Candy, Confectionery, Fondant.*

GRITTY, SUGARY

This time: A few drops of lemon juice or vinegar, a dash of cream of tartar, or a teaspoon of light corn syrup can remedy the situation. Add flavoring after one of these stabilizers. See *Candy, Confectionery, problems of basic sugar cooking in candy making.*

Next time: Allow egg whites to be cooked by the hot syrup to produce a creamy texture. Never put an icing that needs warming before using (such as fondant) over direct heat; the sugar at bottom will crystallize. Use a double boiler or bowl over warm water to obtain gentle, steady heat. Never scrape in hardened parts that adhere to side and bottom of pan. Beating many icings increases volume and overall texture.

HARDENED

This time: When the syrup hardens too quickly, add a few drops boiling water or lemon juice. The same can also help soften a firm icing after mixing. Once on the cake and hardened, store, tightly covered, with a piece or two of bread, cut moist fruit, or a small glass of water. Icing should regain moisture in several hours.

Next time: Overcooking icing causes excessive hardening. Use a candy thermometer to help determine just when the right temperature is reached. When frosting a dry cake, a professional trick is to spread top with a thin layer of hot apricot jam, which serves as an insulator, preventing the dry layer from sponging up the icing's moisture, and binds loose crumbs to enable smooth application. Nonfat icings harden very quickly in dry hot weather. That's why you find glycerine bottles in a pastry chef's kitchen. A few drops, or egg whites, stirred into the icing during mixing help retain a smooth, pliable consistency. See *Weather.*

RUNNY

This time: Place icing in top of double boiler or in heatproof bowl over hot water while beating until proper spreading consistency is reached. If you're lucky enough to have a sunny kitchen, strong sun rays might eliminate the need for hot water. When icing runs off cake, stop; chill cake and further heat and beat icing.

Next time: Boil syrup longer. Check accuracy of thermometer. When adding nuts, raisins, citrus rinds, coconut, or other ingredients with oil or acid, wait until last moment to incorporate them. The oils and acids thin icing. Be sure cake is thoroughly cooled before icing is applied.

Adjustment for high altitudes: Add ⅛ tsp. glycerine to sugar and allow longer cooking period.

Uncooked: Cream cheese, buttercream, quick chocolate, confectioners sugar, or plain water glaze.

GRAYING

It's natural for many icings to develop a grayish cast during preparation. A tiny amount of blue vegetable coloring whitens the icing, much the way bluing whitens the wash. When there's no blue dye, enhance the grayness by decorating with silver dragees or completely cover with coconut, chocolate shavings, chocolate shot, or ground nuts.

HARDENED

This time: When the icing is hardening quickly in the bowl, stir in a little more water, lemon juice, cream, or flavoring, depending on recipe. Once the cake is iced, place under a cake saver with cut fruit, a slice of bread, or a small glass of water. Several hours or overnight should soften the icing.

Next time: Add a little liquid next time. Store iced cake tightly covered to preserve moisture.

THICK

This time: Gradually stir in a little cream, milk, or water, according to recipe.

Next time: Add dry ingredients (usually sugar) gradually; entire amount may not be necessary. Amounts vary with weather. See *Weather.*

THIN

This time: Stir in more sifted confectioners sugar until right consistency is reached. If icing is running off cake, chill. Spoon up drippings, add more sugar, and give cake a second coating. Decorate to cover any flaws.

Next time: Add liquid very slowly; entire amount may not be necessary in humid weather. A very buttery icing should be spread on thoroughly cooled cake; most other quick icings spread better on warm cakes.

Jam—See Canning.

Jelly—See Canning.

Jerusalem Artichoke—These homely, knobby underground tubers taste better than they look. They are no relation to the lovely thistle commonly called globe or French artichoke, and they are not native to Jerusalem!

DISCOLORED

This time: After cutting, raw Jerusalem artichokes discolor rapidly. Drop slightly discolored pieces into cold water to prevent further darkening. If badly darkened already, cook in water with some lemon juice or vinegar added, then use in a cooked dish.

Next time: Immediately drop cut pieces into cold water after cutting. To prevent discoloration when cooking, cover with acidulated water in noniron utensil, about 5 to 7 minutes, until just tender. Avoid alkaline water or substances in cooking liquid.

OVERCOOKED

This time: Purée mushy Jerusalem artichokes and use in cream of vegetable soup (p. 315) or chop and use in casserole.

Next time: Allow only 5 to 7 minutes for pieces cooked in boiling water. Test to see when tender, and do not allow to sit in hot water.

OVERRIPE

This time: Shriveled, soft-textured tubers are over the hill. Avoid using raw. Cook following directions under *Discolored,* then purée and use in cream of vegetable soup (p. 315) or chop and serve with cream sauce.

Next time: Select firm heavy tubers without any soft, decay spots or shriveled skin. Store in cool, airy, dry place or chill in plastic wrap up to 1 week. Some have lasted for months in my refrigerator crisper.

Juice—*See Canning; Punch;* or name of specific fruit.

Kabobs—*See Meat.*

Kale—*See Greens.*

Kidneys—*See Meat.*

Kiwi Fruit (Chinese Gooseberry)—Originally from China's Yangtze valley, the fuzzy brown tropical fruit today comes from New Zealand and California. The rather ugly exterior hides a most decorative fruit within. Its subtle flavor and bright green translucent pulp with its intricate seed pattern have made it the darling of French chefs.

OVERRIPE

This time: Chop very soft fruit and fold into sweetened whipped cream or gelatin with whipped cream. Mushy fruit can be cooked with fruit juice and a little sweet wine for a dessert sauce; purée and sieve for a more refined sauce or glaze.

Next time: Select a firm, ripe fruit that is slightly soft; store in refrigerator up to 4 days.

UNDERRIPE

This time: Ripen at room temperature, or simmer firm fruit in sweet fruit juice (with a touch of kirsch or other favorite liqueur) and mix with other fruits for compote. Cook with spices and raisins for chutney.

Next time: Choose soft-ripe fruit.

Kohlrabi—Kohlrabies are deliciously crisp when young, but can be fibrous when old. Eat before full grown, when about 2 to 4 inches in diameter.

DISCOLORED

This time: Mash with a little cream or milk, season and top with shredded cheese or minced parsley. Or purée and use in cream of vegetable soup (p. 315).

Next time: Pigmentation turns gray-brown when cooked too long, or green-brown when cooked in iron. Add a little acid to cooking water to cover. Avoid overcooking.

OVERCOOKED

This time: If mushy from overcooking, mash with a little milk, butter, and seasonings; top with minced green onion and sunflower seeds. A nice substitute for turnips or potatoes, or good combined with either as well. Or purée and turn into cream of vegetable soup (p. 315).

Next time: After trimming tops and paring more mature bulbs, cook uncovered in boiling water to cover 20 to 25 minutes, until just tender. Julienne strips and slices take less time. They are good steamed and buttered. Cook tops (leaves) separately, then chop and serve with knobs.

OVERRIPE

This time: See Overcooked.
Next time: Select small bulbs with thin skin and fresh leaves. Avoid large knobs with wilted tops and cracks or bruises. Store in cool, dry, airy place or chill in plastic bag up to 2 weeks—sometimes longer if very fresh.

OVERMATURE

This time: The overmature kohlrabi is woody. Remove the tough rind, cook uncovered in boiling water to cover until tender, about 25 to 30 minutes; allow less time for sliced or chopped. Serve with cream sauce or purée for cream of vegetable soup (p. 315).
Next time: See Overripe.

Kumquat—Tiniest and least juicy of all citrus fruits. Must be very ripe to be tasty raw. Kumquats were eaten by the ancient Chinese; preserved, they are still very popular in that cuisine. Delicious cooked into a compote with other fruits, as a relish, candied, or preserved in marmalades or conserves. Beautiful as a garnish for meats and fowl.

OVERRIPE

This time: Stew slightly soft fruit in water until tender, then cook in syrup (about 1 cup water to 2 cups sugar) and chill. To make sauce purée kumquats, adding fruit juice or water plus a little liqueur to taste; season with spices, cook until tender, chill and serve over ice cream or cake. Or cook in sweetened water with ginger, nutmeg and cloves; makes a great accompaniment for roast poultry.
Next time: Select firm fruit, heavy for its size. Store in plastic bag in refrigerator up to a month.

UNDERRIPE

This time: Follow a favorite conserve recipe (kumquats are good paired with cherries). Or make preserves: boil in water until tender after piercing fruit with cake tester. Drain, then cook in syrup until transparent. Let sit in syrup one day. Cut fruit, seed, return to syrup and pack in hot sterilized jars. Seal well, and process 10 minutes at simmer.

Next time: Select well-colored resilient fruit.

Lamb—*See Meat.*

Langouste—*See Shellfish.*

Lard—*See Fat.*

Lasagne—*See Casserole; Meat; Pasta.*

Leavening—See individual names.

Leek—*See Onions, Green.*

Leftovers—See individual foods.

Legumes—*See Beans, Dried; Peanut.*

Lemon—Thought to have come from China or India, this sour citrus fruit high in citric acid made its mark in the Arab world by A.D. 1000. Soon after, the lemon was introduced to the Mediterranean, where it is used prolifically. This powerful yellow fruit has a long history of medicinal uses, and does a lot of doctoring in our kitchens today. A squeeze of its potent juice puts an inimitable zing into salads, soups, fish, asparagus, a variety of fruits and vegetables, and tea. A grating of rind, which contains very concentrated citric oil, enlivens cakes, puddings, sauces, and dressings.

BITTER

This time: Once you've cut a bitter lemon, use it in dishes where salt, sugar, and/or seasonings may be added to alter its taste. Exceptionally sweet juices or dessert mixtures can be enhanced by a touch of bitter lemon juice. Pucker up.

Next time: Select yellow-skinned fruit, avoiding any that are greenish. This does not apply to green lemons other countries grow, however.

DRY

This time: Roll lemon with hand on flat, hard surface to make the fruit yield slightly more juice. When you know the lemon is dry by its shriveled appearance, simmer the entire fruit in water for several minutes.

Next time: Select firm, fine-textured lemons, heavy for their size. Store at room temperature 1 or 2 days, or store in plastic bag in fruit bin of refrigerator up to a month.

SQUIRTY

This time: To gracefully squeeze a lemon wedge or half over your plate without squirting yourself or a companion, cover the lemon with your hand, rind against fingers, and with the other hand holding a fork, insert tines and squeeze. A nice touch at formal dinners is to wrap small pieces of muslin cloth around lemon halves and tie at the top. Prevents seeds from falling into food.

Next time: Use the same tips, or slice lemon instead of cutting into wedges or halves. Slices don't squirt as much—they can be pressed with knife and fork over the food.

OVERRIPE; SHRIVELED

This time: Slightly overripe lemons give good juice. When shriveled roll on flat, hard surface to yield more juice, or boil whole fruit for several minutes. Avoid using overripe lemon fresh. Instead, slice or chop the pulp and use in lemon chicken, fish in lemon-butter sauce, or avgolemono soup.

Next time: See *Dry*.

Lemonade—The magic quench words "ice-cold lemonade" on a sign bring the hot and thirsty in from the heat. The very thought of a tall, frosty glass revives body and soul. My first plunge into the business arena was at the age of five, when my mother helped me set up a lemonade stand in our front yard. One customer liked Mom's lemonade so well he told me to keep the change from a nickel for the two-cent drink. Each little paper cup was garnished with a mint sprig from the rock garden mint patch. Today's frozen concentrate is of course available throughout the year, but nothing can compare to the freshly made pitcher ritual on a summer day.

Leftovers: Can be covered and stored in the refrigerator 1 week. For longer storage, freeze in ice cube trays up to 1 year. Grated outer yellow lemon rind portions (zest) can be frozen and used to flavor icings, cakes, fruit sauces, etc.

RAN SHORT: Mix with iced tea, fruit juice, or carbonated beverage.

STRONG: Add more cold water or ice cubes or blend in fruit juice, club soda, or iced tea.

SOUR: Add more sugar, sugar substitute, or sweet fruit juice to balance an acrid lemon tang. When making lemonade frequently throughout the summer, it's convenient to make this syrup to keep on hand: boil 2 parts sugar and 1 part water for several minutes, cool, add lemon juice in equivalent amount to water, strain, and chill in covered jar. Use about 1½ tbsp. per glass, fill with water and ice.

SWEET

This time: Add more lemon juice, or the juice of any sour fruit—limes and grapefruits are fine. Club soda's bitter carbonation or a dash of bitters helps cut sweetness too.

Next time: Add sugar gradually while tasting. It's better to under- than oversweeten. Have extra lemon juice on hand.

WEAK

This time: Add more lemon juice and sugar, or blend in fruit juice and garnish with mint or fresh fruit.

Next time: Avoid diluting drink with ice; use lemonade ice cubes. Use syrup (see *Sour*).

Lentils—See *Beans, Dried.*

Lettuce—Iceberg and romaine are best used in chunkier preparations with heavier dressings—the softer, more delicate butterhead type (e.g. Boston and Bibb) and leaf lettuce are better when lightly dressed.

WILTED

This time: Use in cooked dishes, especially lettuce soup (see cream of vegetable soup, p. 315) or creamed lettuce (p. 334). You might make wilted salad, but it is better prepared with fresh, crisp leaves that can hold up to a hot bacon dressing.

Next time: Iceberg and romaine should be crisp and firm with fresh leaves; avoid brown spots, seed stems or excessive outer leaves. Select iceberg heads heavy for their size; very large, whitish heads are overmature. Look for romaine with bright green-topped outer leaves. Select fresh, tender butterheads with clean leaves. Looseleaf is best with crisp, crinkly foliage. Avoid any lettuce with bruises, rust spots, excessive tip burn, or wide spaces between outer leaves at the base, indicating seed stems. Wash in several changes of cold water or under cold running water. Drain in basket of salad spinner; spin dry. Or drain in a wire basket, shake off excess moisture, dry on paper toweling or kitchen towels. Roll up in toweling, which can be tucked into a plastic bag, and store in vegetable crisper of refrigerator. The crisper varieties store better (a few days) than the softer.

Lima Beans—*See Beans.*

Lime—The famous limes grown on the Florida Keys from which Key lime pie takes its name are small, round, yellow, and acrid. Can be used interchangeably with lemons, although flavor is not quite as sharp. For problems with bitter, dry, squirty, or overripe, see *Lemon.*

YELLOW

This time: Yellow limes, except Key variety and other yellow varieties, tend to lack acidity and flavor. If you have other green limes or lemons around, use half and half with yellow limes to add strength of flavor. Bottled lemon or lime juice also adds a fillip to bland juice. Or use the less acid juice in milder dishes.

Next time: Look for heavy, firm green limes, free of irregular-shaped purplish-brown spots.

Liver—*See Meat.*

Lobster—*See Shellfish.*

Lopsided—See specific baked item.

Lumpy—See specific item.

Lunch Meat—See Meat.

Macaroni—See Pasta.

Macaroons—See Cookie.

Mackerel—See Fish.

Madrilene—See Soup.

Mango—At best, its flesh is luscious and juicy with a rich tart sweetness. At worst, it may be firmly and acidically premature. But even in this state, it possesses the ability to wow discerning palates in curries and chutneys. Small wonder it has been cultivated for thousands of years in warm climates. In India it is a staple ingredient and the tropical tree is considered sacred. Mango chutney is as important a condiment to Indians as catsup is to Americans—and, I must add, of far greater palatability. The fruit turns a yellowy orange-red upon ripening, indicating sun exposure. Can be a challenge for the novice to eat, since the pulp clings to the large stone amid fibers.

DISCOLORED

This time: If the darkened part is the surface of a halved mango, it can be scraped away easily enough. But if slices or chunks have darkened, stew them with spices in sweetened water or fruit juice along with vanilla and the color won't matter. Or mash mango and blend with softened ice cream, whipped cream, pudding, or perhaps even a spicy main dish.

Next time: Rub lemon, lime, or grapefruit juice over cut surface and cover with plastic wrap before refrigerating. Use soon to prevent loss of aroma and flavor as well as color.

FIBROUS: Slice pulp from fibrous pit, sieve or purée flesh. Because the flesh sticks to the fibers which cling to the stone, cut the skin in a circular fashion around each end, slice lengthwise around the pit and horizontally next to the stone to loosen slices, remove peel, and lift the sections. The stone is worth chewing on to get all the bits of fruit stuck to it, but fibers do stick in the teeth. When the flesh is already cut from the stone and fibers cling to it, peel them off. Otherwise, run mixture through a sieve to remove fibers or purée it to break fibers down.

OVERRIPE

This time: Very soft mango is delicious peeled in sections and eaten with a spoon. It's also desirable for mashing or puréeing, to be used for jam, sauce, sherbet, mousse, pudding, or pie, mixed with sugar and frozen, or turned into any number of poultry or Indian spicy dishes. It also makes a rich nectar.

Next time: Select firm fruit that yields slightly when pressed, with orange-yellow-red color. Soft or brown spots indicate overripeness. Refrigerate ripe mango, use within a week.

UNDERRIPE, GREEN

This time: To quicken the ripening process place in paper bag and store in warm, dark place. Or use mature green fruit for a spicy chutney: chop with onion, garlic, and chilies and boil with vinegar, sugar, and raisins.

Next time: Select orange-yellow-colored mangoes that feel slightly soft when pressed gently. If rather firm, leave at room temperature until riper.

Manicotti—See *Pasta.*

Maple—See *Syrups.*

Margarine—See *Butter; Fat.*

Marinade—See *Sauces.*

Marmalade—See *Canning.*

Marrow (bones)—See *Soup; Stock.*

Mayonnaise—See *Sauces.*

Meat—The most recent available figures show the average American consumes about 63.1 meat pounds (purchase weight, excluding processed products) annually. And since this country's beef is world famous, it's no contest which meat is the favored at 37.1 pounds per person. Pork is second preference—around 25 pounds and increasing. Surprisingly, veal and lamb average only about ½ pound per capita. Meat is not only well liked, it is also rich in protein, minerals, and B-vitamins, and almost all of it is digestible. Although tender cuts from younger animals are more highly prized, the food value from older, tougher animals is comparable. Parents can keep this in mind when their teen-age sons try to convince them they need steaks to build muscles. Hamburger and meat loaf will make them just as strong and athletic. Meat accounts for the biggest share of the grocery bill, so it's important to get the most value from your purchase. By preparing it properly, you avoid waste. And even if the meat turns out tough or overbrowned, it can be salvaged creatively.

General Meat Problems

BLAND

This time: The spice rack is the salvation here, for every type of meat can be enhanced by one or several herbs or spices. A classic sauce like bordelaise will elevate the meat to new heights. But even the simple touches of crushed garlic, minced onion, Worcestershire, and hot or steak sauce all add quick flavor. Leftovers can be marinated or sliced and tossed into a piquant salad.

Next time: Most recipes are conservative in seasonings. Adjust according to taste during cooking and just before serving. For long-simmering meat use whole spices and herbs, as the ground seasonings cook out quickly. When browning meats, season afterward, unless seasoning is mixed into a coating. Marinate blander cuts, allowing enough time for flavors to absorb.

CURLING (CHOPS, SLICES, STEAKS)

This time: Slash fat in 1-inch intervals around edges during cooking to prevent even further curling. For already cooked curly meat, cut into bite-size pieces and serve with vegetables over rice with a sauce, or incorporate into a casserole.

Next time: Slash fat around edges before cooking.

DRY

This time: Slice thin and cover with gravy or sauce. Or use thin slices or ground in casserole. Cover while baking so steam can penetrate meat and soften. Or grind and make nalesniki (p. 320).

Next time: Add fat to lean meat cuts before broiling or pan-broiling. Lay bacon strips across top of veal before broiling, for instance. Time meat carefully, as overcooking dries it out. After browning pan-fried meats, cover and allow moist heat to build up.

FROZEN

This time: Quick-thaw in microwave oven. Or place under cold running water or in cold water bath, wrapped, allowing 2 to 5 hours total. In a pinch, meat can be cooked frozen, allowing about one-half as much additional time for roasting and one-fourth to one-half more for broiling and pan-broiling. Place broiler pan farther from heat source.

Next time: The safest and best way of thawing meat is slowly in the refrigerator, allowing about 6 hours per pound.

HARD TO SLICE

This time: It's important to allow a roast to rest 15 to 20 minutes after cooking before slicing. Make sure knife is very sharp. Use crumbled pieces for sandwich spread, in casseroles, or in salad.

Next time: Time meat to allow for resting period after roasting. Make sure carving utensils are in prime condition.

NOT ENOUGH

This time: Thinly slicing the roast or steak or cutting or chopping helps distribute the amount. Embellish with vegetables, such as mushrooms and onions, and serve with a sauce over rice, toast, or noodles. Turn into a casserole with numerous other ingredients plus some protein foods like egg and cheese, and no one will ever guess the meat ran short. Try pairing meat with seafood for an elegant duet; steak and oysters or shrimp are delicious.

Next time: Allow for shrinkage and waste when calculating servings per pound.

OFF FLAVOR

This time: When meat has absorbed flavors from the refrigerator, reheat in a spicy sauce (barbecue, mustard, horseradish, etc.) or well-seasoned marinade.

Next time: Store meat tightly covered in meat keeper away from other aromatic foods. Cover and wrap all foods in refrigerator.

OVERBROWNED

This time: Trim off overbrowned and hard edges and cut up; serve with sauce or grind and turn into a casserole, nalesniki (p. 320), or stuffing.

Next time: Calculate length of cooking and use proper temperature. Check periodically during cooking. If you notice overbrowning, cover top or edges with foil.

OVERCOOKED

This time: Overcooking toughens meat; thin slices make it more tender. Moisture in the form of a relish or sauce adds palatability. Even very overcooked meat can be revived by grinding or chopping and combining with textured foods and a moist binder. Overdone beef, for example, takes on new life when chopped and tossed with celery and olives for a salad bound with mayonnaise.

Next time: When roasting meats, do not turn up oven to quicken process; meat is liable to shrink and become overdone. A 325-degree oven is recommended for most meats. A meat thermometer inserted into the fleshy part of muscle is the only exact way to test internal temperature. Remove meat from oven just before thermometer indicates desired doneness, because cooking will continue a while from contained heat. To avoid overcooking smaller cuts, turn and check frequently. Long-simmering cuts should be cooked over very gentle heat and timed. Allowing pot roast to cook an extra hour will not make it better, but rather will result in an overcooked, fall-apart disaster.

SALTY

This time: A raw potato absorbs a lot of salt, so quarter it and add to the saline meat sauce, stew, or pot roast as it simmers; then remove. The salty tuber can either be used in another bland dish or cooked with other potatoes. For larger cuts cooked by dry heat, rinse briefly in wine, water, or milk or juice, depending on your taste. Don't soak meat a long time in water, because it washes away juice and flavor. To remove salt from ham and other smoked meats, slice and soak in milk about ½ hour, then rinse in cold water. All meats are delicious fruited, so try soaking or marinating a salty cut in a fruit-juice blend. Adding additional spices and herbs also helps.

Next time: Salt at end of cooking after tasting. Sometimes the salt from ingredients such as capers, olives, and bouillon is sufficient. Salting before cooking draws out essential juices and can make the meat dry.

STICKING TO PAN

This time: It can be disappointing to break up a lovely large cut; but when there's no way to keep it together after scraping it from the pan, present it attractively in pieces over rice covered with a sauce. Or stir-fry with vegetables for a Chinese-style entrée.

Next time: Lightly grease broiler pan when broiling lean cuts. Leave on some border fat as lubrication when trimming. Reduce oven temperature when roasting, or burner heat when frying or pan-broiling. Add some fat to pan first before browning meat. Turn frequently to prevent sticking.

TOUGH

This time: Even "shoe-leather" meat becomes chewable when thinly sliced, chopped, or ground. This problem usually is accompanied by dryness and occurs from overcooking or improper cooking. The less-tender cuts may be tough because they need further simmering. In this case, return to the pot. Once-tender meat that has toughened probably did so during overcooking. The fastest solution is to slice the meat paper thin and cover with gravy. Another is to chop and use in a casserole or toss with both dry and moist ingredients for an Oriental stir-fry dish. Grinding tenderizes the most hopelessly unchewable mass. It then can be used for forcemeat; as fillings for stuffed peppers, eggplant, or nalesniki (p. 320); in stuffings; and for numerous other dishes using ground meat. It's important to moisturize tough meat.

Next time: When not sure what part of carcass a particular cut comes from, ask the butcher. The more tender cuts come from the rib and loin sections. Tougher cuts can be tenderized numerous ways: by marinating, pounding with a mallet, long simmering, and when short on time, using a commercial tenderizer. Unless the cut is of good quality and has already been tenderized by one of these methods, do not attempt to cook by dry heat. Broiling, roasting, frying, and pan-broiling should be reserved for the more tender meats. In general, avoid overcooking and high temperatures. Quality, indicated by U.S.D.A. grades, also affects tenderness. Prime and choice have more marbling of fat and yield better eating.

UNDERCOOKED

This time: Slice off outer edges and serve those while finishing the rest. Put a pot roast or other meat cooked by moist heat in a pressure cooker to hasten the procedure. A microwave oven could save a dinner party; follow manufacturer's directions to complete the dish. Another quick trick is to slice the meat and sauté, then cover and cook (with or without liquid, depending on recipe). By increasing size of surface area, the meat cooks much more rapidly.

Next time: Carefully calculate cooking time, allowing a little extra for resting period.

WON'T BROWN

This time: With paper toweling, wipe all surfaces very dry, especially marinated meats. Sometimes moisture collects (as with thawed meat), creating steam and preventing browning. If meat is fully cooked but still not darkened, a sure-fire way to induce browning is by rubbing the surface lightly with a spicy-sweet sauce or by smearing over a little fat. Then zap it under high heat. For microwave, follow directions for browning mode or pan and/or use browning seasonings.

Next time: Drying meat before cooking and lightly flouring, breading, or smearing with a spicy-sweet sauce encourages beautiful browning. Have pan hot enough before adding meat.

Basic meat cookery methods

1. Roasting: cooking in an oven or Dutch oven in meat's own juices; recommended for large, tender meat cuts, such as rolled rib roast of beef, center loin of pork and leg of veal or lamb.

2. Broiling: cooking by direct heat at a moderate temperature over hot coals or under an electric or gas heat source in the home broiler; the fat from the food being broiled drips down through holes in the upper pan into a lower pan, producing a relatively low-fat product. Use this method for tender steaks and chops at least ¾-inch thick; ham slices at least ½-inch thick; and ground meat patties at least ¾-inch thick. Lean or thin steaks and chops should be braised or broiled with some fat added to prevent drying.

3. Pan-broiling: cooking meat uncovered in a moderately hot, heavy skillet, turning meat occasionally to brown on both sides, pouring off fat as it accumulates. No fat or water is added, but the pan may be lightly greased to prevent very lean cuts from sticking. The same cuts suitable for broiling when cut 1 inch or less thick are recommended for this method. Pan-broiling takes about half the cooking time as broiling.

4. Frying: cooking in fat. When a small amount of fat is added to a pan, or allowed to accumulate during cooking, the method is pan-frying. The meat is browned on both sides, then cooked through while turned occasionally over moderate heat. Small, rather thin and tender meat cuts are suitable for pan-frying: cube steaks, beef and veal round steaks, pork blade and arm steaks, lamb arm and blade chops, patties and veal loin chops. When a large amount of fat is used and the meat is completely immersed, the method is deep-frying, and usually used for organ meats (brains, sweetbreads, and liver) or croquettes. The meat is usually dipped in batter or coated with egg and crumbs or corn meal, fried until golden brown and cooked through, then drained.

5. Braising: browning meat slowly, pouring off drippings, then cooking covered, slowly, in small amount of liquid until tender. This method is especially appropriate for less tender cuts such as short ribs, shanks, and beef flank steak; but it is also suggested for some tender cuts, such as pork and veal steaks and chops and beef and pork liver.

6. Cooking in liquid: browning large, less tender meat cuts and stew meat, then covering meat with liquid and simmering, covered, until tender. Meats usually cooked by this method include stews, beef brisket and beef plate, smoked picnic ham, shank portion of smoked ham, pork hocks and feet, spareribs and backbones.

Servings: An average serving of cooked meat is about 4 to 6 ounces. Allow ⅓ pound raw per serving for boneless cuts; about ½ pound or slightly more per serving when there's a little bone, and about ¾ to 1 pound per serving for bony cuts or those with much fat.

To store in freezer: Fresh prepackaged meat may be frozen up to 2 weeks without rewrapping. For longer storage or for fresh meat not prepackaged, wrap tightly in freezer paper or foil.

In refrigerator: Fresh meat can be stored in meat keeper or coldest part of refrigerator for a few days. Ground meat, stew meat, and variety meats are highly perishable and should either be used within a day or frozen. Prepackaged meat can be left in wrapper; others should be loosely wrapped in wax paper, foil or butcher's wax-lined paper. Cooked meats keep about 5 days.

To thaw: Thaw wrapped meat slowly in refrigerator, allowing 6 to 7 hours per pound. Thawing is much faster in the microwave oven or by placing wrapped meat under cold running water or in cold water bath. Allow 2 to 5 hours for latter, depending on size.

Types of meat: The main types of meat are listed here with selection and leftover tips and any specific related problems.

Beef: Select well-marbled, lean, red, firm meat with a firm white or cream-white outer fat cover. Well-aged beef should have a purplish tone. Leftover roast can be slivered or chopped for a hearty cabbage slaw or spinach salad with blue-cheese dressing; thin slices or shavings can be creamed and served over toast, bite-size chunks can be incorporated into a casserole.

Canned meats: There are numerous processed products such as hash, luncheon meats, sausages, stews, chili, etc. Many tend to be oversalted (see *Salty*). Because there's no waste or shrinkage, figure fewer ounces per serving than other meats.

Ham: There are so many styles that it is best to check with the butcher or read the label carefully to select one suited to your needs. Generally hams are pink-fleshed and have a nice, firm coating of surface fat. Avoid those with excess fat. Thin ham steaks or slices can curl when broiled (see *Curling*). To remove excess salt, soak in milk about ½ hour, then rinse in cold water before cooking. A sweet glaze or sauce counters saltiness (see *Salty*). Leftover ham can be incorporated into omelets, scrambled eggs, and many casseroles, especially those flavored with mustard or fruit. Thinly sliced, it can envelop a fresh asparagus for an elegant appetizer or form a surprise filling in a veal cutlet. Because of its robust taste, ham pairs well with veal and poultry. Grind up scraps for the popular ham sandwich spread; use along with any leftover bone for flavoring soups, beans, or lentils.

Lamb and Mutton: Fresh, good-quality lamb should be firm and well textured with lean that can range from pink to deep red. It should be very well marbled and have a brittle white fat cover. Mutton is an animal more than 1½ years old; it may be substituted for lamb but requires about 5 to 10 extra minutes cooking per pound. Use leftovers in pilafs, in tossed salads with curry dressing and on sandwiches with chutney.

STRONG FLAVORED

This time: Some people object to a "lamby" taste, which might be from mutton instead of lamb. The fell (white brittle fat coating) also adds strength of flavor. The robust taste will diminish when served piping hot with a fragrant, tangy mint, hot curry, or sweet chutney sauce or with a fruited rice pilaf.

Next time: When you prefer a lighter taste, make sure you're buying lamb, not mutton. Remove the fell before cooking or marinating. Older lamb can be marinated in a spiced or fruited mixture, allowing the meat to take on new flavor characteristics.

Pork: Choose firm, pinkish pork lean with some marbling and firm, white outer fat. Many people, still fearing the outdated trichinosis (disease caused by eating insufficiently cooked infected pork) cook this meat to death. It should be cooked only until the juices run clear when the flesh is pricked. An indication of finished meat is an even grayish color without pink. The National Live Stock and Meat Board now suggests cooking pork slowly to only 170 degrees instead of the former conservative 185 degrees for more palatability. Add leftover pieces together with preserved kumquats and pineapple chunks to an Oriental sauce (see Gingered sweet-sour sauce, p. 329) and serve over rice, or use in stir-fry dishes and dumpling fillings. Ground pork mixed with mayonnaise and olives makes an excellent sandwich filling.

Sausages: The selection is mind boggling. When buying fresh sausage (as opposed to smoked or cooked deli-style) avoid a slimy or dried and shriveled appearance. Sausages need some fat to be tasty, but avoid links that look excessively fatty. Dry sausages can be kept almost indefinitely in a cool, dry place if properly made and casing is intact. After opening, smoked or cooked sausage can be refrigerated about 1 week, the semidry and dry sausages 2 weeks or even longer. Leftovers can embellish pizza, soup, beans, lentils, and eggs. Links or 3-inch lengths make wonderful lunches tucked into crusty French bread with hot peppers or a spicy mustard relish.

BURSTS, CURLS

This time: Sausages that have exploded inside out or have twisted during cooking are not very appetizing. Slice and stir-fry with vegetables or incorporate into scrambled eggs or omelet. Or chop and add to beans, soup, or casserole.

Next time: Pierce or slash sausages well before cooking. When frying, add a small amount of water to the pan first, or blanch, then dry and flour lightly before frying.

FATTY

This time: Pierce whole sausage in several places and squeeze gently between paper toweling. Drain very well before serving. Or slice and drain well.

Next time: Pierce or slash before cooking whole so fat can escape during cooking. Then boil or broil. Another choice is to slice sausage and fry, draining off fat as it accumulates. Drain all cooked sausage well on paper toweling before serving.

Smoked and cured meats (see also *Ham; Sausages*): Select bacon that has good proportion of red-brown lean to firm white fat. Most smoked meats have a reddish color, and should look fresh and feel firm. Avoid cuts with slimy, shiny surface or dried, shriveled appearance. Leftovers from these meats lend good flavor to bean dishes and soups, eggs, sandwich fillings, and salads. A common problem here is saltiness (see *Salty*). Do not store longer than recommended in freezer, as freezing increases the problem.

BACON, CURLED

This time: Any heavy heatproof weight can be used to keep bacon strips flat while frying. Shriveled bacon can still be served unless you're trying to impress a discriminating guest. In that case, crumble and sprinkle over eggs, casseroles, or salads.

Next time: Bake bacon strips in 400-degree oven 10 to 15 minutes. When curling begins during frying, dust lightly with flour to stop it. The microwave oven also produces attractive, delicious bacon.

Variety meats: Liver, tripe, sweetbreads, heart, kidneys, and brains are extremely perishable, so purchase from a reliable source. They should be kept well chilled at all times and used soon after purchase, or frozen. Leftovers are especially good in stews and soups, or chopped and incorporated into casseroles, stuffing, or eggs. Taste drippings; if too strong, dilute with broth, wine or water. Ground leftovers can be made into forcemeats and sandwich spreads. Many of these specialty meats can toughen easily from cooking too long or at too high a temperature. Grinding or fine chopping is the solution.

BURSTING, SPATTERING

This time: The organ meats have a different density from other animal parts, and pressure builds up with heat and bursts through the outer membrane. This can be alleviated by piercing in several places with fork tines. Use medium heat and make sure meat is dry before frying, to reduce spattering. Once already burst and unattractive, chop or grind and use in a casserole, soup or stuffing.

Next time: Pierce and dry well before cooking. Slight flouring before frying also helps.

Veal: Select veal with gray-pink flesh with a small amount of fat. Veal has no marbling; any fat should be creamy white and firm. This is the most delicate of meats and should be treated with low heat. Leftovers can be reheated gently or sliced and paired with ham. Use chopped in casseroles or over rice with mushroom or lemon sauce. Because veal has so little fat, some moisture should be added, even after browning thin scallops. This baby animal is bland (see *Bland*). It is extremely compatible with lemon, mushrooms, and delicate herbs.

DRY

This time: Depending on preparation, moisten with a favorite sauce. Breaded cutlets take well to a sprinkling of fresh lemon or orange juice. Or turn chunks into a casserole, perhaps with mushrooms and peas, bound with a light wine-herb sauce.

Next time: Wrap bacon strips or salt pork around or across top of veal cuts when browning or pan-broiling. Or cook with a little moisture.

To whiten: Milk-fed veal usually needs no whitening, but it's hard to get in the U.S. Soak older veal in milk overnight in refrigerator. Some chefs blanch meat briefly starting in cold water, then soak in lemon juice for 1 hour before cooking. This both whitens and tenderizes.

Meat Loaf—Too often maligned as a throw-together cheap main dish, meat loaf actually should stand proud. No doubt the disparaging remarks stem from the bland institutional meat loaf of steamy texture topped with catsup. No wonder some of us grow up never wanting anything to do with it again! But how sad never to try the European veal loaf smothered with creamy mushroom sauce or tangy sweet-sour ham round or beef and pork blend stuffed with cooked egg and wrapped in pastry. The typical American mixture of beef, pork, and veal can be dressed up with a frosting of cheesy mashed potatoes, or baked in a ring and filled with vegetables. With a delicious sauce, an unusual shape, and a surprise ingredient, you'll renew your family's appetite. For a crustier top, shape into a loaf or round and bake out of a pan on a baking sheet.

CRUMBLY, STUCK TO PAN

This time: Reluctant edges and corners can be persuaded to let go with gentle, firm prodding from a spatula. If a few cracks appear, reassemble loaf with gentle pressure and serve with a sauce. When the loaf really falls apart, serve chunks over rice, noodles, or waffles covered with a compatible sauce.

Next time: Grease pan well, use a nonstick pan, or place partly cooked bacon strips across bottom before packing meat mixture in. If partly cooked, the bacon flavor shouldn't overpower and the meat will not sizzle in fat. About 1 medium egg binds 1 pound meat mixed with about ½ cup crumbs.

DRY, OVERCOOKED

This time: Moisten dry slices with a favorite sauce. Or simmer in the sauce, allowing the steam treatment to do its work. Bite-size pieces bound with a sauce can be served over rice or noodles. Thin slices dressed with a piquant relish make a nice sandwich on moist bread; toast is too dry.

Next time: Bake a 2-pound meat loaf in a 350-degree oven about 1 hour; do not overbake. Add more liquid ingredients.

FATTY

This time: Most of the excess fat accumulates at the pan bottom, so drain off before unmolding loaf; drain each slice on paper toweling before serving.

Next time: Use leaner meat. Ground round or chuck are better choices than ground beef. The blend of beef, pork, and veal is a dependable choice.

HEAVY

This time: A compact loaf slices nicely when chilled; spread with mustard, horseradish, or relish for sandwiches. Or moisten by serving with a sauce.

Next time: Use 1 egg per pound meat; a filler (crumbs, oatmeal) helps give a lighter texture.

Melons—Cantaloupe is reportedly named after a castle called Cantelupe in Italy, and muskmelon supposedly takes its name from Persian-perfumed musk oil. Surprisingly, no melon is named after Roman Emperor Tiberius, who loved melons so much that one of history's first greenhouses was designed so he could enjoy the fruit even during winter. Legend has it that he ate a melon a day, as some of us eat an apple. However frequently you indulge, most of the melon advice that follows applies to all varieties. Specific characteristics are mentioned where germane.

BLAND

This time: Melon flavor is enhanced by a squeeze of lemon or lime. Cubes or balls of melon marinated in fruit juice sparked with liqueur or rum, or bathed in salad dressing will add a nice taste dimension to a fruit salad.

Next time: Picking a fully ripe melon does not guarantee good flavor, but it certainly increases the chances. A rich aroma usually indicates full flavor, especially in cantaloupes and Persians.

Here's a rundown on selecting the various melons and what characteristics to look for:

Cantaloupe—a smooth, depressed scar at stem end indicates easy separation from stem, thus adequate maturity. Softened blossom end, lightened grayish rind color, and strong aroma indicate full ripeness.

Casaba—rough, wrinkled rind goes from light to dark yellow upon ripening.

Crenshaw—rind deepens in color and blossom end softens when melon is ripe.

Honeydew—blossom end should be slightly soft to insure readiness for eating. Fragrance is faint.

Persian—look for softening at blossom end and lightening of rind to indicate ripeness.

Watermelon—the trickiest to choose for ripeness. Very hard melons are probably underripe. Look for well-shaped (large oblong) melons with bloom over smooth, deep green to grayish rind. Bottom side will be yellowish. Flesh should be dark pink to red, juicy and sweet. Avoid those with white, fibrous streak throughout pulp.

OVERRIPE

This time: Slightly overripe melon can be marinated in a piquant dressing for several hours or overnight; it makes a flavorful addition to salads. Soft melon pulp can be puréed for any number of dishes, especially frappés, sherbets, and icy drinks or soups.

Next time: Make sure melons have no very soft spots or decay areas. Once ripe, store in cool place or chill, wrapping in plastic wrap or other cover, up to 1 week. Wrap all cut melons, as well.

UNDERRIPE

This time: Store a hard melon at room temperature until ripe. Some recommend a paper bag. If preferred, cut up and use for chutney or pickles; hard melon is better for these condiments.

Next time: Avoid very hard fruit.

Meringue—Whether billowing across a pie or delicately holding a filling, meringue is an exquisite culinary phenomenon. The meringue shell piled high with whipped cream garnished with chocolate or fruit is a common sight in Europe. Individual meringues, or the softer meringue pie-topping version, are more familiar in this country. True to prima donna form, meringue is beautiful and often temperamental. Conditions must be just right for it to give a grand performance. When things don't go according to script, the suggestions below should enable you to carry on the show.

General tips on making meringues

Unless you know professional techniques, don't attempt on a humid day. Moisture is one of meringue's worst enemies. See *Weather*.

Make certain bowl, beaters, and other utensils are very clean, dry, and free of the smallest speck of fat.

Best results come from using an unlined copper bowl and balloon whisk; however, a heavy-duty mixer does an excellent job. Avoid using hand mixer or rotary beater, which produces less volume.

Use fresh large (2-ounce) eggs, or make adjustment when using different size.

It's easier to separate whites from yolks when eggs are cold. If even the tiniest trace of yolk falls into whites, scoop out with eggshell, not fingers. Skin oils will prevent whites from being beaten to fullest volume. Bring whites to room temperature.

Cream of tartar, a stabilizer, should be added to egg whites at foamy stage, when large opaque bubbles begin to form.

Extra-fine granulated sugar is recommended, although superfine also produces an acceptable product. Because volume measurements vary with the grain, it is more accurate to weigh the sugar.

Always add sugar gradually while beating when egg whites reach the glossy, soft-peak stage. Marion Cunningham, San Francisco baking and cooking expert who teaches classes with James Beard, shares this stabilizing technique for soft meringue. She credits Chef Bruno of Stanford Court Hotel for it: gradually stir sugar into egg whites over very hot water before beating until stiff. The meringue holds up for two days, even in that foggy city. Meringue is at correct consistency when stiff and glossy and will support a whole egg in its shell. French meringue will have stiffer peaks than soft meringue.

Soft meringue: The type commonly used for toppings; made by adding 2 tablespoons extra-fine granulated sugar per large egg white. For more accuracy, use the weight ratio: ⅛ lb. sugar (about ¼ cup) for every 2 egg whites (large, 2-oz. eggs; ¼ cup total whites).

GUMMY, STICKING TO KNIFE

This time: Measure about ½ to ¾ teaspoon granulated sugar and carefully sprinkle evenly over meringue surface. Or dip a sharp serrated knife in very cold water between slices. Both methods prevent clinging. Sprinkling surface with toasted coconut or slivered almonds helps hide a gummy appearance and often facilitates slicing too.

Next time: Be sure egg whites are at soft-peak stage before adding sugar; stabilize with salt and cream of tartar; gradually add sugar, using about 2 tablespoons per large egg white. Or add less sugar; when too much is beaten into meringue it may turn gummy and "bead out." Avoid making meringue in humid conditions, including steam in kitchen. Tightly cover (in pie saver) to prevent moisture absorption when refrigerating.

SHRUNKEN, SHRIVELED

This time: Decorate edges with whipped cream and/or fruit slices, nuts, and chocolate curls.

Next time: Spread meringue to completely cover filling, sealing well to edges. Do not use high oven heat. The usual temperature for baking meringue pie toppings is 350 degrees F. for about 12 minutes, depending on thickness. A hotter oven will shrink the egg protein. Cool in warm place free of drafts.

SLIDING OFF PIE

This time: When meringue refuses to adhere, serve wedges of pie in a deep dish topped with a sauce (lemon meringue pie and raspberry sauce are an exciting duet; try vanilla sauce over chocolate). Another trick, and attractive garnish, is to spear compatible fruit (orange slice for orange meringue) with a decorative pick and place through center of wedge to hold meringue in place.

Next time: Quickly spread a thin layer of meringue over hot filling as soon as it is poured into baked pie shell, using a spoon or rubber scraper. Once meringue has a grip on filling, add more, piling higher in center.

SOFT (NO BODY)

This time: A tangy fruit or liqueur sauce poured over enhances the pie and draws attention from the meringue texture. Sprinkling top with nuts, coconut or chocolate curls also helps add substance.

Next time: When mixing meringue, be sure to use clean bowl and beater without a trace of grease. Have fresh egg whites (old are runny) at room temperature so they reach maximum volume. At the foamy stage add salt and cream of tartar to stabilize. Whisk or beat until creamy with soft peaks; gradually beat in 2 tablespoons extra-fine granulated sugar per egg white, making certain each addition is well dissolved before adding more. Beat mixture only until peaks are glossy and pointed (or see Marion Cunningham's tip, p. 162). Most pie meringues are baked in preheated 350-degree oven. Store tightly covered (in pie saver) in refrigerator; meringues absorb moisture easily and will disintegrate.

WEEPING

This time: Surface droplets are easily covered by sprinkling with chocolate bits, ground nuts, or grated coconut. Or serve with ice cream or sauce.

Next time: Sift confectioners sugar lightly over meringue before baking. Cool very slowly in turned-off oven. Quick cooling causes the beading effect. Once cooled to room temperature, pie may be tightly covered and chilled.

French Meringue: A hard meringue used as meringue shells, cookies, vacherins (usually fruit-and-whipped-cream-filled cylinders), dacquoise (usually buttercream-filled crisp layers) or various decorative shapes. Made by adding 4 tablespoons extra-fine granulated sugar per egg white. For more accuracy, use the weight ratio: ¼-lb. sugar (about ½ cup) for every 2 egg whites (large, 2-oz eggs; ¼ cup total whites). This type of meringue can be prepared by following the procedure for soft meringue, beating until stiff and glossy, or by gradually adding ⅔ to ½ the castor or extra-fine granulated sugar at the soft-peak stage, beating until stiff and glossy peaks form, then folding in remaining sugar. The latter method makes a crisper, more tender meringue.

BROWNED

This time: When meringue browns, disguise appearance by serving with ice cream. When quite dark, crumble and mix with nuts and a cream for a delicious crunchy cake filling or use as pudding topping.

Next time: Meringues must be baked in a very low preheated oven, about 225 degrees, so they dry out without coloring. Use bottom heat.

MIXTURE RUNNY

This time: When the meringue mixture is runny, make another small meringue batch and incorporate into the softer one. A mixture that is too soft to hold shape can be supported by baking in little, lightly oiled paper cups.

Next time: See *Soft Meringue* for procedure. Do not add more than 4 tablespoons extra-fine granulated sugar per egg white. Make sure egg whites are at soft-peak stage and stabilized with salt and cream of tartar before gradually adding sugar.

SOFT, CHEWY

This time: Return to a low oven for further drying, or serve topped with, or crumbled over, ice cream.

Next time: See *Mixture Runny.* For meringues without additional color (e.g., vacherins, meringue mushrooms), bake in preheated 200- to 225-degree oven (no higher). Baking in preheated 250-degree oven gives some color and a crisper product. When adding nuts and coconut to meringue, make sure ingredients are drained or toasted and dry; incorporate at very end, because nut oils and other moist flavorings can thin the meringue.

STICKING

This time: Pry up with sharp, flexible thin-bladed knife. Crumbled pieces can serve as ice cream or pudding topping or can be incorporated into cake filling.

Next time: Pipe meringue shapes onto waxed or lightly oiled parchment paper on baking sheet. Before piped meringue cools completely, gently loosen with spatula before further drying in cooling oven. Other causes may be insufficient sugar in recipe or too high an oven temperature.

Italian Meringue: A "softish" meringue that is slightly stiffer and has more body than soft meringue, and requires no baking because the egg whites are cooked by hot syrup. Proportion of ½ lb. extra-fine granulated sugar (about 1 cup) per ½ cup water and ¼ teaspoon cream of tartar, cooked to 238 degrees F. (soft ball stage), and poured very gradually over 3 egg whites (large 2-oz eggs; 6 tablespoons total whites) beaten to soft-peak stage. Used for buttercream frosting, candy, chantilly meringue cake topping.

RUNNY

This time: Make another batch and incorporate into softer one. If too soft to use as intended, serve as topping over pudding and parfaits.

Next time: Make sure egg whites are beaten to soft-peak stage before gradually introducing syrup in a thin stream. If added sooner, the meringue will have no body.

Milk—Milk in this country means cow's milk, whereas other people around the world drink milk from different animals. Middle-Eastern desert dwellers rely on the camel, an amazing creature that can be milked even after traveling for days without food or water. Egyptians drink the product of their work animals, water buffalo. And in Italian and Greek villages, it's still possible to see goat herdsmen milking their flocks in the street for customers carrying pails. Some African tribes are almost completely milk-dependent; other cultures shun the drink. The Chinese consider it unfit for consumption.

Called "nature's most perfect food," cow's milk contains all the known vitamins except vitamin D, and today's milk is vitamin D fortified. Milk and milk products are the best source of the mineral calcium, which is necessary for development and maintenance of bones and teeth and other important body functions. However, gourmet James Beard, considered to be the single most important American food expert confesses an aversion to milk in his *Delights & Prejudices* (Simon & Schuster). "My earliest hate was milk. I loathed milk, cold or hot. . . . Eventually, though, I came to accept milk when it was combined with other ingredients and turned into a modest but delectable dish, clam soup." I heartily endorse his last point for nonmilk drinkers. Why not combine milk with other ingredients, or *eat* instead of drink it? Use it in cream soups, sauces and custards, and eat it in other dairy forms such as yogurt and cheese.

FROZEN

This time: If the milk accidentally freezes, thaw it slowly in the refrigerator. Stir if fat separates and use as usual within a couple of days. If you plan to cook with it, thaw more quickly by slowly heating in top of double boiler over hot water, stirring occasionally. Avoid chilling the heated thawed milk, since the temperature changes shorten its life. Yet another alternative is to keep it frozen and break off milk ice chips to chill milk punch or a frosty milk drink without diluting.

Next time: When trying to freeze milk for frozen cubes, pour into ice-cube trays and freeze. Keep milk in refrigerator at about 40 degrees for best quality.

SKIN FORMATION

This time: Skim off or strain.

Next time: Use steady, moderate to low temperatures when heating milk in a covered pan, and you'll see no skin. Other preventive measures are diluting the milk or adding a little fat to the surface (such as butter in oyster stew). High temperatures produce a tough skin formation.

SOURING

This time: Milk that is just beginning to sour will last another day or two with the addition of about 1½ teaspoons baking soda per quart. Slightly sour milk can be used for pancakes, breads, cakes, dips, and soups (see *spinach—sour-milk soup*, p. 317). I've mixed a little tangy milk with yogurt or sour cream, blue cheese, mustard, lemon juice, and herbs for a tangy salad dressing.

Next time: Always store fresh milk in refrigerator at about 40 degrees. When removing it to pour, return to refrigerator immediately. Once removed, do not return milk to original container. Try to use within 3 to 5 days; protect from sunlight, which causes vitamin B loss, and keep covered to prevent absorption of surrounding odors.

Substitutes: You can substitute any of the following for 1 cup whole milk:

½ cup evaporated milk plus ½ cup water

1 cup skim milk plus 2 teaspoons cream, butter, margarine or oil

1 cup reconstituted nonfat dry milk plus 2½ teaspoons butter or margarine

¼ cup sifted dry whole milk powder plus ⅞ cup water

1 cup buttermilk plus ½ teaspoon baking soda

For 1 cup buttermilk or sour milk, place 1 tablespoon lemon juice or distilled white vinegar into measuring cup, then fill to 1-cup mark with fresh milk or equivalent. Let stand 5 minutes at room temperature.

Millet—*See Cereal.*

Molasses—"Slow as molasses" depicts the pace at which the viscous liquid pours. First known to the Chinese, it was brought to the West Indies by Columbus and soon became a prime sweetener in America. Considered an essential part of early New England cookery, molasses flavored doughnuts, cakes, breads, and good old baked beans.

TOO ROBUST

This time: The tangy, robust flavor is natural in blackstrap molasses. Intended mainly for cooking and baking, this type is perfect for spicy Indian pudding or a rich gingerbread. To use as table syrup, dilute with light molasses or corn syrup.

Next time: Become familiar with various labels and select light molasses for table use.

STUCK TO MEASURING UTENSIL OR CONTAINER

This time: Some maneuvering with the rubber scraper will get all clinging bits. If you can't fit a scraper into the container, remove cover and heat slowly in pan of hot water on burner or in low oven until molasses thins slightly.

Next time: Oil measuring utensils lightly before measuring molasses to prevent sticking.

To substitute: In most recipes, 1 cup molasses may be replaced by a scant ⅔ cup honey or maple syrup, 1⅔ cups corn syrup, or ¾ cup packed brown sugar.

Mold—*See Bread; Cheese; Food Spoilage, Poisoning.*

Mollusks—*See Shellfish.*

Moose—*See Game.*

Mostaccioli—*See Pasta.*

Mousse—*See* individual ingredients.

Mousseline—*See Dumpling; Sauces;* or individual ingredients.

Muffins—*See Bread, Quick.*

Mush (corn meal)—*See Cereal.*

Mushrooms—These fungi varieties are among the simplest plants, but not simple to grow. They reproduce from spores, instead of flowers or seeds, and need no sunlight. The cultivated mushrooms most common to our tables are grown in temperature- and air-controlled houses—one reason for their comparatively high price.

DISCOLORED

This time: Darkened raw mushrooms to be eaten raw can be lightened by wiping with a damp cloth, sprinkling with lemon juice and refrigerating. Darkened raw mushrooms to be cooked may become lighter in color if dropped into boiling water with some lemon juice (or other acid) added; cook about 1 minute. Or poach lightly in milk or butter to cover, about 15 minutes. Darkened cooked mushrooms can be lightened by cooking further (gently) in an acid solution (lemon juice, vinegar, wine) or milk. If very over-browned use in a brown stock or sauce, or in a dish where the color will not matter; browned mushrooms are still a flavorful addition to meaty dishes.

Next time: Select clean, fresh, firm, white to creamy-colored mushrooms, free of discoloration, opened caps, and shriveled appearance. They are very perishable and need air in storage. Keep in open plastic bag or on tray covered with damp paper towels in refrigerator. Use within 2 or 3 days. Do not wash until ready to use. To ensure preserving white color it's preferable to wipe with damp cloth and sprinkle with lemon juice. Or dip trimmed mushrooms quickly into cool water with lemon juice added (1 cup water, 1 teaspoon lemon juice), drain and dry. The flavor of lemon juice is light, and tends to leave no aftertaste. Vinegar and some white wines may leave a flavor that is undesirable for a particular use of the mushrooms. Avoid cooking light-colored mushrooms in black iron or aluminum, which darkens them. Overcooking darkens them, and alkali (baking soda or alkaline water) yellows them. Sauté in butter over medium-low heat, stirring, for short period of time to prevent overbrowning.

FLAVORLESS

This time: Remember that mushrooms eagerly absorb oils and other fats and cream mixtures. Marinate them in dressing for ½ hour or more if you intend to serve them raw in salad. When using raw mushrooms with a dip, sprinkle them with lemon juice and a compatible seasoning; refrigerate at least ½ hour before serving. When using in cooked dish for the mushroom flavor (as in mushroom sauce or soup) fortify with a little mushroom powder or soaked dried mushrooms, which have a stronger taste.

Next time: You can't predict flavor of fresh market mushrooms. So when using mushrooms for their essence, a bit of dry mushroom is more reliable—flavor is more intense.

OVERCOOKED

This time: Chop or purée for cream of mushroom soup (p. 315) or sauce.

Next time: To blanch, time carefully, allowing about 1 minute for small and 1½ to 2 minutes for large. Remove and immediately dip into cold water to stop cooking. Add mushrooms for several minutes at end of cooking period, just enough for them to impart flavor without losing texture.

POISONOUS: Even experts have trouble discerning safe varieties from poisonous. *When in doubt, do not eat.*

SHRIVELED

This time: Some flavor will be lost, but when appearance counts, peel. (Save peelings for sauce or soup.) If flavor is more important, then dip shriveled mushrooms in acidulated water, swirl around, wipe with damp cloth, dry, and chop and use for cooked mixture. If possible, poach in a little milk, butter, or white wine, or blanch in acidulated water for a minute or two.

Next time: See Discolored.

TOUGH

This time: Remove peel, slice or chop, and simmer in stew, wine, or cream sauce.

Next time: Select young, firm specimens, with closed caps; avoid long stems (more woody) and dark gills.

WATERY (EXPELS MOISTURE TO MAKE DISH WATERY)

This time: Drain, thicken. Drain off liquid; add appropriate thickener, e.g., 1 tablespoon flour to a small amount of the liquid, stir until smooth, then blend into entire sauce mixture; cook until thickened, while stirring. Then pour over ingredients and mix well. If using cornstarch or another thickening agent see *Thickeners.*

Next time: Blanch or sauté mushrooms before adding to a dish; add at very end of cooking. Sauté mushrooms quickly, stirring, in uncovered pan. Or allow for release of water if adding raw, using more flour or other thickener, or cooking longer to reduce mixture.

Substitute for fresh: Use 2½ to 3 ounces dry for 1 pound fresh. To reconstitute dry mushrooms, wash in tepid water (some need 2 or 3 waters) to remove grit and dirt. Soak in lukewarm water to cover for at least ½ hour or more until softened. Use soaking water as a liquid for cooking, since it has good flavor. If mushrooms still not softened, pour boiling water over and soak longer, or simmer.

Muskmelon—*See Melons.*

Mussels—*See Shellfish.*

Mustard—*See Spices.*

Mustard Greens—*See Greens.*

Mutton—*See Meat.*

Napoleon—*See Puff Paste; Pudding, Custard.*

Nectarine—Like their fuzzy relative the peach, nectarines will not ripen if immature when picked. Avoid very green, hard fruit; but ripe nectarines usually have a greenish tint to their red-blushed yellow skins. The juicy fruit tends to lose its delicacy in cooking, so is at its best eaten fresh and fully ripened. However, it can be substituted for peaches in cooking. For problems with discoloration, greenness, and over- or underripeness see *Peach*. Incidentally, the nectarine is not a cross between a peach and something else. It's a member of the same family, but definitely has its own identity. Like its cousins the apricot and peach, its history goes back to China. In recent years nectarines have increased greatly in popularity here. Most of our supply comes from California, where the modern variety has been developed. Its peak season is July and August, with some on the market from early summer to early fall.

Nesselrode—See *Pudding, Custard.*

Newburg—See *Cream.*

Niçoise à la—See *Salads; Sauces.*

Noisette (boneless lamb chop)—See *Meat.*

Noodles—See *Pasta.*

Nougat—See *Candy, Confectionery.*

Nuts—Nuts and berries were diet staples for early man. Many wilderness dwellers like our American Indians depended on nut nourishment for survival. Ingenious uses included grinding meal from dried kernels to make breads and puddings. Plentiful nut supplies helped to fill out the early colonists' sparse diet. Among the native American varieties they found were chestnuts, pecans, hickory, acorns, beechnuts, and black walnuts. Nuts are high in protein and fat, making them no-nos for serious weight watchers. They tend to be costly, so best values are obtained by knowing how to store and salvage them whenever possible. See also *Chestnut, Peanut,* and *Pistachio.*

BITTER

This time: Bitterness usually develops from age and overbrowning. Give shelled old (but not rancid) nuts a boiling-water bath for 2 to 3 minutes, then drain and dry, or oven-crisp. Overbrowned nuts can also develop a bitter taste, but chopped fine and used sparingly, they will add a robust taste touch to many foods, including ice-cream toppings, puddings, casseroles, and sauces.

Next time: Nuts keep best in the shell. Their natural coverings protect them from heat, humidity, light, and air—conditions that hasten rancidity. Roasting and salting also shorten their life span, as do shelling, chopping, and grinding. The more surface area exposed, the faster the nuts will deteriorate. Select nuts that don't rattle in the shell; shells should be smooth, unbroken, without holes or cracks. Generally, fresh nuts in the shell can be kept about one year at cool room temperature. Shelled and tightly wrapped or stored in closed container, they'll keep in the refrigerator several months. Fresh shelled nuts can be wrapped and frozen about a year. To prevent overbrowning or toasting, arrange blanched or unblanched nuts in shallow baking pan in 300-degree oven for 15 to 20 minutes, stirring occasionally. Remove when they look slightly underbrown, since they darken and crispen upon cooling.

CRUMBLY OR HARD TO CRACK

This time: Walnuts, pecans, and Brazil nuts crumble easily when being shelled. This usually happens when you're bent on retrieving nut halves to decorate some creation. Pour boiling water to cover the unshelled nuts and soak 5 to 15 minutes; this should make shells easier to remove. Or use coarsely chopped nuts instead of halves—no tragedy.

Next time: Soak unshelled nuts in salt water overnight, or try a boiling-water bath.

MOLDY

This time: Slight mold can be cut away, and the nuts will freshen after a 3-minute boiling-water bath. Drain, dry, and roast at 300 degrees for 10 to 15 minutes to recrisp.

Next time: See *Bitter.*

PASTY (GROUND NUTS)

This time: The recipe calls for ground or finely chopped nuts, you turn on the blender, and suddenly you have a crunchy nut butter. If this was your whole supply and the cake batter is ready to go into the oven, spread the nut paste over a shallow baking pan and heat in the oven (300 to 350 degrees) for 5 to 8 minutes, stirring frequently and watching carefully. Do not overbrown. The heat should dry out the nuts enough for cake batter.

Next time: Use a special nut grater or grinder or a food processor to turn out fluffy grated nuts. Avoid using any utensil that presses out the nut oils instead of grating.

STALE, OLD

This time: Blah-flavored nuts that have lost their crispness can be rejuvenated in a hot bath. Cover shelled nuts with boiling water and set timer for 3 minutes. Drain, dry, and use; or, if crunchier texture is desirable, roast at 300 degrees 10 to 15 minutes, stirring occasionally. Nuts may be left in a little longer to toast.

Next time: Buy according to your needs. About 1 pound nuts in shell yields about ½ pound shelled. (See *Bitter.*)

Substitutes: Unless nuts are a major ingredient, as in a nut butter or nut torte, they often can be omitted from cake, cookies and puddings. Like people, one nut can be substituted for another, but of course personalities will vary with the choice. When you want the texture chopped nuts provide in baked goods, but your supply has run out, toasted rolled oats or coarse bran make crunchy substitutions.

Oats—*See Cereal.*

Oatmeal—*See Cereal.*

Octopus—*See Seafood.*

Odors—See individual foods.

Oil—*See Fat.*

Okra (gumbo)—Called gumbo because it's used to give substance to the Creole stews of the same name. The interior substance of the slender pod becomes gelatinous when cooked, making it a natural thickener for soups, stews, and saucy dishes. Okra is also good steamed, fried or pickled in salads.

DISCOLORED

This time: Darkening on raw okra is an indication of age, so use now. Try a tomato sauce base with other compatible ingredients, such as a chicken gumbo or vegetable stew with eggplant, onion, and chopped tomato. Olive-green cooked okra may have turned from an acid solution (lemon juice or vinegar, or very acidic tomatoes), or it may be overcooked (you can tell by the soft, gooey texture). Camouflage color by combining okra with other ingredients in a tomato-sauce base.

Next time: Select firm, crisp pods that snap readily and have no hard seeds. Store loosely wrapped in refrigerator up to 5 days. To cook, barely cover with boiling salted water and simmer 10 to 12 minutes, or until just tender. Or steam until just tender. Overcooking will cause okra to disintegrate and become very gummy. In gumbos or stews, where the thickening effect is desired, cook it longer, according to recipe directions. Add acidic ingredients toward end of cooking.

GUMMY, OVERCOOKED

This time: Use in gumbo or stew.
Next time: See *Discolored.*

OLD, SHRIVELED

This time: Use in soup or stew. Avoid pickling and using for salads.
Next time: See *Discolored.*

Olives—These small, hard-stoned fruits of one of the oldest trees are picked at various stages of ripeness—the riper containing more oil. They are processed numerous ways, frequently soaked in lye and then in brine. To remove excess salt from olives, soak briefly in clear, cool water, or use in a cooked dish without adding more salt. When a large quantity of olives must be pitted, arrange them over a large piece of wax paper and roll them firmly but gently with a rolling pin. This loosens the pits and gentle squeezing usually does the trick.

Omelet—The French omelet whisks whole eggs together. It is folded before serving, and can be filled with various meats, cheeses or vegetables. Or flavorful ingredients might be incorporated into the eggs. The finished product is browned outside and runny inside. The puffy version gets its name from the stiffly beaten egg whites folded into beaten yolks; it becomes fluffy and firm when cooked and also is folded before serving. As with all egg cookery, a proper result depends upon careful timing and temperature control.

OVERBROWNED, OVERCOOKED

This time: Top a slightly overcooked omelet with a sauce to moisturize and to disguise an overbrowned appearance. When the omelet has become quite firm and dark from long cooking or high heat, lightly brown the other side and chill for appetizers, served warm or cold in wedges, like the *tortilla de patata a la Española* (Spanish potato omelet). This delectable hors d'oeuvre, which includes potato, onion, and ham and is browned on both sides in olive oil, was served to me many times in Spain with olives, almonds, and sherry. A very dark outer crust on an omelet can be peeled off with the tip of a paring knife if necessary. Then cover top with a light coating of mayonnaise or another sauce before cutting. Another use for overcooked omelet is egg salad; chop with onion, celery, and pimiento, then coat well with mayonnaise.

Next time: Give an omelet your full attention when it goes into the sizzling pan. The edges should set first. Using a fork or spatula, pull the thickened mixture at edges toward center, then lift in several places to allow uncooked portions to flow underneath. Tilt pan to help distribute mixture. As soon as omelet is set but surface is still moist, increase heat to quickly brown bottom.

STICKING, BREAKING

This time: Drizzle a little oil or butter around the edges of hot pan, gently lifting omelet with a wide spatula to allow fat to flow under. With careful prodding, a wide spatula may ease up the stubborn omelet in one piece. If it falls apart, trim edges of break and serve with parsley covering any ragged edges. Or smother with sauce or sautéed vegetables (green pepper, onion, and mushrooms are good choices). Crumbles can be tossed with sautéed chopped vegetables and served as scrambled eggs. Or chop for egg salad (*see Overbrowned*).

Next time: Use well-buttered, seasoned omelet pan or skillet with sloping sides for easy turning. Nonstick surfaces should be cared for according to manufacturer's directions. To season regular pans to prevent sticking, scour well, fill with cooking oil to within an inch from top. Heat slowly until threads of oil move about. Turn off heat and allow to cool completely. Oil may be saved for reuse. Wipe pan with paper toweling. Try to reserve pan for egg cookery. Do not wash after using; merely wipe with paper towel, adding salt and rubbing if necessary for cleaning.

Onion—From soup to tart to stuffed onions, the bulb shows its versatility. Pungency varies greatly—those grown in warmer, sunnier climates are sweeter and milder. The sweeter onions actually sweeten a cooked dish, and caramelize when browned.

DISCOLORED

This time: Trim darkened spots and use soon in a cooked dish, or cook and store in refrigerator a day or two. If greenish-brown, cooked onions may have discolored from iron pan. If simmered in liquid, add a bit of lemon juice or vinegar to bleach onion. If over-browned, incorporate in a rich onion soup with brown stock.

Next time: Select firm, hard onions with crackly-crisp skins and small necks. Avoid those with soft spots and blemishes, or any that have begun to sprout. Store in a cool, dry, airy place—up to 1 month at room temperature. Once cut, cover surface with plastic wrap and refrigerate. In cooking, add a bit of acid, such as lemon juice, to the liquid to preserve whiteness. Avoid using a cast-iron pan, and do not overcook. Chopped onion will cook to tenderness in just a few minutes. When sautéing, or lightly browning, use medium-low heat; onions darken quickly over high heat. Stir frequently. To bake onions, parboil first 5 to 10 minutes, then stuff and bake in 375-degree oven 30 to 40 minutes, depending on size.

FRIED RINGS (BATTER WON'T STICK)

This time: Chop or crumble and use as casserole topping.

Next time: Peel 2 large white onions, slice ¼-inch thick, soak in equal parts milk and water for about 1 hour. Drain and dry. Dip into batter (⅔ cup flour, 1 egg yolk, 1½ teaspoons oil, and about ⅓ cup flat beer or other liquid). The batter should ripen, covered, at least a couple of hours in refrigerator. Fry in hot deep fat, about 370 degrees, until golden-brown. Drain on paper toweling.

FRIED RINGS (OILY)

This time: Press out excess oil. In doing so, shape will be altered considerably, so incorporate in casserole, or chop and use as casserole topping.

Next time: Follow frying directions above, making certain oil is hot enough. Do not crowd pan; too many rings at one time will lower oil temperature.

OVERCOOKED

This time: Mushy onions can be incorporated in cooked, saucy dishes, where their presence will be valued more for flavor than texture. Purée and use in cream of vegetable soup (p. 315).
Next time: See *Discolored.*

MUSHY, SPONGY

This time: This problem indicates age. Cut away any soft spots and use rest as usual. If most of the onion has become rather soft, rinse off well, dip quickly in ice water, and cook, then purée.
Next time: See *Discolored.*

PEEL (DIFFICULT TO): If onion is to be chopped or sliced into strips, cut in half, then peel. It's easier than peeling a whole onion. Or drop into boiling water for a short time, then into cold water before peeling.

SMELLY

This time: If onion is extremely pungent, simmer cloves in a bit of vinegar to remove odors. To remove from breath, eat fresh parsley. To remove from hands, rub skin with lemon juice, salt, or vinegar.
Next time: Chill onion first. When the volatile oil is cold, it is not as odorous.

SPROUTING: See *Mushy.*

TEARS: See *Smelly.*

Onions (Green)—(Includes scallions, leeks), also known as spring onions. These are onions that are harvested young, when tops are still green. Leeks have flatter, thicker leaves than scallions. In the same green onion category are shallots, with clusters of bulbs similar to garlic cloves, and chives.

OVERCOOKED

This time: If overbrowned, chop fine and use in soup, stew, or sauce with brown stock base. Green onions that have been overcooked in liquid tend to be mushy, so use them in casseroles or other saucy dish where the texture doesn't matter much. Or purée along with other cooked onions and some thickened stock for an onion sauce over meats; or add to other puréed vegetables for a soup (see *cream of vegetable soup*, p. 315).

Next time: Sauté green onions quickly over medium heat, stirring, until soft but not browned. To cook whole green onions, simmer in small amount of boiling salted water for about 3 minutes. Drain and season.

WILTED

This time: You can replant wilted green onions in a flower pot or your garden. They'll take root and revive. Or trim off badly wilted green parts, and peel outer skin of white section. Then chop and use.

Next time: Select green onions with firm, white bulbs and fresh green tops. Avoid shriveled, soft, or yellowed leaves. Store in plastic wrap in hydrator of refrigerator and try to use within 3 days.

Orange—Juice of this citrus fruit has gained the reputation as the American eye-opener, but it's better to eat rather than drink the orange. For about the same amount of calories, you know that you've eaten something and gotten important dietary fiber. The rind is edible too. Instead of adding to your garbage, grate skin and freeze so you can add a spoonful now and then to spark up the flavor of some dish. Or cut into strips, and candy. There are few problems surrounding this golden apple, since they usually are in good condition at groceries and store well.

DRY

This time: Occasionally you cut into an orange and discover it to be pithy and lacking juiciness. There's nothing to do but use it for cooking in a saucy dish or marinate pieces in fruit juice flavored with liqueur, rum, or brandy.

Next time: Select oranges that are heavy for their size, indicating good juice content. Avoid fruit that looks puffy, spongy, shriveled, or withered; dryness indicates age.

GREEN: No problem. Green can be as ripe as orange or yellow. In fact, sometimes regreening occurs in fruit picked when golden ripe. California fruit is natural colored, while the Florida industry sometimes adds orange color. All fruit is required by law to be picked mature, depending on sugar, acid, and other indicators besides color.

HARD TO PEEL

This time: Place in boiling water for a few minutes to loosen peel. Oranges can be soaked, then refrigerated until ready to peel.

Next time: Select oranges of the loose-skin eating varieties, such as navels and Valencias.

OVERRIPE

This time: Use immediately. If soft and over the hill in flavor, marinate in liqueur or cook into a sauce with seasonings. Orange is adaptable from appetizer to main course, salad, or dessert. At the moment of writing this, I'm sipping orange cappucino. For a great soup, hot or cold, combine orange juice and rind with white wine and lemon juice slightly sweetened, spiced with cinnamon and thickened with cornstarch.

Next time: Choose firm, heavy fruit with fine-textured peel. Color is not a factor, since green or russeted are as ripe as orange. Can be stored at room temperature for a couple of days, or will keep for a month or more in the refrigerator or cool, airy, dry place.

Overbrowned—See individual foods.

Overcooked—See individual foods.

Overripe—See specific item.

Overseasoned—See *Herbs; Too Salty; Spices.*

Oxtail—See *Meat; Soup.*

Oyster—See *Shellfish.*

Oyster Plant—See *Salsify.*

Pancakes—A weekend morning can easily be ruined when you must struggle with difficult griddlecakes for the family. This information should help prevent your pancake problems from stacking up too high.

HEAVY, TOUGH

This time: The tough exterior on a pancake can be softened by steam, so one remedy is to place on rack in covered steamer until softened. Or sprinkle with fruit juice and wrap in foil before reheating in oven. Pancakes too tough for eating the conventional way can be turned into a successful bread pudding, especially with lots of custard and fruit. A quicker dessert is too break or cut up the disasters, soak in fruit sauce, and top with fresh fruit.

Next time: Frequent turning and overcooking cause a tough crust. Never turn pancakes more than once, and flip only after holes appear on the surface. Cook on griddle just until golden.

STICKING TO PAN

This time: One or two stuck cakes can be taste-testers. But when half the batch has stuck and fallen apart, that's the time to change your serving plans. Layer bite-size pieces in dessert dishes with jam and fresh fruits, perhaps with a drizzle of liqueur or fruit juice. Or mix pieces with syrup and melted butter; top with fruit. Quite an inventive brunch item! Pancake fragments also can be used for bread pudding or sautéed with a sweet sauce and quartered bananas.

Next time: Griddle may need reseasoning, or oil pan and heat to proper temperature before adding batter. At the correct temperature, a drop of water will bounce around. If it disappears, griddle (or pan) is too hot. If water drop flattens out and sizzles, griddle is not hot enough.

TOO THICK (BATTER)

This time: A little milk, water, fruit juice, or another compatible liquid will thin down a thick batter. Add gradually!

Next time: Use less flour or other thickener. Allow for batter to thicken as it ripens (waits to be cooked). Reserve some of the flour and add it as needed later.

TOO THIN (BATTER)

This time: Allow batter to ripen for about ½ hour. If still too thin, a little more flour, corn meal, oatmeal, or other thickener will help get the batter to a working consistency.

Next time: Compare recipes, selecting one with a slightly higher proportion of dry ingredients to liquid. Or adjust the recipe to use less liquid, and allow enough time for ripening. Make sure any fruits added are well drained.

Papaya (also pawpaw, not to be confused with the North American pawpaw)—Papaya spread quickly from either its native Mexico or the West Indies to other tropical lands. Most of America's supply comes from Hawaii and Florida (larger) or, to a lesser extent, from Mexico and Texas. It may come as a surprise to those familiar with the 1- or 2-pound fruits that they also grow as big as 20 pounds. The plant contains an enzyme, papain, which breaks down protein. Dried papain is an ingredient in commercial meat tenderizers and is used as a digestant. Even juice, seeds, and leaves are capable of transforming tough meat into a tender pièce de résistance.

DISCOLORED

This time: If more darkening has occurred than you can trim away, soak in rum or brandy, cut up and cook with other fruits or in a spicy poultry or seafood dish. Mash or purée and use for mousse, soufflé, pudding, dessert sauce, or tropical rum drink.

Next time: Select firm but resilient ripe fruit with yellow-orange skin and nice aroma. Avoid specimens with soft, dark spots. Store fully ripened fruit in refrigerator up to 2 to 3 days. When using only a part of the fruit, rub lemon juice over cut surface of remainder and tightly cover in plastic wrap before refrigerating.

GREEN

This time: Let green fruit ripen at room temperature; refrigerate when ripe. Fullest palatability comes from fully ripe fruit, but when short of time, underripe fruit also can be good baked, basted with fruit juice and margarine; or peel and boil, then slice or chop for piquantly dressed tossed salad. Preserve puréed cooked pulp in jam or conserve, or chop and cook with raisins and spices for chutney, or pickle.

Next time: Avoid green, hard fruit. (See *Discolored.*)

SOUR

This time: Lime juice, sweetened to taste with honey, does wonders for sour papaya. Poach slices in wine and glaze with guava or quince jelly. When there's at least an hour before serving time, combine papaya chunks with chopped figs, pineapple chunks, berries, orange segments, lime juice, honey, and rum. Vary fruits and liquor to taste.

Next time: One insurance is tasting before buying. Another is to select only fully ripened fruit. (See *Discolored.*)

UNDERRIPE: See *Green.*

Parfait—See *Ice Cream.*

Parsley—Bunches of parsley sprigs are part of a bouquet garni, and the minced leaves are an ingredient in fines herbes—a delicate blend of fresh herbs used to season cheese and egg dishes and savory sauces. Chopped, parsley delicately flavors many foods, from soups and meats to stuffings and salads. It is good fried, and can be dried or frozen for future use. Curly leaf is the most common type found, but some markets sell the more flavorful flat-leaf or plain-leaf variety. Very high in vitamins A and C.

DISCOLORED

This time: Yellowed parsley indicates aging. Chop or mince and use immediately in a dish where its appearance won't matter much.

Next time: Select fresh, bright green sprigs with an aroma that can be sniffed from arm's length. If you must put your nose to it for a mere faint smell, forget it for flavoring. If still fresh-looking, however, it might be used for garnishing. No matter how fresh, it wilts quickly if not stored properly. By far the best way to keep a bouquet lively for weeks is to refrigerate with stems in a jar of water. Cover top with plastic wrap; secure with rubber band. It has amazed me to discover how healthy parsley has remained during even a two-week absence.

FROSTBITE

This time: Parsley leaves sometimes freeze accidentally in a cold part of the refrigerator. When that happens, chop coarsely and pack into freezer containers, leaving ½ inch headspace and freeze. Use for cooked dishes only. You can intentionally freeze parsley following these directions, but best to choose fresh leaves.

Next time: Store in warmer part of refrigerator.

WILTED

This time: Parsley often revives by storing with stems in water. If past restoring, however, chop or mince and use at once.
Next time: See *Discolored*.

Parsnip—Our early New England settlers believed that parsnips were poisonous until after freezing, which may explain why they are not as popular in this country as they are in France or England. For ages these edible roots were food for the poor of Northern Europe. The roots are completely underground and can survive throughout a winter. In fact, their flavor depends on frost, as the cold weather changes the starch to sugar. Used here primarily to flavor soups and stews, parsnips are delicious braised, creamed, or fried, alone or with potatoes.

DISCOLORED

This time: If raw, may be an indication of freezing. Cook in water with some lemon juice or cream of tartar and serve with a sauce to disguise the off-color. Brown spots usually indicate decay, which must be cut out. When cooked, the discoloration may be a sign of overcooking (especially high heat), or of alkaline mixture or iron. Cook in water to cover with about 2 teaspoons lemon juice or 1 teaspoon cream of tartar per quart. This should have a bleaching effect. If still not white enough incorporate the parsnips into a stew or soup, or serve with a sauce so color is not so evident. Or mash, along with potatoes if desired, and sprinkle with chives, parsley, paprika, or cheese.
Next time: Select small to medium-size, firm parsnips that are clean and smooth. Avoid soft, shriveled, discolored roots. Large ones tend to be woody. Cook in water to cover with acid added, about 2 teaspoons per quart, and do not overcook. Allow about 15 to 20 minutes for whole; less time for pieces.

MUSHY, OVERCOOKED

This time: Mash with butter or sour cream and herbs—good blended with potatoes. Or purée and use for cream of parsnip soup (*see cream of vegetable soup*, p. 315).
Next time: See *Discolored*.

SOFT, PITHY

This time: See *Mushy.*
Next time: Choose firm parsnips (see *Discolored*).

TOUGH, WOODY

This time: Cook longer to tenderize. Mash or purée for numerous treatments (see *Mushy*).
Next time: Avoid large parsnips (see *Discolored*).

Partridge—*See Poultry, Game Birds.*

Pasta—With my first buttery mouthful of fettuccine Alfredo at the famous namesake restaurant in Rome I became a devotee. Newly made melt-in-the-mouth pasta strands were gently turned with sweet butter (fresh from the owner's nearby farm) and fluffy grated Parmesan, then sprinkled with minced parsley. It was almost impossible to stop eating this delicious first course (Italians usually have pasta before the main course). The success secret of this very simple dish is freshness; hours-old pasta, and the freshest butter, fresh aged cheese, and parsley. Make the same recipe with older ingredients and it's no longer memorable.

More than 100 pasta varieties exist in Italy, and specialty shops here carry many sizes and shapes. Whatever type you choose, it is important to know quality and to cook it al dente. Pasta is produced from semolina (or hard wheat), the best of which is durum macaroni wheat, which here is grown mainly in Minnesota, South Dakota, and Montana. This wheat is required as the basic ingredient for some European pasta and is the standard of quality in the United States. A 100-percent durum product retains firm texture, taste, and a golden color after cooking. Because of the current homemade-pasta craze, certain problems involving the making of it have become common. See *Pasta Dough.*

BROWNED (ACCIDENTALLY)

This time: Make noodle pudding or fry. Find a good recipe for a Jewish kugel; some blend raisins and sweetened cheese or fruit in the baked noodle dish. Or season pasta and fry until completely browned.
Next time: Hot pasta in a covered heavy pan will retain heat for

about 10 minutes or longer in a warm oven. When holding cooked pasta, coat with oil or butter. When reheating, use low burner and stir well.

CLUMPING, STICKING

This time: Transfer pasta to colander and pour boiling water over. Drain and lightly coat with oil or butter. Return to pot to keep warm until serving. If the larger pasta shapes break apart when separating, combine in a casserole with vegetables and a sauce and it won't matter. Or chop pasta and use in soup.

Next time: The addition of 1 or 2 teaspoons of oil to the boiling water helps prevent sticking.

OVERCOOKED

This time: Even mushy pasta can be salvaged in a casserole. When using for a noodle pudding, bake long enough to develop a crisp golden-brown topping. Another remedy is to coat soft strands gently with buttered crumbs and perhaps some grated Parmesan, then brown lightly in butter until they gain substance.

Next time: To cook pasta properly, boil 2 to 3 quarts water for each ½ lb. pasta; when it comes to a full boil, add about 1 tbsp. salt and a little oil. Add pasta all at once to rapidly boiling water. Cover to return to boil, uncover, and stir occasionally, checking carefully until pasta is al dente—firm-tender. The time varies with the size, but start testing after the third minute for tiny shapes, a minute or so later for larger sizes. When done, immediately remove from heat and drain in colander, shaking to remove excess moisture. Just as quickly, sauce the pasta and serve.

TOUGH

This time: Further cooking in boiling water or in a soup or casserole should help soften the texture.

Next time: Be sure to measure salted boiling water accurately for the amount of pasta cooked (see *Overcooked*). Hardness could result if there's not enough boiling water or if it doesn't boil rapidly. The problem also can be related to the quality pasta. Fresh, good-quality pasta is resilient; a bunch of spaghetti springs back and forth. It should have a yellowish-ivory color (except for green spinach pasta). Avoid brittle pasta with a grayish tone.

UNDERCOOKED, UNEVENLY COOKED

This time: Return to boiling water and keep testing until done. Pasta intended for further cooking in casseroles and other baked dishes should be slightly undercooked.

Next time: Bring water to a full rolling boil and add pasta all at once without disturbing vigorous boil.

To cook in advance: Stop cooking just before the pasta is al dente; keeping pasta warm or reheating cooks it further. When holding cooked pasta, keep moist with butter, oil, milk, bouillon, or tomato or another sauce. For a 10-minute-delay, pasta will keep nicely if buttered or oiled right in the cooking pan. To keep warm up to ½ hour, or to reheat, place buttered (or oiled) pasta in covered casserole or ovenproof pot in warm oven. Serve with a hot sauce.

Equivalents: Allow 2 ounces uncooked pasta per first-course serving; 4 ounces for each generous main-dish serving.

Leftovers: Add enough oil or butter to coat each piece of pasta, then store covered in refrigerator. Make macaroni salad with smaller shapes; larger sizes may be chopped and used in soups or seasoned and fried. Almost any size can be cut for a casserole; noodles can be paired with compatible vegetable-meat-sauce trio. Try thicker pasta with heartier ingredients, such as bits of roast beef, broccoli and a piquant blue-cheese sauce; blend the more delicate pasta with lighter fare, like chicken, peas and a light mushroom sauce.

Pasta Dough

STICKY (on hands and board during kneading)

This time: Add flour; keep kneading until the dough is firm.
Next time: Add less moisture during the initial mixing process.

TOUGH TO HANDLE (KNEAD)

This time: Add a tablespoon of water and knead for 5 minutes more. Continue adding water as needed.
Next time: Double-check quantities of flour, eggs, oil, and water. The consistency of the dough should be similar to firm Play-Doh. Getting the right feel of it is important. Add sufficient moisture at the initial kneading stage.

LUMPY

This time: Knead, knead, knead. Continue until smooth.
Next time: Allow at least 10 minutes of good firm muscle power
for ample kneading.

STICKS TO ROLLING PIN OR MACHINE (when forming)

This time: Let dough surface dry to touch, about 10 minutes. If
still too sticky, dust with extra flour.
Next time: Use less moisture or more flour in the recipe. Avoid
pasta making on hot, humid days. A dry day will bring better results.

DIFFICULT TO PIN

This time: Allow the dough to rest in a cool place for 15 minutes
longer and pin again.
Next time: After kneading all doughs, it is necessary to allow the
gluten strands to soften (relax). This is accomplished by placing the
covered dough in the refrigerator for a short time. The elasticity
(toughness) is thus reduced and permits easier pinning to take
place.

UNEVEN THICKNESS

This time: Apply even pressure to the rolling pin. The technique
becomes easier with practice.
Next time: Use a larger and heavier rolling pin.

Paste—*See Pâte à choux; Puff Paste; Tomato.*

Pastrami—*See Meat.*

Pastry—*See* individual types.

Pâte à choux (pouf paste)—Much easier to prepare than its
puff-paste relative, but also dramatic in its own right. It is the basis
for cream puffs, which become building blocks for the spectacular
towering croquembouche with a mortar of caramelized sugar. The
eggy dough is formed with a spoon or piped through a pastry tube
into various shapes, such as the elongated éclair, round tiny cream
puffs, profiteroles, and the graceful swans that hold fluffy sweet
creams.

COLLAPSES

This time: Serve filled halves garnished decoratively and your pride need not fall with your puffs. If badly misshapen, chop puffs and float on light soups or sprinkle over ice cream with a sauce.

Next time: Bake in preheated 400- to 425-degree oven for about 20 minutes, then reduce heat to 375 degrees and bake another 10 minutes or so for large puffs. Reducing oven temperature too soon will cause steam to escape and collapse the puffs. Puffs should be hard before leaving the oven.

FLAT, DIDN'T RISE FULLY

This time: Slice into halves, remove soggy centers, and fill shells with a selected mixture. Serve in dishes with sauce poured over instead of in the usual cream-puff style.

Next time: Check recipe; perhaps more egg is needed. Be careful not to overcook or overmix dough once it becomes smooth and forms a ball, leaving the sides of the pan during cooking. Continue to cook and stir another minute. At this point remove from heat, let rest, then vigorously beat in each room-temperature egg one at a time. Use dough at once as soon as it holds its shape when scooped at the end of a spoon. Sprinkle puffs lightly with glaze or water to make the shells crisp. Bake in preheated hot oven until firm to the touch.

HARD (PASTE)

This time: If the paste is too firm to spoon or pipe, mix in more egg until it holds its shape but is still spoonable. Remember, the more egg the better the puffing during baking.

Next time: Check recipe proportions; have extra ingredients on hand if necessary to correct paste consistency.

SOGGY CENTERS

This time: Cut off the top third, scoop out moist centers, and fill shells. Roll the soggy interiors into 1-inch balls with confectioners sugar and bake in 400-degree oven about 5 to 8 minutes for a sweet little snack.

Next time: Unbleached all-purpose flour is best. Don't use soft flours. Sogginess may also be caused by excess liquid in recipe. Be sure to start the baking in a preheated 400- to 425-degree oven. Pierce sides of pastries with point of small, sharp knife. Turn off oven and leave small shells in 10 additional minutes, larger ones 15 to 20. This method allows inside steam to evaporate and helps prevent sogginess. This is best done right after baking, although shell interiors can be dried later in a low oven.

SOFT (PASTE)

This time: Place soft dough without eggs over very hot (not boiling) water in a double boiler for several minutes, stirring continuously until dough stiffens and leaves sides of pan. This condition is caused by undercooking and undermixing. When it is the result of too much egg, it is risky to return to heat. Do so only in the top part of a double boiler over hot water; stir constantly and watch very carefully. Remove as soon as dough is thick and solid enough to hold its shape. Generally it's best not to return dough to heat once eggs have been added. A wet spoon or pastry bag makes dough easier to handle. Or make another small but stiff dough, adding soft dough to it.

Next time: Assuming a reliable recipe, follow directions carefully when mixing and cooking ingredients. Add lukewarm eggs only after dough leaves sides of pan in a ball. Correct choux paste is solid enough to hold its shape; check consistency before adding last two eggs. Or make proper adjustments, such as using medium rather than large eggs.

Pâté—A spread or paste made of fish, fowl or meat, sometimes enclosed in a crust. Liver pâtés are among the most popular.

Pâté en croute—Pâté in crust is a general term for any number of pâté mixtures wrapped in a pastry or bread crust, baked, then often chilled and sliced. Some of the best anywhere are prepared at the incomparable Le Français Restaurant in Wheeling, Illinois. Owner–chef Jean Banchet, a mischievous Burgundian, is revered as a genius innovator by gourmets and experts in French cuisine. His restaurant has been called the best French dining spot in the country. Below, Jean shares his secrets for preventing sogginess—the most common problem—in the crust around pâtés.

SOGGY

If the "en croute" has become hopelessly soggy, discard and rewrap pâté in fresh pâte (paste), or pastry dough. Jean uses a *pâte brisée* (short paste) with egg, a dough made of all-purpose flour, butter, whole egg, and water. Roll it ½-inch thick, wrap it around the pâté, glaze with egg yolk and water wash. Bake in preheated 475-degree oven about 25 minutes, until dough is slightly browned. Reduce oven to 400 degrees and bake until browned and dough is dry when pierced with cake tester. Dough should be thoroughly cooked. Chill thoroughly for easier slicing. If no time, serve hot.

Peach—Like its smaller relatives, the apricot and nectarine, the peach originated in China; it then moved on to Persia and supposedly was the fruit referred to as Persian apple. It's doubtful that any other country has as large a repertory of peach dishes as the Persians; together with lemon and spices, this succulent fruit enhances meat and fowl. After apples and oranges, peaches are the most important U.S. fruit crop. Our country produces about 50 percent of the world's supply. Georgia, the peach state, grows the famous Elberta, one of the most popular of the yellow-fleshed freestone varieties. This and other freestones are grown for eating; the clingstones go into cans.

DISCOLORED

This time: If you want to use peaches raw, trim away darkened area, then spread with cream cheese or use in fruit mélange. Great with raspberries, salad or rum pot (p. 337). Broiling halves filled with cranberries and brown sugar covers discoloration. Or cook slices for compote. When sliced or chopped peaches have darkened, mash or purée for milkshakes, cooked meat, or poultry dishes or a dessert, such as soufflé or pudding, which incorporates other ingredients that will blend with the discolored peaches.

Next time: Select firm, fresh fruit with a red blush on yellow, free of soft, dark spots. Fruit should yield to gentle pressure. Do not buy green peaches which will never ripen properly—they just shrivel. Keep at room temperature until soft enough for your purposes, then refrigerate. Chilled, they will keep from several days to two weeks, depending on freshness. Once fruit has been cut, rub surface lightly with lemon or other citrus juice and store tightly covered with plastic wrap. Sliced fruit keeps best in syrup, acidulated fruit juice, or a thickened sauce in covered container.

GREEN, IMMATURE

This time: Store at room temperature a few days to soften slightly. Hard green fruit can be cooked to softness, then combined with spicy ingredients to help develop flavor; good uses are chutneys and curried sauces for meats and poultry. To hasten cooking, chop or mash fruit. Good pickled, too.

Next time: Steer away from green peaches—even those showing some greenish tinge. They're unsatisfactory and will shrivel instead of ripening.

HARD TO PEEL

Drop into boiling water for a minute, rinse in cold water, and the skin should slip off easily.

OVERRIPE

This time: Fruit that is too soft for slicing or eating can be crushed for jelly, baby food (plain or combined with other fruit), cereal, or sauce (for poultry or sweetened for puddings and cakes). Add to ice cream, thicken for cheesecake glaze, or add to tapioca or rice puddings, parfaits or shakes. Especially delightful paired with strawberries or raspberries.

Next time: Choose peaches that are firm but yield to gentle pressure. Overmature fruit is very soft, bruises readily, and must be used immediately. Refrigerate fruit as soon as it is ripe.

UNDERRIPE

This time: Poach slightly underripe peaches whole in wine or syrup flavored with spices and liqueur. Firm fruit needs more cooking than ripe fruit to soften. Tenderize sliced peaches by simmering in syrup, then combine with other riper fruits that require less cooking. Sliced firm-ripe peaches are used in the classic peach Melba. Crushed or puréed fruit can be cooked and thickened for poultry or dessert sauces.

Next time: Select fruit that yields to gentle pressure (see *Discolored*).

Peanut—A legume, like the pea and bean, but treated like a nut rather than a vegetable. Its alternate names groundnut and ground pea come from the plant's ostrichlike peculiarity, after flowering, of burying its stalks several inches into the earth, where the brown pods mature. Peanuts grow either on bushes or on extended low-lying runners. The maturation process is the same for both. Peanut traces were discovered in tombs of ancient Peruvians, so the legume is believed to have sunk original roots in South America. Later, peanuts were cultivated by the Aztecs and Mayas. Exploring Spaniards introduced them to their motherland and Africa, where the legumes were called *nguba*—hence the southern term, goober. The peanut returned to colonial America with the 17th-century slave trade. But rather than food for people, it became pig fodder and responsible for the good taste of the famous Virginia hams.

In 1896, George Washington Carver first used peanut production to restore the depleted soil at Tuskeegee, Alabama raising the agricultural South from a suffering one-crop cotton region to a thriving area of crop diversification. The domestic peanut industry was born. Packed with protein, iron, minerals and calories, the peanut is a powerhouse of nutrition for just pennies. Recent soaring prices are considered temporary. May this vegetable snack jump out of the nut bowl and peanut-butter jar to enrich more of our foods.

Since the smaller, milder Spanish peanut is used almost exclusively for peanut butter, the following material refers to the large Virginia type.

TOO BROWNED

This time: Chopped slightly overbrowned peanuts add a robust crunchy topping to ice cream sundaes and casseroles. Use darker ones in small quantities for concentrated roast-peanut taste to meat loaf, and after cooking, to stews and Oriental stir-fry dishes.

Next time: Toast shelled peanuts in flat pan in 325- to 350-degree oven, stirring occasionally, about 15 to 20 minutes. They tend to get crisper and darken upon cooling. When browning in a skillet, stir frequently to prevent overbrowning.

SOGGY

This time: Restore crispness to soggy peanuts by heating a few minutes in moderate oven. If light color need not be preserved, brown peanuts following roasting directions above. Allow less time for peanuts already roasted. Or use soft nuts in creamy goober soup (p. 316) or for baking.

Next time: Select nuts with clean, uncracked shells and that do not rattle. Store in tightly covered container in refrigerator. Shelled keep well about 3 months, unshelled about 9. Freezing is an even better method of preserving their freshness. High humidity turns them soggy.

STALE

This time: Flat-tasting, chewy peanuts can be revitalized by heating, in the shell or out. Spread them on baking pan and place in 325-degree oven, a few minutes to enliven or 15 to 20 minutes to roast. Browning brings out the flavor, so shell and stir occasionally while roasting until desired browning is almost achieved; they darken and crispen upon cooling. Very rancid nuts can't be salvaged. But slightly rancid nuts benefit from a 3-minute boiling-water bath; then drain, dry, and oven-crisp for renewed quality.

Next time: For longer storage, buy unsalted, unroasted peanuts in the shell. Store in refrigerator or freezer.

Peanut Butter—Whatever would we do without the popular nutty spread? Addicts owe their gratitude to a St. Louis doctor who in 1890 first ground roasted peanuts in his search for a high-protein, easily digestible food for some of his patients. Little did he know the delicious ramifications of his experiment. Today peanut butter is big sticky business sold in jars and incorporated into cookies, cakes, and candy. When grinding your own peanut butter, remember Spanish peanuts make the best.

SEPARATED

This time: When oil parts company with the peanuts, stir the two back together, then store in refrigerator. Cold prevents separation.

Next time: If the separation bothers you, buy homogenized commercial brands. True connoisseurs, however, insist on the nonhomogenized type, and enjoy the stirring as a kind of ritual preceding the tasting.

STALE

This time: Heat briefly in low oven. Allow to cool before using for sandwiches, or use for dips and cooked dishes, such as African stews or a spicy Indonesian sauce. (See *creamy goober soup*, p. 316.)

Next time: Keep peanut butter tightly closed in a cool, dry place, or in refrigerator for long periods of time and during hot spells.

TOO THICK

Add small amount of peanut or other oil, softened margarine, warm water—or for slightly altered flavor, orange juice or syrup.

Pear—One of the few fruits that should be ripened after picking. Removed from the tree when hard but mature and stored in a cool, humid place, the fruit develops in flavor and texture. The pear season spans almost the entire year, with off months usually from May to July, when the Bartletts begin. Winter varieties—Comice, Anjou, and Bosc—are available from October to May. The tree grows in temperate climates all around the globe. Most varieties in this country come from the European pear or are hybrids of that and the China pear. The fruit was eaten by ancient Greeks and Romans. Today, France is the leading country in pear cultivation.

BLAND

This time: Flavorless pears will soak up the flavor of liqueur or liquor; for extra pear taste, pour over some Poire William or another pear alcohol. An hour in the bath should do it. When there's more time, poach pears gently in slightly sweet wine or fruit juice with spices. Serve warm or cold. A quick remedy is to toss chunks or slices of the fruit into a salad, perhaps along with apple chunks and nuts. If there's time, let the fruit absorb a bit of the dressing before serving.

Next time: Difficult to gauge flavor by looking, but full flavor develops only when pears are allowed to ripen completely. Select firm, not hard, fruit. Store in cool, slightly humid place until fully ripe, and yields to gentle pressure. Anjou remains green when ripe, Bartlett turns yellow. Refrigerate ripe pears and use within several days to 2 weeks, depending on stage of ripeness.

DISCOLORED

This time: Darkened pear may be trimmed of discolored areas and cooked with other ingredients, such as in a casserole or in a sauce for poultry or meat.

Next time: Rub cut surfaces with lemon or other citrus juice, cover with plastic wrap, and store in refrigerator.

OVERRIPE

This time: Peeled, puréed, and spiced, soft pears add delicious substance to gelatins and puddings. Or cook them with sugar, water, lemon juice, rind, and spices for a delicious sauce over warm pudding or spice cake. Pair pears with apples, rhubarb, cranberries, or other fruits for pie fillings, custards, puddings, and sauces. Pears are also compatible with some vegetables (have you tried them with spinach or kale?), poultry, and seafood.

Next time: Be sure to refrigerate pears that have fully ripened. Avoid selecting fruit that is shriveled or has soft spots.

UNDERRIPE

This time: Continue storing at room temperature in a fairly cool, humid atmosphere until fully ripe. If underripe pears have been refrigerated, though, they'll never ripen properly. Best thing to do is cook into a sauce or use in baking. Poach in spicy juice (such as leftover spiced-pear liquid) or light syrup and use as poultry or meat accompaniment, or cook slices or chunks along with other fruits in a sauce or meat or pilaf.

Next time: Allow very firm fruit to ripen at room temperature before refrigerating. Select fruit that yields to slight pressure.

Peas (fresh)—The green garden pea is the most common. The tender snow or sugar pea, naturally packaged in its soft edible pod, is a familiar Chinese cuisine ingredient. And the newest addition, the sugarsnap pea, is my favorite. It's the sweetest and most tender—I love it raw. Peas were an important part of the central European diet by the time our first settlers brought the seeds with them to America. There's no comparison between the sweet taste of fresh and the processed.

DISCOLORED

This time: Mash or purée for vegetable timbales (p. 333), or cream of vegetable soup (p. 315). Or mash with butter, cream, and seasonings and top with minced parsley or cheese or mushroom sauce.

Next time: Select plump, unwrinkled, bright green pods that snap easily and are uniformly filled with tender peas. Like corn, peas are best eaten soon after picking. If you must wait, place unshelled peas in plastic bag and refrigerate. They keep best when cold and humid. Try to use within 2 to 3 days. To be sure of preserving green color, add a dash of baking soda to boiling water, add peas, bring to boil again and cook uncovered until just tender, about 4 to 6 minutes. Even without the baking soda, a short cooking time gives the best results. If to be served cold in salad, rinse hot peas with cold water to stop cooking process; drain and chill. Very tender young peas can be eaten raw, or cooked just 1 to 2 minutes. Add any acidic ingredients such as tomato at very end of cooking.

OVERCOOKED

This time: Mash or purée with minced parsley (which adds more green) and onion, and perhaps a bit of butter or milk. (See *Discolored.*)

Next time: See *Discolored.*

OVERMATURE

This time: Add a teaspoon of sugar to small amount of cooking water. Cook uncovered 1 minute. Should be tender in 4 to 6 minutes. Drain and season with butter and herbs (mint, basil, and marjoram are especially good) or serve in cream sauce, perhaps with tiny onions.

Next time: See *Discolored.*

SHRIVELED: See *Discolored.*

Pecans—See *Nuts.*

Pepper, sweet green bell—Sweet and mild-flavored, this pepper variety is used both as a seasoning and a vegetable dish in its own right. Bell shape makes a natural container for stuffing. Sweet peppers are green when mature; they turn red with further ripening, which explains why red peppers are sweeter. Some less common varieties are white to yellow. The following information on discolored applies only to green bell peppers. Everything else applies to red and yellow also.

DISCOLORED (green bell peppers)

This time: Camouflage in a tomato or cheese sauce, or chop and use in a dish. Or grill or broil them until charred. No one will ever know!

Next time: Cook peppers in nonacid liquid and do not overcook. Since most water is slightly alkaline, cover peppers with water, but uncover pot to prevent fading. This method allows the vitamin C to escape, but will ensure a bright green coloration. When preparing pepper shells for stuffing and baking, drop stemmed, seeded peppers into boiling water for only 1 or 2 minutes, depending on size.

MISSHAPEN

This time: No problem unless you're using the peppers for stuffing. If they don't stand up, trim bottoms flat until they do, then fit them into a snug casserole for baking. Scoop up each one onto a serving plate carefully, to prevent filling from escaping.

Next time: Choose big, well-shaped peppers for stuffing, and use the misshapen ones (sometimes cheaper) for dicing and chopping.

OVERCOOKED

This time: When green peppers are soft and don't hold shape very well, chop or dice and turn into a casserole or dish where presence will be tasted but otherwise well concealed. If mushy, use in soups or sauces—especially tomato-based. Or purée and use for vegetable soups or sauces.

Next time: See *Discolored* for blanching shells before stuffing. Sauté strips or chunks until crisp-tender, only a few minutes.

SHRIVELED

This time: Avoid using raw. Drop into boiling water for 1 to 2 minutes, then dip in ice-cold water to loosen skin. Or hold over open flame or broil until charred, then wrap in damp towel until skin loosens. Peel, chop or dice, and use in cooked dish. Or stem, seed, and quarter peppers and grill or broil until charred. This conquers the shrivels.

Next time: Select firm, sturdy, glossy, bright green peppers with no soft or shriveled spots. Old peppers get dull in color and soft in texture. Store unwashed in vegetable crisper of refrigerator; use within 1 week.

Persimmon—Captain John Smith wrote, "If it is not ripe it will drive a man's mouth awrie with much torment; but when it is ripe, it is as delicious as an apricock." It is the high tannin content in the underripe persimmon that causes the mouth so much irritation. This acid develops into sweetness as the fruit ripens. The skin is indigestible until after frost.

ACIDIC

This time: Rinse mouth with baking soda solution, seal fruit tightly in plastic bag with a piece of ripe apple or pear, leave at room temperature and wait a few days.

Next time: Don't taste fruit until it's reddish and spongy-soft to touch. Green or yellow is not ready for eating.

DISCOLORED

This time: Mash pulp, removing seeds and skin, and turn into a custardy pudding or blend into softened ice cream, then refreeze.

Next time: Stir about 1½ teaspoons lemon juice (or lime or grapefruit juice) into each cup of mashed persimmon pulp if not to be used immediately.

UNDERRIPE: See *Acidic.*

OVERRIPE

This time: Scoop out soft or mushy pulp and blend with honey, citrus juice (or other favorite), and a bit of liqueur and fold into whipped cream for an excellent dessert. Soft pulp can be blended with another fruit juice or sugar, water, and spices and cooked until saucy. Use over pudding, cake, gelatin, or ice cream. Can also be used for jams or preserves, and in compotes.

Next time: When fruit turns reddish and is soft to the touch, refrigerate if you cannot use it immediately. Keep no longer than 2 days. Or sieve pulp, mixed with ascorbic acid, pack into freezer containers, leaving ½-inch headspace, and freeze.

Petits Fours—See *Cake; Icing, Glazes.*

Pheasant—See *Poultry, Game Birds.*

Phyllo (Filo) Leaves—Commercial pastry sheets can be bought (especially in Greek shops), and are a shortcut certainly worth taking for Middle-East dishes.

CRUMBLY, DRY

This time: It's difficult to resurrect the original texture and impossible to shape crumbly leaves, so rather than fight it, turn a free-standing pastry into a different type of dessert where shaping isn't necessary. Use fragments to line bottom of pan, add filling, then top with more pastry pieces. Trace individual portions on top layers and bake as directed in recipe, allowing a little more time for a pan instead of individual serving portions. Serve in dishes with appropriate sauce.

Next time: Cover opened pastry with foil or a damp towel while working quickly with one portion. Use opened package immediately, or overwrap and refrigerate or freeze. Phyllo sometimes sticks together in its package. Open the box before buying to see if the layers appear to be separated. When in doubt, gently squeeze phyllo two inches from the top with thumb and forefinger. If leaves don't separate, select another package. Despite these precautions, phyllo sometimes sticks together in the middle. In that case don't try to make individual pieces. Layer pastry and filling in pan (see *Crumbly, Dry*).

To freeze: Overwrap package tightly in foil or freezer paper; freeze up to 2 or 3 months.

To refrigerate: Wrap well in foil or plastic bag; refrigerate up to 1 day.

To thaw: Defrost slowly in wrapping; do not use until thawed.

Pickles—See Canning.

Pie—The medieval version often contained meat mixed with dates and currants between two crusts. John Russell, in his Boke of Nurture, describes a "Feast for a Franklin" (Chaucer's country squire); a capon pie was one of six dishes for the first course, and a small meat pie or pastry was one of several second-course specialties. Frequently live or mechanical birds would emerge from Middle Ages crust for the amusement of diners, as in "Sing a Song of Sixpence." Research indicates, however, that the blackbirds were not actually baked in the pie, but tucked under the finished pastry. I presume the pastry was wasted after the birds did their number. Who would want any part of it after four and twenty nervous birds were held captive for a spell?

Crumb Pie Crust (the unbaked is faster and easier; the baked is crisper).

CRUMBLY

This time: An unbaked crumb crust can be reworked with more butter to hold it together. If crust is too thin, prepare more mixture and press into pan, then rechill. Even a baked crust can be crumbled, remixed, and rebaked, but it is easier merely to crumble the unfilled pie crust and use as a pudding base or topping. When the crust is discovered to be crumbly after it already holds the filling, serve chunks of the pie in a dessert dish topped with ice cream, custard sauce, or whipped cream.

Next time: For a 9-inch pie crust, use about 1⅓ cups crumbs to ¼ to ⅓ cup melted butter. Chill unbaked crust well before filling and slicing.

OVERBROWNED (BAKED CRUST)

This time: Overbrowned crust has a bitter taste; but crumbled and incorporated into a sweet bread-custard pudding, or sprinkled over a fruit pudding or pie, it can add a nice taste counterpoint. Do not salvage burned crust.

Next time: If crust was very thin, make it thicker. Avoid black pans. Use a shiny metal or enamel pan, which reflects heat. Check oven thermostat; do not overbake.

SHRUNKEN (BAKED CRUST)

This time: When time permits, remix the crumb crust with more of the same ingredients and press evenly into pie pan. An easy and sure method of doing this is to press another pie pan of same diameter firmly into the crumbs, then remove top pan; bottom crumbs will be evenly distributed. A quick remedy is to fill the shrunken pie shell and pipe whipped cream or some other border decoratively around edges.

Next time: Avoid using a larger size pan for the crust recipe. Distribute crumbs evenly (see *Shrunken*).

SOGGY

This time: Usually the crumb crust becomes soggy from a moist filling. Unless the filling can easily be removed and the crust re-mixed, the best remedy is to serve the pie as pudding, topped with a sauce or ice cream. An unfilled crust can be remixed with more crumbs and baked. Heat crisps it.

Next time: Unbaked crumb crusts should be thoroughly chilled before filling. Baked crumb crusts are best if cooled before filling. Bake crusts at 300 degrees about 15 minutes.

Flour Pie Crust

BROWNING UNEVEN

This time: Uneven browning of a bottom crust won't show; just make sure lighter areas are thoroughly cooked. The best cover-up for a splotchy top crust is an egg glaze. Beat a whole egg, then paint top crust with a pastry brush dipped into it. Return to oven until egg and heat combine to form a shiny surface. Melted butter or mar-garine, vegetable oil, cream, milk, or evaporated milk can be used. Tart fruit pies sometimes benefit from a sprinkling of coarse sugar over an uncooked glaze such as melted butter, cream, or milk. Another camouflage for an unevenly browned top crust is to serve the pie topped with cheese, ice cream, or sauce.

Next time: Roll pastry evenly. Place in nonshiny pan for best browning. Flute or pinch and finish edges of single crusts to prevent uneven browning around sides. Avoid overhandling dough. Place pie in middle of center oven rack to bake; space several pies at least 2 inches apart and from oven sides. Check oven heat to make sure it's even—there might be hot spots. Let crust cook until golden brown. For best browning and most decorative finish, glaze top crusts (see *Browning, Uneven*).

CRUMBLY, DRY (DOUGH/BAKED CRUST)

This time: Add a little more water to an unbaked dry dough at room temperature, being careful not to overwork. Or make an additional smaller dough; undermix; crumble first dough (kept at room temperature) into it, and mix together very gently. When you're confronted with a very dry baked pie shell, it can be crumbled, tossed with shredded cheddar, herbs, and/or spices, then baked until blended and warm—a delicious snack. Crumbled pie crust can be sprinkled over fruit puddings and custards for an upside-down-pie dessert. A filled pie shell that crumbles under the knife can be spooned into a dessert dish, topped with ice cream or sauce, and served as a deep-dish dessert.

Next time: When mixing dough, butter should be finely cubed and about 70 degrees F. Refrigerating dough at least 30 minutes before rolling helps hold it together. When it still has a dry, crumbly texture, add a few drops of water and rework gently. If the problem is the result of too much shortening add a bit more flour; rework gently. It is important not to overmix or a tough pastry will result, but a crumbly dough is sometimes the result of undermixing. Ingredients must be blended thoroughly but never kneaded. Handle as little as possible once it rolls itself into a ball around side of bowl. Rolling pastry too thin also can cause it to fall apart.

PUFFED PIE SHELL

This time: Fill shell with Bavarian cream or mousse and decorate sides; use a soft filling (not custard) that will adhere to crust. But if pastry is very misshapen, crumble and use to top fruit or custard puddings or similar single-crust pies.

Next time: Roll dough evenly. With fork tines, pierce pastry bottom and sides very well *before baking*. Another insurance against puffiness is to bake pastry shell filled with uncooked dry beans to weigh it down. Bake until set; remove beans; continue baking pastry. Keep beans and use repeatedly for pie crusts.

SHRUNKEN PIE SHELL

This time: Remove shrunken tart or pie shell to platter or pie holder. For fresh fruit tart, for instance, arrange fresh fruit on top; pipe whipped cream around edge. Camouflage in similar ways for different recipes. If badly shrunken, crumble for toppings.

Next time: Chill dough after mixing; roll evenly. After rolling, loosen from board with spatula and allow to relax about 5 minutes. Do not stretch dough to fit pan.

SOGGY CRUST (FRUIT AND CUSTARD PIES)

This time: For a pie that can be baked a little longer, turn up oven to crisp pastry. Individual slices of fruit pie can benefit from heating before serving. When the soft bottom holds a gelatin or other chilled mixture, remove the bottom pastry and place slice of "crustless pie" in deep dish. Top with ice cream or a sauce and call it pudding pie. Try a caramel sauce with apple pie, a spicy rhubarb sauce with strawberry filling, and a rum-raisin sauce with a custard or vanilla pudding. A rich custard sauce shows remarkable compatibility with both fruit and gelatin fillings. The soggy pastry that was trimmed away can be crisped in an oven and crumbled over a fruit or custard pudding or ice cream.

Next time: Assuming a good recipe, a prebaked shell works for all pies. In fact, it's a must for all custard pie mixtures. Don't be afraid of overbaking; at 350 degrees for ¾ to 1 hour, a filled prebaked crust will not overbake. Before baking, pierce pastry dough well with fork to allow steam to escape, but avoid tearing or overpiercing bottom crust, because filling can seep through. Bake assembled pie immediately to prevent pastry from absorbing juices. Too low an oven or an overly juicy fruit filling can also cause the problem. A sprinkling of bread or cookie crumbs over the bottom pastry before adding filling helps absorb juice. Glazing a bottom crust with egg white and prebaking a short time also works. Refrigerator storage of leftover pie causes the pastry to soften too. Whenever possible, reheat individual pieces before serving.

TOUGH, NOT FLAKY

This time: If the compact pastry could ruin your baking reputation, cut it into small pieces, sprinkle with cinnamon-sugar or cover with confectioners icing, and serve to the kids as cookies. A quicker solution is to let the blender make crumbs, which can be mixed with chopped nuts and spices for an ice cream or pudding topping.

Next time: A recipe short on shortening or heavy on flour (usually a ratio of 1 shortening to 2 flour is best) could have caused the problem. Butter has good flavor, and creates a fine crust if in the correct proportion to flour. Lard was rated as top place shortening for yielding the flakiest pie pastry in my University of Illinois food chemistry class. A little butter mixed in to replace part of the lard makes an excellent, flavorful crust. Shortening (in the can) also yields a decent texture. Overhandling or rerolling can cause an unpalatably hard pastry, so remember to handle pastry as little and as lightly as possible.

Meringue Pie Crust (see *Meringue*).

Filling (Fruit). For other fillings see *Gelatin; Ice Cream;* for mousse, see *Egg* or *Cream; Pudding.*

DRYING OUT DURING BAKING

This time: A piece of macaroni inserted vertically in center of pie allows heat to escape instead of boiling the juices away. Add moisture to pie by pouring over a little rum, brandy, liqueur, or fruit juice, or by dotting with a little butter.

Next time: Use less thickener in fillings, add more liquid; dot with butter or use a lower temperature. Another solution for a single-crust pie is to cover with foil, especially during last part of baking.

GUMMY, GELATINOUS

This time: A little fruit juice, liqueur or lemon juice, or more of the fruit in the filling will improve consistency.

Next time: Some fruit is juicier than other types; adjust proportion of thickener to liquid. Make sure oven is not too high.

SPILLS OVER

This time: A funnel inserted in the center allows the juices to bubble up in it to eliminate a messy spillover. If the pie is oozing over the edge, place a baking pan on the rack beneath to catch drips.

Next time: Do not overfill the pie. If the fruit used is very ripe and juicy, add extra thickener. Cut sufficient air vents in the top crust toward center to let steam escape. Cutting them near the edge could cause a boil over. To prevent filling from leaking out the side, be sure bottom and top crusts are well sealed together.

TOO SWEET

This time: Sprinkle lemon or lime juice over to cut sweetness, or serve with a sour lemon sauce.

Next time: Reduce amount of sugar called for in the recipe. Ripe fruit requires very little. Taste, then add more sweetener if needed.

TOO THIN

This time: Add a little more tapioca and cook further until thickened. Or serve in deep dish as pudding pie with ice cream or custard sauce over.

Next time: Drain excess juice, add enough thickener; slash top crust to allow steam to escape.

Pig—*See Meat.*

Pilaf—*See Rice.*

Pimiento—*See Pepper.*

Pine Nuts—*See Nuts.*

Pineapple—Named for its resemblance to a pine cone, this fragrant, sweet fruit was growing on the West Indies island, Guadeloupe (where Indians called it "nana," or "fragrance"), when Columbus sailed there in 1493. It was not introduced to Hawaii until about 300 years later, and there is no record of exactly how or when it arrived. The first recorded planting was on January 21, 1813. By the mid 1800s, pineapples were plentiful in Hawaii, and today our 50th state grows most of the pineapples in the world. Fresh *pina* (as the Spanish call them) come to us from Mexico and Puerto Rico as well, so they're available the year round.

ACIDIC; UNDERRIPE

This time: Marinate in a sweet mixture of 1 or more fruit juices, perhaps with honey or liqueur. Straight liquor also adds a more emphatic flavor. Rum is especially compatible—cut fruit into chunks and use for rum pot (p. 337); then wait a couple of months. You'll never recognize the sour fruit.

Next time: Let your nose and eyes guide you to the best ripe pineapples. A fully ripe one has a distinctively fragrant odor and fresh green leaves. Select one with clean, fresh appearance with flat, almost hollow eyes. Usually heavy mature fruit is better quality. Avoid dull, yellowish pineapples with rather pointed, poorly developed eyes. Contrary to popular opinion, when the top spikes can be pulled out easily, doesn't necessarily mean the fruit is ripe. And color is a poor indicator, too, as ripe fruit varies from all green to all yellow. It's important to choose a ripe pineapple, because those picked too soon will never ripen properly. Refrigerate ripe pineapple and use within a few days.

OVERRIPE; SOFT

This time: Crush and use for juice or for sauce, for ham or fowl. Sweeten the sauce and use over puddings, ice cream, cake, or fruit, or make a glaze for cheesecake. Because of the fresh fruit's enzyme, bromelain, which tenderizes meat, crushed pineapple or the juice makes an excellent marinade for tougher meat cuts.

Next time: See *Acidic* for selecting ripe pineapples. Avoid those with brown, soft spots or dark decay around the base. Refrigerate perfectly ripe pineapple and use within a few days.

Pistachio—Graceful thin green seed of an evergreen tree, related to the cashew and believed to have originated in Asia Minor. Grows well in dry climates, such as California and the middle and southern parts of our country. The green pistachio nut is covered with a reddish skin and enclosed in a hard, two-part brownish shell. Salted and roasted in the shell, the nuts can become addictive. Shelled, they are used extensively for both color and subtle aromatic flavor in baked goods and ice cream. *See Nuts* for other nutty problems and tips.

TO PRESERVE COLOR: Cover shelled pistachios with cold water, bring to boil, drain, and rinse with cold water. Remove skins, dry at room temperature or in very low (about 200-degree) oven, stirring occasionally, about 30 minutes. Storing nuts in covered, lightproof container also helps them retain color. Nuts keep well up to 3 months in refrigerator.

Pizza—It's hard to believe the pizza institution is post-World-War II. We can thank the GIs for the importation of this Neopolitan specialty. After they discovered pizza in Italy, it didn't take long for the craze to catch on. The open-face pie has undergone such Americanization that the young believe it started here along with McDonald's hamburgers and Kentucky Fried Chicken.

RUNNY, SOGGY

This time: Reduce oven temperature to prevent pizza from baking too quickly, and bake longer at reduced temperature to allow sauce to thicken and crust to crisp. Or run under broiler quickly. Another way to firm up bottom crust is to brown wedges in a hot skillet just before serving.

Next time: Pierce dough with fork to allow heat to circulate. Some pizza pans have holes for heat penetration. A light sprinkling of corn meal on pan helps give coarseness to crust. Dough may be lightly brushed with oil before adding sauce, or place cheese over crust first, then add sauce, other ingredients, and more grated cheese. Use slightly less sauce if it was runny, and layer ingredients evenly. Bake long enough to attain desired brownness.

STICKS TO PAN

This time: When the crust sticks to the pan cut pizza into small pieces instead of slicing into wedges to reduce risk of tearing. Use kitchen shears and cut bite-sized squares—a perfect appetizer and easier to eat at a stand-up party. Cut larger squares for a sit-down supper. Break custom again and serve with knife and fork.

Next time: Lightly grease or oil pizza pan. Another insurance against sticking is sprinkling pan bottom with corn meal before adding dough. Roll dough thick and evenly enough so filling doesn't penetrate and bake onto the pan.

CRUST TOO THICK

This time: Best to add more filling ingredients before baking the pizza. If you only notice the too-thick crust after it's out of the oven, then cook more tomato sauce with herbs, green pepper, onion, mushrooms, and whatever. Pour over pizza, add browned sausage and more cheese, then return to oven until cheese melts. Very thick edges can be trimmed; use trimmings for crumbs or bread stuffing.

Next time: Pat and stretch dough evenly in pan. Pinch up a collar around edge to hold filling, but make sure the wall of dough is not too thick. Pierce dough thoroughly with fork to enable heat to penetrate and bake it through. Use leftover dough scraps to make little individual pizzas.

Plantain—Larger, starchier and less sweet than the typical banana, it is served baked, fried, or boiled by Mexicans and by Puerto Ricans and other Caribbeans. For problems with discoloration, over- and underripeness, *see Banana.*

Plum—Ranging in color from yellow and green to red, blue, and purple, plums also vary in texture and flavor from firm and tart to juicy and sweet. Plums in this country are of two general types: European (most popular being Italian, or prune) and Japanese (heart-shaped red on yellow background). The latter probably originated in China, where the fruit is associated with age and wisdom. Some varieties, like Damsons, are best for pickles and preserves.

DISCOLORED

This time: Cut away soft brown spots or darkened cut areas, then use fresh in salad or fruit mixture. Or make plum dumplings, or stew with other fruits for compote; also can use for pie, pudding, kuchen, plum butter; or mash and cook with sugar, lemon juice, and spices for a sauce to serve over puddings, cake, and ice cream.

Next time: Select plump, fresh-looking fruit that is firm but a little resilient. Avoid those with brown spots or with a very soft texture. Refrigerate in loosely closed plastic bag about one week. Once cut, rub surface with lemon or other citrus juice and tighten plastic wrap around halves or slices, or store in salad dressing, marinade, or syrup to preserve color and texture.

OVERRIPE

This time: Soft fruit mashes or purées easily in a blender, then can be sieved to remove skins and blended with lemon juice, spices, or extracts and sweetened—a great topping for spice cake or ginger-bread and fruit gelatin. Start with the same mashed plum mixture, but this time add garlic and herbs for a delicious basting sauce for roast poultry or meat. Soup can be created from the same basic purée; it can take on various characters depending on added ingredients, from sweet wine and spices to robustly seasoned chicken stock and dumplings.

Next time: See Discolored.

SOUR

This time: Sour fruit drinks up the liquid in which it marinates, so give it a bath in a sweet nectar of your choice (juice, wine or liqueur). You might not want to eat a sour plum out of hand, but it can be a tart addition to a tossed salad, especially if first soaked in a piquant dressing. Also adds just the tangy touch to many a meat or poultry sauce or casserole.

Next time: See Discolored.

SUN-BROWNED

The brownish spots on plum skins usually indicate a sunburn, which also signifies lesser quality. Taste to determine the problem. Then marinate in anything from piquant to sweet, depending on your preference. When texture is affected, use fruit for cooking or purée and follow one of suggestions above in *Overripe.*

UNDERRIPE

This time: Slight underripe plums will come to fuller maturity if left at room temperature a few days. Do not refrigerate until fully ripe. When time is short, cook to soften and use in numerous ways; bake in fruit juice for meat accompaniment; poach or stew with other fruits; purée and cook slowly for a sauce or soup.

Next time: See Discolored.

WATERY

This time: Purée and follow suggestions above (*see Overripe*). If you've discovered the watery plums after you've already baked a kuchen, serve the soggy cake in dishes with a sauce.

Next time: Italian plums are a great choice for dumplings and kuchen.

Poisoning—See *Food Spoilage, Poisoning.*

Pomegranate—This heavily seeded fruit, one of nature's wondrous works, symbolized fertility in many ancient cultures. Like an exploration to eat, and definitely worth the trouble. Usually marketed from September through December. Believed to be indigenous to Persia, this flat-sided roundish fruit thrives in warm, dry climates. Its rough skin, which ranges from yellow to pink to brownish red, is used for wool dye in the Middle East. The pulp goes into the making of grenadine syrup.

OVERRIPE

This time: When skin has darkened, but flesh is still juicy, use reamer to extract juice, which then can be strained and sweetened with a dash of lime juice, a great refreshment when chilled and poured over ice with soda. Or freeze mixture until slushy, stir, and refreeze for a tasty ice, which resembles the first-known sherbet, made from the juice and snow. The juice also makes a delicious addition to curries and stuffings. If pulp is browning and drying, remove any badly discolored parts and add usable portion to cooked dishes, such as soup or sauce for chicken. Sauté seeds or seeded pulp in butter with chopped onion and garlic, then add tomato purée or apricot nectar and water to get the right consistency.

Next time: Select pomegranates heavy for size with fresh, bright-colored, thin skins. Keep in cool, dry place or refrigerate several days.

To eat: Presents a problem, since its red juice can squirt over clothes and face. Now I can understand why my mother was upset when, as a ten-year-old, I would buy a pomegranate to eat on the way home from school. The fruit is messy for out-of-hand eating.

Slice off the end opposite the stem, peel back the skin and divide fruit into natural segments; then it's easier to bite a section of fruit, eating the red pulp and spitting out the seeds. Avoid the white, bitter membrane. Another trick is to roll the pomegranate against a flat surface, or squeeze, then make a hole at one end and drink the juice—best done on a beach in a bathing suit with a towel handy.

Popcorn—Remnants of popcorn kernels thousands of years old have been found in Central America. And at the first Thanksgiving, the Indians shared bushels of popcorn with the Pilgrims. This habit-forming snack is easily made at home with merely a large pot, hot oil, and lots of motion, or a popper. The moisture and air inside literally explode the kernels inside out soon after the dry heat and agitation begin. Quality depends on corn variety and processing. The more hull-less, the better.

Tip: Keep pan moving constantly during popping.

SOGGY AFTER POPPING

This time: Spread on baking pan and heat in 250-degree oven a few minutes until crisped.

Next time: Remove cover immediately after popping. Do not let popcorn stand after it is finished, because the steam causes sogginess. Eat soon after popping. Leftover popcorn can be crisped in a low oven.

WILL NOT POP

This time: When the pot is not overloaded and heat is high enough and there is no popping noise, or very little, stop the process and plan on popcorn tomorrow. The kernels probably do not have enough moisture content, so soak them in water for several minutes, drain, and freeze overnight. The next day use them while frozen and you'll see how a little coaxing brings them to life.

Next time: Store both opened and sealed packages in a cool, dry place. An unopened package can be kept about 1 year; once opened, use within 2 or 3 weeks.

Equivalents: ½ to ¾ cup kernels will pop into about 1 quart popcorn.

Popovers—Properly made popovers are thin, crisp, evenly browned shiny shells with moist yellow interiors. Steam inflates the egg-rich batter into balloonlike shells that become firm and brown from a hot oven. High heat is essential to form steam rapidly, while the egg enables the batter to expand and the outer crusty walls to coagulate. Good popovers are easy to make. No need to pop over any problems.

COLLAPSED

This time: Fallen popovers are still delicious split open and served warm with honey, fruit preserves, or creamed vegetables. They may be served in a dish, then filled with any favorite compatible mixture such as sautéed sausage and onion slices, hot tuna salad, or chipped beef.

Next time: Use a high oven temperature of at least 375 to about 450 degrees. Make sure shells are dry and crisp before removing from oven; when detained, turn off heat and allow popovers to remain in oven to dry slightly.

FLAT, DIDN'T RISE

This time: Even popovers that never rose are perfectly good to eat when fully baked. Cut in half and top with creamed chicken or turkey, vegetables in cream or cheese sauce, or a favorite stew.

Next time: Before making popovers, make sure oven temperature is accurate and that it is preheated to at least 375 to 450 degrees, depending on recipe. Temperature should either be increased from 375 degrees or maintained at a higher setting. Batter should be smooth and no heavier than whipping cream. Fresh large eggs should be used for best volume. Use heavy-weight pans (cast iron or ovenproof glass), and grease and preheat them before adding batter.

MUFFINLIKE TEXTURE; NOT HOLLOW

This time: Cake-textured popovers make a tasty, eggy base for many dishes, such as chicken à la king, hash, or hot turkey-grape salad.

Next time: Do not fill cups more than ¾ full.

STICKING TO PANS

This time: Stubborn, clinging popovers can often be persuaded to leave the pan with gentle pressure from a thin-bladed spatula or knife. When they come apart, serve in a dish as a base for favorite compatible meat or vegetable mixtures.

Next time: Grease and preheat heavy-weight ovenproof glass or cast-iron pans before adding batter. When popovers have popped, and are brown and firm, turn off oven and let them dry. When using highly glazed (e.g., ceramic) custard cups, grease and dust with flour or sugar so batter can climb the sides.

Pork—*See Meat.*

Pot Pies—*See Pie.*

Pot Roast—*See Meat.*

Potato—The number one crop in the U.S., versatile, bland, and inexpensive. High in vitamin C and carbohydrates, and considered the most economical source of vitamin B_1.

DISCOLORED

This time: Strip off another layer of raw, pared potatoes to remove darkened parts and immerse immediately in ice water. If already shredded (as for potato pancakes) toss with lemon juice or cream of tartar. If still quite dark, serve pancakes with lots of sour cream or apple sauce to camouflage. Or use for cream of potato soup (*see cream of vegetable soup,* p. 315). Green spots on raw potatoes indicate light exposure; the spots can be toxic in quantity and bitter, so scrape away. If potatoes have been cooked after discoloring, add some cream of tartar or lemon juice to water and cook further for a short time. If still too dark to be served, mash, season, blend with mashed turnips, rutabaga, or carrots and serve with a cheese or green herb sauce. Or put mashed potatoes with egg yolk through pastry tube, making individual swirls, then bake until browned. If cooked cubes of potatoes have darkened, they can be turned into stews and casseroles.

Next time: Drop pared potatoes in cold water to prevent darkening. Add a dash of lemon juice to water when boiling to help prevent discoloration. Avoid selecting potatoes with any green color.

EXPLODED

This time: When the potatoes baking in your oven have a dynamite reaction, retrieve larger pieces; clean oven when slightly cooled. If you really need to serve this fallout, scoop into a casserole, top with cheese, and bake or microcook until cheese melts. Call it twice-baked, and don't expect compliments. Add a dash of white wine and perhaps some herbs for a finer flavor.

Next time: Pierce or cut a cross in baking potatoes before putting in oven.

MEALY

This time: Mash and serve one of several ways: plain with butter, piped through pastry bag and browned in oven, or mashed with another vegetable, placed in casserole, topped with cheese, and browned. If potato skins are still intact, mash interior with sour cream and chives, put back into skins, top with cheese and broil until tops are browned. Or serve skins broiled as separate item.

Next time: Russets, also known as Burbanks or Idahos, are fairly thick-skinned and starchy and best for baking, mashing, and French frying. The flattened white, thin-skinned, shallow-eyed potatoes and the red round or oblongs are best suited to pan-frying, salads, and boiling because they hold their shape. The first are mealy and fluffy; the last two are less starchy.

OILY

This time: If fat isn't hot enough or potatoes are too mealy, fried potatoes can absorb too much fat during cooking. Press out excess between layers of paper toweling. This procedure will undoubtedly also destroy the shapes, so invent a new dish—put the squeezed potatoes into a casserole, layer with sautéed onion slices, sliced mushrooms, minced parsley, fine crumbs, grated Parmesan, or a little light cheese sauce (1 tablespoon each butter and flour cooked, ½ cup milk added gradually and cooked, ⅓ cup dry white wine, and ¼ cup grated Parmesan or shredded Cheddar).

Next time: Oil should be 285 degrees before and during frying; do not crowd potatoes in pot. Select Russets for fries; soak in cold water first. Choose round red or white for pan frying.

OVERSIMMERED

This time: Mash with sour cream or a sauce, then season and serve, or bake or broil until brown on top. They can be piped around a meat loaf, planked fish, or a platter of meat.

Next time: Boil scrubbed, unpared new potatoes or pared older potatoes in boiling salted water to cover just until tender, depending on size, 20 to 40 minutes. Quarter to quicken cooking. Drain and use water for soup, stew, or yeast bread. Dry potatoes over low heat in saucepan; season and butter. To bake, scrub skin, remove any eyes, rub skins with a little shortening. Pierce in 2 or 3 places. Bake on oven rack or baking sheet in 450-degree oven about 40 to 50 minutes, depending on size. When soft, slash top and press up potato through top. Serve topped with butter, sour cream and chives, blue cheese crumbles, or chili sauce.

SPROUTING

This time: Remove sprouts and eyes, pare, and boil, then serve with a sauce, in a stew or casserole, or mashed and blended with other ingredients.

Next time: Select firm, clean, well-shaped tubers without sprouts, cuts, or bruises. Avoid those with a wilted look or with green spots. Store in a cool, dry, airy place. Light can cause greening, and refrigeration or low temperature converts the starch to sugar. Fresh potatoes will keep 2 months or more. New potatoes (freshly dug, which have much less starch) keep only about 2 weeks in a cool place.

STARCHY

This time: Soak in cool water for 45 minutes or slightly more to get rid of some of the starch (along with some of the nutrients, unfortunately).

Next time: Choose new potatoes; avoid the older, starchier tubers. Select round white or red unless using for baking or mashing, when Russets are the best.

UNDERCOOKED

This time: If the rest of the meal is about ready and the baked potato is still hard, wrap in foil and increase the heat, or insert potato nails. The microwave oven would solve the problem; one potato takes about 4 minutes total. For boiling, cut into smaller pieces; boil rapidly.

Next time: See Overcooked.

Poultry, Game Birds—As a little girl, I remember accompanying my mother on grocery expeditions. Even blindfolded I would have been able to identify which shop we were in at a given moment: the sausage shop with wall-to-wall garlic and smoky aromas; the bakery filled with sweet strudel warmth. But the odors from the poultry place, where freshly killed chickens, capons, and ducks were displayed in full feather for customers to inspect, always stopped me in my tracks even before the entrance. I held my nose while Mom made her purchase.

Today's supermarket-era children don't even know that the pre-packaged turkey or duck their parents buy once had feathers. The modern bird is nonodoriferous, neatly wrapped, and ready to cook. The birds themselves have changed, too. They've been bred to be meatier and more tender; even new, leaner ducks have made their debut. I witnessed the amazing mass-production proficiency at one large chicken packing house in Jackson, Mississippi. When the broiler is packed for market it is less than 2 hours from slaughter and only about 7 to 9 weeks old. The term *poultry* encompasses all domesticated birds raised for consumption. Wild birds are considered game. The following information applies to both groups, with specific references to one or the other where applicable.

Basic cooking methods: Following are types of poultry suggested for each cooking method.

1. *Roasting:* The most common way of preparing whole birds. Even works well for lean birds if they're larded or a little liquid is added.

2. *Broiling:* Suggested for cut-up or split birds, especially split duck and goose.

3. *Panbroiling:* Recommended for birds with moderate fat content.

4. *Frying:* Best for smaller more tender poultry pieces.

5. *Braising:* Especially appropriate for older and drier birds, but also used for the more tender specimens.

6. *Cooking in liquid:* Recommended for stewing hens and some tough, old game birds.

BATTER DOESN'T ADHERE

This time: When the batter comes off like a glove, place bare chicken in a casserole, drizzle with melted butter or a sauce and top with crumbled batter. Or brush chicken lightly with egg, then cover with crushed batter and bake. Topping should then adhere.

Next time: Make sure bird pieces are dry before dipping in egg batter or egg and coating. Also allow a rest period of about 15 minutes between dipping and frying.

BROWNISH SPOTS

This time: If the bird has no off-odor, the brown spots are freezer burn, and indicate drying. Rub with oil or margarine before roasting.

Next time: This condition indicates dehydration from long, improper freezer storage. When freezing poultry at home, cover and seal well in freezer wrap.

DRY (ESPECIALLY TURKEY)

This time: Slightly dried poultry can be salvaged by topping with an herb or lemon butter or a sauce. When bone dry, it's best to shred for soup or stew. Or dice for chicken (or other fowl) à la king, creamed on toast, soup, or a sandwich spread. Sliced dry bird can become more palatable when simmered gently in a buttery broth for a few minutes.

Next time: Except for the new lower-fat duck, domestic duck and goose are no worry, because they're fatty. Wild birds tend to be dry; greasing them on the inside helps retain juices. Game birds benefit greatly from marinating and larding before roasting; braising is another method that ensures moist tenderness. Turkey should be basted during roasting, then served with a gravy or sauce. The quick bath in a buttery broth after cooking and slicing allows it to absorb moisture.

FROZEN, MUST USE (ESPECIALLY LARGER BIRDS)

This time: Quick-thaw in microwave or under cold running water.

Next time: Allow 6 to 7 hours per pound of frozen bird to thaw in the refrigerator, the best method.

GAMY TASTE

This time: Freshly squeezed lemon or lime juice helps cut gamy flavor. Another remedy is a robust herb-wine sauce, gingered sweet-sour sauce (*see* p. 329) or sweet wine sauce (sweet vermouth with tomato paste and thyme).

Next time: When bagging your own, select younger birds for a preferred milder taste. The less-developed birds have softer bills and sharper claws. It's important, especially in warm weather, to draw the bird soon after killing. For best flavor, it should be hung at least 10 days at a temperature just above freezing. Marinate more mature birds or those suspected of having a gamy taste in wine or an oil-vinegar blend before cooking. Rub inside cavity with lemon or ginger, or add a carrot, onion, celery stalk, potato quarter or a cored, pared apple to attract off-flavors during cooking. Discard fruit or vegetables after cooking.

GREASY (ESPECIALLY FATTY DUCK OR GOOSE)

This time: Pierce the skin and administer high heat to make fat ooze out; drain well. Or simply remove the skin with its fatty under-layer and slice, chop or shred meat for casseroles or salads, or serve with sauce.

Next time: Preroast a duck or goose about 20 minutes before stuffing. Pierce frequently all over before roasting or broiling to allow fat to escape, especially around legs and wings. Begin fatty birds breast side up in a hot oven, 375 to 400 degrees; temperature can be lowered toward end of roasting if becoming overbrowned.

Another foolproof method for succulent, moist duck with crisp skin comes from chef Carolyn Buster. She and her husband, Jerry, own The Cottage, a creative, elegant restaurant in Calumet City, Illinois. Duck is one of the specialties and this is her secret. Place a 4- to 4½-pound duck breast down on a bed of chopped vegetables and herbs (onion, celery, carrots, garlic, bay leaves) in roaster. Sprinkle with chef's salt (salt, white and black peppers, paprika, and a touch of garlic); add 5 or 6 black peppercorns and ½ inch water to pan and put some rendered duck fat or lard over bird. Cover tightly; place in 325-degree oven about 2½ hours. The fat melts down, sealing the surface of the water, which prevents a "boiled taste," and the bird picks up moisture and flavor. Cool duck to room temperature on rack; split in half. Bird may be cooked hours in advance to this point. When ready to serve, brush skin with a little vegetable oil if desired; roast in 450-degree oven 20 minutes. Perfection!

NOT ENOUGH: Slice and serve with sauce or gravy over stuffing, rice, or pasta; pair with smoked meats, which add compatible flavor.

OVERCOOKED

This time: Serve oversimmered poultry that is falling off the bone in a sauce over waffles, rice, toast points, or pasta. An over-roasted bird, on the other hand, can be bone dry. Simmer gently in a buttered broth or serve smothered with sauce.

Next time: Weigh bird and carefully calculate cooking time. Use a meat thermometer—inner thigh should reach 185 degrees F.; stuffing should reach at least 165 degrees.

SALTY

This time: Simmered or braised fowl can be slightly desalted by adding a cut-up potato to the cooking liquid. The salty tuber may have to be discarded. A bird fully cooked by dry-heat method can be quickly rinsed or soaked in milk, unseasoned stock or water. Sweet balances salty, so serving with a fruit sauce or glaze helps diminish the problem.

Next time: Add salt toward end of cooking after tasting. This also prevents juices from being drawn out.

STICKING TO PAN

This time: Scrape up pieces and serve over rice with a sauce or in a casserole or soup.

Next time: Lightly grease pan when cooking lean birds. Game birds need larding or added moisture during cooking. Turkey also usually needs lubricating during roasting or broiling. Too high a temperature also may cause sticking. Turn pieces frequently to prevent them from adhering to the pan.

TOUGH

This time: Cutting a tough bird into small pieces or thin slices helps chewability. Grinding helps a great deal. Moisten with sauce or broth, depending on use. Spread slices with mustard or some relish for sandwiches, or serve hot with a cranberry sauce or gravy. Chunks take on moisture from a sauce in a casserole, when tossed with greens and a dressing, or stir-fried with vegetables and soy sauce. Ground poultry is great in stuffing or blended with mayonnaise, onion, and chopped pimiento for salad.

Next time: Select young birds. Flexible bones (especially breast) on most birds generally indicates youth. A young turkey has black feet, a middle-aged gobbler pink, and a senior citizen gray. Hanging wild birds helps to tenderize them; old birds can be held longer than young ones. Humidity accelerates ripening. Generally they should hang about 10 days at a temperature just above freezing. To ensure palatability, old birds should be braised, stewed, or otherwise cooked with moisture. Marinating in an acidic medium also tenderizes, as does cooking in milk. Meat tenderizers also work on fowl.

UNDERCOOKED

This time: An undercooked large whole bird, such as a turkey, can present an embarrassing problem when guests are waiting for dinner. If there's no microwave oven in which to finish the bird, then carve and braise the pieces to save time using outer slices first. Serve over stuffing or rice with the gravy.

Next time: Carefully calculate cooking time, then add extra time.

Preserves—*See Canning.*

Pretzel—To crisp soggy pretzels, place on baking pan in a 350-degree oven for several minutes, until warm and crisp. For other problems, see *Bread.*

Prosciutto—*See Meat.*

Prune—Prunes are made from several particular types of plums that can be dried without fermentation. They were sun-dried by the Turks and Mongols long ago, who found they traveled well and provided much energy. Today, commercial prunes are subjected to controlled dehydration, leaving enough moisture in them to remain soft. The natural laxative quality probably comes from their high cellulose content. As my grandmother used to sing, "No matter how young a prune may be, it's always full of wrinkles!"

DRIED

This time: After storage, prunes sometimes dry out. Pour boiling water (cold water also works, but slower) over prunes to cover; refrigerate one day to plump. If cooking, use any remaining soaking liquid. For faster plumping, steam for 20 to 30 minutes. Or simmer in water to cover (especially nice when spices or wines are added) about 15 minutes.

Next time: If bought in plastic bags, make sure they're plump and soft. Store in dry, cool place at home; refrigerate in hot weather. Try to use within 6 months.

STICKY WHEN CHOPPING: Dip scissors or knife in flour periodically.

Pudding—The word inspires Englishmen to yearn for Yorkshire or steamed plum pudding, Scandinavians to dream of their baked-fish version, and New Englanders to build appetites for the Indian-inspired molasses-corn meal favorite. There's a great variety of boiled, steamed or baked food mixtures called pudding. Served cold or hot, they can be the main dish, an accompaniment, or dessert. Today's popular English steak-and-kidney pudding is an outgrowth of the suet-covered 14th-century "puddynges." Plum pudding, another suet-based recipe, contains not even one plum! Rich in brandied currants, raisins, nuts, and citron, however, the dessert hardly misses it. Corn, onion, and noodle puddings are popular in this country. And a meal may end with bread pudding or any of the soft, creamy spoon puddings of chocolate, vanilla, or butterscotch. For clarification here, puddings have been divided into two main types: the custard-based and creamy dessert-type, which have similar behavior patterns; and suet-based baked or steamed.

Custard (flan, rice, Indian, bread, fish, Yorkshire) and *Creamy Dessert* (chocolate, vanilla, butterscotch)

CURDLED, LUMPY

This time: When just starting to curdle, transfer at once to a cold bowl or set in bowl of ice water. Beat with wire whisk until smooth. When already curdled, add 1 teaspoon custard to 1 teaspoon milk (or liquid in recipe). Beat until smooth and creamy, then slowly beat in more broken custard. Gradually beat the smooth mixture into curdled. An egg yolk instead of the milk also works as a binder. A little cornstarch mixed with cold liquid, then stirred into the separated custard, also pulls it together. After the mixture is smooth again, stir while heating gently in top of double boiler over hot water. A curdled mixture can be passed through a sieve to remove the lumps.

Next time: Low heat and stirring are very important in producing smooth mixtures. Before adding eggs, temper by stirring in a little of the hot milk mixture before gradually returning to remainder. Cook slowly, stirring constantly, in top of double boiler over hot water. Direct heat or thin cookware may cause mixture on bottom to get overheated and lumpy. When using pudding mix, be sure to add the powder to the milk, not the reverse. If the milk was mistakenly added to the dry ingredients, a blender or food processor can take most of the lumps out. In cornstarch-thickened mixtures, make sure cornstarch is well blended with liquid before cooking.

FLAN STICKS, WILL NOT UNMOLD

This time: Custard flans baked in caramel sugar molds need to set at least 6 hours in refrigerator before unmolding.

Next time: Allow adequate setting time.

SKIN FORMED

This time: Remove skin with rubber spatula or back of spoon. It's tasty, but makes pudding less appealing. Cover top of pudding with fruit, whipped cream or ice cream.

Next time: A light sprinkling of sugar over the surface helps prevent skin formation. For a cornstarch pudding, lay a piece of wax paper or plastic wrap directly on top until pudding has cooled. Cool pudding gradually at room temperature before chilling, unless otherwise directed in recipe.

SOGGY, WATERY

This time: Drain excess liquid with baster if awkward to tilt entire pudding. Soft, runny puddings need not be lost. Serve a soupy fish or vegetable type as a sauce over another fish or vegetable. Everyone will love the bread pudding when it seeps into the bowl and intermingles with melting ice-cream or whipped-cream topping.

Most of the sweet mixtures can be used as sauces over fruits, gelatins, cakes, and even other puddings. A liquidy custard or vanilla cornstarch pudding makes a great sauce over a hearty bread pudding, for example.

Next time: Whole eggs for custards should be just lightly mixed, enough to blend whites and yolks together. Custard should be cooked until it's thick enough to coat a metal spoon. Strain and continue stirring after cooking to release steam. When steam is permitted to condense it makes the texture watery. Allow enough time for pudding to set; chill cold ones thoroughly. Refrigerating custard for a while can cause the same problem. Be sure to cool before chilling, then cover well. In puddings with dry ingredients, add less liquid or more of the bread, corn meal, or thickener. Underbaking also prevents certain puddings from firming. Avoid overbaking, which causes the eggs to "break."

THIN (MIXTURE BEFORE COOKING)

This time: More recipe thickener can be added either before or while the pudding is cooking. Be sure to temper the egg to any hot mixture (see *Curdled*). It's best to mix a little cornstarch or flour into a paste with a small amount of liquid before gradually stirring into the mixture. Check proportions in recipe, using the following guide:

Soft or stirred custards: 1 cup milk requires 1 egg, 2 yolks, or 2 whites to thicken.

Molded custards: Double eggs in soft custard above or use ½ tablespoon gelatin powder per cup milk.

Creamy puddings: 1 cup of milk needs about 3 tablespoons flour or 1½ tablespoons cornstarch to thicken it.

Molded puddings: Use 4 tablespoons flour or 2 tablespoons cornstarch per cup liquid.

Next time: Use the above guide to check proportions in recipe before beginning. Some recipes (bread pudding, etc.) may need more dry ingredients. Give pudding enough time to cook and set.

THIN (MIXTURE DURING COOKING OR COOKED)

This time: If the mixture in the saucepan is not thickening, stir in a little cornstarch, arrowroot, or flour-water paste and cook, stirring, until thickened. (See *Thickeners.*) If you're faced with a runny cooled pudding, use as a sauce (see *Soggy*).

Next time: Avoid overcooking puddings or starch granules will rupture and thin out. Other causes might be too much sugar in proportion to starch and the introduction of acidic ingredients, such as lemon juice, during cooking. Add acid ingredients last, after mixture has thickened and been removed from heat.

THICK (MIXTURE BEFORE COOKING)

This time: Gradually stir in more liquid to thin to correct consistency; continue to cook and stir.

Next time: Use less of the thickening agent (see *Thin*).

TOUGH

This time: Extra-firm custard serves nicely when diced and combined with gelatin cubes and a sauce. Some especially good custard combinations are coffee gelatin and vanilla sauce, orange gelatin drizzled with curaçao, and raspberry gelatin with peach sauce. Another way to lighten custard is chopping and blending into whipped cream, then topping with chopped nuts or crumbled macaroons. When a dessert pudding gets tough, slice thin over a plain cake (pound, angel, chiffon, etc.) and top with a creamy sauce. Or cut pudding into chunks and serve with warm cake and topping as a pudding cake.

Next time: Always use a double boiler for cooking. Excessive heat will toughen the mixture and prevent it from holding the liquid in suspension. Add more egg yolk, which tenderizes. Once pudding has reached proper consistency, quickly stop cooking by setting pot (or custard cups with baked custard) in pan of ice water.

For brown crust: To get a rich-colored crust on custard pudding, beat eggs until frothy before adding milk.

To reheat: Puddings and custards reheat nicely without further cooking by covering them with lettuce leaves and placing in a warm oven until serving. The large outer leaves are best. What do you do with hot lettuce? See creamed lettuce (p. 334). Once-used leaves will also blot off fat from soups (see *Soup, Greasy*).

To unmold: Baked or cup custards that are to be unmolded need a larger quantity of eggs; beat slightly before adding.

Suet-Based (baked or steamed plum, fig, carrot, steak-and-kidney):

CRUMBLY

This time: Serve in deep dishes topped with a sauce. Plum pudding is traditionally topped with a brandy hard sauce, but try the thinner custard, lemon, and vanilla sauces. They bring out hidden qualities of this pudding type and camouflage the crumbly appearance. Chunks of pudding mix well with vanilla ice cream and others too.

Next time: Use more egg or suet to bind dry ingredients together. Sticky dried fruits (raisins, figs, dates, etc.) also help hold the mixture together. Steam the pudding; do not allow it to cook uncovered or it will get dry and crumbly. Allow sufficient ripening time. Like fruitcakes, puddings usually improve with aging. Slicing them when immature causes crumbling.

DRY

This time: Bathe a dry pudding in a thin sauce to inject moisture. Sprinkle or inject pudding with rum, brandy, or a good whiskey before saucing. Before storing remainder soak well, wrap in liquor-soaked cheesecloth, overwrap tightly in foil and refrigerate. Water the pudding every few days, as you do plants, but with a liquor instead. After a week or two the pudding should be moist and *very* spirited.

Next time: Add more fruit or liquid, less flour, meal, or other dry ingredients. Steam tightly covered to prevent drying during cooking.

SOGGY

This time: Remove unwrapped pudding from pan or mold, place on a baking pan in a low oven to dry slightly. Watch carefully to avoid overdrying.

Next time: Add fewer liquids and fruits or more dry ingredients. Make certain cooking temperature is high enough, or cook longer if necessary.

Puff Paste (pâte feuilletée)—The true test of the pastry chef. Capable of rising 8 times its original size, it's used for Napoleons, cream rolls, vol-au-vent, bouchées (small vol-au-vents), turnovers, and patty shells. Reasonably good commercially prepared butter products can be found, but for those of you facing the from-scratch challenge, here are some solutions that may further inflate your puff-paste knowledge.

COLLAPSED WHILE BAKING

This time: Fill a low-rise vol-au-vent with a savory mixture and cover with sauce and garnish. Or serve a fruit mélange or scoop of ice cream with whipped cream or fresh fruit sauce over the flat pastry in a dessert dish—it will look like a specialty.

Next time: Use flour with high gluten content. Some good recipes combine these with pastry or cake flour, but never rely *solely* on cake flour. Sprinkle parchment paper or baking sheet lightly with water; the steam helps layers to expand, increasing volume. Check oven temperature for accuracy; make sure oven is fully preheated. Chef Jean-Pierre Capelle of Gascony emphasized this distinction between general puff pastry and another form of it called mille feuilles: "Although puff pastry is never pricked to release air or moisture, mille feuilles is pierced over its entire surface so it doesn't rise too high. Mille feuilles is a long strip of the same puff paste, pierced all over and baked longer until very dry; it's always served cold, whereas other puff pastries are often served warm."

CRACKS, TEARS WHILE ASSEMBLING

This time: Quickly mend tears to keep butter encased; the openings release air, which, like punctures in a balloon, prevent it from expanding. The pastry tends to be uneven after patching. The paste must be very cold; rechill if necessary. If paste and icy-cold butter are not the same waxy, pliable consistency, butter may rupture paste in rolling process.

Next time: Allow sufficient chilling time. Check consistency of paste and butter before attempting rolling.

FAT RUNS OUT DURING BAKING

This time: Once this problem occurs and the pastry is baking or is baked, it's too late to improve it; pastry will be flat and tough. Depending on its condition and form, it might be merely camouflaged and topped with a filling or sauce. Or crumble and use as topping for puddings and desserts or to decorate cakes.

Next time: Usually occurs because paste wasn't turned and folded enough, so give it one additional turn and fold. A break in the paste will also cause this calamity (see *Cracks, Tears*), as will too cool an oven. Usual baking temperature is 425–450 degrees.

FLAT, TOUGH PASTRY (WITHOUT FAT HAVING RUN OUT)

This time: See *Fat runs out during baking.*

Next time: If you suspect that the dough was overworked, cut one rolling and folding from the procedure. Too much flour used in recipe, or in rolling and turning the paste, will also produce this poor quality. Check oven temperature; it must be hot enough.

SHRINKAGE DURING BAKING

This time: Pastry chef Jolene Worthington says, "When my 9-inch circle shrinks to 8 inches, I just make a smaller cake. Or I cut out triangles or other shapes to use as decoration."

Next time: Resting time is very important for the "worked" paste. After it's made up, allow paste a 2-hour refrigerator rest; allow shaped pieces a 30-minute to 1-hour rest before baking. Shrinkage even occurs with commercial puff pastry sheets.

STICKY (PASTE)

This time: A combination of flour and cold should do the trick. Chill hands in ice water and work quickly, adding more flour if necessary. Warmth will soften the dough and make it sticky.

Next time: Unless your kitchen is air-conditioned, do not attempt to make puff paste during hot weather. Puff paste recipes usually start with, "Choose a bright, chilly, windy day." Be sure to chill ingredients thoroughly.

UNEVEN LAYERS

This time: Slice horizontally and layer with thick filling; or spoon casserole or dessert filling over individual layers.

Next time: Roll all layers evenly and equal, keeping corners square. Chill both paste and butter to the same cold, waxy, pliable consistency—not oily and not yet hard. Always cut paste with a very sharp instrument, making clean cuts for the best-proportioned layering. Handle carefully, using a spatula; avoid finger indentations, which will cause unevenness.

To store: Puff paste can be stored in the refrigerator for several days when well wrapped in plastic wrap. For longer storage, shape and freeze, well wrapped, up to 3 months.

Pumpkin—*See Squash.*

Punch—The featured item at many festive occasions, this potable might have a champagne base for toasting newlyweds or a milk and fruit base for a children's party. Many adult punches contain alcohol. These tips can add spirit to any punch bowl.

TOO ALCOHOLIC

This time: Add more of nonalcoholic ingredients, such as soda, tea, fruit juice, fruit, sherbet, ice cubes, or water.

Next time: Stir in liquor gradually, tasting as you mix. Try using a lower-proof alcohol. Wine punches are less potent than those made with hard liquor, and the recipe possibilities are limitless.

DILUTED

This time: Add more lemonade, fruit punch, juices, sherbet, alcohol, etc., depending on the recipe.

Next time: Prepare ice cubes of some of the punch ingredients to prevent watering down. Taste while gradually mixing. Embellish punch with stronger flavors. For example, adding more fruit to a fruit punch gives a richer, more concentrated taste.

SOUR

This time: Add more sugar, honey, fruit, sherbet, syrup, soda, or sweet wine. When using a viscous or concentrated sweetener, dilute it first in a small amount of punch before stirring into the bowl; this ensures a more thorough blending and uniform flavor.

Next time: Adjust ratio of sweet to sour ingredients according to personal preference. Add fewer acidic products (lemon, lime, etc.). Taste while mixing.

SWEET

This time: An extra dose of lemons, limes, oranges, club soda, bitters, and the like will do the job.

Next time: Check proportions in recipe before adding all the sweet ingredients. For my personal taste, most recipes tend to be too sweet.

Quail—*See Poultry, Game Birds.*

Quenelles—See individual ingredients.

Quiche—*See Pie; Pudding, Custard; spinach quiches* (p. 330).

Quick Breads—*See Bread, Quick.*

Quince—How could a fruit this astringent and hard have gained mythological significance as a sign of love? The Romans and Greeks considered the quince sacred to the Goddess of Love. In modern slang, its name connotes an undesirable, sour personality. Cooked, however, the quince takes on a delightful new character, in anything from sweet jellies and pastes to the Mediterranean beef stews. The delicious Iranian quinces are a rare taste experience, stuffed with meat and split peas in a sweet-sour sauce.

ACIDIC: Astringency is its nature; do not eat raw. If not using for jellies, jams, or marmalades, cook with spicy meat stews, add a few slices to apple or pear pies or simmer with citrus and other fruit compotes. Or make the concentrated paste so popular with Latin Americans, who eat it with queso blanco (bland white cheese) and crackers. Seed and steam fruit until soft, then sieve; blend with equal part sugar and cook, stirring, until pasty and candylike. Pour ½ to ¾ inch deep in pans to cool, dry in low oven or in sun; may take several days to dry well. Keep in tins and slice with cheese and crackers.

HARD

Softens upon cooking; slow simmering or steaming is best.

OVERRIPE

This time: Seed the fruit and cook until very soft, then sieve pulp for a sweet sauce, delicious over puddings and cakes. Or make paste (*see Acidic*).

Next time: Look for quinces with light yellow to yellow-green color, avoiding any with soft spots and bruises. Be wary of little holes, which usually indicate worms. Store in cool, dry place. Refrigerate after ripening.

UNDERRIPE

This time: Store at room temperature until ripe for use. Slightly underripe fruit can be used for jellies and jams. Or bake in fruit juice or sweetened water until deep-red, about 2 hours in low oven; simmer slices along with vegetables and meat in long-cooking dishes; or steam until tender.

Next time: Avoid very hard fruit. Do not refrigerate until ripe.

Rabbit—*See Game.*

Rabbit, Welsh—*See Cheese.*

Raccoon—*See Game.*

Radish—Most radishes we see are small round or oblong shapes with white interior and red skins. Occasionally we see the larger black radishes, which tend to be more pungent. The Orientals grow much larger varieties, while the Germans have huge carrot-shaped white varieties. The problems dealt with here relate to our commonest variety.

DISCOLORED

This time: If the dark spots go through the root, radishes are no longer usable. If the spots are merely on surface, cut them out and pare, if necessary. After this surgery, the radishes will not be attractive enough for relish trays, so plan to cut them up to perk up a curried chicken dish, an Oriental stir-fry mixture, or a spicy soup.

Next time: Select firm roots with no decay spots. Greens should look fresh. To store, remove tops, wash and dry. Store in plastic bag in refrigerator crisper. Use within 1½ to 2 weeks. When cooking, avoid using alkaline water or any alkaline solution, which tends to yellow white radishes. If brownish, they may have been cooked too long. A greenish-brown color indicates they've picked up iron from a utensil. Use another metal. Cook in a little water with a dash of acid (lemon juice or vinegar) added; cover and cook just until tender.

OLD

This time: To crisp pithy radishes, trim off tops and bottoms and place in ice water in refrigerator. An hour's soaking should do the trick. Soak longer if necessary. If the soaking still doesn't produce a radish crisp enough to be used in salad, then cook and turn into a dish (see *Discolored*).

Next time: Select firm, smooth, well-shaped roots, preferably with tops on. Look for fresh green tops. Store in refrigerator crisper in plastic bag, up to 2 weeks.

Ragout—*See Stew.*

Raisins (problems and solutions also apply to other dried fruits)—Thousands of years ago, when Egyptians left grapes on the vine too long, they found that the fruit shriveled and grew sweeter. All or most raisins we add to baked goods and eat from boxes come from the San Joaquin Valley in California, the world's biggest producer. The golden color of the sultanas is preserved by a sulphur treatment and controlled dehydration. The brown muscats are sun dried. Available seeded and seedless.

DRIED

This time: For baking purposes, soak in liquid required in recipe. After 15 minutes (more if brandy for fruitcake) raisins should be plump. Soak shriveled raisins in water several minutes before eating plain or using in dish where no additional flavors are desired. When intended for cooking, simmer in water, a sauce or broth, or rinse with water and heat in a 325-degree oven until puffed.

Next time: Store raisins tightly covered in dry, cool place. Refrigerate in summer; then they can be kept almost indefinitely.

SINKING IN BATTER

Lightly toss with flour before turning into the batter; it helps to keep them suspended instead of sinking to the bottom. Another solution is to stir three-fourths of the raisins into batter, sprinkle remainder on top of batter after it's in the pan.

STUCK TOGETHER

This time: Heat in low oven or soak in water for several minutes.

STICKY WHEN CHOPPING

Toss lightly with flour, dip scissors or knife into flour or cold water before chopping.

Rancid—See *Fat.*

Rarebit, Welsh—Same as *Rabbit, Welsh;* see *Cheese.*

Raspberries—See *Berries.*

Ratatouille—See *Eggplant* and other specific ingredients.

Ravioli—See *Pasta.*

Red Snapper—See *Fish.*

Reduction—See *Sauces; Stock.*

Reheating—See individual foods.

Rhubarb—Also called pie plant, because of its delicious reputation between the crusts. Not a fruit, although the plant is used as one. Good for homemade jams, jellies, and wine. Native to Asia and of the family known as docks in England, this perennial has edible reddish stalks and *inedible poisonous leaves* containing oxalic acid. Because of their tartness, stalks usually are poached or baked with sugar and honey. A harbinger of the spring fruit season, it's usually the first to appear on the market, peak season being April and May.

For centuries actors backstage have chanted "rhubarb" to create a mob sound, a practice reputedly begun by Shakespeare. May the following information prevent any rhubarbs over your rhubarb.

MUSHY, OVERCOOKED

This time: Mix 2 teaspoons cornstarch in a little cold water or juice, then stir into 2 cups cooked mushy rhubarb and simmer until thickened. Or combine with a thick applesauce and serve over a fruit gelatin. Macaroon or cookie crumbs soaked in rum might be blended into overcooked rhubarb to lend both substance and good flavor. You may always overcook your rhubarb to serve it this way.

Next time: Cook firm, crisp 1-inch lengths of the stalks with a little water until just tender. Add about ⅓ to ½ cup sugar per pound, or to taste. Can also be seasoned with cinnamon, nutmeg, ginger, or allspice.

OVERRIPE

This time: Cook up for sauce, perhaps with another fruit, such as strawberries, pears, or oranges. Flavor with spices and sweeten to taste.

Next time: Choose young stems that sound crisp when pierced. Store fresh rhubarb in plastic bags in refrigerator for up to 3 days. When you have more than you can use, freeze by packing 1-inch lengths into freezer containers, covering with a cold simple syrup, and cover, allowing ½-inch headspace.

TOO TART

Sweeten to taste with honey, sugar, or a little artificial sweetener. If you know the batch of rhubarb is extremely tart before cooking, cook in a sweetened fruit juice. Soaking it for a few minutes in heated water with a bit of baking soda helps remove acid.

TOUGH, STRINGY

This time: When already cooked, sieve mixture to remove fibrous parts. Before cooking, remove the coarse strings with a paring knife.

Next time: The hothouse variety tends to be more tender with thin pink or light red stalks and greenish-yellow leaves, and usually can be cooked without peeling. The hardy field rhubarb can be identified by thicker deep-red stalks and green leaves; try to pick the young reddish stalks of this type. For the most tender and delicate rhubarb, look for young stems and immature leaves. Avoid oversize stalks, or those that are wilted or flabby. Pierce the stalk with something sharp to detect crispness.

Rice—This amazing seed of a cereal grass is the staple food for over half the world. Many reasons account for its wide use, including the grass's ability to grow in places where other grains cannot and its comparable high yield per acre. Another advantage is its usability without the need for extensive milling. This ancient grain is a descendant of a southeast Asian grass. In some parts of Asia, it is still the main diet ingredient. The many varieties and the blandness of rice make it versatile in any language. The white, fluffy grain forms the foundation for Spanish paella (the seafood saffron-rice national dish), Greek rice soup, Indian biryani, and jambalaya from our own South. And, of course, most Japanese and Chinese meals include bowls of sticky rice that can be eaten with chopsticks. Northern regions of China grow wheat, so dumplings and noodles are more common there than rice. The Chinese have a charming New Year's greeting: "May your rice never burn." But even if it does, these same rice lovers have devised a delicious solution. Read on.

Basic types: Information that prevents problems caused by using wrong rice for a particular dish.

1. *Brown (natural):* Has rich, nutty flavor from the nutritious bran coat and germ. Requires longer cooking time than regular white rice.

2. *Converted:* Creamy-colored whole-grain rice that has been parboiled before milling. Retains many nutrients otherwise lost in milling. Requires longer cooking than regular.

3. *Long-grain:* The Carolina type, which produces separate, fluffy grains when cooked. Cooks faster than short-grain. Use as meat accompaniment, soups, stuffing, or molding.

4. *Precooked (instant rice):* Partially cooked long-grain rice that has been dried and packaged.

5. *Short-grain:* Unless package specifies, most rice is short. Moist and tender after cooking, it is ideal for puddings, sauces, and croquettes.

6. *Wild:* Not a true rice, but the seed of a marsh grass. Dark color, robust flavor, nutlike quality. Requires longer cooking. More costly than the true rices because of the difficulty in harvesting.

BLAND

This time: Blandness is one of rice's virtues, making it compatible with a host of other ingredients. Often it is intentionally served as a foil for highly seasoned, saucy foods. But when served as a separate side dish, it requires more flavor. After cooking, try adding minced parsley or scallions for a pretty color contrast as well as a flavor fillip. Depending on the dinner, soy sauce or hot pepper sauce, grated cheese, chutney, or a creole sauce can be sprinkled over rice. One of my favorite presentations was passed along by a Middle Eastern friend. His pilafs sometimes were as simple as sautéing slivered almonds and raisins in butter, tossing with the rice, and seasoning with curry spices and rosewater. Plain rice transformed into lovely aromatic pilaf—a great addition to any table, but especially Middle Eastern fare.

Next time: Cook in bouillon or stock instead of water, with a little butter, salt, and herbs or spices to taste.

BOILING OVER

This time: A dab of butter prevents a spillover. Reduce heat at same time.

Next time: Use a larger pot for the same quantity rice. Rice triples in volume when cooked. When water is brought to a boil after rice is added, reduce heat to simmer and cover. Do not let rice cook in rapidly boiling water.

BROWNED, BURNED

This time: A resourceful Chinese cook must have invented sizzling soup after the rice burned to a crust in the pot. The renowned soup gets its name from the snap-and-crackle noise when hot soup meets hot crusty rice in the bowl. No need to make the soup at the time of the rice mishap. Dried, browned rice can be stored in a tin until needed. Chunks of the rice can be deep-fried and salted for a type of rice patty snack. Browned but separate grains give good texture to a fried rice; stir-fry, season with soy sauce and add eggs and any leftover cooked meats and vegetables. Grains that have hardened together can be broken into 3-inch pieces and used as individual pizza crusts. Or kept intact, the entire mass can be topped with mozzarella, tomato sauce, and the usual pizza fixings. Bake in a pizza pan just until cheese melts and ingredients are heated.

Next time: Follow directions on package and check rice just before end of cooking time. A little more hot water may be needed to prevent crusting. (See *To cook,* below.)

DRY

This time: A little hot water or broth stirred into the dry rice should do the trick. Re-cover and allow to cook further until water is fully absorbed. Or place in rice steamer (a makeshift utensil can be constructed with a sieve or fine mesh basket on a rack over water in a large pot) and allow dry rice to absorb moisture from the simmering liquid under it.

Next time: George Kuan, owner of Szechwan House and Hunan Palace restaurants in Chicago specializing in four Chinese cuisines, suggests steaming rice as the solution to the quandary of how much water to add. Cooked in a steamer, rice absorbs the moisture necessary to make it swell and become tender. In southern China rice is frequently steamed right in serving bowls; rice and water are in the bowls, then placed on a rack in a pot holding water that comes to a level partway up the bowl. It is covered and cooked. When boiling rice, add about twice the amount of water as rice used. (See *To cook,* below.) Keep simmering liquid beside the cooking rice to add as needed. Do not add cold liquid to hot rice.

DULL COLOR AFTER COOKING

This time: Taste and texture are not affected when rice dulls, so use as intended. If the loss of sheen and whiteness bothers you, camouflage by topping with a saucy mixture or turning into a soup, casserole, or pudding.

Next time: To keep rice bright white add 1 teaspoon lemon juice or 1 tablespoon vinegar to cooking water.

HARD, CHEWY

This time: Stir a small amount of hot liquid into the cooking rice, cover, and simmer a little longer. Brown and wild rice need longer cooking and are chewier than white.

Next time: Keep a pot of simmering liquid near the rice during cooking and add as needed.

GUMMY, STUCK TOGETHER

This time: Steam over hot water. Serve in a heated bowl or on a hot platter to avoid further softening. Slightly sticky rice is perfect for picking up with chopsticks; serve in little bowls with an Oriental dinner, or turn into Spanish rice. Good for rice fritters or waffles, too. Browning rice before cooking keeps grains separate. Frying cooked, gummy rice gives it substance (see *Browned*).

Next time: Use less water—about double the amount of rice, or slightly less. Do not overcook and use the right size pot for quantity cooked. Rice cooks better in low, wide pans than in high, narrow pots. Washing raw rice 2 or 3 times before cooking removes excess starch and ensures a light, fluffy product, but destroys nutrients.

OVERCOOKED, SOGGY

This time: Stir-frying soft rice firms up the texture; add chunks of leftovers and season for a quick side or main dish. Or add to soup, custard pudding, fritters, or casserole, where the overcooked quality will go unnoticed. The Chinese make a kind of porridge called jook from deliberately soggy rice mixed with chicken or fish and sauce.

Next time: Setting a timer a minute or two before rice is supposed to be done helps you save it from unnecessary longer cooking. Follow directions on package for best results. If necessary, add more hot liquid toward end of cooking. Japanese new crop rice requires much less water than usual dry rice, so check type when buying.

UNEVEN COOKING

This time: When some rice in the pot seems underdone while other grains are soft, stir thoroughly, cover with tight-fitting lid, and continue cooking until all grains are tender. Better to risk some being overdone than trying to bite through hard grains. Allowing rice to stand a few minutes in covered pot after removing from heat firms it up a bit.

Next time: Stir well when adding rice to boiling water. Make sure all grains are well covered with liquid. Do not overfill pot. Check burner or utensil used; some heat unevenly. In this case, turning pot occasionally might help distribute heat better; or oven-bake rice.

Equivalents
1 cup raw white rice yields about 3 cups cooked.
1 cup raw brown rice cooks up to 3½ to 4 cups.
1 cup precooked rice gives 2 cups cooked.
1 cup parboiled rice yields 3½ to 4 cups cooked.
1 cup wild rice makes 3½ cups cooked.

To cook: Double-boiler, steamer, and oven-baked methods all work well. The saucepan two-to-one method, which I use for long-grain, produces fluffy rice with separate grains. Bring slightly less than 2 cups water or stock plus 1 tsp. salt (less if using bouillon) to a boil. Add 1 cup rice, stir well to moisten all grains. Bring to a boil again, then cover and simmer over low heat 13 to 14 minutes. *Do not lift cover until then.* Check rice. If dry but not quite tender, add a little more hot liquid, cover, and continue cooking another 2 minutes or so. If rice looks very moist when checked after 13 minutes, cover and continue cooking another 2 or 3 minutes. Let stand removed from burner about 10 minutes before serving.

Ricotta—*See Cheese.*

Roast Beef—*See Meat.*

Rock Cornish Hen—*See Poultry, Game Birds.*

Roe—*See Caviar.*

Rolls—*See Bread.*

Romaine—*See Lettuce.*

Roquefort—*See Cheese.*

Rosette—*See Deep-fried Foods.*

Roux—*See Thickeners; Sauces.*

Rutabaga—Like other root vegetables, this sturdy, storable crop has sustained many through cold winters in northern and central Europe. No one seems to know why it's called "the Swede," since it's not indigenous to Sweden.

DISCOLORED

This time: If raw, discoloration could be the result of improper storage—dehydration or heat. If cooked, it may have been caused by overcooking, or iron utensil. Pare, slice, or dice and cook in water to cover; add 1 to 2 teaspoons molasses to cooking liquid. After 12 to 15 minutes, depending on size of pieces, rutabaga will be an attractive gold. Molasses also sparks up flavor. Use in soups and stews instead of (or along with) potatoes. When you're out of molasses, cook in an inch of salted boiling water same amount of time, then mash with Cheddar and paprika, or with cinnamon, nutmeg, sugar, and butter or evaporated milk. Can be made into a pudding.

Next time: Buy firm roots, heavy for size, without blemishes or cracks. Storage vegetables are usually waxed to help preserve them.

Keep in cool, moist room, or in plastic bag in refrigerator, about a maximum of a month for best quality.

OVERCOOKED

This time: Mash and mix in butter, orange juice, cinnamon, and nutmeg—and perhaps coriander or curry spices—or butter and/or cream, herbs, salt, and pepper. Place in casserole, top with cheese and broil quickly. Rutabaga is compatible mashed with sweet potatoes or carrots, or orange rind and juice. Also good mashed with potatoes, parsley, butter, and sour cream.
Next time: See *Discolored.*

OVERMATURE

This time: Overgrown, lightweight roots tend to be pithy and tough. Cook according to directions (see *Discolored,* above), allow more cooking time and a *bit more molasses.* Sugar also helps to restore flavor. Serve in casserole with other vegetables and a sauce (white and cheese are good choices). Or mash as directed above in *Overcooked.* Turning it into a pudding with eggs, cream, spices, and sugar camouflages any mature taste and texture.
Next time: See *Discolored.*

SHRIVELED: See *Overmature.*

Rye—*See Bread.*

Safety—*See Fires, Burns; Food Spoilage, Poisoning.*

Salad, Salad Dressing—The word *salad* is a derivative of *sal,* Latin for salt. The dish was so named after ancestral versions eaten by ancient Romans: vegetables with salt, the only available preservative then. Salting was a method of long storing. Most of the tips below apply to tossed green salads, which are more perishable and fragile than others. For information on other salads, turn to particular ingredients.

BLAND

This time: If the salad lacks taste after tossing, it's not too late to sprinkle on more herbs, spices, lemon juice, or whatever seasoning might enhance it. Sliced olives or green onions, nuts, capers, seasoned croutons, grated cheese, pickles, and numerous other tasty additions can be made at the last minute. Or try mixing a little more dressing with a higher concentration of seasonings, then pour over and toss.

Next time: Make sure herbs and spices are fresh. Shop for quality oils and vinegars. Add seasonings to the oil first before gradually adding the vinegar; the oil holds the flavors better than vinegar. The usual proportion is 3 or 4 parts oil to 1 part vinegar, lemon or lime juice. Personally, I prefer a more even ratio, especially when using the milder lemon juice. Explore the vast array of oils and vinegars. Try a robust French walnut oil or a tart black-currant vinegar.

For a different taste sensation, select a rich olive oil and a flavored wine- or herb-vinegar or whisk a rich Dijon mustard into a vinaigrette. Taste the dressing when combining, adding complementary ingredients as needed. Allow dressing to stand for flavors to blend.

DRESSING DOESN'T ADHERE

This time: Remember the basic premise: oil and water don't mix. Salad dressing will slip off wet ingredients. If the dressing is sitting in the bottom of the bowl under greens, remove vegetables and blot dry on paper toweling. Then return to bowl, toss, and watch how dressing and ingredients cling together.

Next time: Allow enough time for drying after washing greens. One easy method I like is to spread washed and drained greens on a clean kitchen towel lined with paper toweling. Roll up and chill until ready to prepare. They emerge from the refrigerator crispy cold and dry, ready to absorb your dressing.

LEFTOVERS

This time: Little remainders of tossed bean and potato salads or slaw make a nice base for sandwich spreads; mash and add to a little mayonnaise, sour cream, or cheese spread. Most salads can embellish an omelet; chop and add directly to the eggs or use as filling. One of my favorite combinations is cottage cheese flavored with a bit of leftover tossed or bean salad—a quick dieter's lunch. Several kinds of leftover salad can be served on a relish tray as an appetizer. Or try tossing together for a salad mélange.

SPICY, VINEGARY

This time: You thought the spice or herb bottle had a shaker—it didn't. Now half the contents are on the salad. When you don't have more salad ingredients to stretch out the seasoning, remove the top layer and rinse off. Dry and return to the bowl. When the seasonings are already incorporated, or the strong taste stems from a heavy vinegar, add more oil, sour cream, or yogurt. These help buffer the flavor. A touch of sweetness helps to counter an acid vinegar.

Next time: Try milder and better aged vinegars. Judiciously add seasonings to the dressing instead of the salad. Always taste before tossing. It's easier to stretch or adjust the dressing than the entire salad.

WILTED

This time: Slightly wilted greens can look rejuvenated when some new ones are added to the mixture. When they have really given up, shred, sauté, and serve as a hot vegetable. Nice mixed with leftover rice. Or chop and use as a flavorful omelet filling. Chopping diminishes the droopy appearance. Try tossing chopped salad with a heavier one, such as kidney bean or macaroni.

Next time: Add moist ingredients just before serving. Cherry tomatoes are better than sliced large ones in a tossed salad. Drain any fruit well before adding. Add just enough dressing to coat ingredients lightly; don't drown them. Try to estimate how much salad will be used, and make just about what is needed.

Salmon—*See Fish.*

Salmonella—*See Food Spoilage, Poisoning.*

Salsify (oyster plant)—Its juicy but firm milky flesh and taste undoubtedly gave this herb root its secondary name. The kind most commonly used is white skinned; scorzonera is the black-skinned type with a similar interior. Both varieties can be used interchangeably.

DISCOLORED

This time: Like Jerusalem artichokes and other white-fleshed vegetables, salsify darkens upon cutting. Sauté and cover with a creamy sauce or turn into casserole or stew.

Next time: Drop slices or cut pieces immediately into cold water containing a little lemon juice or vinegar. Cook (not in iron pot) in a little boiling salted water to which 1 to 2 teaspoons lemon juice or vinegar have been added. Cover and cook 5 to 8 minutes, until just tender, depending on size and age. Do not overcook, and avoid alkaline water; both discolor.

OVERCOOKED

This time: Mushy salsify can be puréed and mixed with a little cream, butter, and seasonings and served as a vegetable. Or purée and use for cream of vegetable soup (p. 315).
Next time: See Discolored.

OVERMATURE, WOODY

This time: Cook longer with more acid in water; chop, cut into strips, or mash and serve with a creamy sauce, like a béchamel or a hollandaise. Can be puréed for cream of vegetable soup (p. 315).
Next time: Select clean, firm, medium-sized roots, free of soft spots. Avoid the large ones, especially shriveled. Store in plastic bag in refrigerator up to 4 to 5 days.

Too Salty—One of four basic tastes. Generally, very salty foods (e.g., anchovies, olives, etc.) become less so after a rinsing or brief soaking in clear water. A raw potato absorbs excess salt when allowed to simmer in an overseasoned broth. See individual foods.

Sandwich—The sandwich takes its name from an 18th-century gambler, the Earl of Sandwich, who ate cold roast beef on bread so he could remain at the gaming table. Having a meal without silverware was a return to the more primitive eating with the hands. The convenient sandwich rapidly became the answer for eating on the run and for workers, schoolchildren, and picnickers. Sometimes the filling is placed on one slice of bread, and the result is called an open-face sandwich, like the Danish smørrebrød. In Denmark I watched experts construct this beautiful sandwich art form with varied colorful ingredients: cheeses, cucumber, tomato, tiny shrimp, and smoked eel. Whatever calories one saves from eating only one piece of bread are canceled out by the thick slathering of rich local butter on the single slice. Besides, the smørrebrød are so delicious, no one stops at one.

DRY

This time: Add lettuce, tomato slices, relish, or spread.

Next time: When using dry sausage, roast meat, or cheese, toasting the bread makes the sandwich even drier. Use either fresh, moist bread, or add some moistening agents: butter, mayonnaise, relishes, tomato slices, etc. When packing sandwiches, wrap moist vegetables separately to prevent sogginess.

SOGGY

This time: Butter outside of sandwich and fry on both sides to brown, or broil, browning both sides. Another delicious solution is dipping into a milk-egg mixture before browning in butter—a version of the French croque monsieur (dipped and fried ham-and-cheese sandwich).

Next time: Serve immediately after adding juicy ingredients. When packing or freezing sandwiches avoid using juicy meats or moist relishes. Select drier sliced meats, sausages, and cheeses. Spread bread with butter or mayonnaise (or a sandwich spread made with one of them) to seal bread from moisture. Toasting helps bread retain crispness.

To freeze: Most sandwich fillings emerge from the freezer in good shape; the exceptions are hard-cooked eggs, raw vegetables, jelly and preserves, sour cream, and mayonnaise.

Sardines—*See Fish.*

Sauces—French cookbooks begin with them, indicating their importance in one of the world's most sophisticated cuisines. And as with all great genealogies, the classic sauce family begins with several "hot mothers:" basic brown sauce or sauce espagnole (a richer, simplified modern version is demi-glace), white sauce or velouté (like the brown except made with white stock) and béchamel sauce (a thick white sauce made with milk). Also important in the *hot* category is tomato sauce. The two major cold sauce varieties are mayonnaise and oil and vinegar. Once the basic techniques for the essential categories have been mastered, they may be applied to all members of the family. Contemporary, simplified nouvelle cuisine sauces are lighter and flourless, thickened by reduction of liquid, often stock or cream. "The preparation of sauces requires a great deal of care," wrote the late legendary "haute cuisine" French chef Auguste Escoffier in *Les Sauces*, first published in 1934. "It is through the subtlety by which our sauces are constructed that the French cuisine enjoys such worldwide supremacy." French sauces, in particular, do indeed require much attention and skill. But once a relatively few basic principles are mastered, they are not that difficult. And the trouble is more than worth it. A great sauce has the power to transform an ordinary food into a spectacular experience. Even the most problematic sauce challenge need not intimidate you when armed with the following facts. Both French and non-French sauce varieties are treated here with problems peculiar to the particular type.

Butter, emulsified (beurre blanc, beurre rouge as examples). Beurre blanc, the darling of modern French cuisine, is an emulsion of a small amount of acid (usually white wine vinegar or white wine reduced with shallots) and a large amount of butter. The rouge sister sauce is made with red wine or red wine vinegar. Many techniques and variations exist. Related to the other emulsified sauces (hollandaise, mayonnaise, etc.), these have no egg, so they are in a separate class. Beurre blanc is especially compatible with poached light fish or chicken and vegetables, the rouge with richer fish and light fowl or meats.

SEPARATED

This time: When the sauce just begins to break, remove it from the heat and whisk in an additional two tablespoons cold butter. If the sauce has thoroughly separated, bind it by whisking in a tablespoon of whipping cream or crème fraîche; sauce may be slightly thinner. Or stir some of the broken sauce into an egg yolk, then gradually whisk into the sauce, heating gently while whisking. The sauce will not be a true beurre blanc, but will be delicious.

Next time: Use very low heat and a saucepan that is a good heat conductor (not aluminum). The most common preparation method is to remove the acid reduction from the heat, then begin introducing bits of cold butter. Return to low heat while whisking in the remaining chilled butter in small amounts. When thickened, serve immediately, or set in bowl of warm water to hold awhile. Sauce will decompose upon cooling. Leftovers may be refrigerated, brought to room temperature, blended in a mixer and served over hot food, which will melt the sauce.

Butter-Based and Egg-Thickened (hollandaise and its offspring, béarnaise, as examples)

CURDLED

This time: There are several ways to uncurdle a hollandaise. Here are my recommended methods:

1. By far one of the best methods is the addition of arrowroot or cornstarch. (Use arrowroot only if sauce will be served within minutes and not reheated.) Remove the curdled sauce from the heat immediately and cool with 2 to 3 teaspoons cold milk per 2 cups sauce. Blend in a scant teaspoon arrowroot starch or cornstarch and observe how the sauce pulls itself together. I received this handy tip from a Montreal French Canadian at a Chicago Black Hawks hockey game. His date told me that only the day before he had rescued a friend's sauce.

It seems those French Canadians know their cooking every bit as thoroughly as their hockey. I never found this cornstarch cure in any book; most of them recommend the egg-yolk method listed below. But I found some chefs who depend upon cornstarch for preventing and rectifying curdling both in hollandaise-type sauces and cream soups. When Carl Peralta was the executive chef of the Chicago Press Club, he made hollandaise daily. He used a cooked cornstarch-water paste to whisk into curdled sauce over low heat. "Hold the metal bowl over a steam table or place sauce over hot water in a double boiler and whisk until the cornstarch brings it back together," said Peralta. "Add a little at a time until the right consistency is reached. The egg-yolk method works too, but cornstarch makes it hold up better over a long period of time," he explained. When you catch the sauce "just breaking," he advised adding a drop or two of hot stock or water and whisking quickly; no heat is necessary. This is a preferable remedy if you're planning to glaze the sauce (run it under the broiler). Once the cornstarch is added, he claimed the sauce doesn't glaze well. But that should not concern most home cooks anyway.

2. The most common book method is to beat an egg yolk with a pinch of dry mustard, then gradually add the curdled sauce to the

fresh yolk. This produces a richer and quite presentable sauce, although some visible flecks remain.

3. Another good egg-yolk remedy is to beat 1 yolk with 1 teaspoon cold water, stir in about ¼ cup warm curdled sauce; gradually add this mixture to the rest of the sauce and reheat gently in top of double boiler over boiling water.

4. At the first sign of the sauce breaking, remove from heat and briskly stir in a little boiling stock or water, a few drops at a time. This does not yield a presentable sauce once it is very curdled. Food consultant-writer Marina Polvay adds 1 teaspoon hot water per cup of curdled sauce, beats for 2 minutes, then places it over hot water and beats until warmed through. More water added thins the sauce.

5. Chef Carolyn Buster of The Cottage Restaurant (Calumet City, Illinois) shares these tips: "Immediately place curdled egg-thickened sauce in food processor or blender and blend a few seconds until smooth. If a sauce begins separating because it's too hot, remove from heat, let stand a few minutes, whip with wire whisk." She has held this type of sauce for up to 3 hours in a thermos or vacuum bottle.

6. When sauce just begins to curdle, remove from heat. Quickly whisk in 1 to 2 tablespoons heated whipping cream. This addition changes the character of the sauce somewhat, but is still quite a distance from mock hollandaise, a mixture of cream sauce and the real thing.

Next time: Briskly stir melted clarified butter, drop by drop at first, then in a fine trickle, into the thickened yolk mixture. Although each yolk can absorb a maximum of about 3 ounces butter, most recipes use the proportion of 2 ounces per yolk. Cook, whisking constantly, over low heat in heavy enameled or French copper pan; if using a double boiler, cook over a little hot, not boiling water (water not touching top part). Uninterrupted preparation is important. Try to avoid making hollandaise-style sauces on a humid day; if you must, use clarified butter. Keep sauce barely warm in pan of lukewarm water until needed. Reheating usually causes curdling (see *Leftovers*).

THICK

This time: Whisk in very gradually up to 1 or 2 tablespoons hot water, stock, vegetable cooking liquid, milk, cream, or wine, depending on how sauce will be served.

Next time: Heat egg yolks slowly while stirring continuously so they will thicken into a smooth custard. Whether you beat them over hot water or low heat makes no difference, as long as the process is gentle. Add about 3 ounces butter and ¼ teaspoon lemon juice to each medium yolk. A proportion higher in yolk may result in a sauce too thick. Or use a whole egg for a lighter sauce.

THIN

This time: Measure 1 teaspoon lemon juice and 1 tablespoon sauce in a mixing bowl rinsed out with hot water. Beat the two with a wire whisk briefly, until thickened. Gradually beat in remaining sauce, ½ tablespoon at a time, beating until each addition has thickened before adding next.

Next time: Add butter very gradually to the sauce. Egg yolks must be allowed time to absorb each addition of fat before another is presented. Too much butter added at a time will prevent sauce from thickening.

Leftovers: Store in covered container up to 2 days in refrigerator. Bring to lukewarm by beating 2 tablespoons sauce over very low heat or hot water, then very gradually beating in remaining sauce. Keep warm in pan of (or over) lukewarm water. Also may be frozen in freezer containers. To thaw, place closed container in bowl of lukewarm water and let warm tap water run over until sauce becomes lukewarm.

Cold (mayonnaise and vinaigrette)

CURDLED, SEPARATED (MAYONNAISE)

This time: The same egg-yolk procedure used for hollandaise works for mayonnaise. Beat 1 egg yolk slightly with dash of mustard. Spoon off excess oil at top; stirring aggravates separation. Then gradually beat the separated cold sauce into the beaten yolk, a tablespoon at a time at first, then gradually increase the doses, treating the curdled mixture as if it were oil. A separated sauce will also recombine by substituting vinegar, prepared mustard, or even 1 tablespoon water for the yolk, depending on desired piquancy.

Next time: Extreme cold and warm storage temperatures cause curdling and separating. Have ingredients at room temperature and add oil slowly. Store mayonnaise in warmest part of refrigerator. Serve sauce separately rather than risk its coming apart over hot food.

VINEGARY (ESPECIALLY APPLIES TO VINAIGRETTE)

This time: Add more oil, even a different, compatible kind. A pinch of sugar or dash of fruit juice also helps to offset a sharp vinegar taste. Or add more sweetness for a sweet-sour dressing.

Next time: Use a finer, more delicate vinegar, such as a fruity peach or an aged wine type. Do not expect plain distilled white to be anything but harsh. The classic proportions of oil to vinegar are 3 to 1. Personally, I prefer oil and vinegar to be about equal for most green salads. For a more delicate dressing, use lemon or lime juice instead of or as well as vinegar.

WON'T BIND (MAYONNAISE)

This time: Any cold ingredients should be allowed to come to room temperature before beginning the sauce. It is essential to add oil drop by drop at first, beating constantly, then in a slow trickle. After each ⅓ cup, stop and beat. A tablespoon of boiling water beaten in at the end (or directly into yolks at the start) binds the emulsion. If a thunderstorm is brewing outside, stop everything and wait until it blows over. It will prevent your mayonnaise from binding. Remarkable, but true. (*See Weather.*)

Next time: Plan ahead when making mayonnaise. Avoid a stormy day; allow all ingredients to come to room temperature; then follow a dependable recipe carefully. Finishing the sauce with boiling water thins it at first, but the sauce thickens after standing.

Dessert: There are numerous types in this grouping: the high-sugar sauces, such as butterscotch and chocolate, for ice-cream toppings; the fruit mixtures, based on fresh, frozen, dried or preserved fruits; those stemming from soft custard thickened with egg, starch, whipping cream or a butter base; and the flavorful syrups. These are among the least troublesome of the sauces. Sweet and hard sauces do not separate and can be refrigerated, tightly covered, for more than a month. The high sugar content prevents spoilage organisms from developing. Custard sauces are an exception: they should be used within a few days and do not freeze well. Most others can be frozen.

TOO THICK

Add slightly more liquid to thin out a viscous mixture. Add gradually while stirring. Chef André Daguin of Gascony suggests thinning a crème anglaise by beating in more cream. However, "The best ice cream is made with a thick crème anglaise," he says.

TOO THIN

Thicken cooked sauces with arrowroot starch, cornstarch or flour; make a paste of the starch and a little liquid, then gradually blend into sauce and cook until thickened. For uncooked sauces, add more of whatever thickener is used or compatible (whipped cream, drained puréed fruit, etc.).

Gravies: The three basic gravy types are dish, kettle, and pan. The first is meat juices from carving; the others are composed of fat, starch, and liquid. The tips that follow should smooth out all your gravy worries.

Tip: Lightly grease pans before roasting meat to prevent any dripping juices from burning before the meat fats have coated pan bottom.

CURDLED, LUMPY

This time: Straining through a medium-fine sieve will remove most lumps. To make it even smoother, or for only slightly curdled gravy, gradually add small amounts of hot water, whisking or stirring continuously until smooth.

Next time: Either too much fat or flour can cause a separation or curdling. Too much flour, or adding it improperly, can result in a thick, pasty, lumpy mass. Try using equal parts flour and fat, stirring together until flour is dissolved before gradually adding liquid; then stir continuously during cooking until thickened and smooth. Flour also can be dissolved in a little cool liquid, then slowly stirred into the drippings while stirring and cooking. Always use low heat and stir constantly.

TOO LIGHT IN COLOR

This time: Brown flour by spreading on shallow pan and baking in 250-degree oven about 30 minutes, scraping and stirring frequently until browned. Browning reduces thickening power of all-purpose flour to about half; so replace white all-purpose flour with double the amount of browned flour. Extra browned flour can be stored in a covered container in a cool place. Another remedy to color a light gravy is to cook more roux (equal parts butter and flour) until deep golden brown, but not scorched. Stir in gravy gradually, until well combined. A quick method is to add a little gravy browning sauce to impart both richer taste and color.

Next time: When there aren't many meat drippings to scrape up from pan bottom, use one of the recommended coloring methods above. When using water instead of stock, enrich with a beef bouillon cube or granules. Another trick for darkening gravy is to add about ½ teaspoon sugar to fat before adding flour. The sugar caramelizes and imparts a rich, browned color after cooking several minutes.

TOO THICK

This time: Gradually blend in more pan juices, stock, wine, or water. Simmer, stirring, until well blended and heated.

Next time: Have extra stock or compatible liquid on hand, and avoid cooking gravy down too much. Use less flour. About 1 tablespoon flour per cup liquid makes a slightly thickened gravy. When using browned flour, remember thickening power is cut in half with browning. To ready more liquid, pour off fat after meat is cooked. Add ⅓ cup or more hot water or stock to pan, cook on burner, stirring and scraping up all the succulent solidified, darkened fragments. The addition of wine hastens the process and heightens flavor and aroma.

TOO THIN

This time: Cook the sauce down until it's the proper consistency. Or (if to be used within minutes) add arrowroot, flour, or another thickener, such as potato starch, cornstarch, egg yolks, or tomato paste. When thickening with flour, blend 2 parts water with 1 part flour, then stir in as much of this paste as needed. Cook and stir or whisk gravy until thickened, at least 3 minutes to reduce raw flour taste. Another remedy is to whisk in about 1 tablespoon cold sweet butter, bit by bit, to heated, strained gravy. Rotate pan in circular motion so butter makes a swirl in the gravy as it melts.

Next time: Allow more time for cooking gravy down, or add more flour to the fat. When using pan drippings, strain and remove excess fat. Reheat an amount almost equal to the flour used. Add flour or other thickener to fat and cook until consistency of whipping cream. Gradually add just enough liquid to reach desired consistency.

Hot Butter (drawn butter, lemon butter sauce, or herb butter sauce)

BITTER, SPECKLED

This time: Strain out larger specks through fine sieve or cheesecloth; use remainder for sautéing vegetables, meat or poultry. A little sugar helps remove the bitter taste. Chutney or another sweet, spicy mixture has a similar effect, and can enhance a casserole when drizzled over.

Next time: Use clarified butter. The solids in butter burn easily.

THINNED, OILY APPEARANCE

This time: Remove a spoonful of the sauce to a cold mixing bowl; gradually beat in the remaining sauce by small spoonfuls. Do not reheat, but beat 2 to 3 tablespoons hot liquid into the sauce bit by bit.

Next time: Prepare sauce just before serving. If necessary to hold the sauce awhile, place bowl in pan of barely tepid water, just warm enough to keep butter from congealing; or warm in microwave on lowest (defrost) cycle, following manufacturer's directions. Sauce also can be kept warm near the very faint heat of a pilot light.

Marinades and Specialty Sauces (cooked and uncooked marinades for meats and poultry; barbecue sauce; Chinese hot mustard sauce; tomato sauce; sweet-sour sauce, and other miscellaneous sauces). These mixtures tend to be more intensely flavored than other sauces. Most of them store well in the refrigerator; for very long storage, they can be frozen in sealed containers.

BLAND (MARINADES)

This time: When there's time, add whole spices to a cooked marinade and bring to boil, or quickly season with ground spices. To cold marinades, add more vinegar, wine, lemon juice, crushed garlic or ground spices. Flavor of whole spices must be brought out by heating, but ground spices are easily distributed in cold liquids. Some spice suggestions: pepper (beef), allspice, nutmeg (veal), cloves (ham), curry powder (chicken or lamb), ginger (pork), paprika, and mustard. Herbs that enhance many marinades are thyme (compatible with most meats and poultry), rosemary (especially good with lamb), oregano (beef), marjoram, bay leaf, celery leaves, and mint (lamb). Seeds also add good taste to these blends; a sprinkling of caraway, fennel, or poppyseed does wonders. Hot pepper sauce or crushed chilies add heat without cooking to the sauce.

Next time: Taste after mixing the marinade, adding more seasonings as necessary. Plan ahead and allow flavor to blend thoroughly. Do not add ground spices to slow-cooking dishes, because they lose potency with prolonged heating.

DISCOLORED

This time: Chopped parsley, chives, scallions, and various herbs can brighten up a drab sauce. A darkened tomato sauce can be lightened with the addition of chopped tomatoes and lemon. When you're not pleased with a sauce's appearance, you can sometimes blend it with another sauce (mushroom and cheese are compatible) or incorporate it into a dish where it becomes secondary instead of the showcase.

Next time: Incorporate wine into a sauce before any egg, milk, cream, or butter. A tomato sauce will keep a fresh color if cooked slowly and not too long.

TOO THICK

This time: Thin down with whatever liquid is in the sauce: salad oil, vinegar, wine, lemon juice. Barbecue sauce can be diluted with broth, water, or tomato juice. If a large amount of liquid is added, blend into sauce well and (for cooked sauce only) bring to boil for best flavor.

Next time: Cook down to desired consistency, allowing for thickening upon standing.

TOO THIN

This time: Allow a cooked sauce to heat longer until more evaporation thickens it. Uncooked sauces should be given time to stand, since they thicken upon storage.

Next time: Allow slightly more time for cooking down. Prepare uncooked sauces ahead and refrigerate several days for best consistency and flavor to develop.

Starch-Thickened: The classic French brown and white sauces begin with a roux (cooked flour and fat) and take shape with the addition of a good stock. Some French chefs make these sauces without flour. The velvety-rich sauces of Jean Banchet, chef–owner of the highly acclaimed Le Français Restaurant in the Chicago suburb of Wheeling, never see flour. This impassioned master of cuisine browns the bones first to obtain a dark color. After the stock is added, he reduces the sauce by simmering until the proper consistency is obtained, eliminating the need for a thickener. This flourless method also eliminates any chance of curdling.

CURDLED

This time: Lumps in a flour-thickened sauce can be removed by straining. A blender can help in achieving a smooth texture.

Next time: Blend flour thoroughly into the fat, cooking and stirring until thickened and smooth. Gradually add hot liquid (some cooks add cold with success), stirring continuously during cooking to ensure a smooth sauce. Reducing stock to sauce consistency prevents the problem.

LIGHT (BROWN SAUCE)

This time: When the sauce is already prepared, the easiest way to darken it is to add browned flour (see *Gravies, Light*).

Next time: Brown the bones first before making stock. For other preventions see *Gravies, Light*.

THICK

This time: Gradually stir in more stock, heating gently until incorporated and heated through.

Next time: Stop cooking just when the desired consistency is reached. In a heavy pan that retains heat, the sauce can go on cooking even after removed from the burner.

THIN

This time: Cook longer until desired consistency is obtained for best quality. Or thicken with a little flour-water paste (whitewash) stirred in gradually; cook and stir until smooth and thickened.

Next time: Add liquid gradually until correct thickness is reached. Allow enough time for reduction, which produces a richer and better sauce.

Sausage—*See Meat.*

Scallions—*See Onions, Green.*

Scallops—*See Shellfish.*

Scum (skin)—*See Milk.*

Sea Urchin—*See Seafood.*

Seafood—In this book the broad term applies to all miscellaneous water inhabitants we eat besides those covered in Fish and Shellfish—eel, frog, sea urchin, octopus, squid, terrapin, turtle, and the beleaguered whale. Several of these creatures are quite different from their fish and shellfish relatives. The snakelike eel is popular smoked in northern Europe, but hard to find here except in major East Coast cities. Although the frog spends much of its life out of water, it's classified as seafood. Its flesh resembles that of other fish, although the texture and taste of frogs' legs is often compared to chicken. Octopus and squid are related; both have tentacles and emit a protective black-ink camouflage. Both are popular in the Mediterranean and the Orient. I'll never forget the delicious flavor of baby octopus stewed in its ink, which I first tasted in a Madrid restaurant. Baby eels, quickly sautéed in olive oil, are another specialty of that city. From the pain sea urchins cause when stepped on, one might not expect the great pleasure they can bring to the table.

Happily, my first meeting with an urchin was the latter experience in a Martinique café. It was love at first taste when the steaming, spicy sea urchin soup (with roe) was set before me. Unfortunately, it makes rare appearances in the U.S. Both freshwater turtles and sea terrapins are classified as endangered species. However, from a few more plentiful types, certain turtle steaks and soups are still available at Florida restaurants and other natural-habitat areas of the shelled reptile. The only mammal in the seafood category is the gravely endangered whale. At this critical point in time, I strongly urge readers to delete whale entirely from menu considerations.

BLAND

Select the more robust seasonings and sauces (horseradish, mustard, rémoulade, provençal) for smoked seafood and the sturdier turtle. Batter-fried squid and octopus require only lemon; when served in their own flavorful ink, a touch of minced garlic and parsley are complementary. Sea urchin can be simply boiled and served with lemon or highly spiced in a soup. A favorite preparation for frogs' legs is to dip them in flour or egg and crumbs, then sauté in butter with garlic and parsley. Most edible acids—lemon, orange, lime, pickles, cranberries, etc.—squeezed over or served with most seafood items will greatly enhance flavor.

DRY

Frogs' legs are most compatible with a white wine sauce or a hollandaise. The more robust seafoods can take richer sauces— mushroom, curry, anchovy butter, egg sauce. If you can obtain untreated (unblanched) squid and octopus with their ink still intact, this natural "sauce" lends flavor to the cooking broth and should be used whenever possible.

OVERCOOKED

Moisturize dry, hard pieces by simmering in liquid or saucing. Mushy, disintegrating seafood can be turned into a casserole or mashed and used in a spread or dip.

SALTY: See *Fish*.

TOUGH

This time: Cutting in smaller pieces—especially grinding—tenderizes tough cooked meat. Add moisture; simmer in broth or wine, top with sauce, add to soup or chowder or use in spreads, dips, and casseroles. Lemon juice squeezed over is a boon to chewy seafood. For more information, see *Shellfish, Tough.*

Next time: Allow at least several hours for marinating tougher seafood items in an acidic mixture, and do not overcook. Use lower heat and time carefully.

Seasonings—*See Herbs; Spices.*

Seeds—*See Herbs; Spices.*

Separating—*See* individual food.

Seviche—*See Seafood.*

Shallots—*See Garlic; Onions.*

Shellfish—Includes the crustaceans and the mollusks found in both fresh and salt water. The first group features segmented bodies and crusty shells. Lobster, shrimp (prawn on the West Coast), crayfish and crab are in this class. Mollusks are further divided into univalve (one shell)—including the abalone, snail, and conch—and bivalve (two shells)—among them the clam, oyster, mussel, and scallop. Freshness is essential to good flavor. Growing up in Chicago didn't provide the best opportunities for sampling shellfish. However, my parents made sure we had our share. On hot summer nights, before air-conditioning, my dad frequently drove us to Lake Michigan's shore, where we watched boats and savored the breeze. The evening highlight was always a stop at a waterfront shack that specialized in fried and boiled fresh Louisiana shrimp, which we promptly devoured with tangy sauce and lemon. Somehow, shrimp out of the bag, eaten with fingers, tastes better than when it's on fine china and cut with knife and fork. However you like it, here are some helpful facts to ensure full enjoyment and to use every bit. Shellfish is too delicious and expensive to waste. It also can be rather elusive at times. The first time I was preparing soft-shell crabs three of the critters started moving across the kitchen counter. I, of course, thought they had been killed and cleaned at the fish market!

I hastily scanned a dozen cookbooks before one explained how to kill a soft-shell crab. If you're like most cooks and don't have the stomach to kill your dinner, be sure to have crabs thoroughly prepared at the market. Lobsters and larger crabs are another matter. For best eating quality, they should be steamed or boiled live. Clamp the pot cover down firmly after dropping them in the boiling bath and don't allow guilt to spoil your dinner.

BLAND: See *Fish.*

DRY

This time: Drizzle melted butter or squeeze lemon juice over to moisten (especially important during dry cooking methods). Very dry shellfish can benefit from simmering in, or steaming over, broth, wine, or a sauce. Serve with the liquid or sauce for improved palatability. Or add to soup or chowder.

Next time: Avoid salting before cooking, as salt draws out natural juices. Use lower heat. When broiling, grilling, or baking, be sure shellfish is well lubricated to avoid drying. Basting sauces are essential to have nearby during these cooking procedures. When frying, remove from heat when browned on both sides and cooked through. Overcooking causes drying.

OVERCOOKED

This time: Shellfish that has become dry requires the addition of fat or liquid to reinstate moisture content, so add melted butter, lemon juice or a sauce (see *Dry*). Overcooking tends to toughen seafood, drawing moisture from the flesh. A delicate crustacean can get tough and fibrous from oversimmering. Use disintegrating meat in casseroles, soups, dips, or canapé spreads. Or purée for a pâté or forcemeat.

Next time: When appropriate, check shellfish during cooking and watch temperature carefully. Follow reliable recipes or timetables. An extra minute can mean the difference between just right and overdone. Better to err on the undercooked side, especially if ingredient is to be cooked further in a recipe.

SALTY: See *Fish, salty.*

SANDY (ESPECIALLY CLAMS AND MUSSELS)

This time: The quickest and best way of making clams and mussels part company with their home sand is to give them a bath in very warm salty water with a little lemon or vinegar added. The broth, if there's enough of it, will work well too. Be sure to allow enough time for the sand to settle to the bottom before serving broth. Being careful not to stir, pour or scoop off the top liquid, leaving sandy sediment behind.

Next time: Scrub shells very well with a brush under running water, then soak in salty warm water with a little vinegar or lemon juice, and the mollusks will release the sand. After 10 minutes, water may need changing. The number of baths depends on how sandy the mollusks are. Do not use very hot water or the shells will open and the flavorful liquor will be lost. A mussel tip from Cordon Bleu chef and cooking teacher Alma Lach is to add a handful of flour to the third water rinse. "They love flour," says Mrs. Lach. "There will be a lot of bubbling and gurgling. After 2 hours of the flour cleansing, rinse in clean water again. The mussels will be sandless and white."

TOUGH

This time: Some shellfish varieties are inordinately tough and chewy; abalone, conch, and quahogs are examples. The first two mollusks need pounding before cooking (unless ground or chopped), the third requires fine chopping. California seafood fanciers spend much time beating and flattening their beloved univalve abalone into steaks. Whether marinated or dipped in egg and crumbs, the abalone is addictive when quickly fried or pan-broiled. Another conch-lover and I have spent many hours pounding out aggressions on this stubborn marine snail. Conch always requires much determined elbow grease to tenderize its fibers. Ah, but the effort is amply rewarded. Conch flavor has a rare, sweet, scalloplike delicacy you won't soon forget. During a sojourn in the Yucatan, I culled some tips from an excellent native cook named Miriam in Puerto Morelos. She either pounds the conch slices into steaks and quick-fries them in hot butter, or marinates the chopped raw meat in a hot-chile-onion-tomato-lime-juice mixture for seviche. Both were wonderful. I've tried many conch techniques at home, and one of the best was putting the muscle through a food processor's chopping blade. I shaped the ground mixture into medium patties with a seasoned coating of fine breadcrumbs and quickly fried them in butter. Grinding is one of the best tenderizers and saves much of *your* muscle. As for the hard or "chowder" clams (an alias for quahogs), they are naturally chewy and therefore usually are directed to the chowder pot. A friend and I gathered a bucketful one morning on Cape Cod. We steamed them for brunch, ate them with crusty bread, and washed both down with lemony broth and white wine. Although the flavor was delicious, we agreed the chewy texture would have been better chopped in chowder. Any tough raw or cooked shellfish can be chopped or ground for fritters, soup, or gumbo. Add cooked seafood toward end of simmering.

Next time: Allow plenty of time for preparatory pounding, marinating, or simmering of the tough shellfish. A combination of two or more of these techniques increases palatability. Marinades made with vinegar, lemon or lime juice, or white wine are preferable for seafood. When frying a marinated item, be sure to drain and dry well to avoid splattering and a steamy texture. Overcooking any shellfish will toughen it.

To open tight mollusks: Oysters are more recalcitrant than their cousins, so oyster-shucking serves as a master exam for the bivalves. A special oyster knife or any sturdy short, flat-bladed knife makes the job easier. Hold the oyster flat-side up anchored in a towel with one hand. With the other, insert the flat blade in the hinge of the shell. Twist until the upper shell can be lifted and the hinge muscle cut. The upper shell should now pop open with ease. Warning: this is not an easy process. No two oysters have identical binding characteristics. Each is a separate challenge and can cause many cuts, raw spots, and violent language when in the hands of the novice. (Former novice talking!) When the intention was to serve oysters on-the-half-shell and several still refuse to yield, change plans and steam. Even the most obstinate oyster will succumb to heat. (Take into account that thicker-shelled individuals will require longer, perhaps hotter treatments.) Place on a rack over simmering liquid and be sure to save this seafood liquor. Any mollusks that refuse to open after sufficient doses of heat—or any that are open *before* cooking—should be considered unfit for consumption!

To store:

1. *To freeze:* Wrap fresh uncooked shellfish tightly in moisture-vapor-proof paper and store in 0-degree freezer up to 6 months. At a temperature higher than 0 degrees, chemical changes cause shellfish to deteriorate faster; in a refrigerator frozen food compartment, they can only be kept 1 month.

2. *To refrigerate:* Cover with moisture-proof wrap or keep in original wrap and store in coldest part of refrigerator, 32 to 40 degrees. Keeping shellfish on ice in a warmer refrigerator is a safe insurance. Use within 2 days.

To thaw: Place in refrigerator in wrappings until thawed, allowing about 6 hours per pound; then cook.

Sherbet—*See Sorbets.*

Shish Kabob—*See Meat.*

Shortcake—*See Cake, Foam; Bread, Quick.*

Shortening—*See Fat.*

Shrimp—*See Shellfish.*

Skim Milk—*See Milk.*

Sloppy Joes—Hot sandwiches comprised of a spicy ground beef-tomato sauce filling served in toasted hamburger (or sandwich) buns. See *Meat; Sandwich.*

Snails (escargots)—*See Shellfish.*

Soggy—See individual food.

Sole—*See Fish.*

Sorbets (Sherbets)—Today's sorbets are simply a frozen mixture of sugar-water syrup and fruit purée, sometimes with wine or liqueur. A less sweet version often serves as a palate refreshener between fish, fowl and/or meat courses of a multicourse dinner. Many old-fashioned recipes include either gelatin, beaten egg white or cream to insure a smooth texture. However, these additions are unnecessary when the sugar solution is in balance with the fruit purée or juice. They actually mask the pure, delicate fruit flavors that we have come to expect from sorbets. Adjustments are easy to make when tasting the mixture before freezing: if too sweet, add a small amount of lemon or lime juice. If too tart, add a teaspoon or two of sugar.

COARSE, GRAINY TEXTURE (CRYSTALLINE)

This time: Beat sorbet mixture in very cold food processor container fitted with cold metal blade or in chilled metal mixing bowl with cold beaters until smooth. Immediately freeze until solid. Repeat once or twice for extra smooth texture.

Next time: When processing in ice cream maker, use less coarse salt in proportion to cracked ice (usually 4 to 1). Texture is dependent upon correct salt-to-ice ratio since too much salt freezes the mixture too rapidly, causing large crystals and graininess. For best results, follow manufacturer's directions. When using the metal bowl/still-freeze method, freeze mixture until frozen about two inches from side (almost two hours), beat with mixer until smooth, cover and refreeze. Repeat procedure three times, freezing solid after final beating.

THIN; WILL NOT SET UP (FREEZE)

This time: For a too-sweet mixture add some lemon juice and more fruit purée or juice; repeat procedure. If an ice cream machine was used, perhaps there was too little salt in ratio to crushed ice. Follow manufacturer's directions for ice-salt ratio. When time is short, use runny sorbet as a sauce over fruit or custard.

Next time: Too much sugar is the first culprit in hindering freezing. Many recipes call for twice the amount of sugar needed. Professionals rely on a hydrometer which measures and controls sugar density, but it's possible to get excellent results relying on your taste buds. Add less sugar if fruits are sweet and overripe. Freezing dissipates some flavor, so sorbets are best freshly made. Add a squeeze of citrus juice or a bit of liqueur or wine to perk up flavor of sorbets. However, too much alcohol can also prevent freezing. Most recipes yielding 5 to 6 cups use about ¼ cup liqueur.

Sorrel—*See Greens; Spinach.*

Soufflé—The quintessence of delicate egg cookery. Generally the soufflé begins with a thick sauce (usually béchamel with egg yolks and seasonings added) to which a flavorful ingredient is added. Then stiffly beaten egg whites are folded in and the mixture is baked in a soufflé dish. Those cold-gelatin versions are not true soufflés, although they are of similar finished shape. The real soufflé is a temperamental specialty that waits for no one. Many a beautiful creation has risen to the occasion only to collapse, along with the cook's pride. Many variables affect the outcome of a soufflé: beaten egg whites, method of folding, prepared dish, temperature and baking time. The material here assists in the ups and downs of preparing this elegant dish.

DRY

This time: Serve with sauce. A thin sauce is better since it permits the dry soufflé mixture to absorb more moisture. A zesty orange sauce perks up a broccoli soufflé, or try a crème anglaise over chocolate.

Next time: Add more liquid to the base sauce. Avoid overbeating egg whites to dry stage; peaks should be stiff and glossy. Overbaking also causes the problem. For most 1½-quart 4-egg soufflés, use a 325- or 375-degree oven and bake about 40 to 50 minutes. For crustier top and runny center, as the French prefer, use a 400- to 425-degree oven for 25 to 35 minutes. Cut time by a third when dividing recipe among individual dishes.

FALLEN

This time: Don't let the fallen condition bring you to a similar fate. As long as it's thoroughly cooked, the soufflé is just as delicious. Slice and serve the deflated mixture on plates with a delicate sauce and no one will be the wiser. A quick sauce can be cooked while the covered soufflé keeps warm in a low oven. A cheese soufflé can take a spinach sauce; a spinach soufflé is super covered with cheese sauce. Sautéed vegetables (onions and mushrooms) also do the trick nicely. Or arrange pieces of soufflé over casserole of vegetables; top with shredded cheese; pass under broiler before serving. The desserts are easy to camouflage with chocolate, custard, or fruit sauces or dollops of whipped cream. If there's time, cool and chill the fallen beauty (especially a sweet one). Resembling a mousse cake in texture, it can then be sliced and sauced. Compatible flavors are lemon and cassis, peach and raspberry, and mocha rum and vanilla pecan.

Next time: Bake thoroughly before opening oven and sliding out rack. Resist checking until about 5 minutes before end of cooking. Then open door gently and touch top to see if it springs back. If it does, slide rack out to check color. Keep soufflé away from drafts. Cool air contracts the trapped air within the hot egg mixture, causing collapse. A reliable trick that aids in keeping the soufflé high until serving is a sprinkling of $\frac{1}{16}$ teaspoon cornstarch into the egg whites when beating. Also, the American version of baking at 325 to 375 degrees produces a sturdier soufflé less likely to collapse.

HARD PARTICLES IN SOUFFLÉ

This time: Large lumps can be removed, but the surgery leaves scars. Cover with sautéed vegetables and perhaps a sauce. Sweet soufflés can be topped with fruit and sauce.

Next time: Blend flour and butter well when making roux. Temper yolks with hot mixture and add gradually to basic sauce. Adding yolks too quickly to hot mixture will cause coagulation. Sauce must be blended well with egg whites or more lumps will result.

Leftovers: Cubes of cold broccoli, spinach or cheese soufflé make a colorful, savory addition to numerous soups; heat gently. And leftover soufflé can be delicious as breakfast the next day. The sweet fruit versions are especially good cold this way. Leftovers may be reheated gently by covering with foil and placing in a low oven; a microwave does a fine job in reheating without further cooking. To account for some drying out in reheating, serve topped with a sauce. Vegetable and main-dish soufflés can be scrambled gently over low heat and served over toast with appropriate sauce.

Next time: Serve individual soufflés, allowing about 1 to 1½ eggs per person.

NEVER ROSE

This time: The mixture may be compact, but should be thoroughly cooked. Slice and serve a savory soufflé as side dish covered with sauce or sautéed vegetables. Or cut and scramble gently with other ingredients and serve in pastry shell with sauce over. A mushroom soufflé is a good pastry filling topped with a blue-cheese sauce, for example. Or serve the mixture over waffles. When there's a lot of liquid in bottom of dish, drain off first.

Next time: Folding the egg whites into the sauce base (or the reverse) is perhaps the key technique in soufflé making. I prefer lightening the sauce base first by folding in one-fourth of the beaten egg whites, then folding that into the remaining whites. If the base was made ahead, bring it to room temperature. It's important to incorporate the ingredients well, but excessive folding decreases volume in egg whites (and thus in the finished product). For the best volume, have egg whites at room temperature before beating; use wire whisk or mixer and beat until peaks are stiff and glossy but not dry. Make sure bowl and beaters are clean and free of fat. A touch of acid or alcohol is a booster to rising. Avoid placing soufflé in drafts, since cold air will cause collapse. If added food pieces were large, next time cut smaller or purée. Prepare sides of dish by buttering and crumbing, or sugaring for dessert soufflés; this helps soufflé cling and climb to the top. Never grease a soufflé dish without adding a coarse coating.

RUNS OVER

This time: A cookie sheet or large pan under the soufflé will catch drips. Be careful not to jar baking soufflé. When done, trim rough edges before serving. Cover with sauce if necessary.

Next time: Soufflé dish should never be filled more than ⅔ or ¾ full. When mixture fills dish, it's essential to build a collar around rim of dish to permit higher rising without running over. A collar can be made easily by folding foil to about a 2-inch strip, then pressing around rim and fastening.

Soup—Although menus often bill a bowl of chunky soup and bread as a "peasant lunch," soup is just as often prepared for royalty. Escoffier originated several for Baron Rothschild and the German Kaiser. Whatever a soup's origin and style, every country has certain favorites, from the French pot au feu and tangy Greek avgolemono to sweet-sour Russian borscht, earthy Cuban black bean soup, and Chinese egg drop soup. America has its New England and Manhattan clam chowders, Philadelphia pepper pot, and many others. Louis Diat, the late renowned Ritz-Carlton chef who created crème vichyssoise glacée, claimed he was raised on soup. In *Gourmet's Basic French Cookbook: Techniques of French Cuisine,* Diat wrote: "In our country home in the Bourbonnais, we had soup for luncheon, soup for dinner and always soup for breakfast. For us,

a steaming bowl of thick hearty leek and potato soup was a far
better way to begin the day than the porridge of the British or the
American's strange meal of orange juice and ham and eggs." The
simmering pot can challenge your utmost culinary creativity. For a
soup that will bowl you over, begin with neck and knuckle bones or
fish heads in the stockpot. When time is short, purée vegetables in
the blender for a self-thickened restorative. Feed the soup pot various leftover scraps, but refrain from making it a catch-all. Use vegetable cooking water, but avoid the potently flavored broth of cabbage family members; store these separately and use for soups
based on one of these vegetables. The liquid results of starchy
vegetables and legumes sour rapidly and cloud a broth. They may
be added for flavor to mixtures based on the starch, such as bean
soup. And with a few personal touches, even some commercial
products can become special fare.

Basic classifications: The limitless variety can be divided by the
three main characteristics. The jellied and miscellaneous cold and
sweet variations fall into one of these main categories.
  1. Clear: includes broths (derived from cooking solid ingredients)
and the clarified broths—bouillon (primarily beef-based), consommé (predominantly from light meats) and Madrilène (consommé flavored with tomato).
  2. Light: thin cream soups; bisques; vegetable soups and sieved
and strained purées.
  3. Heavy: poultry and meat soups, chowders and thick cream
soups.

BLAND

This time: Quickly enliven with a sprinkling of herbs, spices,
lemon juice, or wine, or a combination. A flavorful garniture also
enriches a nondescript soup. On jellied and cold soups, float a
dollop of sour cream, yogurt, or whipped cream topped with capers,
chives, caviar, or fruit, depending on recipe. Sprinkle cream soups
with minced parsley, chives, green onions, or grated Parmesan. A
splash of Madeira, medium-dry sherry, dry wine, or lemon juice can
do wonders for clear soups. Try not to use more than ¼ cup wine to
1 quart soup. Bouillons and broths can be strengthened with the
addition of 1 or 2 bouillon cubes. To light soups, add the more

delicate herbs. Chervil, basil, and dill are especially good with tomato and most vegetable soups. Thyme is versatile, very appropriate for thinner cream soups and bisques. Add ⅛ to ¼ cup dry white wine to a fish, crab, or lobster bisque. In heavy soups use the more robust herbs, such as tarragon, oregano, and sage. A cup of beef broth per 3 cups bean or cabbage soup adds character. An oxtail or beef soup takes on a new dimension with the addition of a little full-bodied dry red wine. Seasoned croutons or grated aged cheese also sharpen flavor.

Next time: When beginning with bones for stock, brown in oven first to derive richest flavor. Browning chicken or meat first enriches both color and flavor. Use stock or bouillon instead of water whenever possible. Add salt at start of cooking to extract maximum essence from meat and bones. The best bones to select are from the neck, leg, and knuckles. Bird carcasses, fish heads, and cracked shells (lobster, shrimp, etc.) fortify fowl and seafood soups. Compatible vegetable juices, whole spices, and fresh herbs make their contributions to the pot by slow simmering. Add vegetables toward the end of cooking, sautéing them first in butter to bring out full flavor.

GREASY

This time: My mother always made her soups in advance so there was time to chill them and solidify the fat. I recall being amazed at the hard top layer that formed and could later be lifted off. When you want to serve the soup immediately, float a lettuce leaf or two. These fat blotters are better choices than paper towels, which sometimes disintegrate. Discard and add more if necessary. Another quick solution is to skim the surface with a clean cloth wrapped around an ice cube; the cold hardens the fat for easy removal. A baster also does a decent job, and so do those handy fat-skimmer gadgets, but they need washing.

Next time: Trim or pour off excess fat from meat before using for soup. Skim off excess fat as it accumulates during cooking when not able to chill soup in advance of serving.

SALTY

This time: Slice a raw potato and let it simmer in the soup for a while to absorb salt. It can then be discarded or added to the pot when cooking more tubers. A touch of sweetness or lemon juice helps to counter saltiness.

Next time: Lightly salt from the beginning, but allow for the addition of salty ingredients, such as bouillon, capers, olives, well-seasoned vegetables, and some wines. Reduction during simmering also concentrates flavors. Since many whole spices, herbs, and other comestibles release their full flavor during cooking, it's better to adjust seasoning when tasting at finish.

TOO THICK

This time: Thin with boiling stock, water, juice, or wine, depending on the soup. Let simmer a little longer to blend.

Next time: Avoid rapid cooking, which reduces the soup. Check soup periodically to thin density during cooking. Always add hot liquid, not cold, to cooking soup.

TOO THIN

This time: Gradually stir small amounts of the quart or so of hot liquid into a blend of 2 beaten egg yolks and about 1 tablespoon cream until completely incorporated. Increase yolks and cream for very thin soup. Serve immediately or hold briefly in top of double boiler over hot water to prevent separation. Other methods of giving substance and bulk: add more cooked, sieved, or puréed vegetables, meat, etc., stir in a little instant potato flakes (perhaps their best function), or use one of the usual thickening agents (see *Thickeners*).

Next time: If a soup of substance is desired, make certain that enough bulky ingredients or thickeners are added. Check periodically during cooking. An hour before soup is finished, it can be given a booster shot of 1 tablespoon barley, rice, or oatmeal for every 3 cups original stock.

Clear: (broth, bouillon, consommé)

CLOUDY

This time: Looking-glass-clear soup with sparkling transparency can only result from extracting all floating particles through clarification. For each quart broth, beat 1 egg white until frothy, then mix with about 2 teaspoons cold water; add along with the eggshell.

Acid products (lemon juice, vinegar, and tomato) also help clarify. Bring just to boil and simmer several minutes, stirring constantly. Remove from heat; do not disturb for about 20 minutes. Strain through a fine sieve lined with several thicknesses of cheesecloth wrung out in cold water. Chefs often use a mixture of raw ground beef mixed with egg white. The protein coagulates with gentle heat application; it's important *not* to boil the soup. Hard cooking causes cloudiness. Once the coagulated particles float, reduce heat to a bare simmer and cook about 1 hour. Many pros recommend beginning a consommé with cold stock to ensure transparency.

Next time: Starting with cold stock, cover or partially cover with loose-fitting lid during cooking to avoid the cloudy appearance. Allow enough time for clarification (*see Cloudy*). Never allow consommé to boil rapidly during clarification.

Cream (cream of celery, potato, chicken, etc.)

LUMPY

This time: Passing the soup through a sieve will strain out most lumps. If the soup is still not respectable, stir in a little cornstarch blended with cold water or broth and simmer a short time. It will pull separated mixture together.

Next time: Add ingredients gradually, stirring until smooth before cooking. Simmer, never boil. To be safe, use a double boiler for both cooking and reheating.

Fish (boiled mixtures, bisque, chowder)

FISHY TASTE

This time: The strong flavor emanates from boiling fish fat. Let the soup stand for a period after cooking, then skim off fat. A touch of sherry or ginger or both helps camouflage the fishy taste. Fresh lemon juice squeezed into almost any seafood soup except creamed helps cut a robust flavor.

Next time: Select lean fish for soups. Allow plenty of time for chilling and removing fat. Use fresh fish. Many recipes, such as that for bouillabaisse, call for rapid boiling in short spurts to extract fish essence and to boil off unsavory fish oils. Strain stock carefully to remove shell, fat, and bone fragments.

Jellied (consommé, madrilène)

RUNNY

This time: When there's time, melt down the mixture and blend in more dissolved gelatin, about 1½ teaspoons per 2 cups liquid. (First soften gelatin in cold liquid; dissolve in boiling liquid.) Place container in bowl of ice water; stir until thickened. Or chill in refrigerator.

Next time: Use the right bones and animal parts; veal knuckles and chicken feet have good jelling power. When adding powdered gelatin, be sure it is fully dissolved. There should be no graininess.

TOO STIFF

This time: Although the soup may be too tough to serve jellied, it can add much good flavor and color to other soups, gravies, and stews. When there's time, it can be melted and diluted, then rechilled.

Next time: Avoid reducing too much. Check periodically during simmering. When adding gelatin, use only about 1½ teaspoons per 2 cups liquid. Freezing gives a rubbery texture.

To reheat: Bring soups to be served hot just to the boiling point before serving. To prevent separation, stir and reheat (never boil) the more delicate cream and egg-thickened soups in double boiler over hot water.

TO STORE:

To freeze: Most soups freeze well. Leave about 1-inch headspace at top of container. Thaw slowly in refrigerator before using, or quicken thawing by heating partially thawed soup in saucepan just before serving. The texture of jellied soups often changes upon freezing.

To refrigerate: Most soups will keep well in covered containers 1 week if there's enough fat to rise and coat the surface. Soups can be stored much longer if boiled briskly at least 10 minutes every 2 or 3 days and more liquid is added. Best to use jellied soups within several days.

Too Sour—One of the basic tastes; balanced by sweetness. (See individual foods.)

Sour Cream—When old-fashioned sweet cream fermented, it yielded a thick, tangy substance. Europeans spread it over dark rye bread or spooned it over borscht, blintzes and other Old World dishes. Beef Stroganoff is one specialty that depends on sour cream. (See giblet stroganoff, p. 324.) The modern version is pasteurized, homogenized sweet cream with less fat than its ancestor. A lactic acid culture is added to produce its characteristic piquant flavor.

CURDLED

This time: As soon as you see the sour-cream mixture curdle, remove from heat and cool down by transferring to a cool bowl, adding an ice cube or a little cold milk or cream. Blend gently. If flecks are not entirely gone, add a scant teaspoon arrowroot starch or cornstarch per 2 cups sauce, first dissolved in a little liquid, and mix well. Reheat slowly, stirring. If you don't have arrowroot or cornstarch, sieve and remember that a slightly curdled sour cream sauce is still good to eat.

Next time: Heat sour cream gently. Never boil, even though some new types are hardier. Stir in just before serving. Flour or cornstarch added to a sauce first or condensed canned soup as part of the mixture help prevent the sour cream from curdling or separating when heated. Use very little salt in sour cream recipes since it can cause curdling.

FROZEN

This time: Freezing affects sour cream's smooth texture; it separates upon thawing. When it freezes accidentally, thaw in refrigerator and blend gently. It may be presentable enough for dips or salad dressings. Otherwise, make a sour-cream cake, bread, cookies, or pancakes, or use in cooked dish with arrowroot or cornstarch, which will bind separated cream.

Next time: Store in refrigerator at 40 degrees.

OLD, MOLD ON TOP

This time: Remove surface mold and a good portion of sour cream around it; then use for cooking or baking. The American Dairy Council takes a conservative stance and suggests discarding any moldy cream.

Next time: Store in its carton in coldest part of refrigerator, about 40 degrees. To prevent any entry of air, store carton upside down. Try to use within 2 weeks. Older sour cream develops a sharp flavor.

THINNED

This time: Chill, or thicken sauce. Lemon juice, vinegar, and other acidic foods tend to thin sour cream when the two are blended. Refrigerating returns the cream to its original thick consistency. If the mixture is to be cooked, thicken with flour or cornstarch.

Next time: Add acid ingredients only when there's time to chill the dip or spread. When embellishing a sour-cream sauce with acidic items, thicken the mixture with flour first to prevent a watery mixture. Overstirring also may thin sour cream, so fold it carefully into other ingredients.

SOUR HALF-AND-HALF (Cultured Half-and-Half)

A mixture of milk and cream with 10.5 percent minimum milkfat. Similar to sour cream but almost ¼ fewer calories (20 calories per tablespoon as compared to 26 for sour cream), it also gets its tangy flavor from injection of a culture. (See *Sour Cream.*) Can be substituted for sour cream except in baking, since it is lower in fat.

Substitutes: For use in baking or uncooked dressings, add 1 tablespoon vinegar or lemon juice to 1 cup evaporated milk at room temperature; let stand until it thickens. For use as dressing or garnish, blend 1 cup cottage or pot cheese in blender with about ¼ cup buttermilk and 1½ tablespoons lemon or lime juice. Sour half-and-half may be substituted for sour cream, except in baked products.

To substitute: When using dairy sour cream in an old-fashioned (1940s) recipe, add 3 tablespoons butter or margarine per cup of sour cream to add butterfat equivalent to that in old-fashioned sour cream.

Sour Milk—See *Milk.*

Soybeans—See *Beans, Dried;* see also *soybean casserole*, p. 332.

Spaghetti—*See Pasta.*

Spareribs—*See Meat.*

Spices—Generally, an inclusive term for seasonings, including herbs; specifically, they come from flowers, berries, roots, or fruits of certain plants, while herbs tend to be plant leaves or soft section. See also *Herbs.*

TASTELESS, IMPOTENT

This time: Spices can be rejuvenated by cooking in butter, oil, or whatever fat is appropriate to the dish, or by steeping about ½ hour in a compatible liquid. Use more of an over-the-hill spice. Add ground spices toward end of cooking, and be sure to taste the dish at the temperature it will be served. Cold minimizes seasonings.

Next time: Buy the freshest, best-quality spices available from a store with good turnover. Store in airtight containers in cool, dry, dark place. Try to use within a year. Whole berries and pods last longer than ground, and they should be added at the beginning of cooking, whereas ground spices should only be incorporated toward the end. Crack whole peppercorns or nutmeg just before using to prevent airing out. To bring out spicy flavors in uncooked mixtures, such as marinades, allow flavors to blend for several hours.

TOO STRONG

This time: Dilute by adding more liquid and/or starchy food. Sweet sometimes counters spiciness, so a little sugar, honey, or tomato sauce or purée might help. Cook the dish a little longer uncovered, to help cook off the flavors.

Next time: Add spices gradually and taste as you go. Avoid tasting a sauce cold if it is intended to be served hot, since heating intensifies the flavors.

Spinach—This versatile leafy green was cultivated in ancient Persia and rapidly spread throughout the western world. Immigrants to this country undoubtedly brought their spinach seeds with them in the early 1800s. By the late 1920s, the vegetable developed a reputation as a body-building phenomenon when Popeye the Sailorman attributed his remarkable strength to canned spinach. A true powerhouse of nutrients, especially vitamin A, the green leaves are also rich in iron, vitamin C, and folic acid (a B vitamin). Fresh and canned versions have decreased in consumption over the years, but frozen remains popular—mainly because it's convenient. Many cooks will not bother with the numerous rinsings fresh spinach requires. However, it's well worth the effort. Even the selections sold in plastic bags must often be washed in several waters to remove the sand and dirt that clings to the crinkled leaves.

COOKED DOWN, NOT ENOUGH

This time: Add some cooked frozen; or quickly sauté some mushrooms or onions to embellish the shrunken greens. Or serve the spinach creamed as a topping for artichoke bottoms, cauliflower, or carrots—a pretty color contrast.

Next time: Allow about a pound of spinach for 4 servings.

DISCOLORED

This time: Drain, chop, and use in casserole, omelet, soufflé, or heavily sauced dish. Or purée and use in spinach–sour-milk soup (p. 317) or for vegetable timbales (p. 333).

Next time: Like all green vegetables, spinach becomes a sickly yellowish when cooked with acid. Cook properly to prevent discoloration. Rinse several times in tepid water to remove sand and dirt, trim off coarse stems, shake off excess water. Then, with only the water clinging to leaves, cook tender spinach covered for only 3 to 4 minutes; tougher leaves in rapidly boiling, slightly sugared water about 8 to 10 minutes. Save water for soup if not too strong.

OLD

This time: Do not use for salads, which deserve only the tenderest leaves. If you're not pleased with the texture or flavor when cooked, purée for sauce, for spinach–sour-milk soup (p. 317), or vegetable timbales (p. 333), or use in spinach quiches (p. 330).

Next time: Select fresh, tender green leaves. Straggly, overgrown spinach with seedstalks is old. Avoid yellowed, wilted leaves or those with mushy brownish spots. Place unwashed leaves, loosely wrapped in plastic, in vegetable hydrator of refrigerator. Use within 3 days. Store cooked spinach no more than 2 days; the nitrate content increases with age.

OVERCOOKED

This time: The best thing to do with mushy spinach is to press out excess moisture and chop finely or purée for sauce that can be served with poultry, omelet or vegetable timbale (p. 333), or make cream of vegetable soup (p. 315), or spinach–sour-milk soup (p. 317).
Next time: See *Discolored*.

WILTED

This time: Soak briefly in tepid water, then cold water. (See *Old*.)
Next time: See *Old*.

Spoilage—*See Food Spoilage, Poisoning.*

Spreads—A paste of meat, fowl, fish, cheese, or vegetables that is spread over bread or crackers and usually served as an appetizer, or as a sandwich filling. See *Cheese; Sandwich.*

Squabs—*See Poultry, Game Birds.*

Squash—Of the hundreds of species in this gourd family, many are grown to be eaten as a vegetable. Native to the Americas, they were a staple in the Indian diet, along with corn and beans. Squashes vary greatly in appearance but may be classified into two main categories: summer and winter. The first are smaller, with thin skins and light-colored pulp, marketed before seeds and rinds harden. The second have hard rinds, which are often dark green or orange.

The alphabetical line-up of common summer squash: caserta, chayote, cocozelle, scallop (or pattypan), yellow crookneck, yellow straightneck and zucchini. The most popular winter squash varieties are: acorn, buttercup, butternut, hubbard, sugar or pie pumpkin and turban (Warren). Some varieties of both categories are available the year round, but peak season for summer squash is early summer, and for winter squash it is actually fall.

IMMATURE

This time: Immature summer varieties may be slightly bitter and hard. Salt slices before cooking, drain, and cook well until tender. Season to overcome any bitter taste—a bit of sugar or slightly sweet tomato sauce may camouflage the flavor. Winter squash that is immature can be watery and bland. Cook until tender, then drain off excess liquid, mash, and season well with spices.

Next time: Select fresh, tender-crisp summer varieties that are heavy for their size and free of bruises. Skin should be tender enough to be pierced with fingernail. Refrigerate in plastic bag 3 to 5 days. Winter squash, on the other hand, should be firm, hard and heavy for its size. Store in dry, airy place, 1 to 4 weeks.

OVERCOOKED

This time: Soft, mushy squash may not hold its shape, but is delicious mashed or puréed for soup. Summer varieties can be mashed and seasoned with dill, yogurt, sour cream, onions, and garlic. Winter orange-flesh types are especially good mashed with butter, a little brown sugar, and perhaps ginger, nutmeg, cinnamon, or mace. Purée winter squash and make cream of vegetable soup (p. 311).

Summer squash: Tender enough to be eaten raw. Great in salads. Very little cooking needed, so time carefully. Scrub, *do not pare*; remove stem and blossom ends and cut into thick slices, sticks, or cubes. Cook in small amount of boiling salted water, covered, until just tender, 5 to 10 minutes. Uncover and cook off any remaining liquid, then butter and season. Add garlic and onion to cooking water, if desired.

Winter squash: Can be halved and placed cut side down in baking dish with small amount of water, or placed in a covered casserole. Bake in 375-degree oven for 35 to 60 minutes, until tender, depending on size and type. Uncovered, it takes a bit longer. If mashing, allow to cook slightly; then scrape out pulp, mash and season; then reheat before serving.

OVERMATURE

This time: If tough or summer variety is hard-skinned, pare and cook longer, until tender; season well, perhaps serving with a sauce to make up for what it lacks in texture and flavor. Once developed to hard-rind stage, it's not usable generally.

Next time: Summer squash generally not palatable once matured to the hard-rind stage. Avoid winter squash with soft spots or spotty rind.

OVERRIPE (SHRIVELED, PITHY)

This time: Use as soon as possible. Pare shriveled skin from summer squash and cook until tender, then season well and sauce to compensate for lack of good texture and flavor. Bake or steam winter squash, then scoop from shells and mash; add spices. They have a special affinity for fruits (e.g., orange, apple). Or purée for cream of vegetable soup (p. 315).

Next time: See *Immature* and *Overmature.*

Squid—*See Seafood.*

Steak—*See Meat.*

Stew—The world abounds with bean stews, vegetable stews, stewed fruits, etc. But usually, stews are meat plus vegetable combinations simmered in liquid. And every country seems to have a version. The Belgians have carbonnade à la Flamande, beef stew tenderized in beer; the Irish have mutton stew; the Hungarians their peppery goulash; the French their ragout, boeuf bourguignon, and bouillabaisse. Beef stew with potatoes and carrots is probably the most popular American form, but this country has also produced other notables, such as Brunswick stew, made with pork and squirrel or chicken. Squirrels go into another big pot for Kentucky burgoo, an enormous collection of fowl, meat, squirrel, and vegetable pickings including tomatoes, okra, and corn.

BLAND

This time: Although best seasoned at the start of cooking, stews may be adjusted to taste at the very end. Add herbs, ground spices, Worcestershire, hot pepper sauce, or other condiments.

Next time: Use more onion or garlic, and add more whole spices or bay leaves from the start, since they give off their essence during long simmering. Remove whole spices before serving. For fuller flavor use wine or broth for the liquid instead of water. Lemon juice adds spark to almost any stew.

GREASY

This time: Give the fat 5 to 10 minutes to rise to the top.

Next time: Trim off excess fat from meat or use a leaner cut. Pour off fat after browning meat. Turn meat to brown all sides and to melt off fat.

OVERCOOKED

This time: When the meat is falling apart and doesn't hold its shape, spoon the stew over noodles or rice and the smaller pieces won't matter. Or thin broth and turn into soup. If you are feeding a baby, put soft stew through the blender; many babies love the purée.

Next time: Stir occasionally during cooking to assure that all pieces cook evenly, and to check on meat's progress. Most stews using 1 pound of beef take 2 to 3 hours. Pressure cookers and microwave ovens cut time considerably, of course.

SALTY

This time: Add a raw potato or a pinch of brown sugar. The tuber will absorb much of the salt; cut up and allow to simmer awhile. A pinch of brown sugar or other sweetness also helps counter saltiness. Very oversalted stew needs a radical move: quickly rinse meat and vegetables in water, and dilute sauce with water or unsalted liquid. Use about half, cook down slightly, return meat and vegetables and simmer until heated. Reserve remaining diluted sauce for next stew; freeze in containers.

Next time: Add salt toward end of cooking and season to taste. Avoid cooking the sauce down too much or the flavor can get extremely concentrated. Be sure to count the salty ingredients; cut down salt when adding bouillon or olives, for instance.

THICK

This time: Gradually stir in a little boiling water, tomato juice, broth, wine, or other juices, depending on stew.

Next time: Use more liquid during cooking, allowing for some reduction. Try to include more high-water vegetables, such as celery or zucchini. Use less thickener.

THIN

This time: Let liquid evaporate while cooking without the cover. This method takes a bit longer than by blending in flour or another thickener. Add raw rice (if recipe doesn't already have another starch) and let it cook at least 15 minutes to absorb excess liquid; rice triples, so 1 cup absorbs about 2 cups liquid. An addition of small-shaped pasta also would work; most forms double upon cooking.

Next time: Check proportion of liquid to thickening agents in recipe. At least 1 tablespoon flour per 1½ cups liquid should be used. The addition of raw rice or pasta would help to absorb much of the liquid. Or plan to simmer the stew uncovered for a while to reduce the sauce naturally, a recommended method for best flavor.

TOUGH

This time: Wine and other acids are tenderizers, so a little added to the pot helps soften the meat. Cook slowly afterward to let it do the job. When time is short, finish the stew in the pressure cooker.

Next time: Avoid toughening meat by using high heat or over-browning. Tenderize before cooking by marinating, pounding, grinding, or using commercial tenderizer.

UNDERCOOKED

This time: Cut in smaller pieces and simmer longer; or transfer to pressure cooker or microwave.

Next time: Allow at least 2 hours for a stew with 1 pound of meat. One of the stew's most welcome features is its ability to hold up well after cooking. In fact it *benefits* from a short standing period, a little like the aeration of a good red wine.

Stock—The legendary French master chef Auguste Escoffier once said, "Stock is everything in cooking. Without it, nothing can be done." In this age of convenience, many modern restaurant kitchens that no longer do their own butchering use commercial chicken or beef bases in lieu of stock. Some discriminating home cooks still observe the stock ritual to maintain high-quality cuisine.

Main types

1. Brown: Made from oven-browning beef marrow and other bones (and often veal) before adding to water with vegetables, herbs, spices, and sometimes dry wine.

2. White stock: Blanched veal (frequently a combination that includes poultry and beef bones) bones form the basis for this light stock.

3. Chicken: Obtained from simmering poultry wings, backs, and necks with vegetables and seasonings. Dry white wine is often an ingredient.

4. Fish: Quicker and simpler to prepare, it is derived from poaching fish, and frequently bony parts as well, in seasoned water with dry white wine.

CLOUDY

This time: Chill stock and remove all fat particles. Pour into a clean pot. Lightly beat 2 egg whites and crush 1 eggshell. Add to pot, place over medium heat, and beat with whisk. As soon as stock reaches a hard boil, stop beating, remove pot from heat and set aside. Let sit undisturbed for about 15 to 20 minutes. Pour through a fine sieve lined with 2 or 3 layers of cold, wet cheesecloth. Stock should be sparkling clear.

Next time: Clarification with egg whites is essential to a crystal-clear stock. To prevent undue cloudiness avoid boiling stock vigorously or for longer than recommended periods. Skim occasionally. (Some experts prefer not to skim. They allow the sediment to settle and later use it for stews and thick soups.)

SALTY

This time: Blend in more water and simmer longer. A sliced raw potato method works as a salt sponge (*see Soup, Salty*), but the starch and flavor from the tuber also changes the character of the stock.

Next time: Do not salt a stock. Reduction intensifies flavors and it is used as the foundation for dishes that later may be adjusted to suit taste.

To freeze: Remove congealed surface fat from chilled stock, place in containers leaving head space; freeze. It's convenient to freeze some of the stock in ice cube trays, then cubes can be used as needed.

To refrigerate: Cool stock quickly (in sink of cold water). The fat that congeals over the surface forms a protective seal. Cover and refrigerate. Use within several days.

Strawberries—See *Berries.*

String Beans—See *Beans, Green.*

Strudel—When expert hands finish working it, strudel dough covers the table like a linen cloth and is transparent enough to read a newspaper through. The first skill comes in quickly handling the pliable dough so the result is evenly thinned without rips. The second stage of expertise is in filling, rolling, and baking to get a juicy filling encased in a flaky pastry. These tips from Hungarian pastry experts should help produce the perfect strudel. All problems except the first refer to the baked pastry.

DOUGH BREAKS, DOESN'T STRETCH SMOOTHLY

This time: Assuming you've followed a reliable recipe and used a good bread flour, if you can't stretch the dough without it breaking, let it rest at least 1 hour. Shape into smooth ball; otherwise, when stretched, dough will break next to any thick, doughy seams. Brush surface with oil; cracks will appear at any dry spots. Keep dough covered.

Next time: Use a reliable recipe and appropriate flour. Follow above advice.

CRACKS OPEN, FILLING OOZES OUT

This time: Serve in deep dish with whipped cream or ice cream.

Next time: Especially common with fillings using eggs, such as cheese and poppyseed. For these strudels, allow for expansion; don't tuck ends under. Be sure to vent strudel well by slashing with sharp knife.

CRUMBLY

This time: Allow strudel to cool thoroughly before slicing with sharp serrated knife. Try cutting thicker slices, then dividing in half. When the pastry falls apart hopelessly, serve in dishes topped with lemon custard sauce or ice cream.

Next time: Check proportion of ingredients; perhaps it needs more butter or egg, or less flour. Underkneading and not allowing dough to rest can cause the problem.

DOUGHY

This time: Caky interior layers that haven't fully cooked should be removed with a sharp knife. Cut remaining strudel into chunks, serve reheated in dishes; top with custard or lemon sauce.

Next time: Mix and knead dough thoroughly. Stretch dough evenly so thin it's possible to read through it. After rolling, trim off thick edges; use scraps for patching any tears. Doughiness is usually caused by improper separation of the thin pastry layers, by not brushing with enough butter and baking in too low an oven. Vent assembled strudel well with sharp knife before baking.

SOGGY

This time: A soggy pastry can be revitalized in minutes in a hot oven. Strudel is at its best when warm. An uncrisp pastry becomes less noticeable when strudel is served with a sauce.

Next time: Work dough until it's pliable; brush stretched dough with melted butter and sprinkle with crumbs before adding filling, drained of excess juice. This helps separate the layers for a more tender, flaky pastry. When making fruit strudels, add sugar just before ready to fill. Otherwise fruit will get juicy, resulting in soggy pastry. Bake immediately in preheated *hot* oven. Refrigerator storage can cause sogginess. Reheat individual slices before serving.

Stuffing (dressing)—Stuffing never should be packed so tightly that it truly stretches the food, although one of its functions is to help maintain the food's shape. Stuffing expands during cooking and can burst its container, defeating the initial purpose and creating a mess. It is best to pair a hearty meat or game with a tangy light dressing and to fill a lean bird or fish with a richer blend. For both safety and optimum quality, stuff just before cooking.

BLAND

This time: Cooked stuffing can be seasoned at the last minute with herbs (thyme, parsley, sage, savory, basil), seeds (caraway, sesame, fennel) or spices (allspice, pepper, coriander, ginger, nutmeg). Lemon juice squeezed over helps perk up flavors.

Next time: Crush whole spices or add crumbled bay leaf from the beginning so they can give off their essence during cooking. Add celery with leaves, onion, browned spicy sausage, or sautéed chopped nuts to the original mixture for added good taste. Stuffing should be well seasoned, as its main purpose is to add flavor to the food it fills. It also takes on flavor from the meat or bird during cooking. Stuffing baked in a casserole will not have the same juices to flavor it, and may need added seasonings.

COMPACT, HEAVY

This time: Rice and some bread stuffings can be aerated with a fork. Most heavy mixtures can be shaped into patties or balls and browned in a lightly oiled pan. Sausage stuffings are especially amenable to this treatment.

Next time: Never grind bread for stuffing; use cubes or shreds. Add more textured ingredients, such as chopped celery and nuts, for bulk. Handle lightly to avoid packing it. Stuff bird just before cooking. Allow space for expansion during cooking so dressing can swell and remain light. Never pack stuffing into food, especially rice and bread mixtures, which swell greatly.

DRY

This time: A little melted butter or drippings add both necessary moisture and flavor. Or serve covered with gravy or sauce. A squeeze of fresh lemon or lime juice over some dressings (especially a rice and fruit mixture for fowl or fish) is an excellent moisturizer.

Next time: Do not overfill, or texture will be dense and meat juices will not penetrate to center. Mixture baked separately in a casserole can get dry easily, so drizzle melted butter over top and avoid overbaking. Cover for part of cooking to create steam.

SALTY

This time: Make an extra amount of everything except salt—a fine remedy unless you're out of ingredients or time. Even a few extras will help. Then add a little lemon juice or sweeten slightly to counter the saltiness.

Next time: Undersalt when seasoning; more can always be added later. Allow about ½ to ¾ teaspoon salt per quart bread cubes, about ½ to 1 teaspoon per 1½ cups uncooked rice.

SOGGY

This time: A wet bread stuffing can be revitalized by the addition of toasted crumbs or croutons. Textured items such as nuts and crushed corn chips will aid in rejuvenating other mixtures. Further baking in a casserole until browned also dries it nicely.

Next time: Remove stuffing from fatty bird and bake separately. Or allow enough time to bake further.

Amount estimated: figure about ½ to 1 cup stuffing per lb. bird, fish, etc.

To freeze: Freeze separately from animal it fills; can be frozen in foil lined casserole; when hard-frozen, remove from dish and wrap well in freezer paper. Thaw in refrigerator, then reheat covered in low oven.

Suet Pudding—*See Pudding.*

Sugar—Imagine a pile of 20 five-pound bags—that's the average American's annual consumption of sugar! Which doesn't, of course, even indicate that some may consume only a pound a year while others are shoveling down vastly more than even this staggering national average. Nutritionists view this sugar addiction as both detrimental to health and a major contributing factor to America's high-ranking obesity, dental woes, and a wide range of other medical ills. The fact is that no one *needs* sugar. About all it supplies is carbohydrates and there are many far better sources that offer nourishment as well.

I also believe that prudent use of this sweetener need not be necessarily harmful to a person in good health. Although the extended definition of sugar incorporates dextrose, lactose, levulose, maltose, and other sweet-soluble compounds found in foods, "sugar" as we know it refers to sucrose—the common table variety. Sugarcane (used by East Indians as far back as 1000 B.C.) and the sugar beet (originating in ancient China but now big business in the U.S.) are our two main sucrose sources, producing identical refined granulated substances. The following information will help solve your sugar-related kitchen experiments.

HARD, LUMPY

This time: Slightly lumpy sugar can be mashed easily with a fork or spoon, but when it's really hard or you have a large quantity of lumps, put into the food processor or blender or run through grinder. If you don't mind using a bit of elbow grease, push the sugar through a sieve or food mill or roll it between two sheets of wax paper with a rolling pin. If you have a few days and brown sugar is the problem child, add half a sliced apple to the container and refrigerate. When the intended use is for cooking, place the bricklike sugar in a covered casserole and warm in a moderate-low oven until it softens. Other, more drastic alternatives, which will change its composition, are to steam it in the top of a double boiler or melt it over low heat. Add a flavoring extract of your choice, perhaps a little fruit juice to the liquid sugar, and you have a syrup.

Next time: To prevent solidification, store in airtight canister or jar in cool, dry place. Brown sugar is best kept refrigerated with a piece of apple, orange, or lemon in the container. Replace old fruit with fresh occasionally.

To substitute: When short on granulated sugar, you can substitute the following for 1 cup (½ pound) in most recipes: reduce liquid by ¼ cup and use ¾ cup honey, ¾ cup maple syrup, 1¼ cups molasses, or 2 cups corn syrup; 2 cups corn syrup are equivalent to 1 cup sugar in sweetness, but for best results never replace more than half the required sugar with corn syrup. Without liquid adjustments in recipe, you can substitute for each 1 cup granulated sugar: 1 cup superfine, 1 cup packed brown sugar, or 1¾ cups confectioners sugar. Maple syrup, molasses, and brown sugar impart a more robust flavor than white sugar.

Too Sweet—One of the fundamental tastes, countered by sour and bitter.

Sweet Potato—Interchangeable with yam in cooking, but from an entirely different botanical genus. It is one of the best sources of vitamin A, whereas yam has only a trace of the vitamin. The sweet potato is indigenous to the Americas, having been cultivated by both the Incas and the Mayas before white men arrived. It's very popular in our southern states, where the "potato" or "yam" as it is called is yellow and soft-fleshed. Another main variety grown in the U.S. and popular in the North is the firm-fleshed dry and mealy type.

DISCOLORED

This time: Brown spots on the raw tuberous roots indicate decay. Cut them out and use sweet potato immediately. If surface is uncovered after cutting, sweet potato may darken. Mash and combine with spices, cream and brown sugar. The color pigment is very stable; the sweet potato should not discolor upon cooking. But if it had slight discolorations when raw that went unnoticed in the cooking process, chances are they may be intensified after cooking. Trim off discolored areas and cut up sweet potatoes so the surgery isn't noticeable, and cover with a brown sugar–butter glaze or an orange sauce. Or mash with turnips or regular white potatoes. Another idea is to purée and use for cream of potato soup (1 cup purée to 2 cups chicken stock or bouillon and 1 cup milk, seasoned with nutmeg, cinnamon, and dash mace) or basic vegetable soufflé.

Next time: Select firm, smooth, evenly colored sweet potatoes that are well shaped and free of blemishes. Avoid those with cracks, bruises, or soft decay spots. Store in cool, dry, airy place up to 2 or 3 weeks. Refrigeration damages them. When grating for casserole or pudding, drop into cold water; cover immediately after cutting.

HARD TO PEEL

This time: Dip cooked sweet potatoes quickly into cold water.

Next time: When baking or grilling, first grease skins well, which makes them easier to pare.

MEALY

This time: When the shape is impossible to preserve, then mash or whip, blend with butter, brown sugar, and lemon juice, and bake; or combine with carrots and apple in a casserole.

Next time: Select the Puerto Rican type or another similar variety that is soft-fleshed and moist—better for thin slicing and holding shape.

OLD, SHRIVELED

This time: Rub skins with oil and bake in 400-degree oven 35 to 45 minutes; then pare. Or cook in boiling salted water to cover until tender, 25 to 30 minutes. Drain and skin.

Next time: See *Discolored.*

OVERCOOKED

This time: Purée and make soup (see *Discolored*) or soufflé.

Next time: Cook in boiling salted water to cover 25 to 30 minutes, or grease skins and bake in 400-degree oven 35 to 45 minutes.

UNDERCOOKED

This time: Normally no problem—just cook longer until tender, but it becomes a problem to have an undercooked sweet potato when the rest of dinner is ready and the sweet potatoes are still hard. In this event treat in microwave or pressure cooker to hasten preparation, or cut in small pieces to shorten the cooking process.

Next time: Allow enough time to cook sweet potatoes (see *Overcooked*).

Syrups—Pancake houses frequently offer assorted blends, such as blueberry, cinnamon-honey, and apricot. The most common syrups sold in groceries are molasses (dark and light), corn (dark and light), and maple (pure and blends). See *Honey* and *Molasses* for problems pertaining to those items. The following information applies more to corn and maple syrups.

OLD, MOLDY

This time: Syrup that has been stored for some time might develop little flecks of mold. Strain through cheesecloth or filter to remove all traces. Do not use otherwise. If syrup flavor is stale, heat and flavor with spices or blend with fruit juice and/or liqueur before pouring over griddle cakes. Or use in cooking and baking breads, cakes, frosting, and cookies that call for syrup or where syrup can be substituted. For 1 cup sugar, substitute ¾ cup maple syrup or 2 cups corn syrup and reduce liquid in recipe by ¼ cup. Do not replace more than half the required sugar with corn syrup.

Next time: Keep tightly capped in cool, dry cabinet. Try to use within 1 year.

To substitute: In most recipes ¾ cup maple syrup or 2 cups corn syrup can be substituted by ¾ cup honey or 1¼ cups molasses. Liquid may have to be reduced when using corn syrup. Or increase liquid in recipe by ¼ cup and substitute 1 cup sugar for every ¾ cup maple syrup or 2 cups corn syrup.

Sweetbreads—*See Meat.*

Tangelo—The name of this recent hybrid honors its parentage—the wedding of tangerine and grapefruit (also known as the pomelo). Tangelo pulp is pale yellow, the rind orange. Skin can be either smooth and thin or rough and heavy. Unlike the tangerine, fruit is firm, not loose-skinned. One variety is pear-shaped, another round. All types make delicious eating. The juice is a pleasingly tart, tangy, different citrus experience excellent for both drinking and cooking.

Tangerine—Zipper-skinned citrus fruit with a name from Tangier, Morocco, its ancestor is the Mandarin orange. Tangerines are still popular in China as well as in Japan and the Mediterranean. In this country they have gained a following for their ease of eating and spicy tart flavor. Available an unfortunately short season, from October through January.

DRY

This time: Cook sweetened water or fruit juice spiked with cloves, cinnamon, and a bit of lemon juice for several minutes. Add the peeled tangerine sections, perhaps other compatible fruits, and chill several hours. Or let a favorite liquor, liqueur, or sweet wine replace some of the lost moisture in the segments by marinating overnight.

Next time: Fruit that is heavy for its size indicates juiciness. Look for shiny deep orange to reddish-colored skins. Since the tangerine is loose-skinned, a rather puffy feeling is the norm, but avoid dried skins. Place in plastic bag and store in fruit bin of refrigerator. Very fresh tangerines can be kept for several weeks, but they're more perishable than oranges.

OVERRIPE

This time: Slightly overripe tangerine segments, marinated in a salad dressing or liquor, are a nice touch to salads or desserts; their slightly softer texture is minimized when they are plump with good flavor and combined with other good ingredients. Very soft, over-ripe fruit is still salvageable when cooked into a sweetened, thickened sauce—good with poultry or for dessert. Blend 3 tablespoons honey, 1 tablespoon cornstarch, ½ cup each tangerine juice and water, and cook in top of double boiler over boiling water, stirring until thickened; stir in 1 tablespoon butter, dash salt, about ½ teaspoon grated citrus rind. Stir in about ½ cup tangerine segments, if desired, and use over puddings. Add herbs, if desired, and use with poultry or fish. If juicer is available, make juice and combine with buttermilk, wine, or other liquid refreshment.

Next time: See Dry.

Tapioca—See *Pudding; Thickeners.*

Tea—I love to recall the minted tea in Fez, on my second visit to Morocco. Served with ceremony, it was aromatic, sweet (but not as cloying as most Moroccan tea), and heady. The tea plant originated in China and the drink has been popular there since the T'ang period. It is still the main drink there and throughout the Orient. Tea made its debut in Portugal and Holland in the early 1600s, quickly moved into France and Germany by the 1630s, and then on to England, where the British soon made it their national drink. Like herbs, teas have a history of being medicinal. The Chinese believed that a piping cup of tea without food would erase headache, fever, and stomach ache. Mid–17th-century English tea merchants upped sales by convincing customers that their product was an all-purpose panacea. These cure-all claims aside, the hot brew does have a rejuvenating, soothing effect on a weary body and mind. There are numerous types and blends to choose from, the Chinese generally being the milder and the Indian and Ceylonese being the more aromatic and robust.

Tips. Tea is best made in a china, pottery or glass pot. Stir just before serving to blend the essential oils through the liquid.

CLOUDY (ICED TEA)

Those who suffered from the extreme heat at the St. Louis World's Fair in 1904 didn't mind if their tea was cloudy. In fact, they probably weren't even impressed that they were the first people drinking iced tea. Because of the weather, a tea merchant invented the refresher by pouring his hot brew over ice.

This time: If a cloudy appearance bothers you, restore clearness by stirring in a little boiling water; or, mix the tea with fruit juices and some soda for a sparkling tea punch.

Next time: To preserve clarity, allow brewed tea to cool at room temperature before chilling. Or try the never-cloudy, cold-brew method: mix about 1 teaspoon tea leaves (or add 1 tea bag) per cup cold water in a jar, cover and chill at least 8 to 12 hours; strain (if using loose leaves) and serve over ice. James Beard recommends making extra strong fresh tea and pouring it hot over ice cubes for best flavor. In any case, use fresh, soft water; hard water produces murky iced tea.

STRONG

This time: Add more boiling water, stir and taste until desired strength is reached. Or add milk, as the English do.

Next time: Add about 1 teaspoon tea leaves per 6 ounces water. Don't let the tea steep more than 5 minutes. Serve promptly and remove leaves.

WEAK

This time: When there's time and it's possible to keep tea hot, brew an additional strong pot to reinforce the weak. Otherwise add another tea bag or two to strengthen the pot. Other choices are to add a hot fruit juice or rum, brandy, or some favorite liquor.

Next time: Measure 1 teaspoon tea leaves to 5 or 6 ounces boiling water. Let leaves steep 3 to 5 minutes, then serve immediately, stirring and straining. Be sure to use fresh tea; keep in tightly sealed jar or tin in cool, dry place. Never reuse leaves. Use fresh cold water heated to a boil to avoid a flat taste.

Temperatures—*See Candy, Confectionery.*

Tenderloin—*See Meat.*

Terrapin—*See Seafood.*

Thawed (accidentally)—Raw meat, fish and poultry (when completely thawed) should be cooked before refreezing. Partially thawed small items can be safely refrozen; larger items should be cooked. Baked products can be refrozen but quality may not be as good upon thawing the second time.

Thickeners—Primarily used in sauces and soups, these agents sometimes can enrich color and flavor as well. The information here helps avoid problems from improper use of the thickeners. For particular questions about sauces and soups, turn to those subjects in this chapter.

Arrowroot—This neutral-flavored thickener is the most delicate. Its behavior is similar to that of cornstarch—should be blended in cold liquid or in fat before adding hot liquid—but produces a clearer product and needs no cooking. Since arrowroot doesn't hold or reheat, use only when the sauce will be served within minutes. It should not boil or be vigorously stirred or it will thin. It has no raw taste and thickens at 70 degrees F., a lower temperature than either flour or cornstarch—and so is ideal for egg, fruit, and other delicate sauces. Allow about 1½ teaspoons per 1 cup liquid. To substitute for cornstarch, use ⅔ as much; for flour, use ⅓ as much.

Beurre manie or kneaded butter—Gives body to thin sauces at end of cooking. Not to be used for long-simmering mixtures. Mix equal portions butter and flour into small balls; drop into hot liquid while stirring until well blended and thickened. Simmer only about 3 minutes. Do not boil after adding beurre manie to sauce. Use 2 tablespoons each butter and flour to thicken 1 cup thin liquid.

Browned flour—Fortifies color and flavor. Brown flour by spreading on baking pan in 250-degree oven about 30 minutes, scraping and stirring frequently until browned. Flour also may be browned while stirring in a heavy-weight pan over very low heat. Overbrowning can cause bitterness and total loss of thickening power. Proper browning reduces all-purpose flour's thickening power by half, so allow a minimum of 2 tablespoons browned flour to thicken 1 cup liquid. Store leftovers tightly covered in a cool, dry place.

Butter—A nice finish to sauces after straining and final heating; once added, the sauce should not be reheated. Add cold, sweet butter bit by bit to the sauce, rotating pan over burner so butter swirls as it melts in hot sauce. Remove from heat and continue to swirl until butter is fully melted. Serve immediately. Do not stir with spoon. Usually about 1 tablespoon butter "finishes" 1 cup sauce; it enhances flavor and slightly thickens sauce.

Cornstarch—A starch that adds translucency but no flavor. Commonly used in Chinese and dessert sauces. Mix with about twice as much cold water before stirring into hot liquid. Stir gently but constantly over medium-low to medium heat during entire cooking period, until mixture comes to a full boil and sauce thickens. Cornstarch granules swell to maximum capacity at a full boil; boil 1 minute; remove from heat and serve. Both overbeating and overcooking cornstarch sauces thins them. Adding acid, such as citrus juice, during cooking may cause rapid thinning, so add acidic ingredients after mixture has thickened and is removed from heat. Too much sugar in proportion to starch also can prevent thickening. Egg white added to cornstarch mixtures before cooking might cause lumps, so add only yolks beforehand. On the average, use 1½ teaspoons cornstarch to thicken ¾ to 1 cup liquid, 1 tablespoon per cup for an average gravy.

Egg yolk—Imparts color and flavor as well as thickening. To ensure a smooth mixture, first blend yolks into a little cream, then stir in some of the hot sauce to be thickened. Gradually incorporate this tempered mixture into the remainder of the hot liquid while stirring over low heat until thickened. To avoid curdling, never add yolks directly to hot mixture and never boil sauce once yolks have been added. (For curdled sauce, see *Sauces.*) Unless heat can be finely controlled, add yolks to mixture in double boiler over hot water. Use 2 egg yolks blended with a dash of cream to thicken 1 cup liquid.

Flour—See *flour paste and roux*, below.

Flour paste, whitewash—Resembles its second nickname in appearance. Not as palatable as roux; not recommended for general use; but still a handy stand-in for emergencies. Dissolve 1 part flour to 2 parts water to make a paste. Gradually whisk as much as needed into the boiling stock or drippings and simmer while stirring until thickened. Allow to bubble at least 3 minutes to cook out the raw flour taste.

Miscellaneous—Oatmeal, tapioca, bean, barley, rice, and other farinaceous products are used to thicken soups and saucy mixtures as well as patties, meat loaves, and similar items. Grated raw potatoes often add substance to soups, and breadcrumbs add texture to some sauces or soups.

Potato starch—Renders a transparency to delicate sauces that require less simmering. Serve immediately after thickening. It thins out above 176 degrees F. About ½ to 1 tablespoon potato starch will lightly to moderately thicken 1 cup liquid.

Reduction—An evaporation of liquid by very slow simmering to bring a sauce to its desired consistency. Tomato sauces usually gain substance this way. Finish seasoning after cooking sauce down to right viscosity; otherwise the concentration can yield a salty and overseasoned taste. Flavor will be adversely affected if cooked too fast. Texture of most reduced sauces is improved by straining.

Roux (white, blonde, or brown)—A mixture of flour and fat—usually equal in amounts—blended and allowed to bubble while stirred over low heat until thickened, about 3 minutes or longer depending on color desired. Used as the basis for soufflés, croquettes, and many sauces and for creaming vegetables, fish, and similar dishes. It is essential to blend flour and butter well over heat to allow starch granules to swell evenly; otherwise they are unable to absorb added liquid and will produce a thin sauce. Too high a heat burns the flour, gives it a bitter taste, and makes the starch incapable of swelling. Leftover roux can be stored either in the refrigerator or freezer. The following guide helps to determine the proportions of flour to sauce thickness: 1 tablespoon flour per cup liquid produces a thin sauce; 2 tablespoons, medium; 3 tablespoons, thick; and 4, very thick.

Tomato—Difficult to believe that this number two crop in the U.S. was raised only as a curiosity until the latter half of the 19th century. Although indigenous to the Americas, this fruit (botanically a berry) was not accepted here until long after it was known in Europe. At one time Europeans considered the tomato poisonous. (It is part of the nightshade family, some members of which are deadly.) At another time, this same mistrusted fruit was considered a strong aphrodisiac. The French called it the "love apple." Legend has it that a young man, disappointed in love, decided to end it all by consuming a tomato. But nothing happened. His survival proved that the poisonous love apple was benignly delicious.

ACIDIC

This time: Add a little sugar or cook with another ingredient high in sugar content, like a Spanish onion.

Next time: Selecting ripe red tomatoes increases your chances of getting full, rich flavor. Learn the best types at your market. Often the Italian plum variety and beefsteak are the most flavorful for eating plain.

OVERCOOKED

This time: Purée and use for sauce or soup.

Next time: To stew, peel and place in covered saucepan with onion, garlic, and herbs, if desired; do not add water. Simmer 8 to 10 minutes, adjust seasonings. For tomato halves: dot with butter and season; bake in 425-degree oven or broil for about 10 minutes.

OVERRIPE

This time: Soft, overripened tomatoes do not have the right texture for salads, so cook them for sauce or soup. For sauce, soup, or purée, peel and strain mixture. If really mushy, cut and scrape pulp into the pot while holding skin with one hand.

Next time: Decide when the fruit will be used, then select accordingly. Choose firm, well-shaped tomatoes that are heavy for size. Avoid shriveled, cracked fruit with dark spots. Store fully ripe fruit in the refrigerator several days. Do not refrigerate underripe fruit, since it never ripens properly thereafter.

UNDERRIPE

This time: If you can wait about 4 days, wrap in newspaper and store in a cool place. Do not refrigerate; that interferes with the ripening procedure. Small green tomatoes make excellent pickles and relishes—large ones can be fried in slices. Season thick slices of green tomatoes, dip in sweetened corn meal, fry in butter until browned. Any size can be stewed or made into a green tomato sauce, seasoned with sugar and spices to compensate for underripe flavor.

Next time: See *Overripe.*

Tomato Sauce—*See Sauces; Tomato.*

Tongue—*See Meat.*

Tortilla—The basic Mexican corn- or wheat-bread made into thin, flat rounds and griddle-baked. The tortilla is the basis for numerous Mexican dishes, including tacos and enchiladas. See *Bread, Quick.*

Trichinosis (in pork)—*See Food Spoilage, Poisoning; Meat.*

Trifle—*See Cake; Pudding, Custard.*

Tripe—*See Meat.*

Trout—*See Fish.*

Tuna—*See Fish.*

Turbot—*See Fish.*

Turkey—*See Poultry, Game Birds.*

Turnip—This cabbage family vegetable has been around since America's early years but it has never attained the popularity found in Europe. Delicious fresh in salads. The greens are a favorite southern vegetable, usually boiled and served with pork, barbecue, or black-eyed peas.

DISCOLORED

This time: If raw, the color change is an indication of age or drying out. Instead of using raw, cook pared turnips in water to cover, to which 2 teaspoons lemon juice or vinegar or 1 teaspoon cream of tartar has been added. If that doesn't bleach it enough, then cover with sauce or use in casserole; or mash and blend with potato, butter, and seasonings—perhaps minced parsley. If cooked, the cause could be from prolonged overheating. Follow same advice as for raw, cooking only 1 or 2 minutes.

Next time: Choose smooth, firm, unblemished turnips with fresh greens. Avoid shriveled or soft roots. Very large, overgrown selections are apt to be pithy and tough. Yours should be heavy for size. Remove tops. Store roots in cool, airy place (such as a cellar) or place in plastic bag and refrigerate. Rinse greens, then dry and store in plastic hydrator; use within a couple of days. Roots will store well for several weeks. If storing a cut turnip, wrap well and chill. To avoid overcooking, place whole pared turnips in acid water (about 1 teaspoon lemon juice per cup and 4 turnips) 5 to 8 minutes without cover; then cover and simmer about 20 minutes or until just tender. Cook slices, julienne strips or dice in similar manner, allowing only about an inch of boiling water and approximately 5 minutes.

OVERCOOKED

This time: Mash and serve alone or with mashed potatoes, butter and seasonings. Or purée for timbale (p. 333), or cream of vegetable soup (p. 315).
Next time: See *Discolored.*

OVERMATURE

This time: If overgrown and light in weight for size, cooked result is likely to be tough; certainly both pithy and fibrous when raw. Cook according to directions above (see *Discolored*), allowing more time if necessary. Taste to determine if slices or cubes are palatable enough to be used in a casserole or with a sauce. If too tough or pithy, cook until very soft, then purée for vegetable timbales (p. 333) or cream of vegetable soup (p. 315). Or mash, perhaps with potatoes, butter, cream, and seasoning.
Next time: See *Discolored.*

SHRIVELED: See *Overmature.*

Turtles—*See Seafood.*

Undercooked—See individual foods.
Underripe—See specific item.

Variety Meats—See *Meat.*
Veal—See *Meat.*

Vegetables—See individual names.

Venison—See *Game.*

Vinaigrette—See *Sauces.*

Vinegar—See *Canning; Salad, Salad Dressing; Sauces.*

Waffles—The modern heat-controlled, nonstick-surface waffle makers have made these distant pancake relatives easier to prepare. Much of the guesswork is removed, assuring a more uniform, properly baked product than with the old-fashioned irons that were heated over a burner. Whatever your method, here are some tips that will prevent you from getting burned.

TOO CRISP

This time: Add more flour, corn meal, wheat germ, or other appropriate ingredient to thicken the batter. Never discard crisp test waffles; but since they'll bounce off a plate when cut, soften by steaming briefly (in steamer, microwave oven, by sprinkling with water and heating in covered pan or wrapping in foil and oven-heating). Or break hard waffles into bite-size pieces, arrange in serving dish, and top with a sauce or moist mixture. Main- and side-course ideas are sherried chicken with peas, broccoli with mushroom sauce, or seafood in light white wine sauce. Sweet sauces, fruits, and ice cream can be mixed in any favorite combination. A crisp waffle and ice cream is like having an ice cream cone in a dish. Chunks of crisp waffles also add crunch to bread puddings.

Next time: Irons with high grids close together tend to produce crisper waffles. Thicken the batter, fill the iron more, and do not overbake.

SOGGY

This time: Return soft waffles to the iron for further cooking, or heat in an oven to bake through. As these will not be perfect specimens, tear into chunks and make bread pudding, or top with custard sauce and fruit—chill for a scrumptious dessert. Thin any remaining batter and fill waffle iron less.

Next time: Thin down batter with whatever liquid is called for in the recipe. Avoid overfilling the iron; use slightly less batter to allow waffle to bake through more thoroughly. Check the hinge on the waffle iron; one that's too stiff tends to make soggy waffles.

STICKING

This time: Carefully remove the clinging waffle in pieces and serve as sample or turn into bread pudding. (For other serving suggestions see *Crisp* and *Soggy*.) Before using again, brush grids with unsalted fat, close iron, heat to baking temperature, and let heat for 10 minutes. Allow iron to cool, then use. Waffles may also stick to the iron if batter itself has insufficient fat or if iron is either too hot or cold when batter makes contact.

Next time: Condition grids before using; maintain proper temperature.

Walnuts—*See Nuts.*

Watercress—Its peppery, shapely leaves are an asset to most salads, and it makes an outstanding soup. Most often used as a garnish or served fresh, but cress can be delicious braised as accompaniment to fowl or meats.

OVERCOOKED

This time: Purée and turn into soup, easily done by cooking a short time in chicken consommé with green onions, then adding whipping cream and seasoning.

Next time: Braise by placing trimmed, rinsed cress in covered saucepan with only the water that clings. Cook slowly about 4 minutes, shaking pan occasionally. Add a little butter and chicken consommé, and season to taste. Continue cooking slowly until cress resembles cooked spinach. When cooking cress in consommé for soup, allow about 10 minutes.

WILTED

This time: Place stems in a jar of water and refrigerate a couple of hours.

Next time: As soon as you get cress home, sort and discard any withered, yellowed leaves. Wash in ice water, changing several times until rinse is clean. Store in large covered jar to which a small amount of water has been added, and refrigerate several days at most. Select fresh, bright green watercress with stems that snap easily.

Watermelon—*See Melons.*

Weather—You'll save yourself much aggravation by listening to your weatherman before planning your menus. Atmospheric conditions are important in cooking! During a cooking show on my first professional job after college, I was assisting a colleague during her turn to decorate a Dobos torte. The hot demonstration lights melted the chocolate frosting so it was oozing out of the pastry bag. At the conclusion, she had iced herself even more than the cake. Following a cardinal demo rule, she did not try to cover up the mishap; instead, she called it to the audience's attention, explaining the importance of working in a cool environment. You may not work under hot lights, but you can remain cool and calm when you learn the best temperature and humidity for handling particular foods.

High humidity: Do not attempt to make hollandaise-based sauces on a very humid day unless clarified butter is used. Also avoid making candy and meringues in very damp weather. High humidity greatly affects sugar in cooked food. Cool, dry, and clear "candy days" are also the best for making most pastries. Any crisp baked product becomes soggy in a moist atmosphere. Bread doughs absorb more flour under these conditions.

Low humidity: Although ideal for storing most foods, a very dry climate can be tough on flours, cereals, and baked products. This tends to be a particular concern both in arid climates and during winter, when heat shortens the life span of foods. Any product whose palatability relies on moisture must be protected from extreme dryness.

High temperature: While a yeast bread will rise beautifully on a hot summer day, puff paste could be a total collapse. Do not court disaster by making the delicate paste when the mercury soars, unless the kitchen is air-conditioned. Hot weather also adversely affects the creaming of butter-sugar mixtures and makes it difficult to work with chocolate, ice cream, gelatins and whipping cream. The refrigerator and bowls of ice water become essential aids when room temperature is uncontrolled; keep ingredients and utensils cool enough for proper handling.

Low temperature: Can prevent yeast doughs from rising, butter from creaming, egg whites from beating up high and many frostings and candies from being pliable enough. Warm water and residual heat from a briefly heated oven can give a hand here.

Stormy: Look out the window before making mayonnaise-based sauces. They won't bind during a thunderstorm or its prelude. Stormy weather also bothers butter. If you make your own, wait for a clear outlook.

Weeping—See *Meringue; Pudding, Custard.*

Welsh Rabbit or Rarebit—See *Cheese; Sandwich.*

Wheat—See *Cereal.*

Whip—See *Gelatin.*

Whipped Cream—See *Cream.*

Whitefish—See *Fish.*

Wieners—See *Meat.*

Wild Rice—See *Rice.*

Wilted—See *Lettuce; Salad.*

Wine—To call wine the juice of fermented grapes is technically correct but says nothing of the intricacies, the lore, the pleasures of one of man's oldest and most romantic drinks. Euripides expressed his appreciation: "Where there is no wine, there is no love." The following information merely taps the surface of the subject; it deals with questions and problems concerning wine mainly as a common food.

Leftovers: Wine begins to oxidize once a bottle is opened. For the first hour or so this "breathing" time helps to develop the bouquet, aroma, and flavor of all but sparkling wines. After a prolonged period, however, air causes deterioration and eventual souring. To prevent this condition, transfer any leftover wine into a smaller bottle or decanter so there's little or no air space. Cork or cap it tightly. Chill a white wine; keep a red at cool room temperature or chill also. You can generally count on whites lasting longer than reds. Avoid saving the very old, delicate ones. To be sure, try to use leftovers within a day or two.

When a good wine changes in character during the course of a dinner, it may not be your imagination. Research shows that a chemical in the artichoke alters the palate for wine, as does the vinaigrette that often accompanies the thistle vegetable. Halt wine drinking while eating the vegetable, then cleanse palate with bread and water before sipping again. This point is still highly controversial, however. In both Italy and France I noticed numerous bottles of good wines being poured with artichokes, and no one ever discouraged that combination.

PAST ITS PRIME

There are several uses for that occasional disappointing bottle or the leftovers that turned sour. The wine may be unsuitable for drinking, but it can be used in cooking—especially when a piquant taste is desirable. A rather nebulous wine can be used in that delicious Spanish fruited wine drink called sangria. An acrid wine can be turned into a wine vinegar and is most effective in a marinade; (see lemon-marinated beef, p. 323; substitute wine for lemon juice in this recipe or for vinegar in almost any marinade recipe). An herb-wine vinegar can be made by adding a halved garlic clove, fresh tarragon, a little lemon juice and rind to 1 cup leftover dry red wine. Combine in a jar, cover, and let stand at room temperature about 2 weeks, stirring almost daily. Strain into a clean jar, cover tightly. Use to embellish sauces and gravies. White wine can be substituted for red; garlic can be omitted.

Yam—*See Sweet Potato.*

Yeast—To test activity, dissolve a small portion of the cake yeast with sugar and a little of the dry in warm water (105 to 115 degrees); if active, both should bubble and rise slightly in a short time. When there's no action, yeast is dead and useless. See *Bread.*

Yogurt—Francis I of France claimed he regained his health because of yogurt, and the hardiness and longevity of Balkan peasants has been attributed to the tangy dairy product. The traditional Bulgarian yogurt is rich in butterfat, thick, and quite acidic in taste.

Commercial products in this country have gained popularity since the mid-1960s because of the production of low-fat versions and fruit flavors. The blend of the tart and sweet is most appealing. Plain or flavored, it is spooned out of cartons for a convenient breakfast, lunch, or snack. According to Dairy Research, Inc., recent statistics show Americans eating 566 million pounds of yogurt a year—which translates into 1,132 million cups! In making most yogurt, controlled lactic acid culture is added to a mixture of partially skimmed and nonfat dry milk. There is a variation between types manufactured, but basically yogurt has 1.7 to 3.4 percent milkfat. One cup has about the same calcium equivalent as a cup of milk, and it is believed to be more digestible. The lactic acid supposedly aids digestion and helps assimilate other nutrients.

CURDLED

This time: When you first see the yogurt separating, remove from heat and cool mixture quickly by transferring to a cool bowl, placing in an ice bath, or by adding an ice cube. One trick to pulling it together again is to add a scant teaspoon arrowroot or 1½ teaspoons cornstarch for each 2 cups cooled curdled sauce, mix well, then reheat slowly in light-weight pan, stirring gently. Separated yogurt serves as a good marinade for meats or poultry. Or mix with leftover cooked spinach and onion; serve as a cold relish.

Next time: When cooking with yogurt, gently fold it into other ingredients. Vigorous stirring or beating will break down its texture. Heat yogurt gently in a light-weight pan for a short time to avoid curdling. Stabilize 2 cups yogurt mixture by blending in a small amount of cornstarch (about 1½ teaspoons), arrowroot (about 1 teaspoon) or flour (about 1 tablespoon) before heating.

FROZEN

This time: Plain yogurt doesn't freeze well, because its smooth texture is affected. If frozen by mistake, thaw slowly in refrigerator or at room temperature for 2 to 3 hours. Stir gently to blend after thawing. Use in baking if appearance is not suitable for using as is. Fruit-flavored yogurts can be frozen successfully for about six weeks in unopened containers. Thaw closed containers at room temperature about 3 hours.

Next time: Avoid freezing plain yogurt. Buy or make only what can be used within 10 days.

OLD, MOLD ON TOP, SHARP FLAVOR

This time: Aging yogurt may form mold growth on surface. Discard the mold and a good portion of yogurt around it. Discard heavily molded products. However, the National Dairy Council conservatively suggests discarding any moldy yogurt. Flavor probably will be stronger, so season and use for salad dressing or in cooking. Some flavorful additions to versatile yogurt are chives and other herbs, capers, garlic, spices, tomato sauce, shredded cheese, lemon juice, fruit and honey, anchovy paste, mustard—almost any taste you'd like to give it.

Next time: Store unopened cartons upside down to prevent air from getting into the yogurt. Once opened, store right side up. Keep in cold part of refrigerator no longer than 10 days for optimum eating quality.

THINNED

This time: Overstirring tends to thin it. Refrigerate yogurt mixture intended to be served cold (such as a dip or dressing) and it will set itself up again. Yogurt thins out even more than sour cream in cooking. Adding a little arrowroot, cornstarch, or flour (by dissolving in a little of the cold mixture first, then blending in gradually) and stirring while heating gently in light-weight pan will thicken consistency (see *Curdled*).

Next time: Avoid overstirring yogurt. Gently fold in ingredients. Stabilize yogurt in cooked mixtures by first blending a small amount of arrowroot, cornstarch, or flour, into a little cold yogurt.

Substitutes: Sour cream or sour half-and-half can be substituted for yogurt in recipes other than baked items. Since yogurt's fat content is much lower than sour cream, the recipe for a bread or cake would have to be adjusted to be successful.

To substitute: Can replace sour cream, but finished product will be less rich and more tangy. Cooked dishes in which this substitution is made can be thickened slightly. For gelatins, 1 cup yogurt can replace 1 cup cold water. Yogurt thinned with a little water can take the place of buttermilk in pancakes, waffles, and biscuits. In baked products, it's important to measure ½ teaspoon baking soda per cup of yogurt—the equivalent in leavening strength to 1 teaspoon baking powder per cup of milk.

Yorkshire Pudding—*See Pudding.*

Zucchini—*See Squash.*

Part II

Recipes—
Waste
Control

Introduction

What is the fate in your house of overcooked vegetables, disappointingly tough meat, heavy bread, that soupçon of Sunday's roast chicken too small to serve the family? Do you let cooking liquids, pickle brine, fruit syrups, and minuscule amounts of leftovers slip down the drain? And what about foodstuffs you've overstocked, now on the verge of spoiling, common in every refrigerator—milk that is turning, overmature yogurt, stale bread, overripe fruit? Such problematic but still edible items are all too often consigned to the disposal or the compost heap—a total (and utterly unnecessary) waste of your food and money.

The recipes and tips in this chapter demonstrate how easily, with a little imagination and resourcefulness, a delightful dish can often be made from intended toss-outs. Included are a number of basic "cover-up" sauce ideas that will quickly and completely transform a garbage-bound ingredient into a savory table item.

This is not intended to be a comprehensive collection of recipes "from scratch"—they are included to provide some inspiration for you to use as a launching pad in creating your own delicacies from disasters. The results will often be memorable, and become stock items in your repertory. That is what happened with me and the recipe I have called "Fruit Roll Flop . . . and Pudding" (p. 339). I had the experience of testing a dessert fruit roll that was a truly qualified flop. The result was dough that fell apart, leaving a heap of crumbs and fruit on the plate. The flavor was good, though, so I turned it into a custard bread pudding—and this product of the earlier disaster was one of the best puddings I ever tasted! To repeat it, I had to make the flopped fruit roll first, so I soon developed a short-cut substitute.

Ingredients past their prime and leftovers can be salvaged, too, and by-products of recipes that normally might get thrown out— cooking liquids, tough outer leaves of lettuce, the bones from ham or other roasts. And scraps you thought were too scanty to use can find new life.

This chapter is broken down into conventional cookbook sections—Appetizers; Soups; Meats, Poultry, and Fish; Sauces, Vegetables; Desserts—for example, plus a "Leftovers Roundup" section that provides quick tips and suggestions for a variety of foods, listed alphabetically. Many of the recipes incorporate more than one "problem" item, such as stale bread, dried cheese, souring milk, overcooked or leftover vegetables, and so forth. For that reason there is a special index at the end of the book, in which you can look up individual food items and locate specific recipes for their transformation into a delectable dish.

Yogurt

For years now plain yogurt has been a staple in my refrigerator. Rich in calcium and low in fat if made from skim milk, it's one of the most healthful foods, and my mother introduced it into our family long before it became generally popular. The commercial fruit-flavored varieties are too sweet, and too expensive, for my taste—I much prefer adding fresh fruit to plain yogurt, which I make frequently. The process is simple, and far more economical than buying commercial brands—especially when you consider what an ideal use it is for milk that's beginning to turn sour. Yogurt makers are convenient, but nonessential. All you need is a glass or enamel bowl or casserole. A thermometer is helpful for accurate temperature reading. There is a cultured dairy-food "cooker" on the market that regulates temperature and helps control the process.

Yogurt is delicious straight and with fruit, and is so versatile that it combines well with vegetables, cottage cheese, seasonings and meats, poultry and fish dishes. Mix it with chopped cucumber, dill, and garlic for a relish; use it as a low-calorie substitute for sour cream in cold soups and dips. And experiment with various seasonings, cheeses, citrus juices, and condiments for a myriad of exciting salad dressings.

Homemade Yogurt

1 qt.	skim or whole milk, just beginning to sour
1 to 2 Tbsp.	active culture yogurt

Heat milk to 190 degrees F. (almost boiling) in saucepan. Cool to 110 to 120 degrees F. Do not allow to cool below that temperature (use thermometer for accuracy). Place yogurt in 1½-quart glass or enamel bowl or casserole that has been rinsed in boiling water. Stir in warm milk. Cover and put in warm place (in gas oven with pilot light or oven very slightly preheated, then turned off). Leave about 8 hours, or overnight. Yogurt will thicken. Chill at least 3 hours to set further before serving. Keep a small amount of yogurt to make the next batch. Makes about 1 quart.

Appetizers

Served with sesame crackers, toasted quartered split pita bread (Syrian flat bread), or with crunchy raw vegetables, dips and spreads are great party fare. No one will believe you were rescuing mushy beans or tired eggplant or avocado!

Avocado Spread

Avocados have a sneaky way of getting overripe since the last time you've looked at them. Mushy pulp is perfect for this spread.

*1	overripe medium avocado, pitted and pared
About 2 Tbsp.	minced onion or about ¼ tsp. onion juice to taste
1½ tsp.	lemon juice
	Salt and hot pepper sauce to taste
1	garlic clove, crushed

Mash avocado pulp with fork or in blender. Add remaining ingredients and blend well. Taste and adjust seasonings. Store covered in refrigerator a few hours for flavors to blend.

Serve with buttered cocktail rye bread; garnish with thin lemon slices. Makes about ¾ cup.

*Artichoke pulp may be substituted for avocado.

Eggplant Relish

This "Poor Man's Caviar" is a perfect way of using up over-the-hill eggplant, onions, and tomatoes. One of my faithful standbys, with taste nuances that develop after hours of chilling. It's good as an appetizer with pita bread, on lettuce as a salad, and as one of the items on a relish tray. Because of its acidic content and good keeping qualities, it makes a great addition to a picnic. The proportion of oil to lemon juice can be adjusted to suit your taste.

1 medium	eggplant (about ½ pound)
1	clove garlic, minced
1 medium	onion, chopped
1 to 2 medium	tomatoes, chopped
⅓ cup	chopped Greek or Italian olives
1 large	green onion, chopped
About ⅓ cup	minced parsley
About 1 Tbsp. each	olive oil and lemon juice
	Salt and pepper to taste
	Lettuce
	Lemon slices
	Fresh mint sprigs

Bake eggplant in 350-degree oven 40 to 50 minutes, until it is very soft and can be pierced easily with a fork. Let cool slightly, peel and chop coarse. Drain, pressing slightly to extract excess liquid. Place in bowl. Add ingredients through parsley. Gradually add equal parts oil and lemon juice to moisten. Toss to coat all ingredients. Season to taste. Adjust amount of oil, lemon juice, or seasoning. Cover and chill several hours or overnight. Serve over lettuce. Garnish with lemon slices and mint. Serves 4 as a salad.

Eggplant can be cooked in microwave. Pierce in several places with sharp knife; place on paper toweling. Cook on high power 5 to 7 minutes, turning halfway through cooking for soft eggplant— longer for a firm one.

Bean Dip

When limas are overcooked, tough, or have broken skins, mash and purée them for this scrumptious dip. Other bean varieties can be substituted.

1 cup	cooked lima (or similar) bean purée (about 2 cups cooked or canned beans)
¼ to ⅓ cup	plain thick yogurt
1 small to medium	clove garlic, crushed
1 to 1½ tsp.	lemon juice
Several dashes	hot pepper sauce
½	green onion, minced
1 Tbsp.	chopped parsley
1½ tsp.	fresh dill, coriander or thyme, or ½ tsp. dried

Combine bean purée and yogurt. Add remaining ingredients and mix thoroughly, adjusting consistency and flavor. Cover and chill about 2 hours before serving. Makes about 1¼ cups.

Note: A scoop of bean dip is a nice addition to a composed salad with tomato, pickled corn relish, and cucumber on lettuce.

Brandied Cheese Crock

Save little ends and pieces of dried-out cheese to make this crock. Select several compatible choices (Cheddar, Provolone, blue-veined all enhance each other) and blend with butter and brandy. Add more soft cheese and yogurt to make a crumbly mixture more spreadable.

½ lb.	shredded sharp cheese (Cheddar, Herkimer, Provolone, etc.), at room temperature
2 Tbsp.	softened butter or margarine
Dash	hot pepper sauce
3 to 4 Tbsp.	brandy, to taste
3 to 4 Tbsp.	cream or Neufchatel cheese

Blend ingredients (using 3 Tbsp. cream cheese) in food processor or blender until smooth. Gradually add enough remaining cream cheese to make mixture very smooth and spreadable. Pack into crock, cover, and refrigerate at least 1 day to allow flavors to blend. Keeps for weeks and may be added to whenever you have more dried cheese. Serve at room temperature. Makes about 1 cup.

Variations: Crumble blue-veined cheeses and blend with Swiss or Emmenthaler flavored with mustard. Bland, soft cheeses are compatible when blended with another stronger favorite.

Soups

Soup is a marvelous vehicle for meat and vegetable odds and ends. Whenever you have overcooked vegetables, stale peanuts, tangy milk, tough spinach, a ham bone, or meat scraps, use them in these delicious soups.

Cream of Vegetable Soup

When you've overcooked your family's favorite vegetable, salvage it in this delectable soup and you'll hear praise instead of lamentation. The seasoning and garnish should be selected according to your taste and appropriate for the particular vegetable. Nutmeg is especially good with carrots and winter squash, and the herbs listed in the recipe are versatile enough to be used for most vegetables. Seasoning is a highly personal affair and requires a bit of experimenting. Chicken stock is preferable for most vegetables, but the more robust-flavored ones can take a heartier beef stock. When using a high-water vegetable (escarole, spinach, cabbage, etc.), you may need to increase the flour a bit to prevent a thin consistency.

About 1 lb.	cooked vegetable
2 Tbsp.	butter
½ to 1 small	onion, grated
2 Tbsp.	flour
2 cups	milk

Reserved vegetable cooking liquid plus chicken stock or
   broth to equal 2 cups
Salt and pepper to taste
Grated nutmeg, chopped chives, dill or parsley
Shredded Cheddar, grated Parmesan, or croutons.

Drain vegetable, saving any cooking liquid, and purée in blender
or food processor. Melt butter in medium saucepan. Sauté onion
until golden, 2 or 3 minutes. Stir in flour and cook about 2
minutes. Gradually stir in milk and vegetable-chicken stock, cooking
and stirring until thickened and smooth. Season to taste with spices
and herbs. Stir in puréed vegetable. Heat thoroughly. Adjust seasoning. Top with cheese or croutons before serving to 6.

Creamy Goober Soup

The unusual soup below serves as a great remedy for soggy or
slightly stale peanuts, and/or the remains in the peanut-butter jar.
The peanut flavor is especially good with curry spices, but is also
enhanced by herbs, onion and celery. Hot pepper gives it a zing.
Bourbon gives it a nice kick, too—who cares about soggy goobers?

1 Tbsp.	peanut oil
¼ cup	each minced onion and celery
⅓ cup	peanut butter, crunchy or smooth
⅔ cup	ground salted peanuts
½ tsp.	curry powder, or to taste
About ¼ tsp.	each coriander and cumin
	Freshly grated white pepper to taste
Dash	hot pepper sauce or pinch of red pepper flakes
3 cups	chicken bouillon
⅔ cup	evaporated milk, undiluted
About ¼ cup	bourbon
	Minced parsley
¼ cup	chopped peanuts

Heat oil in saucepan. Sauté onion and celery until soft. Stir in
peanut butter until smooth. Mix in peanuts. Season. Add bouillon,

stirring to blend. Cover and simmer about 20 minutes, stirring occasionally. Stir in evaporated milk and the bourbon. Heat thoroughly. Serve garnished with parsley and chopped peanuts to 4.

Note: For a peanut-butter version, substitute peanut butter for peanuts, or a total of 1 cup peanut butter and no peanuts.

Spinach–Sour-Milk Soup

Use this recipe for spinach stem ends or when spinach leaves are getting old, or for tough outer leaves. A great use for milk that is beginning to sour, too! The soup will have a slightly speckled appearance, which may rule it out as an elegant party soup; but it's a wonderful family supper first course. Fennel seed and tarragon are two distinctive flavoring choices; and a touch of hot pepper adds zest.

1 small	onion, chopped
1 Tbsp.	butter or margarine
1½ tsp.	cornstarch or arrowroot starch powder
¼ tsp.	mushroom powder
½ tsp.	crushed fennel seed or dried tarragon
About 2 cups	coarsely chopped clean spinach ends and leaves
2 cups	chicken stock or bouillon
	Salt to taste
½ to 1 cup	milk just beginning to sour (do not use old)
	Chopped chives

Optional: Dash cayenne or hot pepper sauce

Sauté onion in butter in saucepan until translucent. Stir in cornstarch; cook about 1 minute, then add mushroom powder, fennel, and cayenne. Add spinach, stock, and salt, stirring well (purée mixture if desired). Cover, bring to boil; reduce heat, simmer several minutes. Gradually stir in soured milk, heating gently and stirring; top with chives. Makes 2 (about 1-cup) servings.

Note: Tough outer leaves of lettuce, escarole or endive can be substituted for spinach.

Thick Split Pea Soup

When there's no ham bone, add chopped cooked ham or any
smoked meat. Yellow and green split peas can be used interchangeably in this (and most) recipes; there's only a slight difference
in taste. They need not be soaked for soup. The highly nourishing
peas offer calcium, protein, iron, phosphorus, and the B vitamins.

1 lb. (2¼ cups)	dry green or yellow split peas, rinsed
2 qts.	water
1	meaty ham bone or 1 cup diced cooked ham or smoked meat
2 medium	onions, chopped
4 ribs	celery, diced
3 medium	carrots, diced
3 sprigs	parsley, minced
1 large	bay leaf
1	garlic clove, crushed
Salt and pepper	to taste
½ tsp.	dried tarragon or thyme
Hot red pepper sauce	to taste
3 Tbsp.	lemon juice

Place all ingredients in a large, heavy saucepan with tight-fitting
cover. Bring to a boil, reduce heat, and simmer covered about 2
hours, stirring and skimming occasionally. Avoid overstirring or peas
will mash. Remove ham bone; slice meat off bone, chop, and return
to soup. Discard bone. Remove and discard bay leaf. Taste and
adjust seasonings. Makes 2½ quarts, 8 to 10 servings of thick soup.
For thinner soup, add more hot water.

Note: About 1½ to 2 cups diced mild flavored vegetables such as
green pepper, green beans, kohlrabi or a combination may be substituted for the celery or part of the celery and the carrots.

Meats, Poultry, and Fish

There's no end to the recipes for soups, salads, curries, casseroles, stews, meat loaves, dips, and sandwich spreads that incorporate scraps—or chunks—of leftover roasts of all kinds, not to mention steaks and chops and smoked meats. And another whole area of amazing rescue operations for tougher or blander cuts is marinades and sauces. Let's start with marinades.

MARINADES

Marinades are virtually magical in cookery. They can make tough meat cuts tender—enough to broil, sometimes—and they can impart delicious flavors to otherwise uninteresting cuts. They vary widely in composition, but share an acid medium, which is what does the tenderizing. Wine, vinegar, beer, and lemon juice are the acids usually employed. Papaya extract, a natural tenderizer, is sometimes added. The mixture can be diluted with water, oil, broth, and other liquids, and seasonings and flavorings vary to taste. Even a short soaking of meat in a spicy marinade enhances color and imparts flavor to bland meat.

The best containers for marinating are glass or glazed or impervious metal, such as stainless steel. Refrigerate the meat if it is to be

319

soaked more than an hour or so. Large meat cuts require longer marination, usually several hours or overnight. Delicate meats need only a short bath.

A recipe for a simple marinated steak, made tender for broiling appears on p. 323. Use the top beef round, which is normally too lean for broiling, or chuck-eye steaks, taken from the chuck-eye roast.

LEFTOVER MEAT

You can stretch it in a meat loaf or casserole, add it to soup, curry it with vegetables. And you can make nalesniki, thin Polish rolled pancakes with fillings that vary from sauerkraut to ground meat and spicy cheese.

Nalesniki (Polish Filled Pancakes)

The pancakes envelop ingredients at hand. With a dollop of sour cream, nalesniki become an inventive way of serving leftovers, or tough meat ground to tenderness, with a flair. As my mother and I traveled through Poland, we found the nonmeat versions common main-dish accompaniments; cheese "blintzes" were desserts. Those filled with ground meat were often the substance of a family supper at our house. My mother found nalesniki a nice means of using up leftover roast or soup meat. They're also a great coverup for over-cooked or dry meat. Dillweed is more authentic than thyme, but let your own taste buds be your guide.

NALESNIKI

½ cup	milk
½ cup	water
1	egg, lightly beaten
1	egg yolk, lightly beaten
¾ to 1 cup	unbleached flour

> Dash salt
> Oil
> Ground meat filling (recipe follows)
> Melted butter or margarine
> Dairy sour cream or yogurt

Combine milk, water, egg, and extra yolk in a medium bowl. Stir in flour and salt; mix thoroughly. Cover and let rest about 20 minutes. Batter should be rather thin; add more water if necessary. Oil a 7-inch crepe pan or skillet; heat until quite hot. Pour in 3 to 4 tablespoons batter, rotating skillet rapidly to cover bottom of pan completely and evenly. Cook over medium heat until golden-brown on bottom, then turn and quickly cook second side until lightly browned. Remove to hot platter, cover, and keep warm while repeating process until all batter is used. Divide ground meat filling among pancakes, roll up, and brown each quickly in melted butter. Serve with sour cream. Makes about 6 to 8, or 3 to 4 servings.

Note: ¼ cup buckwheat flour can be substituted for the same amount of unbleached white to give a more robust texture and taste. Yogurt is a good low-calorie alternative to sour cream.

GROUND MEAT FILLING

2 to 2½ cups	(about 1 lb.) ground cooked meat (leftover roast beef, or overcooked meat)
1 medium	onion, chopped
1 Tbsp.	butter
1 tsp.	dillweed or thyme
	Salt and pepper to taste
1 small sprig	parsley, chopped
2 to 4 Tbsp.	beef broth

Brown meat with onion in butter in skillet. Season to taste. Moisten with as much broth as meat will absorb. Cover and cook over very low heat for a few minutes. Use to fill nalesniki above.

Lentil-Cheese Meat Loaf

Stretching and filling can often make meat go twice as far. Soy protein or flour, vegetable protein extender, oatmeal, corn meal, grits, groats, barley, bran, beans, lentils, pasta, rice, seeds, nuts, bean sprouts, and, of course, breadcrumbs, are all wonderful expansion agents for a small amount of leftover meat and a bigger amount of appetites to be satisfied. Here's an example of how a pound of ground meat can serve 6 to 8 by stretching it with lentils, cheese, breadcrumbs, and eggs. The breadcrumbs will use up some stale bread for you; and if you have any leftover mashed potatoes, rutabagas, or turnips, they'll be great spread on top and browned.

1 cup	dry lentils, rinsed
1 lb.	ground beef
2 cups (8 oz.)	shredded Cheddar cheese
2	eggs
1½ cups (4 slices)	crumbled stale bread
1	onion, chopped
1 tsp.	salt, or to taste
½ tsp.	dried basil
¼ tsp.	dried marjoram
	Freshly ground black pepper to taste
Optional:	about 2 cups seasoned leftover mashed potatoes, turnips, or rutabagas

Simmer lentils in 2½ cups broth or water until just tender, about 1 hour. Drain and combine in bowl with meat, 1 cup of the cheese, eggs, breadcrumbs, onion, and seasonings to taste. Mix until thoroughly blended. Shape into 9 by 5 by 3-inch loaf on a foil-lined baking pan and bake in preheated 350-degree oven for 30 minutes. Meanwhile, stir remaining cheese into leftover mashed potatoes or vegetables. Spread mixture over top and sides of meat loaf and bake 15 minutes in a 400-degree oven until lightly browned. Serve with green beans and carrots. Makes 6 to 8 servings.

Lemon-Marinated Beef

Beef top round or 1 chuck-eye steak, about 1 inch thick (about 2 pounds)
½ cup   lemon juice
¼ cup   salad oil
¼ cup   chopped onion
1 clove   garlic, crushed
½ tsp.   each salt and oregano
¼ tsp.   pepper

Trim excess fat from meat. Combine lemon juice, oil, onion, garlic and seasonings. Pour over meat in dish or plastic bag, turning to coat all sides. Marinate in refrigerator 6 hours or overnight. Pour off and reserve marinade. Pat steak dry with paper toweling. Place steak on broiler pan. Broil 4 to 5 inches from heat source 15 to 25 minutes, depending on thickness of steak and degree of doneness desired (rare to medium), turning occasionally. Makes 4 to 6 servings.

Note: For ½- to ¾-inch-thick steak, broil 14 to 20 minutes. Save marinade to reuse for another meat cut. Cover and store in refrigerator. Part of the marinade can be diluted with beef broth and wine, heated, and served over the meat.

LEFTOVER POULTRY

Delicious added to the soybean-vegetable casserole (p. 332) or timbales (p. 333), or cold in curried pilaf salad (p. 335). If your problem is what to do with giblets, store them in the freezer until you have several, then give them this smooth, rich treatment.

Giblet Stroganoff

1¼ lb.	chicken giblets (necks, hearts, gizzards from 4 chickens)
2 Tbsp.	butter or margarine
2 Tbsp.	flour
½ tsp.	salt (omit if using bouillon)
⅛ tsp.	black pepper
1 to 1½ cups	giblet stock or chicken bouillon
½ small	onion, sliced
¼ tsp.	dried leaf thyme
½ lb.	fresh mushrooms, sliced (about 2 cups)
1 tsp.	Worcestershire sauce
3 Tbsp.	dry red wine
1 cup	dairy sour cream or sour half-and-half
	Hot cooked brown rice or ribbon noodles
	Paprika
	Chopped fresh parsley

Put giblets and enough salted water to cover in a medium saucepan. Bring to a boil, reduce heat, and simmer, covered, until fork-tender, 1 to 1½ hours. Drain, reserving stock. Trim giblets of gristle and fat; skin and bone necks. Chop meat coarsely and brown in 1 tablespoon of the butter in a large, heavy skillet. Remove and set aside. Melt remaining butter and stir in flour, salt, and pepper. Cook, stirring constantly, 2 minutes. Gradually stir in 1 cup reserved stock (save remainder for another use). Add onion, thyme, mushrooms, and Worcestershire sauce. Simmer and stir over low heat until sauce is thickened, 10 to 20 minutes. Remove from heat and stir in wine and reserved giblets. Gradually stir a little sauce into sour cream, then gradually stir sour cream into the sauce in pan. Cook, stirring, over low heat; do not boil. Adjust seasonings. Serve over rice, sprinkled with paprika and garnished with parsley. Serves 4.

Leftover Fish—See *Timbale, fish variation* (p. 333).

Sauces

A well-chosen sauce enhances a plain food item or a dish, adding richness, flavor, and moisture. And although some proud chefs find it hard to admit, many a culinary blunder has been covered up by a béchamel or bordelaise. Here are several basic sauces that can be matched with numerous foods that for one reason or another require support. They were selected for their speed of preparation and their adaptability—both vital qualities in the face of a cooking problem. A good one-pot version of the classic béchamel appears on p. 327.

Sauces in Seconds

When time is of utmost importance, rely on canned or bottled items to see you through the culinary crisis. Consider the dish in question and the flavors best suited. Then scan your shelves for some emergency aids. Try to keep several on hand. The choice depends on the foods you tend to serve and your personal taste.

Bottled sauces: Some brands are of quite good quality. Shop selectively and experiment until you find several dependable ones. If you grill a great deal or enjoy broiled meats, you might want to have a good barbecue sauce handy; you can doctor it up. Some Oriental markets sell good Chinese sauces, which serve to make a wok cook more secure. There are canned enchilada sauces and some pretty good French imports, like madeira sauce.

Horseradish: Blend with mayonnaise, crème fraîche, or whipped cream, and a little mustard or herbs for a pungent sauce. Perfect with roast meats and boiled beets; great with cold smoked meat, such as tongue or corned beef.

Mayonnaise (homemade or commercial): This thick sauce is the foundation for dozens of variations, including Thousand Island dressing, which mixes chili sauce, chopped olives, onion, hard-cooked egg, and parsley into the basic sauce. Add Dijon mustard, chopped parsley, and capers and you have the start of two more versions: for rémoulade, add tarragon, chervil, and chopped pickles; for tartar sauce, stir in chopped sweet pickles, hard-cooked eggs, shallots, and olives. Rémoulade is used for shellfish as well as meats and poultry; tartar is usually reserved for fried fish. Crumbled blue cheese can be added for a delicious sauce for broccoli, cauliflower, and similar vegetables. Or add chopped fruits and fruit juice or chutney for a fruit salad dressing or dessert sauce.

Mustard: Our kitchen is never without several varieties of this condiment, to use either straight or blended with mayonnaise, crème fraîche, pan juices, or other compatibles. Try the milder Dijon mustards flavored with green peppercorns, orange or lemon; the robust English or Dutch types; or the fiery Chinese or whole mustard seed–horseradish preparations.

Soups, condensed: I don't endorse them as sauces most of the time, but occasionally they come to the cook's rescue. Try blending two or more quality compatible ones; the basic ones that double as sauces for meats and vegetables are cream of mushroom, cream of onion, cheese, and tomato.

Tomato sauce: Can be fortified with herbs, garlic, onion, and chopped green pepper. Use for meats, sausage, poultry, eggplant, zucchini, and pasta and rice casseroles.

Simplified Béchamel (White Sauce)

2 Tbsp.	butter
1½ Tbsp.	flour
1 cup	milk, half-and-half and milk, or light stock and milk
2 Tbsp.	minced parsley or chives
¼ tsp.	grated nutmeg
	Salt and freshly ground white pepper to taste

Melt butter in small saucepan. Stir in flour, cooking and stirring over low heat until well blended and smooth, about 3 minutes. Slowly stir in milk or other liquid. Season to taste, mixing well. Whisk the sauce as it simmers until thickened and smooth, 7 to 10 minutes. Makes slightly more than 1 cup sauce.

Variations: Stir in ¼ to ⅓ cup grated or shredded cheese (Parmesan, Gruyère, Cheddar, Swiss, etc.) or sautéed mushrooms and onions when seasoning this sauce. When using the sauce for creamed foods use 1 part sauce to 2 parts solid ingredients.

Suggested uses: The plain sauce moisturizes dry poultry, meat, and overcooked vegetables; chopped or sliced solids can be incorporated into the sauce, as in a creamed casserole, or the food in need of camouflage can be topped with the sauce. The cheese version is especially compatible with vegetables, a fallen spinach (or similar) soufflé, and some meats and poultry, while the mushroom sauce makes a nice contrast to spinach and other green vegetables, pasta, rice, meat, and poultry.

Gravy

Many cooks shun gravy, either because they've heard many tales of woe about lumpiness problems or have had the unfortunate experience themselves. These foolproof directions should end gravy worries and enable you to use the gravy to resolve meat problems instead. The rich, flavorful browned pan juices from a roast are incorporated. Gravy makes any roast more palatable, and in the absence of any other sauce is essential to dry, overcooked meat. Follow the same directions for capturing the flavor essence of any roast. Add herbs and other seasonings as desired.

Brown Gravy

¼ cup to 6 Tbsp.	pan juices from roast
¼ cup	browned flour
2 cups	appropriate meat stock or bouillon
	Salt, pepper, and Worcestershire sauce to taste

Measure pan juices in chilled measuring cup to facilitate skimming surface fat. Add ¼ cup skimmed fat to pan. Remove excess fat and reserve for another time or discard. Blend in browned flour. Slowly add meat juices and stock, stirring while simmering about 5 minutes. Gravy should be smooth and thickened. If lumps form, beat with a wire whisk or strain. Season to taste. Makes about 2 cups.

Note: To brown flour, mix 1 cup flour with a little garlic or onion powder (if desired), spread on baking pan, and place in 250-degree oven about 30 minutes, stirring frequently, until browned. Store in jar.

Variation: ⅓ to ½ cup dry red wine can replace part of the beef stock.

Suggested uses: Serve over slices of the roast that produced the drippings. Leftover gravy can be frozen and used later over hamburgers, hash, lamb patties, meat loaf, and other dishes that could benefit from the moisture and flavor.

Gingered Sweet-Sour Sauce

A sweet-sour sauce—this one gingered—has a way of perking up tired chicken or leftover pork and vegetables. The strips of orange rind contribute a sprightly zest and add *eye* appeal as well.

1 Tbsp.	peanut or salad oil
2	green onions, chopped
1 clove	garlic, crushed
	Rind from 1 orange, cut into thin strips
1 tsp.	minced or grated gingerroot
¾ cup	chicken broth or bouillon
1½ to 2 Tbsp.	cornstarch
¼ cup each	sake and fruit juice (pineapple, orange, grapefruit)
3 Tbsp.	cider vinegar
About 1 Tbsp.	soy sauce
1 to 2 Tbsp.	honey to taste

Heat oil in wok or skillet. Sauté green onions and garlic until softened but not brown. Add orange rind and gingerroot. Stir in broth; bring to a boil; cover and simmer 5 to 10 minutes. Blend cornstarch with sake; gradually stir into hot mixture. Bring to full boil, stirring, until mixture thickens. Cook, stirring, 1 minute. Remove from heat. Stir in remaining ingredients. Adjust honey to taste. Makes about 1½ cups sauce.

Suggested uses: I've developed this sauce for chicken with broccoli, carrots, and mushrooms that were first stir-fried in a wok, then simmered in the broth before the cornstarch was added. The sauce is also delicious over shrimp and fish. It has the ability to transform odds and ends of ingredients into a proud Chinese main dish when served over cooked rice.

Vegetables

Whether leftover, overcooked, or just the surplus of an overambitious shopping spree, vegetables virtually never need go down the disposal! The Soybean-Vegetable Casserole recipe on page 332 will incorporate almost any number and variety of leftovers, including meat or poultry scraps. Delicious meatless, too; the soybean protein is complete when served with rice, wheat, or cheese. When meatless, this dish averages out to about 35 cents per serving!

Spinach Quiches in Breadcrumb Crusts

I developed this variation on a quiche when I wanted to use up some very salty ham, leftover spinach, and stale whole wheat bread. The result is attractive individual brunch main dishes. Complete the menu with a tossed green salad, fresh fruit, and coffee.

BREADCRUMB CRUST

*1¼ cups	stale whole wheat breadcrumbs, ground fine (2 to 3 slices)
¼ cup	raw or lightly toasted wheat germ
¼ cup	melted margarine or butter

330

FILLING

4	eggs
1 cup	milk
1 Tbsp.	dry sherry
2 dashes	hot pepper sauce
2 tsp.	chopped fresh dill
½ to ¾ tsp.	freshly ground black pepper, or to taste
½ tsp.	nutmeg
¼ tsp.	ground savory
**¾ cup (4 oz.)	finely chopped lean, salty ham (soaked in milk ½ hour and rinsed)
¾ cup (4 oz.)	shredded mozzarella cheese
***½ cup	well-drained chopped cooked spinach or drained, thawed frozen chopped spinach (about one-half 10 oz. package frozen), water pressed out
1	green onion, chopped fine

Spread breadcrumbs evenly over shallow baking pan. Toast in pre-heated 375-degree oven until dry and slightly browned, 10 to 12 minutes. In small bowl mix breadcrumbs, wheat germ, and margarine. Butter four 8 to 10-oz. round glass baking dishes or rame-kins. Press the crumbs evenly in bottoms and up the sides of the buttered dishes. Bake in preheated 375-degree oven until golden brown, about 10 minutes. Cool 10 minutes.

In a medium bowl, slightly beat eggs. Stir in milk, sherry, hot pepper sauce, dill, pepper, nutmeg, and savory. Mix in ham, cheese, spinach, and onion. Divide filling evenly among baked crusts. Bake in preheated 350-degree oven until knife inserted in center comes out clean, 25 to 30 minutes. Remove from oven. Cool on rack for 10 minutes. Garnish with toasted slivered almonds or sesame seeds. Serves 4.

*If substituting white breadcrumbs, use 1¾ cups.
**Ham can be omitted.
***Kale, broccoli, or other cooked green vegetable can be substi-tuted.

Soybean–Vegetable Casserole

1 cup	soybeans, rinsed
About 2 to 3 cups	broth
1 small	onion, coarsely chopped
¼ tsp.	crumbled dried leaf thyme
1 medium	carrot, sliced ½-inch thick
1 medium	kohlrabi or young turnip, pared and cut into ½-inch cubes
1 medium	green pepper, seeded and cut into ½-inch squares
½ tsp.	oregano
3 Tbsp.	chopped peanuts
1 Tbsp.	butter
1 Tbsp.	flour
1 tsp.	prepared mustard
½ cup	milk
	Pepper to taste
	Several strips (about 1 oz.) mozzarella cheese
	Parsley

Optional: About 1 cup cubed cooked smoked turkey, ham, sausage, or chicken

Cover soybeans with water. Discard any floating bad beans. Soak 20 minutes. Drain and add fresh water to cover. Bring to a boil, remove from heat, cover, and soak until beans soften and absorb liquid, 1 to 2 hours. Add broth (preferably of the same kind of meat you are adding), onion, and thyme. Cook, covered, until beans are tender, 1½ to 2 hours. Add vegetables, oregano, and 2 Tbsp. peanuts and continue cooking covered until vegetables are tender, 15 to 20 minutes. In separate saucepan melt butter, stir in flour, and cook about 2 minutes, stirring. Add mustard and gradually stir in milk, cooking until thickened and smooth. Season with pepper. Stir sauce into bean-vegetable mixture; add meat. Top with strips of mozzarella and more oregano to taste. Bake in a 350-degree oven until cheese is melted and casserole is heated through, about 10 minutes. Garnish with parsley and the remaining tablespoon chopped peanuts. Serves 4.

Vegetable Timbale

Almost any overcooked or leftover vegetable—or even leftover cooked fish or poultry—can be blended into this timbale custard and served plain or sauced. My favorite variation is spinach, which is especially compatible with a cheese, beurre blanc or hollandaise sauce.

1 cup	chicken stock or bouillon
½ cup	half-and-half or milk
4	eggs, lightly beaten
¼ tsp.	salt
1½ Tbsp.	chopped parsley
1	green onion, minced
½ tsp.	dried leaf thyme
⅛ tsp.	lemon juice
*1 cup	well-drained cooked spinach, chopped fine, puréed or sieved
2 Tbsp.	grated sharp cheese (Parmesan, Romano, etc.) Cheese or hollandaise sauce

Blend ingredients through lemon juice with wire whisk. Stir in spinach and cheese. Pour into 6 or 7 buttered timbale molds or 4-oz. custard cups, or a 6-cup ring mold, filling about ¾ full. Arrange on rack in pan of hot water, adding enough water so level is even with top of timbale mixture in molds. Bake in a 325-degree oven 25 to 30 minutes for individual molds, about 40 minutes for ring mold, or until knife inserted in center comes out clean. Loosen edges with sharp, thin-bladed knife and invert onto serving plates. If desired, top with a few watercress leaves; serve with a favorite sauce. Serves 6 as a first course.

*Flaked or minced cooked, skinned, and boned lean fish or chicken, or a combination of vegetable and fish or chicken, can be substituted. Fish or chicken timbales are especially good with watercress, sorrel, or spinach sauce.

Creamed Lettuce

Limp lettuce and those tough outer leaves can be fully utilized for this delectable side dish.

2 Tbsp.	butter or margarine
2	green onions, minced
1	clove garlic, crushed or minced
2 Tbsp.	flour
½ cup	hot chicken stock or bouillon
½ cup	hot (not boiling) milk or half-and-half
*4 cups	chopped lettuce
	Salt and pepper to taste
2 tsp.	grated lemon or orange rind
	Minced chives

Melt butter in medium skillet over medium heat. Sauté green onions and garlic lightly. Stir in flour, cook and stir, allowing to bubble, 2 to 3 minutes. Gradually stir in hot stock and milk; cook and stir over medium heat until thickened and smooth. Add lettuce; cook and stir several minutes. If lettuce is still not tender, cover pan and simmer about 1 minute. Season to taste, stir in grated rind and top with minced chives. Serves 4.

*Escarole or endive can be substituted.

Salads and Salad Dressings

Curried Pilaf Salad

Leftover rice can be made into a hearty side-dish salad or a luncheon main dish. A nice opportunity to use up leftover peas or other vegetables, too, and turkey or chicken.

2 cups	cooked rice
⅔ to 1 cup	parboiled green peas, drained and chilled
2	green onions, minced
2 Tbsp.	mayonnaise (or more if desired)
2 Tbsp.	lemon juice
1½ tsp.	hot Madras curry powder, or to taste
About 1 cup	pineapple chunks
2 to 4 Tbsp.	pine nuts or slivered almonds
	Lettuce
	Raisins
	Chutney
Optional:	about 1 cup turkey or chicken cubes

Combine rice, peas, and green onions in bowl. Combine mayonnaise with lemon juice and curry powder; stir into rice mixture. Cover and refrigerate at least 2 hours. Just before serving, toss in pineapple chunks, poultry and nuts. Arrange over lettuce; garnish with raisins and dollops of chutney. Serves 2.

Orange-Poppyseed-Yogurt Dressing

This dressing can utilize thin or mature-flavored yogurt—delicious over chicken, tuna, vegetable, or fruit salads.

1 cup	plain thin or mature yogurt
2 Tbsp.	orange juice
1 Tbsp.	lemon juice
1 tsp.	poppyseeds
Optional:	1 Tbsp. honey

Blend all ingredients in small bowl or container. Honey can be added when dressing is intended for fruit salad. Cover and chill at least 2 hours. Makes about 1¼ cups.

Blue-Cheese–Yogurt Dressing

Another of my favorite dressings is this blue-cheese version, which camouflages pungent cheese and yogurt and enlivens a bowl of crisp greens dotted with radish slices. You'll also find it's perfect to dress a mixed vegetable salad of red cabbage, greens, cauliflower, olives, and cucumber. For a more piquant taste, tarragon wine vinegar or white wine vinegar can be used in lieu of lemon juice, and milk that has just begun to sour can be blended in as well. Dieters can cut the amount of oil.

3 to 4 oz.	blue cheese
1 clove	garlic, crushed
½ cup	olive oil or salad oil
¼ cup	lemon juice
1 cup	plain mature yogurt
¼ tsp.	thyme
	Salt and freshly ground pepper to taste
Optional:	Dash cayenne

Mash cheese with garlic in small bowl. Gradually stir in oil and beat until thoroughly mixed. Add lemon juice, yogurt and seasonings, mixing well. Cover and chill at least 2 hours. Makes about 1¾ cups.

Desserts and Dessert Sauce

Phylis's Rum Pot

One August day a dear friend, Phylis Magida, brought me a quart jar labeled "RUM POT: DO NOT OPEN UNTIL THANKSGIV-ING." It was sealed with tape to make me resist the temptation of opening. She gave me the directions along with the pot, which explained how to replenish it after it was used. At last the holiday arrived, the jar was uncapped, and a wonderful heady scent emerged. I spooned out a piece of darkened pineapple with some of the liquid and was hooked. Ambrosia! Chunks of pineapple, straw-berries, peach slices, and cherries had gone into the jar with half their weight in sugar and rum. Ten weeks later the separate ingre-dients had merged to form a rich fruit sauce that transforms ice cream, pudding, crepes, or pound cake into a spectacular dessert. Or heat and serve it as a fruit compote with roasted meat or poultry.

Fruit steeped in sweetened rum absorbs it in 10 weeks, so a fresh pot requires at least that much time before being ready to eat. Once the rum pot is opened and used, replenish it almost every time you

337

remove some of its contents. The rum-pot principle is similar to a sourdough starter or yogurt culture; always leave a portion that can be replenished. You can keep a rum pot going for years, as I have, and make enough to give as gifts. Fresh, canned, or dried fruits can be used; see recommended list below. The rum pot is a delicious way of using up leftover fruits or those which are slightly discolored or otherwise pithy and bland.

Buy fresh fruit in any combinations from the list below. Peel, hull, and wash according to directions. Weigh it and half its weight in sugar. Place both in a sterilized large wide-neck glass jar or crockery pot. Cover with dark rum so level is about 2 inches above fruit. Fruit may float for a few days. Seal jar with plastic wrap and rubber band, and label it for 10 to 12 weeks hence and store it in a cool place. When it is ready, mix lightly before serving. As you use the rum pot, add new fruit and sugar. Pour in rum to extend 2 inches above fruit. Allow to steep for ten weeks, during which time you can eat the readied fruit.

Use a combination of any of the following fruits:
Fresh pineapple, pared, cored, eyes cut out, cut in large chunks
Peaches, peeled and pitted, quartered
Plums, either peeled and pitted or left whole, as desired
Apricots, either peeled and pitted or left whole, as desired
Strawberries, washed and hulled
Cherries, stemmed and washed

Note: Dried or canned apricots, figs, pineapple, and peaches may be used; but do not use apples, black currants, billberries, or blackberries.

Fruit Roll Flop . . . and Pudding

Here is the prototypical disaster-into-delicacy recipe mentioned in the introduction on p. 307.

FRUIT ROLL FLOP PUDDING

1	fruit roll flop (recipe follows)
3 cups	heated milk
¼ cup	sugar
3	eggs, slightly beaten
¼ tsp each	salt, cinnamon, nutmeg, and mace

Crumble fruit roll flop in bowl; cover with hot milk. Stir to moisten all crumbs; set aside to cool. Combine sugar, eggs, and spices; stir into fruit roll mixture. Transfer to buttered 2-quart casserole and set in pan of hot water. Bake uncovered in 325-degree oven until custard is firm and top is golden, 1 to 1¼ hours. Serve warm, topped with whipped cream and toasted slivered almonds. Serves 12.

FRUIT ROLL FLOP

3 Tbsp.	oil
¼ cup	honey
1⅓ cups	whole wheat flour
About ¼ cup	cold milk
Grated rind of ½	lemon
1½ to 2 cups	dried fruits, chopped

Blend oil with honey; stir in flour and enough milk to form a smooth dough. Stir in lemon rind. Mix well. Chill about 1 hour. Roll out rather thin on lightly floured board. Cover with chopped dried fruits. Roll up like jelly roll, then shape into a ring. Place on oiled baking sheet. Brush top with milk. Bake in 375-degree oven 30 to 40 minutes. Cool on wire rack set on baking sheet to catch falling crumbs. Use in preceding pudding.

Note: Make this pudding anytime you have a similar flop; or substitute about 3 cups cubed stale bread or pound cake, 1½ to 2 cups dried fruit, 1 to 4 tablespoons honey, and grated rind of ½ lemon.

Jeanette's Mandarin–Ice-Cream Mold

For years my mother has been making this gelatin mold for various occasions. Everyone loves its tangy orange taste and creamy texture. When vanilla ice cream melts accidentally or is growing a bit crystalline, or when the frozen orange juice thaws, serve this delicious mold as a buffet salad or dessert.

2½ envelopes	(the equivalent of 2½ tablespoons) unflavored gelatin
2 cans (11-oz. each)	mandarin oranges or 2 to 3 fresh tangerines or 2 medium oranges, sectioned, drained, liquid reserved
1 can (12-oz.)	frozen orange juice concentrate
1 pt. (2 cups)	vanilla ice cream or orange sherbet, slightly softened or thawed
	Fresh strawberries or grapes

Soften gelatin in a little cold water in medium bowl. Drain fruit; set aside. Add enough water to reserved liquid to measure 2 cups. Bring liquid to boil. Add to gelatin; stir until thoroughly dissolved. Stir in frozen orange juice until melted. Add ice cream and gently fold in until blended. Chill until slightly thickened to consistency of unbeaten egg whites, 30 to 40 minutes. Fold drained oranges into gelatin. Pour into lightly oiled 2-quart mold and chill thoroughly until set, at least 4 hours. Unmold onto platter and garnish with fresh strawberries or grapes. Serves 8 to 10. Recipe can be doubled for larger mold.

Here again, the right sauce can bring through a less-than-perfect cake, cookies, or pudding with flying colors.

Honey Fruit Sauce

1 cup	fruit juice (orange, pineapple, apple, and apricot nectar are good choices)
2 Tbsp.	honey
¼ cup	lemon juice
2 Tbsp.	chopped fresh mint leaves or ½ tsp. crushed rosemary
Optional:	½ cup chopped poached fruit (ideally, to match juice used)

Combine ingredients through mint, adjusting to suit taste. Add fruit, if using over cake or puddings.

Suggested uses: Let dry pound, sponge, or similar cake or cookie crumbs soak up sauce, then top with whipped cream if desired. An overbaked bread pudding derives moisture and rich fruit flavor when the fruit sauce is poured over warm servings. Spoon over a fallen or misshapen dessert soufflé. The sauce, without fruit, lends flavor to bland fruits—soak soft fruits overnight, poach firm ones in sauce, then chill. Fresh and dried fruits can be combined and simmered in the sauce for a rich compote; or use to top a gelatin dessert or ice cream.

Granola

Enid's Granola

This granola recipe from a friend adds a delicious crunchy dimension to your yogurt and fruit for a nourishing breakfast. And it's superb for perking up cereal and nuts that have been on the shelf for a while. Those counting calories can slightly decrease the amount of nuts, honey, and oil, and add fresh fruit.

1 pound (6 cups)	regular rolled oats
2 cups	raw wheat germ
1 cup each	raw cashew pieces, crushed peanuts or Spanish peanuts (skinned), and sunflower-seed kernels
⅛ tsp.	sea salt (omit if nuts and seeds are salted)
⅔ cup	honey
⅔ cup	water
1 tsp.	vanilla
⅔ cup	unrefined peanut oil
About 6 oz. (1¼ cups)	raisins

Combine oats, wheat germ, nuts, sunflower seeds, and salt. In separate bowl, combine remaining ingredients except raisins. Pour over dry ingredients and mix well. Spread out on baking sheet. Bake in 350-degree oven 30 to 35 minutes, stirring mixture every 10 minutes. Remove from oven and mix in raisins. Cool. Store in closed container in a cool place. Serve with milk or yogurt or as a snack. Makes about 3 quarts.

Leftovers Roundup

Here, in alphabetical order by main ingredient, are some tips for swift and skillful salvage operations:

Asparagus stem ends: I peel the tough ends before cooking so the entire stalk can be eaten. If you snap the peeled ends off, though, you can pickle them, following a favorite sweet-sour pickle recipe. Stem ends store well in a plastic bag up to two weeks in the refrigerator until you have enough to pickle.

Bread, stale: Cut into ½-inch cubes for croutons. Arrange on baking sheet and bake in 300-degree oven until golden, about 5 minutes, turning occasionally. If desired, toss with melted butter and seasoning. Use in salads and soups and as casserole topping.

Brine: The brine left from pickled beets or any pickles is tailor-made for preserving other foods like cooked shrimp, hard-cooked eggs, green tomatoes, cucumber slices, and blanched green beans. Add a teaspoon or two of mixed pickling spices and a clove of garlic if desired and cover the food with the brine. Cover jar or dish and chill several days to a week before serving. It makes a great appetizer to have on hand and will last a few weeks in the refrigerator. Here's a sample recipe:

Dill-Pickled Shrimp

1 lb.	peeled, deveined shrimp, cooked
	Dill pickle brine to cover
1 clove	garlic, sliced
¼ tsp.	dillweed
1 Tbsp.	lemon juice
1 small	onion, sliced thin
Optional:	1 hot red pepper, chopped

Place cooked shrimp in shallow glass dish or bowl. Combine remaining ingredients, mixing well. Pour over shrimp to completely cover. Cover dish and refrigerate at least 8 hours. Serve cold on lettuce as appetizer for 6.

Cereals (unsweetened), cooked: Incorporate into puddings, soups, or meat loaves, or use for fried cereal—a nice brunch dish with sautéed vegetables and sausages.

Coffee or tea: Can be chilled or frozen in cubes for iced coffee or tea. Or use leftover coffee to enrich some gravies or turn into gelatins or dessert sauces.

Fruits, poached or canned: Compotes, fruit cups, fruit sauces, gelatins, breads, cakes (especially upside-down cakes, shortcakes, or coffeecakes) all benefit from odds and ends of poached or canned fruits.

Jelly or jam: Can be combined with hard raisins for Cumberland sauce or stewed fruit sauces.

Meat, poultry, or fish, cooked: Use as fillings for sandwiches, for spreads, in salads, in potpies, hash, sauced dishes, casseroles, and the like. Scraps of fish are good in seafood timbales (although usually raw fish is used).

Milk, souring: Milk, buttermilk, or cream that are going off offer a great flavor and texture to biscuits, pancakes, and some cakes and cookies.

Pasta, cooked: Great in casseroles, soups, baked with cheese, meat loaf, or kugels (noodle puddings), or with mayonnaise as salads.

Potatoes, cooked: Fry up leftover boiled potatoes with some chopped onion and diced sausage, or add to soups. Leftover mashed potatoes can be made into croquettes or piped around planked fish.

Rice, cooked: Add to soups or turn into puddings, croquettes, quick breads, or salad. See p. 335.

Sour cream or yogurt: Blend with mayonnaise for salad dressings or turn into sauces for vegetables or meats. Great in many dips, too.

Syrups and juices, canned: Many recipes call for drained canned fruit. What happens to the liquor? Put it to work for poaching hard or pithy fresh fruits or to replace part of the liquid in a fruit soup or a pudding, or thicken it and use to sauce ice cream, gelatin, or stale cake. Kept covered in the refrigerator, it stores well for a long time. It's tasty mixed with club soda or tea as a beverage sweetener, too.

Vegetable cooking liquid: Save small amounts in a covered container and refrigerate or freeze up to 2 months for soups or stews. Or use as part of liquid for a sauce to top the vegetable. Liquids from strong vegetables like broccoli and cabbage are best used separately for a dish requiring the same item.

Vegetables (leafy green), cooked: Use in omelets, soufflés, timbales (p. 333), and soups (p. 315), or cream and serve (p. 334).

Part III

Appendices

Glossary of Cooking Terms

Al dente: Italian term that describes the texture of pasta cooked until tender but still resistant to the teeth.

Bake: to cook by dry heat in an oven or oven-type appliance. Food may be covered or not. For meat cooked this way see *Roast* below.

Barbecue: to cook slowly on a grid or spit over coals or direct heat, usually while basting with a spicy sauce. This term also applies to foods cooked in, or served with, barbecue sauce.

Baste: to moisten food occasionally during cooking with meat drippings, melted fat, fruit juice, sauce or other liquids to add flavor and to prevent surface drying.

Beat: to thoroughly combine all ingredients using a brisk rotary motion that incorporates air, such as with an electric mixer.

Blanch: to preheat food by pouring boiling water over, or by steaming, then immediately rinsing in cold water. This procedure inactivates enzymes and shrinks some foods for canning, drying or freezing. It also is used to remove skins from fruits, nuts and vegetables.

Blend: to thoroughly mix two or more ingredients until smooth.

Boil: to heat a liquid or to cook in water or other liquid until it bubbles thoroughly (212 degrees F., or 100 degrees C., at sea level).

Braise: to slowly cook (usually meat or poultry) by moist heat in a covered utensil with little or no added liquid. Meat may be browned first and the drippings poured off.

Broil: to cook by direct heat under a gas or electric heat source in a broiler or over hot coals. The fat from the cooking food drips away.

Caramelize: to slowly heat sugar or foods containing sugar until the color browns and a caramel flavor develops.

Chop: to cut food into small pieces (usually larger than ½ inch) with a knife or other sharp instrument.

Cream: to soften one or a combination of foods until creamy with a spoon, mixer or other utensil. Usually applies to working fat and sugar together.

Cube: to cut into cubes ½ inch or larger.

Cut: to divide a food using a knife or scissors.

Cut in: to incorporate solid fat in dry ingredients until finely divided by using a cutting motion with two knives or a chopping motion with a pastry blender.

Deep-fry (See *Fry.*)

Dice: to cut into small (usually less than ½ inch) cubes.

Double-boiler cooking: indirect heat over—not in—boiling water. Used for delicate foods such as chocolate, hollandaise sauce, custards, etc.

Dredge: to coat surface of food with flour, corn meal, breadcrumbs or other fine substances before cooking.

Flambé: to ignite a heated food with alcohol and let the flame die, imparting the flavor of the liquor as the alcohol burns off.

Fold: to combine two ingredients or mixtures by gently cutting down through mixture with a spatula, bringing spatula across bottom of bowl, turning over and repeating until well mixed. Used for incorporating beaten egg whites.

Fricassee: to braise serving pieces of meat, poultry, etc., in small amount of liquid in sauce.

Fry: to cook uncovered in fat by one of these methods:
1. *Deep-fry:* to immerse food in hot fat and cook until browned.
2. *Pan-fry:* to cook in small amount of fat in a fry pan.

Glacé: to coat with a thin sugar syrup cooked to the crack stage. For certain breads and pies the mixture may be uncooked; or it may be cooked and contain a thickener.

Grate: to cut into tiny particles by rubbing food against sharp holes of a grater.

Grill: to cook by direct heat over hot coals. (See *Broil*, above.)

Grind: to crush to small particles by putting through a grinder or sharp blade of a food processor.

Julienne: to cut foods in strips about 2 to 3 inches long and ⅛ inch wide.

Knead: to work dough or other mixture by pressing, stretching and folding to make it elastic or smooth.

Marinate: to let foods soak in a marinade (usually an oil-acid liquid mixture) to tenderize or flavor.

Melt: to dissolve with heat application. Butter and chocolate are two examples of foods that melt when warmed.

Mince: to chop into very small pieces.

Mix: to combine all ingredients evenly.

Pan-broil: to cook uncovered in a moderately hot skillet, pouring off fat as it accumulates.

Pan-fry: (See *Fry*, above.)

Parboil: to boil until partly cooked. Food is usually further cooked by another method.

Pare: to peel or trim off outside covering, as with fruits and vegetables.

Peel: (See *Pare*).

Poach: to simmer gently in liquid; properly poached foods retain their shape (e.g., egg, fish).

Pot-roast: to cook large meat cuts by braising.

Purée: to cook and force through sieve or grind to a fine mixture in a blender.

Reconstitute: to restore concentrated foods to their original condition by adding water. The term applies to dry milk and frozen concentrated orange juice.

Rehydrate: to cook or soak dried foods to restore their water content lost in the drying process.

Render: to free fat from animal tissue by heating at low temperatures.

Roast: to cook uncovered in an oven or Dutch oven without added moisture.

Roux: a fat and flour mixture blended gently together over low heat.

Sauté: to brown or cook in a small amount of fat. Same as pan-fry.

Scald: applies to heating milk to just below the boiling point, when tiny bubbles appear at the edges. Also means to dip certain foods in boiling water. (See *Blanch*, above.)

Scallop: to bake foods with a sauce or other liquid.

Sear: to brown meat surface by quick, intense heat.

Shred: to cut into thin pieces using large, sharp holes on a shredder.

Simmer: to cook in liquid just below boiling point, at temperature of about 185 to 210 degrees F. Bubbles form lazily and break below the surface.

Steam: to cook food, usually on a rack over simmering liquid in a tightly covered pot; can be with or without pressure.

Steep: to allow ingredients (usually spices, herbs and flavorings) to stand in liquid below boiling point to extract flavor and color.

Sterilize: to destroy microorganisms, usually done by application of high temperature with steam, boiling liquid or hot air.

Stew: to simmer in relatively small amount of liquid until tender.

Stir: to mix ingredients with a circular motion to blend.

Toast: to brown by dry heat, such as toaster or broiler.

Toss: to tumble ingredients lightly with a lifting motion. A term often applied to salad.

Truss: to tie and bind to ensure holding together during cooking. Usually applied to poultry.

Whip: to beat rapidly to incorporate air and increase volume.

Whir: to whip very thoroughly in blender.

Substitutions

No substitution will yield a product exactly like that made by the item it's replacing. But for baking and cooking purposes, recipes will work with substitutes. This guide is handy to have when your supplies run short.

1 tsp. baking powder	= ¼ tsp. baking soda plus ⅝ tsp. cream of tartar
	= ¼ tsp. baking soda plus ½ cup sour milk or buttermilk when used in a recipe
	= ¼ tsp. baking soda plus ½ Tbsp. vinegar or lemon juice mixed with sweet milk to make ½ cup
	= ¼ tsp. baking soda plus ¼ - ½ cup molasses when used in a recipe
Butter	= same amounts of margarine can be substituted
	= ¾ cup chicken fat, clarified
	= ⅞ cup lard plus ½ tsp. salt
1 cup buttermilk	= 1 Tbsp. lemon juice or vinegar plus sweet milk to make 1 cup, let stand 5 minutes

1 oz. unsweetened chocolate	= 3 Tbsp. cocoa plus 1 Tbsp. fat
1 cup corn syrup	= 1 cup sugar plus ¼ cup liquid in recipe
	= ¾ cup maple syrup
	= ¾ cup honey
	= 1¼ cups molasses
¾ cup cracker crumbs	= 1 cup breadcrumbs
1 cup light cream (18%)	= 3 Tbsp. butter plus ⅞ cup milk
1 cup half-and-half (10½%)	= 1½ Tbsp. butter plus ⅞ cup milk
1 cup whipping cream, heavy (36%)	= ⅓ cup butter plus ¾ cup milk (for baking or cooking only). (For whipped cream substitutes, see *Cream,* p. 78.)
1 egg, whole	= 2 egg yolks (for thickening)
	= 2 Tbsp. plus 2 tsp. dry whole egg powder plus an equal amount of water
1 egg yolk	= 2 Tbsp. dry egg yolk plus 2 tsp. water
1 egg white	= 2 tsp. dry egg white plus 2 Tbsp. water
1 cup sifted all-purpose flour	= 1 cup unsifted all-purpose flour minus 2 Tbsp.
1 cup sifted cake flour	= ⅞ cup sifted, all-purpose flour
1 Tbsp. flour, thickening	= 1½ tsp. cornstarch, potato starch, rice starch, or arrowroot starch
	= 1 Tbsp. quick-cooking tapioca
Herbs	= generally ¼ heaping tsp. ground or ½ to 1 tsp. crushed dried herbs is about the equivalent of 1 Tbsp. chopped fresh. Variables are age and potency.

1 cup honey	= 1¼ cups sugar plus ¼ cup liquid in recipe
1 tsp. lemon juice	= ½ tsp. vinegar
1 cup milk, whole	= 1 cup buttermilk plus ½ tsp. baking soda
	= 1 cup reconstituted nonfat dry milk plus 2½ tsp. butter or margarine
	= ½ cup evaporated milk plus ½ cup water
	= ¼ cup dry whole milk powder plus ⅞ cup water
	= 1 cup skim milk plus 2 tsp. cream, butter, margarine or oil
1 cup milk, sour	= 1 Tbsp. vinegar or lemon juice plus enough sweet milk to make 1 cup (let stand 5 minutes)
	= 1¾ tsp. cream of tartar plus 1 cup sweet milk
Sour cream	= the lower fat sour half-and-half or yogurt may be substituted in most cooked, but not baked, dishes
1 cup sugar (in baking)	= reduce liquid by ¼ cup and use ¾ cup honey, ¾ cup maple syrup, 1¼ cups molasses or 2 cups corn syrup; 2 cups corn syrup are equivalent to 1 cup sugar in sweetness, but for best results, never replace more than half the required sugar with corn syrup
	= without liquid adjustments in recipe, 1 cup superfine sugar, 1 cup packed brown sugar and 1¾ cups confectioners sugar

1 Tbsp. yeast, dry active   = 1 package dry active yeast
                                = 1 compressed yeast cake

Yogurt   = sour cream or sour half-
                                  and-half may be substituted
                                  for yogurt in recipes other
                                  than baked items. Sour
                                  cream and sour half-and-
                                  half have a higher fat con-
                                  tent

Common Volume, Weight, and Temperature Equivalents

Teaspoon, **tsp;** tablespoon, **T;** fluid ounce, **fl.oz;** pint, **pt;** quart, **qt;** gallon, **gal** (all non-metric forms = established U.S.A. and Canadian measures); milliliter, **ml;** cubic centimeter, **cc** (1 **ml** = 1 **cc**); liter, **l.**

¼ tsp = 1.25 ml

½ tsp = 2.5 ml
1 tsp = 5 ml
1 T (½ fl.oz) = 15 ml
2 T (1 fl.oz) = 30 ml
¼ cup (2 fl.oz) = 60 ml
⅓ cup (2.7 fl.oz) = 80 ml
½ cup (4 fl.oz) = 120 ml
1 cup (8 fl.oz) =
   240 ml/0.24 l.
1½ cups (12 fl.oz) =
   360 ml/0.36 l.
2 cups (16 fl.oz/1 pt) =
   470 ml/0.47 l.

4 cups (32 fl.oz/1 qt) =
   950 ml/0.95 l.
2 qt = 1.90 l.
3 qt = 2.85 l.
4 qt (1 gal) = 3.8 l.
*   *   *
100 ml = 3.4 fl.oz
500 ml = 17 fl.oz
1 l. = 1.06 qt
1.5 l. = 1.59 qt

2 l. = 2.12 qt

5 l. = 1.30 gal

WEIGHT/MASS (WORKABLE APPROXIMATES)
Ounce avoirdupois, **oz.av;** gram, **g.;** pound, **lb;** kilogram (1,000 **g.), kg.**

½ oz.av = 14 g.
1 oz.av = 28 g.
4 oz.av (¼ lb) = 113 g.
8 oz.av (½ lb) = 226 g.
12 oz.av (¾ lb) = 340 g.
16 oz.av (1 lb) =
  454 g./0.454 kg
1½ lb = 680 g./0.680 kg
2 lb = 908 g./0.908 kg
1 g = .035 oz./.002 lb.
1 kg = 2.21 lb

5 lb = 2.27 kg
10 lb = 4.54 kg
  *   *   *

100 g. = 3.5 oz.av
1,000 g./1 kg = 2.2 lb
2 kg = 4.4 lb

5 kg = 11.02 lb
10 kg = 22.04 lb

TEMPERATURE
Fahrenheit, **F.;** Celsius (Centigrade), **C.** (rounded to nearest digit).

F.	C.	F.	C.	F.	C.	F.	C.	F.	C.
0	−18	80	27	195	91	275	135	425	218
10	−12	100	38	205	96	300	149	450	232
20	−7	145	63	212	100	325	163	475	246
32	0	165	74	220	104	350	177	500	260
40	4	185	85	238	114	375	191	525	274
50	10	190	88	240	116	400	204	550	288

Temperatures for Control of Bacteria

°F

250 — Canning temperatures for meat and poultry in pressure canner.

240

212 — Cooking temperatures destroy most bacteria. Time required to kill bacteria decreases as temperature is increased.

165 — Warming temperatures prevent growth but allow survival of some bacteria.

140 — Some bacterial growth may occur. Many bacteria survive.

120 — DANGER ZONE. Temperatures in this zone allow rapid growth of bacteria and production of toxins by some bacteria.

60 — Some growth of food poisoning bacteria may occur.

40 — Cold temperatures permit slow growth of some bacteria that cause spoilage.

32 — Freezing temperatures stop growth of bacteria, but may allow bacteria to survive.

0

Inspection, Labeling and Care of Meat and Poultry, U.S. Department of Agriculture, Animal and Plant Health Inspection Service (Revised Jan. 1974).

In Case of Emergency

If power fails or the freezer stops operating normally, try to determine how long before the freezer will be back in operation.

A fully loaded freezer usually will stay cold enough to keep foods frozen for 2 days if the cabinet is not opened. In a cabinet with less than half a load, food may not stay frozen more than 1 day.

If normal operation cannot be resumed before the food will start to thaw, use dry ice. If dry ice is placed in the freezer soon after the power is off, 25 pounds should keep the temperature below freezing for 2 to 3 days in a 10-cubic-foot cabinet with half a load, 3 to 4 days in a loaded cabinet.

Place the dry ice on cardboard or small boards on top of packages, and do not open freezer again except to put in more dry ice or to remove it when normal operation is resumed.

Or move food to a locker plant, using insulated boxes or thick layers of paper to prevent thawing.

Meat and Poultry Storage

STORING CHART

PRODUCT

STORAGE PERIOD
(To maintain its quality)

	Refrigerator 35° to 40° F. DAYS	Freezer 0° F. MONTHS
Fresh Meats		
Roasts (Beef and Lamb)	3 to 5	8 to 12
Roasts (Pork and Veal)	3 to 5	4 to 8
Steaks (Beef)	3 to 5	8 to 12
Chops (Lamb and Pork)	3 to 5	3 to 4
Ground and Stew Meats	1 to 2	2 to 3
Variety Meats	1 to 2	3 to 4
Sausage (Pork)	1 to 2	1 to 2
Processed Meats		
Bacon	7	1
Frankfurters	7	½
Ham (Whole)	7	1 to 2
Ham (Half)	3 to 5	1 to 2
Ham (Slices)	3	1 to 2
Luncheon Meats	3 to 5	Freezing not recommended
Sausage (Smoked)	7	
Sausage (Dry and Semi-Dry)	14 to 21	

STORING CHART

STORAGE PERIOD
(To maintain its quality)

PRODUCT

	Refrigerator 35° to 40° F. DAYS	Freezer 0° F. MONTHS
Cooked Meats		
Cooked Meats and Meat Dishes	1 to 2	2 to 3
Gravy and Meat Broth	1 to 2	2 to 3
Fresh Poultry		
Chicken and Turkey	1 to 2	12
Duck and Goose	1 to 2	6
Giblets	1 to 2	3
Cooked Poultry		
Pieces (Covered with Broth)	1 to 2	6
Pieces (Not Covered)	1 to 2	1
Cooked Poultry Dishes	1 to 2	6
Fried Chicken	1 to 2	4

Can Your Kitchen Pass the Food Storage Test? FDA Consumer, United States Department of Health, Education and Welfare Publication No. (FDA) 74-2052 (March 1974).

Thawing Timetable: Poultry

Do not thaw commercially frozen stuffed poultry before cooking.

Keep poultry frozen until time to thaw or cook.

You can thaw poultry in any of these ways:

In the refrigerator, in the original wrapping or lightly covered with waxed paper if poultry is unwrapped. Place poultry on a tray for easy handling and to catch any drippings. Thaw until pliable.

Here is a timetable for thawing poultry in the refrigerator:

Chickens:
    4 pounds or over .... 1 to 1½ days
    Less than 4 pounds .... 12 to 16 hours
Ducks, 3 to 7 pounds .... 1 to 1½ days
Geese, 6 to 12 pounds .... 1 to 2 days
Turkeys:
    4 to 12 pounds .... 1 to 2 days
    12 to 20 pounds .... 2 to 3 days
    20 to 24 pounds .... 3 to 4 days
    Pieces of large
        turkey (half, quarter,
        half breast) .... 1 to 2 days
    Cut-up pieces .... 3 to 9 hours
    Boneless roasts .... 12 to 18 hours

363

In cold water, in original wrap or other watertight plastic bag. Change water often. Thaw until pliable. Approximate thawing times are:

Chickens, 3 to 4 pounds .... 1 to 2 hours
Turkeys:
    4 to 12 pounds .... 4 to 6 hours
    12 to 20 pounds .... 6 to 8 hours
    20 to 24 pounds .... 8 to 12 hours

You may partially thaw poultry in the refrigerator and complete thawing in cold water.

In a cool room, in a double wall paper bag or wrapped in several thicknesses of paper. Place poultry on a tray for easy handling and to catch any drippings. Thaw at 70° F. or below until pliable. Approximate thawing times are:

Chickens, 4 pounds ....12 hours
Turkeys:
    4 to 12 pounds ....12 to 15 hours
    12 to 24 pounds ....15 to 20 hours

Thawing times with any of the above methods will be shorter if giblets are not packed in the body cavity.

If cut-up poultry pieces are separated by freezer paper, remove outer wrapper, thaw partially in the refrigerator, and then separate each piece for quicker thawing. Or leave poultry pieces in watertight wrapper and thaw in cold water.

After poultry is thawed, prepare for cooking in the same way as chilled, unfrozen poultry. Cook poultry promptly after thawing.

Poultry in Family Meals, United States Department of Agriculture Home and Garden Bulletin #110 (September 1976).

Storage: Fish

STORING FRESH FISH

Wrap fresh fish in moisture-vapor-proof paper, or put it in a tightly covered dish and store it in the coldest part of the refrigerator. If fish is wrapped or covered in this way the quality will be maintained and the odor won't affect other foods in the refrigerator.

To maintain the quality of fresh fish, keep it below 40 degrees F. Better yet, keep it at 30 or 32 degrees F., if you have refrigeration facilities that will do so.

STORING FROZEN FISH

Keep frozen fish in the unopened package until time to use it. Storage life varies with the type of storage compartment. Frozen fish can be stored for a week in ice-cube compartments, a month in across-the-top freezer compartments, and 6 months in two-door refrigerator-freezer units or home freezers. (It will remain in good condition for up to a week in the freezing unit of the refrigerator, provided the freezing unit is operating efficiently.)

Keep frozen fish solidly frozen and don't refreeze fish that has been thawed. Keep in mind the fact that, even though a food is frozen hard, there can still be loss of quality at temperatures above zero degrees F. So, if you want to get the maximum storage life from frozen fish, keep it at zero degrees F. or lower and be sure that it is adequately protected by moisture-vapor-proof wrapping or by glazing with ice.

STORING SHELLFISH

Fresh shellfish should be stored at temperatures near 32 degrees. Much quality can be lost in a couple of hours if the temperature is even a few degrees higher than that. It is very important to keep fresh or cooked shellfish meats from becoming contaminated by bacteria, as they are easily spoiled.

KEEPING FROZEN FISH AT ZERO DEGREES F.

Frozen fish that was of good quality when frozen and that was handled correctly until reaching the storage freezer—and that is then kept at zero degrees F. or lower until used—should stay in good condition for the periods indicated on the chart.

APPROXIMATE STORAGE LIFE OF FROZEN FISH AND SHELLFISH HELD AT ZERO DEGREES FAHRENHEIT

Fatty Fish	**Months**
Mackerel, Salmon, Tuna, etc.	3
Lean Fish	
Haddock, Cod, Swordfish, etc.	6
Shellfish	
Lobsters and Crabs (Meat)	2
Shrimp	6
Oysters, Scallops, Clams (Shucked)	3 to 4

Generally, thaw frozen fish at refrigerator temperatures whenever possible. If a quick method is necessary, thaw in cold running water.

THAWING FROZEN FISH

You can cook frozen fish, fillets, and steaks in their frozen form, if you allow enough additional cooking time. But if fish are to be breaded and fried or stuffed, it's more convenient to thaw them first to make handling easier. Thawing is necessary before preparation if you are going to clean and dress whole or drawn fish.

Here are some methods for thawing fish:

At Refrigerator Temperatures—Thawing at refrigerator temperatures of 40 to 45 degrees F. is the recommended method for thawing frozen fish. Hold the fish at this temperature only until it is easy to handle. A one-pound fillet will thaw in about 18 hours.

Note: Depending on thickness of fish fillet and refrigerator temperature, it has been my experience that it may take as little as 4 to 6 hours for thawing a 1-lb. fillet.

Using Cold Running Water—The quickest method for thawing whole or drawn fish is to put them in cold running water. Leave fillets and steaks in the package while they are being thawed. The thawing time will vary, depending on the shape and size of the fish. It takes about a half-hour to thaw fillets and steaks in cold water.

At Room Temperatures—This type of thawing is not recommended, though it is often used. The thinner parts of the fish, such as the part near the tail, thaw faster than the rest, and if the thawing period is too long, spoilage can start in the parts that thawed earliest. It takes from three to four hours to thaw a package of fillets this way.

Increasing the Satisfaction from Fish and Shellfish, University of Massachusetts, Publication #387 (August 1963).

Storage & Freezer

To use your freezer to best advantage you may want to fill it with a variety of foods: extra quantities of homemade items (use one now, freeze the second); leftovers, and supermarket specials. Whatever the contents, wrap all home-frozen foods well in moisture-vapor-proof paper and label. Keep an inventory of items and rely on the rotation system for best quality. Use oldest foods first.

Home economists at freezer manufacturing companies have thoroughly researched storage periods for various foods. The Ann MacGregor kitchen staff of Amana Refrigeration, Inc., Amana, Iowa, recommends these maximum storage periods.

Recommended Freezer Storage Times (in months) for Miscellaneous Foods

Breads, Quick, Baked	2	Fruits, Except Citrus	12
Breads, Yeast, Baked	4–8	Ice Cream & Sherbet	1–1½
Breads, Yeast, Unbaked	½	Milk, Homogenized	½–1
Butter	6–8	Onions	3–6
Cakes	6	Pastry, Unbaked	2
Cakes, Fruit	12	Pies, Baked	1
Candies	12	Pies, Unbaked	3
Cheese, Hard or Semi-hard	6–12	Pizza	1
Cheese, Soft	4	Salads	2
Cookies, Baked	6	Sandwiches	1
Cookies, Unbaked	4	Soups, Stews	6
Eggs	6–8	Vegetables, Cooked	1
Fruits, Citrus	3–4	Vegetables, Blanched, except onions	12

Amana News, Amana Refrigeration, Inc.

Further Suggested Reading

Ball Blue Book. Muncie, Indiana: Ball Corporation, 1977.

James Beard's Theory & Practice of Good Cooking. New York: Alfred A. Knopf, 1977.

Beard, James. *Delights & Prejudices*. New York: Simon and Schuster, A Fireside Book, 1964.

Burros, Marian Fox, and Levine, Lois. *Freeze With Ease*. New York: The Macmillan Company, 1965.

Child, Julia, and Beck, Simone. *Mastering the Art of French Cooking*, Vol. I. New York: Alfred A. Knopf, 1975.

The Fannie Farmer Cookbook, 12th ed. New York: Alfred A. Knopf, 1980.

Handbook of Food Preparation. Rev. ed. Washington, D.C.: American Home Economics Association, 1971.

Hazelton, Nika. *The Unabridged Vegetable Cookbook*. New York: M. Evans and Company, Inc., 1976.

Jones, Evan. *The World of Cheese*. New York: Alfred A. Knopf, 1976.

Langseth-Christensen, Lillian, and Smith, Carol Sturm. *The Complete Kitchen Guide*. New York: Grosset & Dunlap Publishers, 1968.

Lessons on Meat. Rev. ed. Chicago: National Live Stock and Meat Board, 1974.

MacIlquham, Frances. *Fish Cookery of North America*. New York: Winchester Press, 1975.

Oliver, Raymond. *La Cuisine: Secrets of Modern French Cooking*. Translated and edited by Nika Standen Hazelton with Jack Van Bibber. New York: Tudor Publishing Company, 1969.

Pepín, Jacques. *La Technique.* New York: Quadrangle/ The New York Times Book Co., Inc., 1976.

Rombauer, Irma S., and Becker, Marion Rombauer. *Joy of Cooking.* Indianapolis–New York: The Bobbs-Merrill Company, Inc., 1975.

Sokolov, Raymond. *The Saucier's Apprentice.* New York: Alfred A. Knopf, 1977.

Index to Recipes